ETHICS AND ACCOUNTABILITY IN A CONTEXT OF
GOVERNANCE AND NEW PUBLIC MANAGEMENT

International Institute of Administrative Sciences Monographs

Volume 7

Edited by A. Hondeghem and the European Group of Public Administration

Vol. 6	J.G. Jabbra and O.P. Dwivedi and IASIA (Eds.), Governmental Response to Environmental Challenges In Global Perspective
Vol. 5.	IIAS and the United Nations (Eds.), Public Administration and Development
Vol. 4.	IIAS (Ed.), New Challenges for Public Administration in the Twenty-First Century
Vol. 3.	IIAS Working Group on Social Security Systems (Eds.), Transformations in Social Security Systems
Vol. 2.	M. Garrity and L.A. Picard (Eds.), Policy Reform for Sustainable Development in the Caribbean
Vol 1.	A Halachmi and G Bouckaert (Eds.), Public Productivity through Quality and Strategic Management

European Group of Public Administration

Volume 2

Prepared by: EGPA

Vol. 1.	Hugo Van Hassel, Mihály Hógye and György Jenei (Eds.), New Trends in Public Administration and Public Law, EGPA Yearbook. Annual Conference, Budapest 1996

ISSN: 1382-4414

Ethics and Accountability in a Context of Governance and New Public Management

EGPA Yearbook

Edited by

Annie Hondeghem
Public Management Centre
Catholic University of Leuven, Belgium

and

European Group of Public Administration

Amsterdam • Berlin • Oxford • Tokyo • Washington, DC

© 1998, The authors mentioned in the table of contents

All rights reserved. No part of this book may be reproduced, stored in a retrieval system, or transmitted, in any form or by any means, without the prior written permission from the publisher.

ISBN 90 5199 419 2 (IOS Press)
ISBN 4 274 90244 7 C3034 (Ohmsha)
Library of Congress Card Number 98-73828

Publisher
IOS Press
Van Diemenstraat 94
1013 CN Amsterdam
Netherlands
fax. +31 20 620 3419
e-mail: order@iospress.nl

Co-Publisher
International Institute of Administrative Sciences - IIAS
Rue Defacqz, 1
B-1000 Brussels
Belgium
fax: +32 2 537 9702
e-mail. iias@agoranet.be

Distributor in the UK and Ireland
IOS Press/Lavis Marketing
73 Lime Walk
Headington
Oxford OX3 7AD
England
fax: +44 1865 75 0079

Distributor in the USA and Canada
IOS Press, Inc.
5795-G Burke Center Parkway
Burke, VA 22015
USA
fax: +1 703 323 3668
e-mail: iosbooks@iospress.com

Distributor in Germany
IOS Press
Spandauer Strasse 2
D-10178 Berlin
Germany
fax: +49 30 242 3113

Distributor in Japan
Ohmsha, Ltd
3-1 Kanda Nishiki-cho
Chiyoda-ku, Tokyo 101
Japan
fax: +81 3 3233 2426

LEGAL NOTICE
The publisher is not responsible for the use which might be made of the following information.

FOREWORD

T. Ould Daddah[*]

This second Yearbook is being published at a significant time in the history of EGPA, owing mainly to two reasons:

- The first reason concerns EGPA's willingness to broaden its horizons in time and space; a wise and practical decision to open its doors, first in time, to young European researchers - thus encouraging new talents, establishing a link between generations and ensuring the continuity of scientific research in the field of public administration and management; and then in space, notably owing to the attention given to the specificities of the problems of the Eastern European countries and the dialogue initiated and developed with the Public Administration communities of these countries.

- The second reason is related to the essential nature of EGPA itself. Indeed, EGPA is a homogeneous group of high profile academics and practitioners. These researchers also belong to countries which have both a long tradition of scientific research and the attainment of impressive results in the field of economic development and technological progress, as well as in the field of democracy and respect for human rights.

In consequence, the outcomes, products of studies and research resulting from EGPA's work have, in our era of globalisation, a value whose interest greatly supersedes Europe's borders.

I am proud that the publications policy adopted and implemented by the International Institute of Administrative Sciences (IIAS) has been emulated by its associated organisations, namely IASIA and EGPA. In other words, EGPA could not have done better than to adopt a genuine, realistic and well defined publications policy.

Hugo Van Hassel understood that EGPA, IASIA and IIAS, having the opportunity to constitute a coherent whole, could be mutually strengthened by their synergy and complementary qualities, whereas a dispersion of efforts and overlapping would have made them vulnerable. The scientific autonomy of each of the associations today remains fully intact, but it is being carried out in solidarity in the framework of a common general policy which is mutually beneficial.

Hugo Van Hassel likewise understood that we are living in a difficult world in which competition does not exclusively characterise the market but affects almost all sectors, including those of research and study. No scientific association may thus live and survive if the regularity and quality of its products, namely its publications, are not well known.

Hugo Van Hassel thus took the opportunity of his two successive terms of office as President of EGPA to put to use his high scientific competence and his dynamism in the devoted service of the Group to modernise and professionalise it and to lay down the basis of a publications policy.

---

[*] Turkia Ould Daddah, Director General of the International Institute of Administrative Sciences. Belgium.

This volume brings together remarkable contributions on a theme which today represents a great challenge for contemporary administrations and States.

The administrative revolution which is taking place before our very eyes, the profound crisis of values and the loss of direction of which we are witnesses, just as certain deviant trends arising from an unbridled neoliberalism, necessitate that reflection on questions related to ethics be initiated as a priority and at the highest level.

This volume is therefore an important study, on a significant theme, published at an appropriate moment. We owe this to Hugo Van Hassel's vision and determination, and it is indeed for this reason that as Director General of IIAS, I am taking the liberty of dedicating this volume to him, personally and on behalf of all of the members of EGPA.

FOREWORD

R. Depré[1]

Hugo Van Hassel started his career at the Business Management Centre of the Catholic University of Leuven. This centre was created in 1955 as part of a broad programme for the modernisation of post-war industries in Europe. With Marshall financial support, several national productivity agencies were created within a European framework. The underlying philosophy was that training in management and leadership could be an important tool for the modernisation of the business and industrial world.

Management development centres were set up in 5 Belgian universities. These centres were associated and co-ordinated by the Foundation Industry-University, an institution where representatives of the academic and business world developed research and training programmes.

As soon as the Belgian government understood that not only business managers but also public administrators needed training in management, the University of Leuven was asked to organise experimental seminars for top civil servants. Hugo Van Hassel was in charge of the conception and execution of this project. He went for a year to the United States in order to study the way programmes in management and public administration were run at American universities.

His basic scientific discipline was sociology and political science. At the Indiana University he studied public administration and decision making and also social systems theory and organisational sociology. There he was confronted with the contingency approach and the importance of social and political settings in the understanding of administrative systems.

Therefore, it is not surprising that, when he returned to Leuven, he was interested in the specificity of the public sector, although he worked in a business centre. He believed in a multi-disciplinary approach of public administration, not in a generic philosophy of management which points that only business management is good management. The generic school of management was not able to understand completely the interaction between the diverse and different interests in society neither to consider the power relations as an integrated part of the public sector.

Hugo Van Hassel's basic educational backgrounds have increased his doubt about the pure and simple applications of business management in the public sector. His special interest for the specificity of the public sector was stimulated during his research on the ministerial cabinet in Belgium as a link between politics and administration. This was also the subject of his PhD.

Public administration is more than an amalgam of techniques and methods. Influenced by authors as Max Weber, Selznick and Riggs, Hugo Van Hassel was especially fascinated by the normative aspects and the values of public management.

---

[1] Prof. dr. Roger Depré, professor emeritus Catholic University of Leuven, Public Management Centre, Belgium

Training for top civil servants thus was different than training for business managers. The public managers must above all understand and analyse the institutional and organisational settings in which they are embedded.

Hugo Van Hassel believed strongly in the steering role of government in society and also in the global approach of the system theory. This explains his interest in Planning, Programming, and Budgeting systems as an instrument for integrated policy making. This approach of governmental steering was an important enlargement of the traditional "public administration" in Belgium, which had a strong legal orientation as a result of the French tradition of "droit administratif". It had an influence on research as well as on training in public administration.

This background explains why Hugo Van Hassel was an advocate of a systems approach of government, which aims at integrating as many aspects as possible in order to create a maximum of synergism. This was also his attitude vis-à-vis the International Institute for Administrative Sciences: he understood that EGPA, IASIA and IIAS could benefit from each other.

I have joined the Public Management Centre in 1964 and for more than 30 years, Hugo Van Hassel and myself have run the Centre alternately every three years. The contingency and specificity of the public sector have always been a key characteristic of our approach. Hugo Van Hassel was most interested in the political and international aspects of public management and myself more in the technical and quantitative aspects. This has stimulated a collaboration which has been fruitful for the development of public management in an academic context.

It is a pleasure and an honour for me to write this foreword in a publication on "Ethics and Accountability in Government". Public servants are ethical responsible for their behaviour and their decisions. This supports Hugo Van Hassel's idea and conception of the state and the public service.

From now on Hugo Van Hassel is a professor emeritus. With his retirement the university looses not only a professor, but also a real servant of the state.

Hugo, I wish you all the best ....

Acknowledgments

H. Van Hassel[1]

For their support and contribution, we address here our special homage and feelings of gratitude to

The Flemish Parliament,
The Flemish Government,
The Flemish Community Commission in Brussels,
The City of Leuven,
The Beethoven Academie and their conductor Prof. J. Cayers,
The keynote speakers, the directors of the working groups, and the directors of the study groups,
The complete staff of the Public Management Centre, Vervolmakingscentrum voor Overheidsmanagement en Beleid of the Katholieke Universiteit Leuven, especially Prof. dr. Annie Hondeghem for the scientific co-ordination and Mrs. Christel Vandeurzen for the administrative co-ordination.

We also express our warm feelings and sympathy towards Mrs. Turkia Ould Daddah, IIAS, director-general, for the firm moral support she always gave to the EGPA conferences, especially to this one in Leuven.
Our gratitude also to Mrs. Catherine Coninckx, our executive secretary in EGPA for her accurate and persistent work in preparing the conference, notwithstanding her absence in Leuven, because of the birth of her son Benjamin.

---

[1] Prof. dr. Hugo Van Hassel, President of EGPA, Director of the Public Management Centre, Belgium

This book is dedicated to Prof. dr. Hugo Van Hassel, as president of EGPA, as professor, and as former director of the Public Management Centre.

Contents

Foreword
Turkia Ould Daddah v
Roger Depré vii

Introduction
Annie Hondeghem 1

Setting the Scene: Keynote speeches

Remedies for Misgovernment: changing the mix, but not the ingredients?,
Christopher Hood 9

Ethics in the Public Service - Current Issues and Practice, *Maria Maguire* 23

New Public Management in the Flemish Administration: new ethical
and political dimensions for civil servants, *Jos Van Rillaer* 35

Working Group on Responsibility

Report of the Working Group on Responsibility, *Mark Bovens & Andrew Massey* 41

Towards Reflexive Responsibility. New Ethics for Public Administration,
Barbel Dorbeck-Jung 45

Les réformes comptables et budgétaires et la responsabilisation des agents
de l'État en France et en Grande-Bretagne, *Raphaelle Fabre* 59

Vers une refonte du régime de la responsabilité des fonctionnaires en Belgique?,
Odile Daurmont 73

Fuzzy in Theory and Getting Fuzzier in Practice: post-modern reflections
on responsibility in public administration and management, *Wayne Parsons* 87

Working Group on Transparency, Openness and Service to the Public

Report of the Working Group on Transparency, Openness and Service
to the Public, *Werner Jann and Bernard Hubeau* 107

Political and Administrative Innovations as a Social Project. The Belgian Case,
Rudolf Maes 111

The Impact of Performance Management on Transparency and Accountability in the Public Sector, *Christoph Reichard* — 123

Baromètre de qualité dans le cadre de la Charte Belge des Utilisateurs des Services Publics, *Patrick Staes* — 139

The Gatekeepers of the Common Good Power and the Public Service Ethos, *David Richards & Martin J. Smith* — 151

Working Group on Integrity

Report of the Working Group on Integrity, *Bertrand De Clercq & Gyula Gulyàs* — 167

The Civil Servant, Society and the Citizen in Quest of Good Ethical Behaviour, *Philippe Vermeulen* — 171

Searching for a Set of Values in the Ethical Behaviour of the Public Sector, *Luiz Montanheiro* — 189

Moral Powerlessness in Relations of Subordination. Moral Responsibility and Organisational Culture, *Koen Raes* — 197

Nouvelles perspectives de la lutte contre les conflits d'intérêts dans la fonction publique française, *Didier Jean-Pierre* — 207

The Recent Debate on Curbing Political Corruption, *Katrien Robben* — 219

Reports of the EGPA Permanent Study Groups

Report of the Study Group on Agriculture, *J. Chr. Van Dalen* — 233

Report of the Study Group on Informatization in Public Administration, *Ignace Snellen & Wim Van de Donk* — 235

Report of the Study Group on Personnel Policy, *David Farnham, Sylvia Horton & Annie Hondeghem* — 239

Report of the Study Group on Quality and Productivity in the Public Services, *Geert Bouckaert and Hilkka Summa* — 243

Report of the Study Group on Public Budgeting and Accounting, *Mihaly Hogye & Francisca Sabbe* — 245

Report of the Study Group on Co-operation in Continuing Education, Training, Research and Consulting between Eastern and Western Europe, *György Jenei* — 247

L'évolution de la contractualisation dans le secteur public depuis 1980,
Yvonne Fortin and Hugo Van Hassel 253

Selection of Papers of the Permanent Study Groups Related to the Conference Theme

Risks in Value for Money-related Performance Measurement, *Jarmo Vakkuri & Pentti Meklin* 263

Contracting in the Public Services: the case of transport in the UK, *Enid Wistrich* 279

About EGPA

The organisation, its objectives and activities 293

Publications of EGPA 295

Author Index 299

Introduction

A. Hondeghem[*]

1. Introduction

Ethics and accountability in government have become an important issue during the last years. Actually government is evaluated on criteria of efficiency, effectiveness and economy. Shrinking budgets and growing expectations of citizens have indeed forced government to offer value for money and to do better with available resources.

Increasingly, there is a feeling, however, that the criteria mentioned have to be broadened with social and political parameters. Other values have to be brought in as markers for government. For politicians and public servants, ethical responsible conduct should also be an important criterium for evaluation, referring to a generally accepted system of norms and values.

As to the ethics, however, there is a problem. For several reasons the traditional bureaucratic ethics are too narrow for modern government.

The EGPA Conference aimed to investigate new ethics for the public service, taking into account the actual development in governance and new public management.

2. Influence of governance and new public management on ethics

During the last decade, society and public service have experienced important new trends.

Firstly, the idea of government steering society from a central and hierarchical point of view has been abandoned. Government has become a partner among other partners (public as well as private). The boundary between the public and the private sector has shifted and blurred as a result of privatisation, public-private partnership, accountability, etc. An important extent of governmental activities is now carried out in networks of organisations, each of them executing a part of the activities. Because of the involvement of different actors, the relation between the results and the contribution of each actor has blurred. It is therefore difficult to define responsibilities. This is called the problem of 'different hands' since different actors are commonly involved. Also direct lines are established with client groups seeking quality in the provision of collective services.

Secondly, processes of decentralisation and devolution are taking place within government. In order to follow the dynamics of society, direct response and steering are needed to tackle specific issues. This implies more autonomy for different parts of government. Huge bureaucracies are separated in to more autonomous entities. Policy formulation and

---

[*] Dr. Annie Hondeghem, Catholic University of Leuven, Public Management, Belgium.

execution are split; on the one hand policy formulation is located in core departments; on the other hand implementation is transferred to autonomous responsible units. Traditional hierarchical steering is supplemented with new steering mechanisms, such as contract management and autonomous agencies following up managerial responsibilities.

Thirdly, there is a trend in government to accept business-like managerialism in the public sector. Greater emphasis is put on results, efficiency and effectiveness in relation to specific groups of citizens. Competition is injected into service delivery. Public services must become more self-supporting. Performances are measured and controlled. Input control is replaced by output control. Budgets are established referring to precise objectives commonly agreed on. The idea of customer orientation is intensified. In short, environment-bound and market-oriented action has also become the norm for government.

These developments have important consequences concerning the ethics of public servants.

While in the traditional Weberian bureaucracy the responsibility of public servants is restricted to the execution of orders given by the legitimate power, public servants now have a broad spectrum of responsibility. Also public servants have become more accountable: the traditional hierarchical accountability has been supplemented by new forms of accountability towards other stake-holders, e.g. concerned citizens. Citizens charters, internal and external audit mechanisms have supported this development. The trend towards decentralisation and devolution also poses the problem of ministerial responsibility: the question is to what extent a minister can be held responsible for the acts of more or less autonomous organisations, unless the latter accept partial political responsibility.

In emphasising customer orientation, government has been transformed from a closed bureaucracy towards a transparent body. Service to the public has become a central value for all public servants. The traditional discretion has changed into a duty of transparency, information and openness. Public servants have the right and the duty to inform and to communicate.

In core departments, public servants are closely involved in policy development, decision making and evaluation. This runs counter to the public servant's traditional political neutrality.

Finally, as a result of business-type managerialism, public servants have become more or less public entrepreneurs striving for results. If results, however, become more important than the means to reach these results, traditional public service values such as honesty, fairness, equity and equality are threatened; at that time, legitimate means are no longer taken into account. The greater the ties between the public and the private sector can also enhance fraud, influence pressure and corruption. This explains why more attention is paid nowadays to the question of integrity in all countries.

3. In search of a new ethics for public servants

The traditional ethics of public servants is outdated. The question, however, is: what kind of a new ethics? Which values to guide the behaviour of public servants in the future and how might these values be operationalised in practice?
In the literature on the subject, some new values for public servants may be found.

First of all, there is the value of responsibility. Public servants are expected to behave in a 'responsible' way. This means that they take up their role as a public servant seriously and are aware of the consequences of their behaviour. More than in the past, decisions will have to be based on personal judgement. Indeed, as a result of decentralisation and devolution, the discretionary power of public servants has increased. Decisions must be made within a broad framework defined by politics. Also the variety of situations and the rapidly changing environment necessitate personal judgements by public servants.

A second important value is transparency, openness and service towards the public. Public servants are to serve the public, not vice versa. They must do all they can to inform and to help the public, to provide an optimal service.

Thirdly, there is the value of integrity. This means that the general interest and not personal interest must determine the public servants' behaviour. Although integrity was also an important value in the traditional ethics of public servants, this value needs to be updated and defined in a new way in the context of the business orientation of government.

The development of the new ethics of public servants is supported by changes in law and regulations, by structural changes and by changes in the organisation culture.

In the field of law and regulations, modifications are being made in civil service statutes, legislation (administrative law, criminal law, disciplinary law, ...). Codes of ethics are being rewritten. As to the structural changes, we see a trend towards contract-management and self-governance which supports the idea of the responsible public servant. New structures are being set up to enhance the transparency and openness of the public service. Measures are being taken to prevent corruption and to disclose and punish abuses (e.g. whistle-blowing structures, internal auditing). As to the organisational culture, new values are being introduced. This is supported by training programmes (e.g. integrity programmes).

In short, the new ethics of public servants need changes in different fields. This is only possible if the environmental setting of the public servant moves in the same direction.

4. EGPA Conference

The Conference theme has been elaborated in three Working Groups which have concentrated on the three central values of a new ethics for public servants: responsibility; transparency, openness and service to the public; integrity.

The Working Groups have treated theoretical topics as well as empirical studies or practical matters. Emphasis has been made on changes in regulations and legislation, changes in structures, or changes in organisational culture. Comparative studies as well as case studies were presented.

Below, the problems and topics which have been treated in the different Groups are summarised.

Working Group 1: Responsibility

The different aspects of responsibility have been discussed: responsibility as competence, accountability, and responsible behaviour. The following questions have been examined:

- to what degree can public servants be juridically accountable?
- must public servants be politically accountable?
- what is the impact of decentralisation and devolution on ministerial responsibility?
- what are the dysfunctions of the 'responsible' public servant: to what extent can this lead to an escape of responsibility, apathy and delay in the administrative process?
- to what extent can a code of ethics promote responsible conduct?
- how can loyalty towards different stake holders be integrated into one system?
- how can the 'responsible' public servant be supported by management (personnel management, financial management, ...)?
- in what cases is the disobedience of public servants considered legitimate?

Working Group 2: Transparency, openness and service to the public

This working group has treated the different aspects of transparency, openness and service to the public. Questions here were:

- is there a typical public service orientation?
- what are the boundaries of the right of public servants to inform and to communicate?
- how can the rights of public servants be combined with loyalty to the legitimate power?
- how can the privacy of citizens be protected in a transparent administration?
- what are the experiences with citizens' charters; how has this influenced the behaviour of public servants?
- what are the experiences with ombudsmen?
- what are the experiences with whistle blowing: when and how is whistle blowing legitimate, what are the effects on the transparency of the public service?

Working Group 3: Integrity

This Working Group has treated the problem of corruption in the public sector and the way in which the problem is handled.

- has the business orientation of government enhanced corruption in the public sector?
- does integrity have a different meaning for the public sector than for the private sector?
- how can integrity be promoted?

- what are the experiences with new institutions such as ethical codes, hot lines, ethical commissions, ethical agencies, ethical officers, ...?
- what are the effects of integrity programmes?
- are improved ethics and high government performance compatible?
- to what extent are commercial activities and plurality of offices allowed concerning public servants?
- how to deal with gifts/bribes ?
- how can integrity be supported by management concepts and instruments (e.g. auditing, mobility, split functions, ...)?

In relation to the specific problems and topics of the Working Groups, general issues concerning ethics have also been treated, e.g.:

- is there a difference between the ethics of public servants and the ethics of politicians?
- to what extent are the ethics of public servants contingent to functions, organisational setting and environment?
- what are the mechanisms to improve ethical responsible conduct?

The reports of the Working Groups are found in this yearbook, as well as some interesting papers which were presented during the conference.

We hope that this work will contribute to the elaboration of a new ethics for public servants.

Setting the Scene:
Keynote speeches

Remedies for Misgovernment:
changing the mix, but not the ingredients?

Ch. Hood[*]

1. Introduction

1.1. Our conference deals with an old problem in a new context. So this paper aims briefly to review a set of general 'remedies for misgovernment'[1] and then look at them in the context of contemporary public management reform. What are the main available remedies for misgovernment? And how may we need to vary, reconfigure or re-use them in the current context of managerial thinking about public service reform?

1.2. This paper makes three main points. First, there is more than one possible remedy for misgovernment. Four general categories are suggested below. Second, the mix among the different remedies may need to be altered with contemporary changes in public management but it seems unlikely that any of the basic forms can be dispensed with altogether for any length or time. Third, the outcomes of efforts to reshape government may be surprising or ironic for some of the themes that are conventionally associated with stereotypes of 'New Public Management'.

2. Four Basic Remedies for Misgovernment

2.1. The analysis of remedies for misgovernment is a classical concern of political science. One possible way of framing the issue is to draw on the developing literature of grid-group cultural theory (Thompson Ellis and Wildavsky 1990) to identify four basic ways of promoting accountability and keeping malfeasance in check, which can be termed oversight, mutuality, competition and contrived randomness (Hood 1996; Hood and James 1997; Hood, forthcoming). Each of these basic forms, summarised in Figure 1 and briefly described below, incorporates a vision of how accountability should work and how it should be promoted. Each can come in many different varieties and in real life we constantly encounter hybrids and compounds of these types. So the four-part typology is intended as a loose organising framework for discussion, not a rigid or dogmatic scheme.

2.2. Oversight and Review.

2.2.1. One familiar way of promoting accountability and ethics in public services involves self-conscious oversight in some form (an approach which in previous work [Hood 1986] I have termed 'comptrol'). It involves formal overseers of some kind to whom officeholders or other public service providers are to be answerable for the operations they perform. The aim is to promote desired behaviour by some sort of code of good behaviour associated with an institution or agency whose job it is to further that behaviour.

---

[*] Prof. Dr. Christopher Hood, London School of Economics and Political Science, United Kingdom.

Figure 1. Four Basic Remedies for Misgovernment

BUILT-IN RANDOMNESS

OVERSIGHT AND 'COMTPROL'

COMPETITION

MUTUALITY

2.2.2. This remedy for misgovernment is long-standing and comes in many different variants. It stretches back to the days of procurators and censorates, such as the famous Imperial Censorate of pre-1911 China which for more than a thousand years played the role of inspecting and checking the imperial public service, impeaching wrongdoers and even criticising imperial policy (Kamenka 1989). Modern European states, albeit in different forms, make substantial use of regulatory oversight over and inside government, including waste-watchers (like public audit offices), quality checkers (like ombudsmen and inspectors) and 'sleazebusters' (like anti-corruption commissions). Put together, these various overseers can amount to a substantial regulatory 'industry'. In the UK that industry seems to have been growing substantially over the past twenty years, at a time when the public service as a whole has been substantially downsized (Hood et al 1997).

2.2.3. Oversight and review as a method of checking misgovernment comes in many different forms. Five of the most common types are <u>inspection</u>, <u>audit</u>, <u>arbitration</u>, <u>authorisation</u> and <u>certification</u>. <u>Inspection</u> involves direct observation of the regulated institution by some sort of visit, often concerned with the process by which the organisation does its job; <u>audit</u> involves primarily examination of documents to assess performance in relation to fiscal regularity or some other criterion; <u>arbitration</u> involves handling disputes or complaints to arrive at determinations of what constitutes good administration or proper procedure; <u>authorisation</u> involves the requirement that the regulatee organisation obtain the permission of the regulator organisation for a particular course of action; and <u>certification</u> involves a formal declaration of fitness for a specified purpose. Commonly we find the regulators of government mixing and matching these approaches, and this list is far from exhaustive.

2.2.4. Such overseers also vary in terms of the sanctions available to them, how much discretion they have, and how the different players relate to one another, particularly in terms of the social distance between the regulators (whoever they are) and the regulated. The Chinese Imperial Censorate (referred to above) was extreme in this dimension in that there were draconian measures to ensure social 'distance', notably by prohibiting anyone from joining the Censorate who had a close relative in the public service (to prevent conflicts of interest) and by recruiting Censors only from fresh graduates who had not served in the public service (Hsieh 1925: 98). Very few contemporary regulators of government approach this level of 'relational distance' (Grabosky and Braithwaite 1986: 205-7).

2.2.5. When something is perceived as going wrong in public services - whether it is 'sleaze', police malpractice, organisational failings exposed by some post-disaster inquiry or other shortcomings - the normal reflex reaction is to set up or step up internal regulation in the form of oversight (or 'comptrol') of one kind or another. And it would be surprising if it were otherwise. After all, that is how regulation over business typically grows and develops, as a set of 'tombstones' to past disasters, and regulation inside or over government might be expected to follow a similar pattern. If there is an 'ethics problem' in contemporary government, the conventional reaction is to seek some reconfigured form of oversight to deal with it.

2.3. 'Inspector-free' Controls: Mutuality

2.3.1. Even - or perhaps especially - in an age of 'managerialism', oversight or 'comptrol' in all its various forms is unlikely to disappear as a remedy for misgovernment. But it is by no means the only available ingredient. There are 'inspector-free'[2] forms of control (Beck Jørgensen and Larsen 1987) whose importance has often been stressed from the viewpoint of cybernetics, institutional economics or cultural analysis but which can easily become invisible if we adopt an exclusively 'comptrol' mentality to the regulation of government. One of the best-known 'inspector-free controls' is mutuality, which involves accountability to a peer-group rather than to an external regulator, and shapes individual behaviour by group influence. In such a system the 'regulator' is immanent: there is no institutional distinction between regulator and regulatee, and the regulatory 'rules' are part of the social fabric rather than externally enacted.

2.3.2. Mutuality is a central feature of the burgeoning literature on policy networks and communities and it is a well-known regulating mechanism in the world of the traditional professions (of which a central defining feature is that decisions on granting or withholding permission to practice and on discipline and ethics are arrived at by members of the profession themselves). 'Public management' is rarely a profession in quite that form, but mutuality can be important as a form of regulation inside government at many levels, and is often seen as the real key to public service ethics, at every level from police patrol on the beat to the highest mandarins in the chancelleries and topmost offices of government. For example, it is sometimes said that the ethics questions that are dealt with in other countries by administrative law have traditionally been resolved in many of the Westminster model countries by 'conversations' between Ministers and civil servants (Foster 1996), and even in Germany, with its 'constitutionalized' approach to civil service conduct, the importance of Beamtenethos maintained by a professional dynamic and going beyond the letter of the law, has long been recognised.

2.3.3. Like oversight, mutuality can come in many different detailed forms. It can be built into formal structures (notably in collegial institutions or teams in which power is divided among several co-participants and each member has a 'seat and voice') which require interactive processes of decision-making. It can be built into formal decision-making procedures, as in the famous ringi system in the Japanese civil service and its analogues. Or it can work in a wholly informal way, through service cultures and working relationships (like two police officers sharing a patrol car). Mutuality is harder to 'engineer' than oversight, but we can hardly leave it out of any discussion of public service ethics and accountability.

2.4. Competition and Rivalry

2.4.1. A third classic remedy for misgovernment - much stressed in recent rhetoric about public service reform, but in fact seldom absent from the institutional architecture of public services in one form or another - is competition and rivalry. Competition among candidates for office, notably through electoral rivalry, is an important recipe for exposing corruption and personal failings and keeping rapacity in check. Competition for titles, medals and honours is a traditional device for prompting public service and individual self-sacrifice. Competition for promotion and preferment within bureaucracies is an important way of putting the onus on to public officials to demonstrate that their work furthers the goals of the organisation and not just their own private gain (cf. Horn 1995: 112ff). Competition among bureaucracies or contractors for tasks or functions can also be an important remedy for misgovernment, for instance in the form of rivalry between police forces whose abuses would be harder to check if they monopolised their policy domain, or even among magistrates or auditors. Competition is therefore another powerful 'inspector free' form of control and a traditional remedy for checking abuse of power. In some conditions, a gram of rivalry can be worth a ton of codes of ethics (cf. Bentham 1931: 361).

2.4.2. In recent discussion of public management, much attention has been paid to methods of introducing more competition for custom through outsourcing, quasi-markets and other forms of rivalry among producers. The famous 'Tiebout model' of competition among rival governments for mobile taxpayer-citizens (Tiebout 1956) has also been much discussed as a regulating mechanism. Indeed, contemporary literature on regulation highlights competition among governments themselves, over tax, regulation and services, both at federal-state or local level and between states in the international arena (cf. Sun and Pelkmans 1995). And the forms of misgovernment to which competition can be a remedy go beyond bureaucratic waste in a narrow sense. Competition within the state is a central mechanism for checking abuse of office (notably in the division of power among rival branches or institutions within government). Competition between the state and private business has historically been an important way of checking market abuses, as in the case of 'metaphytic competition' when the state is used as a check on the market rather than vice-versa (Corbett 1965). Competition in some forms may present ethical problems in contemporary public management, but rivalry in some form cannot be dismissed as a potential solution, too.

2.5. Built-in Randomness: A Wild Card?

2.5.1. A final mechanism for checking malfeasance - albeit little 'theorized' or recognised in the literature of public management, or indeed any kind of management - is the deliberate use of chance in organisational design to constrain the opportunities for members of an organisation (or its clients) to promote private or sectional advantage. The basic logic of built-in randomness is to make public service organisation unpredictable in its operation. It is a familiar feature of relationships between public service organisations and their clients, for instance in the widespread use of a random term in tax audit systems or other random search mechanisms. But it also appears within the public service, for example in semi-random posting systems that (albeit at the expense of continuity) make working relationships unpredictable and apparently inscrutable internal inspection or oversight by central agencies such as Finance ministries.[3] And such an approach can even extend to oversight over those who provide public services (for example in unpredictable Parliamentary questioning or media 'feeding' patterns). 'Random agenda selection' is often deplored as working against a tidy vision of rational policy-making (Breyer 1993: 19ff), but it is also an important and often overlooked mechanism for keeping public officeholders in check.

2.5.2. Building randomness into the way public services work has at least two effects. First, it serves to ensure that corrupt conspiracies have an uncertain payoff. If decision procedures are hard to forecast, so are pressure-points for bribery or extortion (Rose-Ackerman 1978: 183-6). Collusion among colleagues for corrupt purposes will be more difficult if no single individual has complete authority over the deployment of resources (for example in the traditional separation of authorisation and payment in financial procedure and other 'dual key' procedures), but yet no-one can predict who his or her colleagues, subordinates or superordinates will be over any length of time. Second, and relatedly, it means that individuals - whether citizens, street-level bureaucrats or high public officials - who want to 'beat the system' in unauthorised ways have in effect to play a game of roulette against the organisation, facing an apparatus that works more like a gaming machine than a determinate slot-machine. That is not quite what the orthodox theory of bureaucracy (with its stress on predictable rule-following) teaches us, but it is a familiar feature not only of traditional public administration but also contemporary multinational corporations.

2.6. Mixes and Matches

Each of the basic remedies which were briefly described above has a long history, and each undeniably has its built-in drawbacks. But, unless quite new ways to check misgovernment can be invented (and that seems unlikely), those four basic types are the general materials which any contemporary attempt to reinvent or reengineer public services needs to employ. Even so, each of the four types referred to earlier contains many different possible variants, and there are possibilities of mixing and matching that further extend the range of alternatives through combinatorial complexity. Space precludes a detailed exploration of all the variants and hybrids of these four basic types, but it can be noted in passing that at least six pairwise combinations are possible, namely peer-group review (mutuality/oversight), peer-group competition (mutuality/competition), randomised review (oversight/contrived randomness), randomised competition (competition/contrived randomness), quasi-markets (competition/oversight) and demarchy (mutuality/contrived randomness). These variants, summarised in Figure 2, may also provide important materials for remedying misgovernment. An example is John Burnheim's (1985) argument for a mix of randomness and other forms of control, in the form of policy-setting for public services by randomly-selected citizen committees. In conditions when no-one can predict exactly who their colleagues will be, he argues, the fundamental conditions for corruption and its diminutives within government (namely close-knit organisation and secrecy) essentially disappear. Accordingly, in those conditions the traditional obstacle to outsourcing most public services (namely corruption in the tendering or contract management process) would also disappear. So on this reasoning, if only we could build enough randomness into public service direction, much of the need for large public bureaucracies and the ethical problems that go with them would disappear.

Figure 2. Compound Remedies

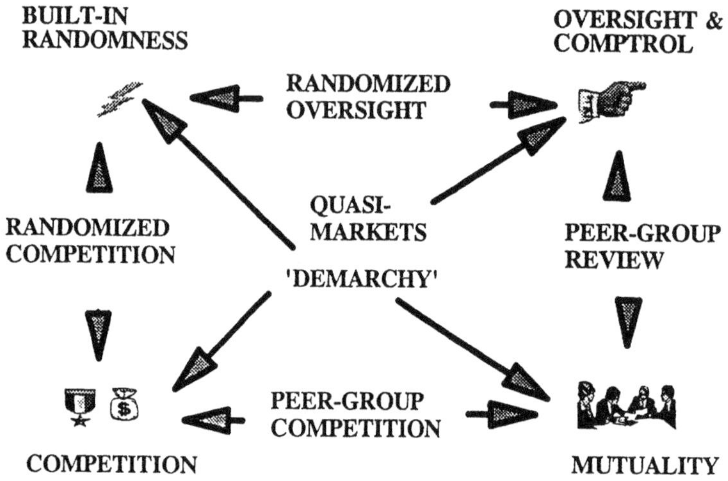

```
BUILT-IN                                          OVERSIGHT &
RANDOMNESS                                        COMPTROL
              RANDOMIZED
              OVERSIGHT
                    QUASI-
RANDOMIZED          MARKETS                       PEER-GROUP
COMPETITION                                       REVIEW
                   'DEMARCHY'


              PEER-GROUP
              COMPETITION
COMPETITION                                       MUTUALITY
```

3. Contemporary Public Management Reforms - Changing the Mix ?

3.1. Many of the themes involved in contemporary reforms of public management have implications for each of the four families of remedies against misgovernment discussed above. Some of those general remedies fit much more obviously into a conventional 'managerialist' agenda for reshaping public services than others. But there are variants of all of them - as well as hybrids among them - that relate to such an agenda. Indeed, it seems doubtful if any fully satisfactory system for promoting accountability and checking malfeasance can do without any of these four basic ingredients, at least for long.

3.2. Oversight, at least in its traditional form, can be problematic for any managerial agenda whose central thrust is to increase the ability of individual managers to 'add value' to public services through initiative and discretion (Moore 1995). Part of the thrust of the reform agenda in a number of countries (such as the USA, New Zealand and the UK) has involved the idea of 'deregulation' within government (Dilulio 1994) to liberate public service managers from the shackles of process controls and egregious public-service-wide rules, particularly over pay and the handling of staff, and to increase the pressure on those managers to achieve substantive results. Viewed from the perspective of 'deregulating government', public sector-specific oversight may at first sight seem to be more part of the problem of blurred accountability and 'management avoidance' in government, than part of the solution. From that perspective, traditional inspection and the regularity of audit systems tend to be criticised as obsessed with process and detail rather than results, authorisation systems as sapping managerial initiative, and the whole structure of oversight in government as excessively complex and contradictory in its demands, creating endless 'double binds' (Hennestad 1990) allied with high compliance costs that interfere with effective public service management.

3.3. From an orthodox managerial perspective, it may therefore be questioned whether much of the organisation of public services really needs a special heavy-duty regulatory framework to govern it, as distinct from the general framework of employment law, health and safety law and the general laws against bribery, racial discrimination and the like (although such an agenda is by definition harder to realise in the public law countries than the common law countries). But to the extent that public sector-specific oversight is needed, an orthodox managerialist agenda suggests a need to refocus such oversight systems from a process-dominated towards a more result-oriented perspective (as has happened in New Zealand with the 'contractualization' of oversight and less dramatically in the UK over the last decade or so when the Audit Commission, with an 'output' and 'value for money' policy-evaluation perspective has been encouraged to work alongside the traditional professional inspectorates with their traditional focus on process and method). A managerialist perspective also suggests a more critical examination of the structure and purposes of the various overseers and regulators working inside government (including more attention and calculation of the compliance costs they impose on their charges in the same way as has developed for the regulation of business in the EU through its fiche d'impact assessments). Further, to prevent oversight systems within government from stultifying public service operations, a managerial perspective would suggest a need to move internal regulation from an emphasis on simple steering and/or universal checking (the search-every-suitcase approach to regulatory oversight) to more reflexive approaches which rely on institutional self-regulation as the default position (Ayres and Braithwaite 1992) and give more play to managerial initiative.

3.4. Mutuality is also a remedy for misgovernment which is potentially problematic for a conventional 'managerial' recipe for reshaping public services. After all, one of the driving themes of recent public management reform rhetoric has been a deep distrust of the capacity for effective management built into the governance of the traditional professions, particularly in education and health care. Collegial self-government in many public service professions has been perceived as a cosy, self-perpetuating world which entrenches expensive work demarcation practices and makes effective cost control and responsibility difficult. Managerialist thinking tends to endorse at least part-replacement of such structures by more conventional corporate hierarchies, linked to external oversight mechanisms focusing more sharply on 'value added' and a 'customer' perspective. Certainly, you do not need to be a dyed-in-the-wool 'New Public Management' zealot to recognise that mutuality can at least in some conditions work as a conspiracy against the laity, as in the often-cited case of police 'canteen culture' working to reinforce police behaviour that diverges sharply from official goals or ethical standards taught in police college. For elected politicians too, there appears to be sharply decreasing public faith in the capacity of parliaments and political parties to regulate themselves in a collegiate style, in the face of the 'sleaze' scandals that have erupted in many of the OECD countries over the past decade. Mutuality in such cases can be seen as too often supporting the wrong kinds of ethics and working against individual accountability.

3.5. At the same time, a vision of reshaping public services in a more managerialist direction can hardly do without mutuality in some form. After all, while pure mutuality in its traditional collegium form in public service professions often attracts managerialist criticism, so do the fragmented and isolated work patterns of many traditional bureaucracies. And favoured remedies for such failings include team structures cutting across traditional grade levels, boards of management to inject a strategic management perspective at the top of public organisations and for the empowerment of front-line staff. Mutuality cannot be avoided for 'think tank' or special project organisation, and often appears indispensable for effective organisation in many other contexts. So from a managerialist perspective on reshaping public services, mutuality is less an element to be removed altogether than to be linked with other ingredients for restraining malfeasance and promoting accountability.

3.6. Competition, unlike oversight and mutuality, is an institutional ingredient which on the face of it is much more aligned to an orthodox managerial agenda for reshaping public services. As noted earlier, competition through market-testing and quasi-markets has been much advocated over the last two decades as a means for cost containment and increasing service quality. The problem is that competition in that form can be more of a source of than a remedy for malfeasance if it leads to corner-cutting, side-payments or even sabotage of rivals for competitive advantage, and fear of such practices underlies many of the worries that have been expressed about the potentially negative ethical effects of 'New Public Management' practices. Just as increased competition in science can increase the incentives to commit scientific fraud in order to establish 'discovery claims' and increased competition in electoral politics can increase the incentives to sabotage the operation of rivals by 'dirty tricks' campaigns, so increased competition within bureaucracies can increase the temptation to sabotage the work of rivals for promotion or appointment (cf. Horn 1995: 128) and increased competition for tenders or contracts can increase incentives and opportunities for bribery and extortion.

3.7. Accordingly, the challenge for a managerial vision of public service provision is to make use of competition in ways that prevent rather than encourage corner-cutting. One such application of competition is what Andrew Dunsire (1990) calls 'collibration' processes in government (where control is achieved by interpolating among rival and contradictory processes). That fundamental process can easily be dismissed as 'inefficient' from a perspective which equates control solely with homeostatic negative feedback systems focused on clear-cut targets, but many of the fundamental ethical issues in government do not lend themselves to point-settings. Indeed, in view of the alleged domination of 'new right' thinking over recent decades, surprisingly little attention has been paid to some of the traditional uses of competition to foster an ethic of public service, such as honorific rewards in the form of medals and honours, 'adversary bureaucracies' or even the kind of pecuniary competition once advocated by Bentham to keep public service salary costs down (in which candidates selected for technical competence to hold office then had to engage in a bidding process involving how little they would accept in terms of salary for the job[4]).

3.8. Randomness as a method of public service regulation is not so much attacked as ignored in conventional managerial reasoning about reshaping government. And one can see why. The idea of designing organisations to approximate to gaming machines at least ostensibly runs against the grain of purposefulness, 'proactivity' and managerial discretion that lies at the heart of any orthodox managerial agenda. And certainly some of the organisational changes associated with contemporary reforms in public services would seem to be reducing the scope for the 'gaming-machine model' within public organisation in its traditional form. Those changes include the trend to downsizing public bureaucracies and outsourcing service delivery, especially at the field level, together with heavier emphasis on control through key 'strategic' targets rather than process checks. If public bureaucracies become too small and 'limbless' to incorporate any substantial element of unpredictability in their operations, extra demands are inevitably thrown on to the other regulatory mechanisms to keep public services in check.

3.9. The challenge for a vision of a managerialized public service is how far malfeasance can be successfully restrained and public service providers held in check without substantial elements of unpredictability and randomness in processes such as budgetary review or financial operations. In an ideal managerialist world, would randomness disappear altogether in organisational functioning, putting more pressure on the other remedies for misgovernment? Or, as with the other remedies, do we need to rethink organisational randomness and refocus the way it works?

4. Potential Paradoxes

4.1. The last section briefly sketched some of the ways that contemporary public management changes may change the mix and emphasis of the four basic remedies for misgovernment, and some of the challenges that poses. But the changes may not be stable or predictable. A number of 'revenge effects' (in Edward Tenner's [1996] phrase) are possible. The effects of a managerialist agenda on the range of remedies for misgovernment discussed here are harder to establish than might be supposed on the basis of the many confident pronouncements that have been made about that agenda. That is because it is hard to anticipate the consequences of action in complex institutional systems and the unintended side- or even reverse effects that attend most forms of social intervention in human affairs (Sieber 1981). Far from being immune to such processes, the complex of changes that goes under the slogan of New Public Management can be expected to be quite vulnerable to them.

4.2. In the case of **oversight**, changes associated with the managerialist agenda will not necessarily achieve the ideal of 'deregulating government' embodied in the idea of control through a few strategic indicators. On the contrary, many of the themes associated with contemporary changes in public management can easily increase rather than decrease the density of oversight as a method of regulating government, for at least three reasons. First, increasing preoccupation with 'sleaze' and 'the proper conduct of public business' across many of the wealthy democracies is quite likely to produce new or enhanced 'ethics regulators' to police the boundaries of acceptable conduct by those in public office. Second, separating policy-making and implementation by outsourcing, 'agencifying' or contractualizing service delivery can produce more formal external regulation of service delivery agencies, for instance in heavy-duty oversight of 'quasi-markets' in health and education. Third, to the extent that a managerial philosophy of 'letting managers manage' does take hold in public services, there is likely to be a counter-reaction in the form of enhanced pressures for uniform treatment from law courts, ombudsmen or similar bodies. Regulatory oversight may be ideologically questionable from the viewpoint of those who aim to deregulate government to make it more businesslike, but ironically the restructuring of public services into corporate and competitive units many in fact have the opposite effect, of enhancing internal regulation rather than diminishing it. That has certainly been the UK's experience over the past two decades, which has displayed in effect a mirror-image process of increased managerial freedom being offset by increasing formal regulation for many public service operations (Hood and Scott 1996).

4.3. There are several related pitfalls here for a managerial agenda for public service reform. One is the risk that a movement intended to empower public service managers can instead turn out to empower middle-level 'bean-counting' regulators[5], with performance auditing systems turning into paper trails that stifle performance and creativity. Attempts to clarify objectives at one level can be foiled by the establishment of regulators with contradictory objectives at another level within government. And the expansion of oversight systems extending the notion of financial audit into new, more nebulous areas of public service performance does not necessarily mean that public service professionals will be subject to more effective checks. It may have the reverse effect if the response to enhanced regulatory pressure is to weaken internal collegiate processes of self-regulation, and thus turn hitherto responsible professionals into cheating or even defiant regulatees (Power 1994). How to avoid such pitfalls, without throwing out the managerial baby with the bathwater, is one of the major challenges for contemporary public service reform.

4.4. As suggested in the last section, pure **mutuality** is at least as unfashionable as oversight as way of regulating public services, with the managerialist assault on professional self-government and collegiality, but the result of that assault is typically a hybrid of mutuality and other mechanisms rather than unalloyed corporate managerial control in domains like health and education. The reason for that seems to be that mutuality can be as hard to live without as it is to live in such domains. In the UK, some of the worst excesses of university mismanagement over the last decade or so have tended to come from university principals or vice-chancellors whose institutions involved no effective element of mutuality in their internal structures, such that the only check on self-serving or ill-judged decisions by top management lay in scrutiny from outside auditors and regulators, who proved better at uncovering the mess afterwards than in checking it before serious damage had been done. The result has been a partial return to a stress on mutuality rather than a corporate management model as a recipe for good governance in universities.

4.5. A managerial vision of public service transformation needs to create effective hybrids between mutuality and corporate control by managers (for example in the development of clinical audits in health care or of university 'league table' rating exercises conducted by top academics) without discrediting the peer group element of the process by the major new conflicts of interest and ambiguities over accountability that such hybrids can introduce. How to engineer such hybrids without ending up with neither effective peer-group accountability nor effective answerability to external authorities is a second major challenge for contemporary public service reform.

4.6. For **competition**, the challenge for the managerialist agenda in reshaping public management is to harness competition for public services in ways that have ethics-enhancing rather than ethics-reducing effects in the conduct of operations. As noted earlier, competition can be an important recipe for checking misgovernment, through devices like division of power among rival institutions, races for election, appointment or promotion, institutionalised role-antonyms (like prosecutor and defence counsel), and even prizes and medals for public spiritedness and 'superogation'. Given current concerns about ethics and accountability, there may be a need for as much attention to be paid to competition as a remedy for misgovernment as has been paid to it in recent years as a means of cutting costs in public services, for instance in establishing a public management equivalent to the Nobel Peace Prize, to reward outstanding instances of ethical behaviour by public servants.

4.7. It was suggested in the previous section that many of the changes associated with contemporary public management reform - particularly outsourcing and downsizing of public bureaucracies - have the effect of removing the conditions for, and generally discrediting, **contrived randomness** as a remedy for misgovernment, at least in its traditional forms. But ironically, this recipe may be re-entering the public management stage in unexpected and unintended forms. While core public bureaucracies are reshaped in ways that give decreasing scope for the traditional gaming machine approach to organisation, institutional randomness may reappear in at least two other forms. First, increased reliance on multinational corporations, replacing traditional public bureaucracies as providers parts of public services through contract, may reintroduce this recipe through the back door, since contemporary multinationals make much more use of the random method of control through postings across their 'empires' than many contemporary bureaucracies do. Second, while randomness of relationships within individual bureaucracies and even in particular oversight mechanisms may be reduced by downsizing and 'going strategic', they may reappear in other forms. New forms of randomness may arise through development of new oversight mechanisms and in the interrelationships both of 'corporatized' or 'agencified' units as they bump up against one another in response to the changing policy environment. For example, as 'performance management' regimes develop into extended batteries of performance indicators, managers may in practice be unable to predict which of the large (and potentially contradictory) indicators will in practice carry the heaviest weight in the policy process. To the extent that that happens, performance indicator regimes, ostensibly offering a way to clarify managerial objectives, may turn into another 'gaming machine' element - and possibly for good reasons, given the well-known tendency of managers to skew organisational behaviour in relation to performance indicator regimes. A final challenge for contemporary public management is how to avoid unintentionally creating new forms of randomness in public service operation that buttress a culture of fatalism rather than can-do management.

5. Conclusion

5.1. The analysis above is necessarily brief and limited. It suggests that the available remedies for misgovernment can be thought of as rather like basic dance steps or plots for novels - consisting of a relatively unchanging basic set of approaches, from which we can form an infinite number of detailed applications and variants can be formed. It argues that some of the analytic thrusts of contemporary managerial thinking about how to reshape public services - its aspiration to liberate managers to 'create public value', its distrust of traditional collegiate governance in professional-dominated services like health and education and its association with measures likely to reduce the element of randomness built into traditional public bureaucracies - may well change the mix among those basic approaches, and create challenges for reshaping them for the new conditions. But it also suggests, following a long tradition of social-science analysis of institutional reform - that the application of the managerialist agenda to public service reform may well produce some unintended effects on the mixture of remedies for misgovernment described earlier. Taking oversight, mutuality or even randomness out of public service institutions is easier said than done. Putting all the weight on competition as a regulatory device is not likely to be a feasible long-term strategy, but the creative use of the other three basic remedies for misgovernment in the current conditions have been surprisingly little discussed. A robust agenda for public service reform needs to incorporate all of them.

Notes

[1] The term is Jeremy Bentham's (1931: 444-66) and he surveyed a range of remedies with his usual energy and thoroughness, though the list he produced was an uncharacteristically ad hoc one.

[2] More strictly, datum- or effector-free.

[3] Bentham (1983: 281) in his Constitutional Code points to 'the advantage, derivable ... from the use of chance, for the purpose of securing unexpectedness to inspection visits, and thence constancy of good order in the places visited'.

[4] Bentham (1983. 337-8). Bentham distinguished reductional bidding (to take a job at less than the appointed pay), emptional bidding (to pay money to take a job) and compound bidding, combing elements of reductional and emptional processes

[5] A frequent criticism of the executive agency programme in the UK (cf. Trosa 1994: 10, §2.26 and 28ff).

Bibliography

Ayres, I and Braithwaite, J (1992) Responsive Regulation: Transcending the Deregulation Debate, Cambridge, Cambridge University Press

Beck Jørgensen, T and Larsen, B (1987) 'Control - An Attempt at Forming a Theory' Scandinavian Political Studies 10 (4): 279-99.

Bentham, J (1983) Constitutional Code Vol 1, ed. F. Rosen and J.H. Burns, Oxford, Clarendon.

Bentham, J (1931) The Theory of Legislation, ed. C.K. Ogden, tr. R. Hildreth from the French of E. Dumont, London, Routledge and Kegan Paul.

Breyer, S (1993) Breaking the Vicious Cycle: Toward Effective Risk Regulation, Cambridge, Mass., Harvard University Press.

Dilulio, J (1994) Deregulating Government, Washington DC, Brookings.

Dunsire, A (1990) 'Holistic Governance' Public Policy and Administration 5 (1): 4-19.

Foster, C D (1996) 'Reflections on the True Significance of the Scott Report for Government Accountability' Public Administration 74 (4): 567-92.

Grabosky, P and Braithwaite, J (1986) Of Manners Gentle: Enforcement Strategies of Australian Business Regulatory Agencies, Melbourne, Oxford University Press.

Hennestad, B. W. (1990). The Symbolic Impact of Double Bind Leadership: Double Bind and the Dynamics of Organizational Culture. Journal of Management Studies, 27(3), 265-80.

Hood, C (forthcoming) The Art of the State, Oxford, Oxford University Press.

Hood, C et al. (1997) 'Regulation of the UK Public Sector: Mapping the Terrain' Bureaucratic Gamekeeping Discussion Paper No.4, London, LSE Department of Government.

Hood, C and James, O (1997) 'The Central Executive', Ch 9 in P.J. Dunleavy et al (eds) Developments in British Politics 5, London, Macmillan: 177-204.

Hood, C (1996) 'Cultural Variety and Institutional Control over Bureaucracy' Journal of Public Policy 15 (3). 207-30.

Hood, C and Scott, C (1996) 'Bureaucratic Regulation and New Public Management in the United Kingdom: Mirror-Image Developments?' Journal of Law and Society 23 (2): 321-45.

Hood, C (1986) 'Concepts of Control over Public Bureaucracies: "Comptrol" and "Interpolable Balance"' Ch 36 in F-X. Kaufmann, G. Majone, V Ostrom (eds) Guidance, Control, and Evaluation in the Public Sector, Berlin, de Gruyter: 765-83.

Horn, M J (1995) The Political Economy of Public Administration: Institutional Choice in the Public Sector, Cambridge, Cambridge University Press.

Hsieh, P C (1925) The Government of China (1644-1911), Baltimore, Johns Hopkins UP.

Kamenka, E (1989) Bureaucracy: New Perspectives on the Past, Oxford, Blackwell.

Moore, M (1995) Creating Public Value: Strategic Management in Government, Cambridge, Mass., Harvard University Press.

Power, M (1994) The Audit Explosion, London, Demos

Rose-Ackerman, S (1978) Corruption: A Study in Political Economy, New York, Academic Press, Ch 9 'Bureaucratic Structure and Corruption': 167-88.

Sieber, S (1981) Fatal Remedies: The Ironies of Social Intervention, New York, Plenum.

Sun, J-M and Pelkmans, J (1995) 'Regulatory Competition in the Single Market' Journal of Common Market Studies 33: 67-89.

Tenner, E (1996) Why Things Bite Back: New Technology and the Revenge Effect, Fourth Estate.

Thompson, M, Ellis, R and Wildavsky, A (1990) Cultural Theory, Boulder, Co., Westview.

Tiebout, C (1956) 'A Pure Theory of Local Expenditure' Journal of Political Economy 64: 416-24.

Trosa, S (1994) Next Steps: Moving On (An Examination of the Progress of the Next Steps Reform against a Background of the Recommendations in the Fraser Report [1991]), London, Cabinet Office.

Ethics in the Public Service - Current Issues and Practice

M. Maguire[*]

Public sector ethics has become a high priority concern for governments throughout the OECD area and indeed in many other countries across the globe. The last few years have witnessed a spate of new ethics initiatives both nationally and internationally, ranging from comprehensive new ethics regimes to more limited measures designed to close gaps in the existing systems.

Does this concern with ethics mean that standards in public life are perceived to be more at risk now than in the past, or that the existing frameworks for ensuring high standards of conduct are inadequate? Is it a response to fears or evidence of increasing corruption? Or is it because government is subject to much more public and media scrutiny and is concerned not only to maintain high standards, but to be seen to be doing so? All of these factors are working to varying extents, but the more fundamental issue driving the current debate is what impact public management changes are having on values and ethics and how ethics regimes may need to be rebalanced and revitalised in the changing public sector environment. As noted in a recent report by the OECD's Public Management Service, it is perhaps in the area of ethics that the tensions between traditional notions of public administration and new public management approaches are most evident, and much of what I have to say this afternoon will focus on how these tensions are being resolved in practice.

The Public Management Service - PUMA for short - is working closely with OECD countries both to analyse the nature of the ethical challenges facing the public sector and to help put in place effective and appropriate solutions. I will be drawing extensively on this work in the course of my remarks, not with the aim of reviewing in detail what is happening in individual countries, but more to give a flavour of overall trends and issues.

I want, firstly, to summarise briefly what appear to be some of the main areas of concern about ethics, as expressed in recent reviews and initiatives in OECD countries.

Secondly, I want to focus more specifically on the implications of public management reforms for public sector ethics and how OECD governments are dealing with new ethical challenges. I will conclude by drawing on PUMA's work in progress to outline some issues relating to implementing ethics regimes.

1. Concerns about ethics

The renewed focus on ethics and standards in the public sector is, first and foremost, a response to widespread evidence of declining public confidence in government, a decline

---

[*] Dr. Maria Maguire, Public Management Service, OECD.

fuelled by concerns about the integrity and standards of behaviour of public officials. While it is difficult to say objectively whether standards are in fact falling, what is clear is that public confidence has been severely dented by the exposure of mistakes and misdemeanours, maladministration, shady dealing and outright corruption. As noted in a recent PUMA report on ethics, few, if any, OECD countries have escaped the taint if not the reality of wrongdoing. As a result, ethics and standards in public life have become an important public and political issue, demanding effective action by governments (OECD, 1996).

At the same time, it is important to note that for most countries the issue is not one of wholesale breakdown in ethical standards. It is rather to do with clarifying and reinforcing these standards in a context where public management reforms are transforming the environment in which public servants work. This in itself presents a considerable challenge, and one which is still being worked through in all OECD countries.

Maintaining high ethical standards is important in all spheres of society of course. It is particularly crucial in the public sector because, in the words of a recent Australian government report, "of the position of trust, power and privilege which public servants hold, and the resulting obligation not to breach that trust and not to misuse their power or abuse their privilege. ...The trust protected by ethical behaviour is not just one that exists between the public and the public service. It supports too the public's confidence in the government and in the democratic process." (Management Advisory board, 1996) This point was expressed more starkly by the late Dutch Minister for the Interior, Catherine Dales, when she said "An administration stands or falls with the integrity of the government; any diminution of the integrity of the government means that the government loses the confidence of the public. And without the confidence of the public, democracy cannot work." (Maas, 1996)

The notion of integrity in government goes much beyond eliminating corruption, essential as this is. Trust in government is founded on a shared understanding between citizens and public officials as to the basic principles and standards that are applied in administrative decision-making, the transparency of the decision-making process and the ability of public servants to account for the way they exercise the power vested in them. John Uhr notes, for example, that "The really distinctive quality of public managers derives from their responsibility to act in the public interest and to conduct their official activities strictly according to standards that can survive the closest public scrutiny by those responsible for ensuring the safekeeping of public expenditure.....[There is a] legitimate public interest in being reassured through evidence that public operations are true to merit, and are not being brought down by inappropriate private interests associated with typical breaches of merit -- such as nepotism, cronyism and associated forms of unmerited private access to public facilities." (Uhr, 1997)

This is why issues of public service values and public accountability are at the forefront of the discussion about public sector ethics in so many countries and why public management reforms raise complex questions about values and ethics. Indeed, as James Bowman notes, "..the kind of ethical problems that attract most attention are perhaps the least important. Flagrant, petty abuses and outright criminality are relatively easy to detect and remedy and they often trivialise ethics, distracting attention from the more frequent and genuine ethical concerns - that is choices that involve morally ambiguous situations. Most public servants will confront dilemmas where a simple right and wrong answer is not obvious. Management issues are infused with ethical dilemmas." (Bowman, 1996)

The concern for OECD governments, therefore, is not merely to strengthen their defences against corruption in the public sector, but to come to grips with new ethical issues that are emerging in the context of public management reforms, and to find ways of maintaining sound ethical standards that are consistent with the overall thrust of the reforms.

As countries move from a rules-based public administration to a results-based public management environment, there are an increasing number of "grey areas" where there are few guidelines to inform the actions of public servants and where governments acknowledge the need to provide clearer ethical frameworks. As the PUMA report emphasises, this is not to suggest that reforms have caused an increase in misconduct or unethical behaviour. But they have created a situation in which governments are finding that the systems that have traditionally governed and guided the behaviour of public servants are insufficient for the new, managerial roles public servants are expected to play, and are indeed often in tension with the demands being made on managers and staff in the new public sector environment. The specific problem for ethics management is how to integrate results, risk-taking and managerial flexibility with the appropriate standards of public accountability and due process that are necessary to good government.

Quoting again from John Uhr, "Managerial reforms are generally good as far as they go, but we should not expect them to be self-sufficient in terms of inspiration or dedication to community service. They do not provide a philosophical framework for revitalised public service." (Uhr, 1991)

It is not surprising then that the contemporary debate about ethics in many OECD countries tends to focus on:

- perceived tensions between traditional public service values and new values, and how to reconcile the two sets of values;
- how to rebalance ethics regimes in ways that are consistent with greater managerial flexibility, without undermining essential standards of accountability;
- how best to equip public servants to cope with the more complex ethical issues involved in new ways of delivering public services and new management approaches.

2. Public management reforms

We can trace these three, interrelated concerns through discussions about the implications for ethics of public management reforms. New ways of carrying out the business of government are significantly changing the environment within which public officials operate. The factors at work are well documented. Among the particularly significant developments are:

- the shift in emphasis from process and control of inputs to outputs and outcomes, with associated changes in the focus of accountability;

- devolution of authority and responsibility to managers;
- new forms of service delivery, such as agencies at arm's length from ministerial departments and contracting out to private sector providers;
- a much stronger focus on responsiveness to the interests of public service users, increasingly defined as clients or customers;
- and increased commercialisation bringing with it much more extensive interpenetration between the public and private sectors.

At the same time, public services are having to deliver the same or better services with fewer resources, while pressures for greater transparency in government mean that the actions of public servants are subject to public scrutiny on a scale hitherto unknown. PUMA's work documents an evident concern among OECD countries that the values and systems which regulate the behaviour of public officials may provide an inadequate foundation for ethical behaviour in the context of the modern roles public servants are expected to fulfil.

This point is well expressed by Kathryn Denhardt who notes that "Public administrators are still striving to develop an understanding of the ethics of their profession, not because it is so new, but because the understanding of the profession and its role in government have changed dramatically over the years." (Denhardt, 1989). Whatever stage they are at in terms of public sector management reforms, this is an issue that an increasing number of countries see a need to address.

For example, a Canadian government report on values and ethics notes that public servants feel the need for guidance about how service-oriented, market-driven public services can treat all clients equitably and how the paramount position of the public interest can be maintained. The same report goes on to note that with individual public servants being asked to exercise more judgement and discretion in program decisions and decisions on individual cases, and with greater decentralisation and delegation of authority in staffing, contracting and partnerships, public servants are concerned that in the absence of adequate ethical and accountability frameworks and proper safeguards, the door could be opened for accusations of bureaucratic patronage, favouritism and conflict of interest. The report observes that the greatest difficulties arise in the broad grey area that exists between behaviour that is clearly forbidden and behaviour that is clearly honest or ethical. (Canadian Centre for Management Development, 1996).

In a similar vein a Norwegian report notes that civil servants are exposed to influences and demands of quite a different character than previously and in ways that are more difficult to handle as a result of a focus on the interests of public service users, changes in the way public services are delivered, the transfer of authority from ministers to public enterprises and state-owned companies and the freeing of public officials from the rules and norms that previously governed their behaviour. (Bohagen and Blyme, 1996).

And an Australian report notes that conflict-of-interest situations are becoming more frequent as public service organisations move to a more service-oriented, market-driven approach, for example in agencies that deal with clients in business and industry who are in competition with one another. Staff in front-line social service departments are also being required to exercise greater judgement and discretion in regard to individual cases. The report notes the challenge involved in preserving the essential values of public administration - impartiality, equity and merit - while simultaneously striving for best practice in service delivery (Management Advisory Board, 1996).

As ministries and agencies gain more autonomy and flexibility, concerns are also being voiced that a cohesive public service culture based on shared values may be eroded and that systems of professional socialisation that inculcate these shared values may be breaking down. A number of countries have responded by clarifying the basic values that public servants are expected to espouse and setting broad guidelines for conduct - through new civil service codes, as, for example, in New Zealand and the United Kingdom, or by proposing to include a statement of values and responsibilities of public servants in public service legislation, as in Australia.

There are also concerns that with more recruitment from the private sector public sector norms and values need to be reinforced. Thompson notes, for example, that "As those who serve government come from more diverse backgrounds and begin with fewer values in common, the rules of government ethics are likely to become more important and more explicit" (Thompson, 1992).

If accountability is at the heart of public sector ethics, it is also here that public management reforms are having one of their most significant impacts on the ethical framework. The shift in emphasis, from compliance with rules and administrative procedures and accounting for inputs, to achievement of outcomes and performance is, in the words of the Australian Public Service Commissioner, altering both the standards and lines of accountability. Traditional forms of accountability focusing on detailed rules and controls are being reassessed in the light of efficiency and effectiveness criteria and are being replaced with accountability for results. And lines of accountability are being made more complex by changes in traditional chains of responsibility and hierarchical reporting and central standards of control as public managers gain greater responsibility and more discretion. (Shergold, 1997) In this context, new notions of strategic risk management are balancing uneasily against the conservative, risk-averse approach that has traditionally characterised the public service.

Much of the recent discussion of ethics in the Canadian public service has revolved around similar concerns that the principles governing the relationships between public servants, ministers and parliament are shifting and that public servants do not yet fully understand what the new principles are. (Canadian Centre for Management Development, 1996).

Accountability is further complicated by contracting out government activities to external service providers, with judgements having to be made as to how the ethical standards of government can be met without imposing unnecessary bureaucratic restrictions (Management Advisory Board, 1996).

Problems with assigning responsibility and establishing accountability are not confined to countries that have followed the path of extensive managerial devolution. A Portuguese government report refers to the problems of apportioning responsibility within a hierarchical and traditionalistic public service and notes that in recent years the model of hierarchical responsibility has been breaking down, as those at the top increasingly shirk responsibility, leading to "a severe distortion of public service ethics". (Moniz, 1996)

It is important to underline at this juncture that the point of my remarks is not to suggest that managerial reforms open the door to unethical behaviour by public servants. Indeed if anything public sector reforms have helped to create a climate where there is much more awareness of ethical issues and potential danger zones. This in itself is a healthy sign.

3. New ethics initiatives

I want to turn now to the issue of how OECD countries are responding to the concerns about public confidence in government ethics and how they are integrating ethics into new ways of managing in the public sector.

It is useful to think of the various mechanisms that can be used to reinforce ethics in terms of an ethics infrastructure, as set out in this diagram from the PUMA report. The infrastructure comprises the different elements that go to define public sector ethics, to encourage and maintain high standards of conduct and to combat corruption. The notion of an infrastructure underlines the interconnected nature of the different elements and that they need to be consistent with one another and mutually reinforcing.

The infrastructure comprises eight elements which can be categorised according to the main functions they serve - guidance, management and control - noting that elements may serve more than one function.

- Guidance is provided primarily by three main elements: strong commitment from political leadership; codes of conduct expressing values and standards; and professional socialisation activities such as education and training.
- Management can be realised through co-ordination by a special ethics body or an existing central management agency and also through human resource policies and employment conditions for public servants.
- Control is assured primarily through a legal framework enabling independent investigation and prosecution; effective accountability mechanisms; and transparency and public scrutiny.

Different countries will find their own ways of combining and balancing the various elements of the infrastructure to arrive at a consistent and effective framework in the light of their own circumstances. In deciding where to place the emphasis, countries need to consider both their current context and where they are moving in terms of their approach to public management. For example, if the main concern is to bring ethics management into line with changes in public management overall, it might be opportune to take steps to reinforce the professionalism of the public service and to re-emphasise, clarify or update the underlying values. In contrast, a review that has been prompted by evidence of wrongdoing or corruption will probably put the emphasis on strengthening the oversight and control elements of the ethics infrastructure.

As devolved, results-based management systems take hold, the balance in ethics management in a number of OECD countries appears to be shifting away from an emphasis on rules and policing compliance towards a greater reliance on encouraging high ethical standards through a focus on values and aspirations and through developing a more acute awareness of ethics on the part of public servants. In other words, there seems to be a shift from what is often termed a compliance-based approach to an integrity-based approach. (OECD, 1996) We can see a corresponding shift in a number of countries from service-wide mechanisms to a greater emphasis on the specific roles and responsibilities of individual agencies. These trends are most evident in New Zealand, Australia, the Netherlands, a number of the Nordic countries and the United Kingdom. By contrast, the United States continues to rely heavily on rules and compliance mechanisms.

An effective ethics regime requires elements of both approaches -- the problem is to get the mix right, and the costs of getting it wrong are potentially high. John Uhr encapsulates this well when he says that "Traditional accountability is an instrument of compliance and control, judging performance against the letter of the law. Contemporary public sector ethics is an instrument of motivation and morale, judging performance against the spirit (or motivating values). Accountability regimes are more effective than are ethics codes in combating fraud and corruption. Ethics codes are more effective than accountability regimes in reinforcing administrative professionalism. Both have important roles to play in maintaining democratic governance". (Uhr, 1997)

In seeking to put in place effective ethics regimes, governments are having to remind themselves of a point that may seem obvious but which is often neglected in practice. This is that ethics have to be seen as an ongoing activity, not as a status to be attained. Ethics are not just about establishing a set of rules or a code of conduct. They are, in the words of the PUMA report, an "ongoing management process that underpins the work of government. This essential point is well put by Kathryn Denhardt when she says that "Ethics are not a set of rules or values waiting to be discovered, that provides all the answers. In the complex world of public administration, principles and values rarely provide clear-cut answers to difficult problems. Instead ethics should be thought of as helping to frame relevant questions about what government ought to be doing and how public administration ought to go about achieving those purposes." (Denhardt, 1991)

We can see three main tendencies in recent ethics initiatives in OECD countries:

- In a number of countries - for example, Finland, the Netherlands, Norway, the United Kingdom, the United States - the primary focus is on checking for gaps in the existing ethics infrastructures and reinforcing where necessary, rather than completely overhauling the system. Interestingly, many of these reviews have resulted in measures to strengthen both the aspirational and the compliance sides of the ethics regime. For example, Norway has introduced new rules to close loopholes in relation to contract management while also reiterating basic values and attending to attitudinal development.

- Australia, Canada and New Zealand are among the countries devoting a great deal of attention to refocusing ethics management in relation to overall public management reform, to emphasise the guidance and management aspects and to redefine the nature of accountability. For example, according to a New Zealand report, the objective of recent ethics initiatives has been to "promote ethical conduct....consistent with a devolved management system, using an integrity-based approach rather than a more traditional compliance or rule-based approach". (State Services Commission, 1991).

- For a number of countries - Spain, Portugal, Mexico, for example, the issue is to put in place ethics frameworks as part of the modernisation of the public administration. In the new Eastern European democracies, this process of creating an ethics infrastructure from the ground up is a critical part of the development of their democratic systems of government.

While the focus varies from one country to another, PUMA's work identifies some important common threads running through recent reviews and reforms which it is worth summarising briefly as they clearly link to the types of concerns outlined earlier.

3.1. Redefining and reiterating public service values

At a recent PUMA meeting on ethics, participants from a wide range of OECD countries agreed on the importance of articulating the values that define and underpin public service. This is seen as critical to providing both public servants and the public with a common frame of reference regarding the principles and standards to be applied and in helping public servants to develop an appreciation of the ethical issues involved in the renewal of the public service. Examples of the importance attached to this include the statement of "The Seven Principles of Public Life" by the Nolan Committee in the United Kingdom and the reports on values and ethics issued recently by the Australian and Canadian governments.

And notwithstanding the cultural and institutional differences between countries, there appears to be a good deal of commonality in the values being promoted. These include core public service values such as integrity, impartiality and accountability as well as values that are associated with managerial reforms, such as efficiency, effectiveness and service to clients. Indeed Gilman and Lewis argue on the basis of a wide-ranging review of countries that ethics are conditioned by the existence of "fundamental values...that are closely associated with democracy, the market economy and professional bureaucracy, ... political values of freedom and justice and the administrative values of efficiency, effectiveness and responsiveness ..." (Gilman and Lewis, 1996).

The central concern for governments is to develop a vision of how the traditional values associated with public service can be integrated with the newer management approaches and to carry this through to ethics regimes in a way that provides public servants with a consistent set of signals as to how they should operate. A New Zealand government report acknowledges the need to imbue public servants with a wider range of values than before -- core values usually associated with public service, such as honesty, integrity, fairness and non-partisanship, along with values that have been brought centre-stage by management reforms, such as efficiency and accountability for results. (State Services Commission, 1996).

Indeed in some important respects, public management reforms can be seen as investing traditional values with new life. The previously cited Canadian report on values and ethics notes that service has always been a public service ideal, but one too often obscured by the complexity of government objectives and processes. The emphasis on service to customers or clients has reinvigorated the idea of service. In a similar vein, one of the focuses of ethics education in Australia has been to show how the new culture of customer service can give a more positive orientation to traditional values such as accountability, that hitherto focused largely on process rather than results.

3.2. New codes of conduct

An increasing number of countries have developed new codes of conduct for public servants over the past several years and it is noteworthy that governments evidently see a need to set out more explicitly the standards of behaviour expected of public servants. This can be interpreted on the one hand as a visible response to public concerns about public sector ethics. It is also an acknowledgement that the more complex public sector management environment calls for clearer guidance for public servants and that it is no longer sufficient to rely on public servants knowing the law and absorbing the professional norms as they go along. Codes are one way of providing guidance in the growing grey area between what is clearly forbidden by law and what is clearly ethical. They are also seen as helping to maintain common standards and values in a devolved management environment. In some countries (for example, Australia and New Zealand) there is a trend to supplement service-wide codes with specific codes or guidelines developed by individual departments and agencies, while in others (for example, Norway) the trend is to encourage the development of codes and guidelines by individual agencies rather than aiming for a service-wide code.

3.3. Exposing wrongdoing

Many of the countries in the PUMA study report procedures to facilitate reporting by public servants of concerns about actions that are potentially illegal or unethical. For example, the United Kingdom's new Civil Service Code makes provision for civil servants to report criminal or unlawful activities by others, or other breaches of the code, while the Netherlands has a system of confidential officers in government organisations to whom complaints can be brought (and members of the public can report suspected ethical breaches to the Internal Security Service). And the Canadian Task Force on Public Service Values has called for mechanisms to enable public servants to express concerns and to have those concerns acted on in a fair and impartial manner. Protection for those who disclose wrongdoing has also been strengthened recently in the United States and New Zealand.

3.4. Disclosure of interests

Several countries (Finland, the Netherlands, the United Kingdom) have introduced new measures related to disclosure of financial and other interests by public servants, others, such as the United States and Australia, have had such arrangements in place for some time. Such arrangements are seen as an element of improving transparency in government and also as an aid to identifying possible conflicts of interest.

3.5. Guidance and training

Increased attention is being given to guidance and training in a range of countries, both to ensure that public servants know and understand the standards of behaviour required of them and to alert them to potential "danger zones" and how to handle these. Examples range from a new training programme recently launched in Japan, to new induction and refresher courses in Finland, brochures dealing with integrity targeted at new recruits published last year by the Dutch government and the importance attached to this issue by the United Kingdom's Nolan Committee.

These are just some examples of the types of developments that are taking place and they are indicative of the extent of review and reappraisal that is going on.

PUMA is currently working with OECD Member countries to develop an instrument - a checklist - to assist in reviewing ethics regimes. This distils the concerns of a range of countries and I want to conclude by summarising it briefly as it may provide a useful way of thinking about how to deal with some of the issues I have outlined as you meet and discuss over the coming days.

4. Reviewing Ethics Regimes

Ultimately of course the effectiveness of any ethics regime must be judged in terms of the results it produces for government and society. But there are a number of key requirements against which the mechanisms in place can be checked. These can be expressed in terms of five questions.

4.1. Are the basic principles and standards clear?

Public servants need to be clear about the basic principles and standards they are expected to apply to their work and where the boundaries of acceptable behaviour lie. The basic frame of reference for ethical behaviour is set in a variety of ways -- through statements of the values and principles that guide public service, clear commitment and leadership by politicians, a consistent framework of rules and laws, and guidance on the standards of conduct expected and applying the standards. These are not sufficient of themselves to ensure a robust ethical culture, but they are an essential ingredient.

4.2. What is being done to foster an ethical culture?

Perhaps the most critical part of the ethics infrastructure is the set of activities and elements that can help to foster and sustain an ethical culture which permeates the everyday work environment of individual public servants. Public servants need to develop a strong awareness of ethical issues and norms and of how to apply ethical judgement to their work. Without this awareness ethics will remain an abstract concept; officials may not break any rules, but neither may they positively strive for high standards of professional integrity. Many of the measures that go to create an ethical culture need to be taken at the level of individual government agencies. They range from leadership by senior managers and incorporating ethical standards in management policies and practices, to putting in place a continuous dialogue on the ethical issues that arise in agencies, communication and training and involving external partners. There are also measures that need to be taken at the service-wide level in relating to these instruments and in terms of making sure that public service employment conditions overall are supportive of high standards.

4.3. Are there adequate oversight and accountability mechanisms?

The internalisation by public servants of sound standards and values is one of the best guarantees of an ethical public service. However, professional norms and socialisation processes need to be complemented by oversight and accountability mechanisms, which monitor ethical standards and require public servants to account for how they are discharging their responsibilities of public trust. Ethical standards are safeguarded and the scope for misconduct and corruption is reduced by having mechanisms to scrutinise actions and decisions of public servants both within agencies and at a service-wide level. As discussed earlier, some of the most difficult tensions with establishing an effective ethics infrastructure arise in the area of accountability as governments seek to reconcile the need for appropriate oversight and control with moves to a more devolved, results-based management environment. It is precisely as rules and ex-ante controls are reduced that accountability mechanisms gain in importance, and a review of the ethics infrastructure should seek to ensure both that there are adequate arrangements in place and that public servants are not being forced to work within an inconsistent framework.

4.4. Are there appropriate sanctions for wrongdoing?

Although the core of ethics management is to do with ensuring that public servants internalise and apply desired values and standards rather than with compliance with rules, an ethics infrastructure needs to include a strong capacity to investigate and sanction wrongdoing. Being seen to act effectively against misconduct and corruption is vital for public confidence in government and for the morale of public servants.
Mechanisms for the detection and investigation of misconduct and corruption are a necessary part of an ethics infrastructure.

4.5. Is the public sufficiently well informed?

Transparency in government is a powerful disincentive to corruption and misconduct.
Citizens and civic organisations can act as watchdogs over the actions of public officials if they are encouraged to learn how public management organisations are supposed to operate, if clear accountability mechanisms exist, and if information about the conduct of public affairs is available.

In sum, therefore, countries manage the ethics of public servants through a mixture of these measures and as public management reforms are implemented, ethics infrastructures need to keep pace with the changing environment in which public servants have to work.

In closing, I would like to say that while cross-national comparison can be useful in thinking about possible approaches to ethics management and in providing examples of successful and less successful practice, it cannot provide ready made models or instant solutions, even if these existed. Different countries must define their own approach on the basis on where they are starting from and where they want to move to with their systems of public administration. But regardless of where a country may wish to situate itself in regard to managerial reforms, ongoing attention to ethics will remain essential to public confidence and governments will be judged by their citizens not only on how efficient and effective they are, but on how well they safeguard the public trust invested in them.

Bibliography

BOHAGEN, Odd and BLYME, Oystein (1996), Report on the Management of Ethics in the Norwegian Civil Service, prepared in the context of a study by the OECD's Public Management Service (PUMA). Available on the OECD/PUMA Web site at http://www.oecd.org/puma.

BOWMAN, James S (1996), "Public Service Ethics: Prospects, Problems and Promise in an Age of Reform", Keynote address presented at the Fifth International conference on Public Sector Ethics, Brisbane, Australia, August 5-9, 1996.

CANADIAN CENTRE FOR MANAGEMENT DEVELOPMENT (1996), *A Strong Foundation - Report of the Task Force on Public Service Values and Ethics*, Ottawa.

DENHARDT, Kathryn G (1989), "the Management of Ideals: A Political Perspective on Ethics", *Public Administration Review*, March/April.

DENHARDT, Kathryn G. (1991), "Ethics and Fuzzy Worlds", *Australian Journal of Public Administration*, Vol. 50, No. 3.

GILMAN, Stuart and LEWIS, Carol W. (1996), "Public Service Ethics: A global dialogue", *Public Administration Review*, Vol. 56, No. 6.

MAAS, Johan H. (1996), Report on the Management of Ethics in the Netherlands Civil Service, prepared in the context of a study by the OECD's Public Management Service (PUMA). Available on the OECD/PUMA Web site at http://www.oecd.org/puma.

MANAGEMENT ADVISORY BOARD (1996), *Ethical Standards and Values in the Australian Public Service*, Canberra

MONIZ, Vargas (1996), Report on the Management of Ethics in the Portuguese Public Service, prepared in the context of a study by the OECD's Public Management Service (PUMA). Available on the OECD/PUMA Web site at http://www.oecd.org/puma.

OECD (1996), *Ethics in the Public Service - current Issues and Practice*, Public Management Occasional papers, No. 14, Paris.

SHERGOLD, Peter (1997), "The Colour Purple: perceptions of accountability across the Tasman", *Public Administration and Development*, Vol. 17, 293-306.

STATE SERVICES COMMISSION, New Zealand (1996), Report on the Management of Ethics in the New Zealand Public Service, prepared in the context of a study by the OECD's Public Management Service (PUMA). Available on the OECD/PUMA Web site at http://www.oecd.org/puma.

THOMPSON, Dennis F. (1992), "Paradoxes of Government Ethics", *Public Administration Review*, May/June.

UHR, John (1997), "Ethical Challenges in a Time of Change", background paper prepared for OECD Symposium on Ethics in the Public Sector, (forthcoming).

UHR, John (1991), "The Ethics Debate: Five Framework Propositions", *Australian Journal of Public Administration*, Vol. 50, No. 3.

*Ethics and Accountability in a Context
of Governance and New Public Management*
EGPA Annual Conference, Leuven 1997
IOS Press, 1998

New Public Management in the Flemish Administration: new ethical and political dimensions for civil servants

J. Van Rillaer[*]

On behalf of the Flemish government I would like to wish the President of EGPA, Professor Hugo Van Hassel and Mrs. Turkia Ould Daddah, Directrice-générale de l'Institut International des Sciences Administratives a successful closure of this conference. Furthermore I would like to make a salute to one of the pioneers of the innovation process of the Flemish administration, Honorary Secretary-General Mr. Etienne De Rijck.

Ladies and gentlemen, it is my pleasure to present you in a short notice of time a few considerations formulated by the Minister Vice-President of the Flemish government Mr. Luc Van den Bossche on the subject treated at this seminar.

In recent years, the increasing attention devoted to management in the public sector has already resulted in some significant improvements at every level of government. This is not always obvious to the superficial observer, particularly because the media usually focus most attention on the government organisations which are struggling or failing. Moreover, we must admit that in some cases only "superficial" changes were made, whether consciously or unconsciously, so as to avoid - or delay as long as possible - any real, far-reaching changes.

The public manager, even more than in the past, has become a real entrepreneur, an entrepreneur working on the border area between the political and the socio-economical market. As for any other entrepreneur, this means taking risks. Within the governmental organisation, it will be necessary to combine political rationale with its need for flexibility and sometimes veiled compromises, with the no-nonsense rationale of professional management which requires a steadfast, unambiguous approach. In the relationship with the environment, it will be necessary to combine the traditional demands imposed on government activity which require a solid and predictable approach, with the flexibility and inventiveness required to operate in a more market-oriented society.

Is this an argument for taking over the principles of the private sector in a very direct way ? "Should government," as President Wilson put it, "be run like a business ?" "Is everyone," as Al Gore puts it, "a customer of his government ?" With Henry Mintzberg, I agree that government should not limit its scope to the customers' view, not in the least because customers are not necessarily, by definition, treated well. Business is in the business of selling us as much as it possibly can - and *caveat emptor*; let the buyer beware.

People are certainly not mere customers of their government - no, thank you ! They expect (and have the right to expect) something more than face-to-face trading, and definitely

---

[*] Jos Van Rillaer, Director General, Ministry of the Flemish Community, Belgium.

something less than the encouragement to consume. When one receives a professional service from government (education, for example), the label *client* (and not customer) seems more appropriate for that role. In fact, a great many of the services we receive from government are highly professional in nature.

But, most importantly, one is a *citizen*, with rights that extend far beyond those of customers, or even clients. Most of the services provided by the government, including highways, social security, and economic policy, involve complex trade-offs between competing interests.

Customers, clients, citizens and subjects: these are the four hats that we all wear in society. Government should not consider itself a business corporation, nor should it treat civilians as mere customers.

This implies that public management has its own, much more complex finality than the private sector, which in turn implies that the ethical and political implications are obviously different. The *caveat emptor* principle of business does not suffice in treating clients, citizens and subjects. Governments should treat them in the best possible way, and nothing less will do. This is easier said than done, of course. Good government can perhaps best be defined in reverse: it is not doing bad things. In others words, it is not behaving unethically.

Ethical behaviour is a way of thinking, a way of living. Not a long list of "do's" and "don'ts". I myself am rather intrigued by one of the recommended tests to determine whether an act is ethical. Just ask yourself: "Would you want what you have done to become public knowledge ?" In other words, would you want your neighbour, who might be opposed to you enlarging your house, to know exactly what you have done to obtain your permit, and exactly how you have done it ? Or is there something you might want to hide from public view ? If the latter is the case, something might well be wrong ...

So in the development of modern civil service management, two - at first sight apparently contradictory - main guidelines can be distinguished : rationalisation on the one hand, and attention to values and principles on the other hand.

The first guideline is the way in which the functions of the public sector have become more businesslike and professional. The aim for greater effectiveness and efficiency can be seen in this light. A more clearly defined delimitation of responsibilities and job functions, the measurement of effectiveness, rewarding performance, contract and project management, are some of the management techniques which are examples of this approach.

The second guideline is concerned with matters such as honesty, a sense of ethics, integrity and attention to individual concerns. The responsibility for the welfare of the public domain is not merely a formal matter, but also has the characteristics of a mission, of norms and values, and of personal experience. In addition to effective decision making, working in a team is more and more a bare necessity for civil servants. This presupposes the necessary social and communication skills. Concepts such as an interactive government and the government as a learning organisation should also be seen in this context. To this can be added modern concepts of personnel policy, so that extra emphasis is placed on the personal development of employees, or increased responsibilities at every level, and on learning the skills which are needed to be able to exercise these responsibilities.

These two guidelines apparently constitute a paradox, but they nevertheless belong together. The first guidelines can be experienced in a way through the second, while the second can be achieved through the first. Together, they lead to the modernisation of the organisation of government. There is a place in this for both legitimacy and responsibility, imagination and ethics.

This means that traditional concepts, such as the primacy of politics, will acquire a new significance. For civil servants, both loyalty to government and their own responsibility will have to be priorities. This places high demands on their capacity to operate carefully and effectively in an environment which constantly places them in changing situations and makes them face new opportunities and threats. In future, civil servants will have to perform the impossible, not by way of exception, but as the rule. Professionalism and versatility, business and communication skills, and a basic approach of serving politics and society are some of the key words in the job description for this career as it will be exercised in the coming years.

In the ministry of the Flemish Community a multi-layered process of innovation is taking place :

- the principles of performance budgeting, strategic thinking and planning are being introduced.
- organisational, development, process reenginering is in operation.
- a new appraisal system, bottom-up appraisal and performance- management are being implemented.
- the systematic development of greater accountability and a reorientation of the core competencies.

All these changes have led to a new balance between the needs of the organisation and the wishes of the individual.

This new balance has found its expression in the Charter of the Flemish Community reflecting the new norms and values.

More recently a set of deontological rules were worked out for different professional groups inside the Flemish civil service. By these efforts, the Flemish administration is offering a new ethical basis to the civil servant in his newly defined role.

In conclusion though, I would like to point out, without wishing to belittle the importance of charters and ethical codes, that most importantly a new way of thinking is needed, which can't be enshrined in a virtually infinite series of do's and don'ts. This will require a thorough change of attitude for civil servants and politicians : ethically justified politics and ethics justified by Realpolitik.

I hope that this conference provides us with new, creative answers concerning the successful integration of the principles of equality, justice and fairness with the principles of a result-, quality- and client- oriented approach of civil service.

Thank you for your attention and... *bon appétit!*

Working Group on Responsibility

Report of the Working Group on Responsibility

M. Bovens & A. Massey[*]

This was a well attended Working Group; there were three sessions with 10 to 50 people attending. We also had, what is presumably an EGPA nouveauté: a joint session with the permanent Study Group on Informatisation. This was a very lively and fruitful session and we think it is worthwhile to organise more of these joint sessions in future EGPA conferences.

It is difficult to draw firm, substantive conclusions, as responsibility is such a broad and often fuzzy concept. Moreover, we found that there are quite large semantic differences among the various European languages, as to the meaning and uses of the word 'responsibility' and its various equivalences. Also, national contexts make for very different administrative and political agendas. It is one thing to talk about responsibility in an established liberal democracy, such as the United Kingdom, but quite something else in a new, formerly socialist, democracy such as Croatia. Several contributors and participants stressed the importance of the national, social, political and cultural context. Many of the papers illustrated the similarities experienced by academics researching the area, but they also identified the often wide disparities resulting from the unique factors pertaining to each national case study. It is clear that as well as the common European experience, policy makers and public servants must account for and embrace the diversity found within European Public Administration.

The Group therefore sought to define the different meanings of the word 'responsibility' and to place it within both its European context and the context to be found within individual case studies. We also made a distinction between two different concepts of responsibility, based on a paper by <u>Bovens</u>:

1. Passive Responsibility, which is responsibility in the sense of accountability and deals with questions such as: who can be addressed, who can be held accountable for certain actions or aspects of public organisations? In the workshop several papers particularly focused on the following specific questions:

- to what extent can public servants be juridically accountable?
- must public servants be politically accountable?
- what is the impact of decentralisation and devolution on ministerial accountability?

2. Active Responsibility, which is responsibility in the sense of virtue, which is about questions such as: what is responsible, i.e. appropriate behaviour for civil servants? In the workshop the following questions were raised in particular:

---

[*] Prof. Dr. Mark Bovens, Department of Legal Theory, Faculty of Law, Utrecht University, The Netherlands. Dr. Andrew Massey, University of Portsmouth, School of Social and Historical Studies, United Kingdom.

- what does the rise of QUANGOs mean for the responsibilities of civil servants?
- what are the dysfunctions of the "responsible" public servant: to what extent can this lead to an escape of responsibility, apathy and delay in the administrative process?
- to what extent can a code of ethics promote responsible conduct?
- how can loyalty towards different stakeholders be integrated into one system?
- how can the responsible public servant be supported by management (personnel management, financial management etc.)?
- in what cases is the disobedience of public servants considered legitimate?

Looking at the workshop from this dual perspective, a very interesting agenda for further research in public administration emerged:

Passive responsibility: Several papers, notably the paper by Babac and the papers by Cope & Sweeting treated the classical questions of democratic control and political accountability in the context of national and local government of Croatia and the UK, respectively. A number of other papers reflected on a series of new developments, both within and without the context of New Public Management, which demand for a reflection on issues of accountability:

1. *Independent agencies*: to whom are these politically accountable? This issue was the topic of a comparative paper on France and the UK by Fabre and was also addressed by Massey and Parsons.

2. *Networks*: Similarly, the rising importance of networks in public policymaking raises a number of difficult questions about political accountability. These were treated in the Massey and Parsons papers.

3. *Personal liabilities of civil servants*: Is it possible to hold civil servants personally liable for the mistakes they make in office. Both Belgium and France have made stricter laws in these respects. These were the topic of the Daurmont paper.

4. *ICT*: Who can be held responsible for the mistakes made by computer programmes and IC-technologies that are used by street level bureaucrats? This was the topic of a paper by Van den Hoven.

Active responsibility: These and other developments also raise a number of questions of a more substantive, ethical nature:

1. *Entrepreneurship*: Can you be a virtuous civil servant and an entrepreneur at the same time? This was the topic of a case study by Richardson & Cullen.

2. *Reflexive responsibility*: Can more responsive or reflexive ideas about responsibility, based for example on the work of Selznick, provide us with a new ethic for public administration? This was the topic of a paper by Dorbeck-Jung.

3. *ICT*: The rise of ICT in public administration also raises a number of ethical questions in public administration, for example: do civil servants, using ICT have a duty to make sure these programmes do not fail. This and other ethical issues was discussed in the papers by Van den Hoven and Raab.

4. *Civil disobedience*: Closely related was the topic of civil disobedience. May, or should, a civil servant disobey a superior, or the computer, if he or she thinks they give a very irresponsible assignment? This was the topic of a paper by Bovens.

One general conclusion stood out: the need to identify new supranational structures across the European Union to operationalize 'responsibility', both in its active and passive senses, for European public officials and those national officials implementing European initiatives and Directives. The weakness of existing national structures for dealing with this issue being demonstrated by several speakers. This could be a very appropriate topic for a future conference!

*Ethics and Accountability in a Context
of Governance and New Public Management
EGPA Annual Conference, Leuven 1997
IOS Press, 1998*

Towards Reflexive Responsibility
New Ethics for Public Administration

B. Dorbeck-Jung[*]

The great task of institutional design is to build moral competence into the structure of the enterprise. This is the key to corporate responsibility - private as well as public.
Philip Selznick, The Moral Commonwealth (1992), p.345

1. Introduction

When looking for a theoretical framework regarding the ethical evaluation of decision-making in public institutions, I studied Philip Selznick's moral theory (1992). It seemed to me that Selznick's work provided some basic concepts for the development of new ethics in public administration. I was struck by his concept of *reflexive responsibility*. Considering the challenges to the ethical behaviour of civil servants implied by recent developments in public administration, reflexive responsibility provides a theoretical starting-point for the development of evaluation standards. According to the theory of reflexive responsibility, the established structures, rules, methods, and policies are all open to revision. Such a revision, however, should be based on certain principles, that is, certain values and purposes should always be observed (Selznick, 1992: 338). Due to its dynamic and open approach, the concept of reflexive responsibility seems able to cope with the demands imposed by the current developments in public administration such as decentralisation, public-private partnership, and increasing commercial activities. Since Selznick's theory of moral institutions focuses both on the efficiency, effectiveness and flexibility, and on the stability, fairness and predictability of rules and procedures, it seems to provide the possibility of reconciling the tensions within the ethos of the new managerial state (Bovens, 1996).

This contribution aims to develop standards for the ethical evaluation of decision-making in public administration. In the *second section* the concept of reflexive responsibility will be discussed in the light of basic notions of Selznick's theory of moral institutions. The *third section* consists of an elaboration of ethical standards that will be applied to higher education quality evaluation regulations *(fourth section)*. Finally, we will draw some conclusions on the advantages and disadvantages of the ethical standards we developed in the previous section.

---

[*] Bärbel Dorbeck-Jung, University of Twente, Faculty of Public Administration, The Netherlands.

2. Selznick's theory of moral institutions

2.1. Moral Institutions

In 1992 Philip Selznick published a study of moral and social theory which is regarded as one of the intellectual cornerstones of the American communitarism movement. Taking an 'ecumenical' view, Selznick's aim was to integrate political, legal and moral theory within social theory. Like Emile Durkheim, he felt that sociology was primarily a moral science. He developed a normative theory that identified certain values and looked at the conditions that either advanced or impeded their implementation. Selznick's ideas are largely based on John Dewey's pragmatism, which combined ideas on liberation and social reconstruction with a strong commitment to responsible participation in effective communities. In addition, Selznick refers to the ethics of Aristotle and ideas of David Hume.

At the heart of Selznick's moral theory lies the concept of *moral institutions*. In viewing institutions as a product of social adaptation, "infused with values beyond the technical requirements of a task at hand" (1992: 232), his approach can be classified as a neo-institutional one (DiMaggio & Powell 1991; Etzioni 1994). In Selznick's neo-institutional perspective, formal acts (i.e. the adoption of a rule or statute) are seen as only a 'starting mechanism' of institutionalisation. Beyond the formal structure lies what he calls 'thick' institutionalisation. The idea of 'thick' institutionalisation includes both the official design ('formal structure') and the informal structure ('organic structure'): "Institutions are established, not by decree alone, but as a result of being bound into the fabric of social life" (1992: 232). The informal structure consists of attitudes, relationships, and practices that develop in the course of social interactions. Formal and informal structures together constitute the operative reality of institutions. In Selznick's publications, the term 'institution' refers to groups as well as to social patterns and practices.

Institutionalisation is associated with the realisation of values. In line with Dewey's ideas, values are identified by *moral experience*. Explanation and justification are based on what is learned from experience, and learning is linked to scientific exploration. Selznick identifies certain *core values* on which moral experience is based, such as responsibility, autonomy, integrity, reason, fairness, equality and democracy. Since all experience is regarded as contextual, there are no moral absolutes. Valuation implies a reconstruction and balancing of these multiple interests. The existing tensions between the different values should be taken into account. When conceptualising the morality of institutions, Selznick introduced the term *character*. This concept indicates an awareness of the institution's values and the consequence of its decision-making. In applying the concept of 'character' to institutions, it appears to have a wider scope than 'culture' (1992: 321). Selznick defines *culture* as the symbolic expression of certain common perceptions, values and beliefs. 'Character' includes culture as well as patterns of dependencies and commitments that lie at the heart of the tasks that are performed by an institution.

Selznick's theory of 'moral institutions' is based on the concept of reason. He elaborates his point of view by contrasting reason with rationalism (1992: 39). In his opinion 'reason' defines the 'fair terms of co-operation', while 'rationalism' refers to the advantages sought and perceived by each individual. Rationalism focuses on technical excellence, effectiveness and efficiency in decision-making. Selznick rejects the rationalist approach, stressing that in organisations values should be applied that go beyond the instrumental perspective. His conceptualisation is inspired by John Rawls' distinction between 'the Reasonable and the Rational'. Following Kantian doctrine, Rawls argues that 'the Rational' is subordinate to 'the Reasonable' because its principles limit absolutely the final objectives that can be pursued (1980: 530). According to Selznick, reason identifies the moral framework within which rational action takes place (1992: 59). Reasonable decision-making involves the reconstruction and evaluation of the interaction between ends and means. The consequences to other objectives should be taken into account ('consequentialist reasoning'). Thus, reasonable decision-making is seen as self-critical and self-limiting.

2.2. Organisations, Institutions and Communities

Selznick elaborates on the characteristics of moral institutions by focusing on the transformation of organisations into institutions and into agencies of communities (1992: 231). The idea of 'transformation' offers a comprehensive perspective for communitarian thought. Organisations are viewed as goal-oriented, rational instruments engineered to do a job, concerned mainly with effectiveness and efficiency. When the focus of an organisation shifts from goals to ends, principles and purposes, it is transformed into an institution. When an institution begins to emphasise aspects such as openness, dialogue and participation within decision-making, it is seen as having been transformed into a community. Regarding the form of decision-making and regulation, Selznick distinguishes between *management* and *governance*. While 'management' suggests rational, efficiency-minded, goal-driven organisation, 'governance' rather implies a focus on values, objectives and principles:

> "To govern is to accept responsibility for the whole life of the institution. Governance takes account of all the interests that affect the viability, competence, and moral character of an enterprise" (1992: 290).

According to Selznick, management and governance coexist and interact within institutions and communities. Though he regards both approaches as a continuum, for practical purposes he suggests classifying some decisions and activities as mainly managerial and others as mainly governmental. Governance is viewed as a 'moral necessity' both in private and in public institutions. Private government is also bound by the principles of due process. Regarding the political aspects of private enterprise, Selznick describes the business corporation as a social institution that takes its social function into account when undertaking economic activities (1992: 352).

Regarding the question of *who is responsible* within an institution or community, Selznick introduces the notion of the *moral agent*. In line with his ideas of moral institutions and governance he describes moral agents as follows:

> "To be an agent is to act purposively, and to do so on behalf of a principle or in the service of a goal or policy. To be a moral agent, something more is required. There must be values in play beyond technical excellence, efficiency, or effectiveness In its usual meaning, moral agency presumes a capacity to appreciate and reason from principles that speak (in the context at hand) to fellowship and integrity. Whether the agent does this well or poorly is a separate question." (1992: 238)

In Selznick's view, the term 'agency' connotes competence, intentionality and accountability. Since the moral premises and dilemmas of administration are not merely individual ones, accountability and responsibility can refer to individuals as well as to collectives. In many cases the individual responsibility for a final decision or for initiating and implementing a policy can be determined. Selznick feels that we should also keep in mind that organisations have attributes that can *not* be reduced to individual motivation and behaviour, such as the structure and pattern of decision-making. Since it depends on the social context whether individual or collective responsibility apply, or both of them, he suggests not to make a definite choice. He recommends, for example, if there is a case of negligence on the part of a municipal environmental organisation, that not just this organisation be held liable, but also its individual officials and employees.

2.3. Responsibility

As mentioned above, Selznick's concept of responsibility is reflected by the idea of a union between management and governance. Referring to Kant's 'categorical imperative', Selznick states that "the claims of purpose and efficiency are strong, but they cannot justify practices that reduce human beings to means only" (1992: 319). In this sense, responsibility should provide moral justification as well as effectiveness and efficiency in administrative decision-making. Departing from his concept of reason, Selznick moreover states that the conceptualisation of responsibility should focus on the interaction between the ends and the means. Here it is important that decision-making is based on certain principles. This is reflected by the term *integrity*. According to Selznick, integrity is a test of the moral character of an institution. It means being true to certain self-defining principles (1992: 322). The ideal of integrity is related to the unifying principles and moral claims on which an institution is based. In legislative decision-making, such unifying principles are, for instance, 'generality', 'publicity', 'intelligibility' and 'constancy'. These principles were laid down in procedures based on the values of due process. However, Selznick rejects the purely procedural approach to responsibility that has recently been advocated by many researchers (Habermas, 1992; Wiethölter, 1985). He feels that unless form and substance are unified, procedures become self-defeating (1992: 331). Thus, he prefers to speak of a continuum of procedure and substance. For example, he states that

> "the 'regular and reasonable procedure of weighing claims and counter-claims' is not devoid of moral content. Adjudication as process has its own values, which include impartial judgement, respect for truth, and the opportunity for reasoned argument" (1992: 431).

Selznick recognises that there exists a fundamental tension between instrumental and moral reason. In his view, instrumental rationality, being dependent on definite purposes and clear criteria of cost and achievement, tends to limit responsibilities. Moral reason, on the other hand, makes goals problematic and broadens responsibility, resulting in questions such as: "Are the set objectives worth pursuing in view of the means that seem to be required to achieve these objectives?" and "What is the cost of achieving other objectives and other values?"

To cope with the tension between instrumental and moral reason, Selznick suggests enhancing the awareness of the values of an institution and extending the concept of *accountability*. From the point of view of moral reason, responsibility focuses both on the social function of an institution ('*social responsibility*') and on the way in which such an institution controls its own behaviour ('*moral responsibility*'). For example, it is the task of social responsibility to do justice in the workplace and to care for the environment. Moral responsibility has to do primarily with the *internal morality* of the institution and with the way in which the institution's activities affect the community. It requires an inner commitment to moral restraints and moral standards. In line with Lon Fuller, Selznick describes 'internal morality' as the set of standards that must be observed if the specific task of an institution or a business is to be realised (1992: 324). Internal morality refers to different moral standards including those reflecting the social function of the institution. Accountability, on the other hand, reflects an *external morality*: it refers to external standards that have been designed to hold institutions responsible. According to Selznick, external control can be limited if an organisation has a well-developed internal morality. He is aware that enhanced accountability may lead to formalism (Nonet & Selznick, 1978: 76). For this reason he suggests that the operationalization of accountability should be based on perspectives of social and moral responsibility. This means that evaluation should also examine whether standards of internal morality are appropriate regarding the social function of an institution.

Responsibility and accountability are associated with the notion of *legitimacy*. Selznick describes legitimacy as the acceptance of governmental action on the basis of the belief of citizens that principles of legitimacy are respected (1992: 268, 273). He distinguishes *gross legitimisation* and *legitimacy in depth*. Gross legitimisation, or legality, implies a blanket certification of the source of authority. Legitimacy in depth, by contrast, requires a critical attitude and a continued justification of the use of authority. According to the notion of consequentialist reasoning, justification includes an evaluation of the results and consequences of decision-making. Both social and moral responsibility and extended accountability are based on the concept of legitimacy in depth.

2.4. Reflexive Responsibility

Selznick's moral theory links the concept of responsibility to a quest for the *autonomy* of the institution, as well as to a need for the *integration of conflicting demands*. Autonomy protects both the freedom of an institution and its other values by insulating the institution from outside pressures and manipulation. It also serves to achieve efficiency and effectiveness. Autonomy is affirmed by the constitutional doctrine of the 'separation of powers'. To avoid insularity and inflexibility of autonomous institutions, responsibility requires integration. Integration involves the acceptance of decision-making, adapting the institution's activities to certain social needs and problems. Here, Selznick uses the notion of *responsive institutions* (1992: 336).

Responsiveness in decision-making means trying to solve social problems in an effective way, using various methods and forms of regulation such as legislation, allocation of resources, self-regulation and negotiation (Nonet & Selznick, 1978: 107; Selznick, 1985). Where social problems can be solved more effectively by means of private government, self-regulation is given priority. Responsiveness also implies a selective and controlled adaptation, however, looking critically at social issues and problems from the point of view of the intended objectives. This is implied by the term 'reflexive responsibility'. Reflexive responsibility is based on the virtues of *civility* and *piety*:

"Civility governs diversity, protects autonomy, and upholds toleration; piety expresses devotion and demands integration" (1992: 387).

The concept of civility implies a 'critical' or 'reflective' morality, which is based on reason and certain principles. Piety, by contrast, is characterised by a 'conventional' morality. According to Selznick, the quality of decision-making depends on a proper balance between both these sources of moral integration.

Selznick realises that the strategy of reflexive responsibility entails a risk of opportunism, corruption and abuse of power. Autonomy and responsiveness are conflicting demands. In responsive decision-making, strict autonomy is abandoned in order to be able to respond to social needs and problems. As a result the institutional boundaries in public administration tend to become blurred, jeopardising the integrity of an institution. For this reason Selznick emphasises the importance of countervailing forces and clear social controls (1992: 246). Although self-regulation is given priority within the theory of reflexive responsibility, social standards should not be self-evident; they must be subjected to impartial external controls. If the integrity of an institution is seen to be low, official sanctions must be available. According to Selznick, an appropriate strategy should combine external constraints with moral development. This can be achieved by setting general standards which an institution has to observe and for which it can be held accountable by law and in court. The development of such moral standards could be allotted to an institutional 'charter' which is charged with the formulation of the principles governing the definition of the mission, staff policy, fiscal accountability, and the visibility of decisions (1992: 344).

Summarising, the relations between the notion of reflexive responsibility and other basic concepts of Selznick's moral theory can be depicted as follows (figure 1).

Figure 1. Relations between reflexive responsibility and other basic concepts of Selznick's moral theory

2.5. Discussion

Regarding our stated goal of developing ethical standards for the evaluation of decision-making in public administration, Selznick's moral theory provides us with some inspiring ideas. It seems that the notion of reflexive responsibility offers a perspective that promises to be able to cope with the conflicting objectives of instrumental and moral reason. Selznick's basic concept of moral integration, which results in the right 'mix' of conventional and critical morality (i.e. 'piety' and 'civility') gives an indication how to reconcile the tensions between the demands of stability and flexibility in the managerial state. The standards for ethical assessment are related to the concept of accountability, which is in turn associated with social and moral responsibility. The notion of reflexive responsibility yields the following suggestions with regard to the elaboration of ethical standards:

1. Ethical standards should be based on principles and principles should in turn be based on certain fundamental values;
2. The notion of legitimacy in depth should be applied;
3. Ethical standards should be based on a continuum of process and substance;
4. Principles and values should be contextual and time-related;
5. When specifying the standards, the perspective of responsiveness should be applied;
6. Ethical standards should depart from the concept of self-regulation and self-control;
7. Within ethical standards, appropriate self-correcting measures, external control and the transparency of decision-making should be given priority;
8. Official sanctions should be imposed where institutions do not comply with their charter and external regulations;
9. Institutions should have an ethical charter at their disposal;
10. Ethical standards should be applied to public and private institutions;
11. Responsibility and accountability should refer both to individuals and collectives.

When trying to operationalize these recommendations, however, we are faced with certain shortcomings of Selznick's moral theory, related to the structure, the composition and the operationalization of this theoretical framework (Dorbeck-Jung, 1995, 1997a; Jansen & Klink, 1993). It is not clear how the major concepts of Selznick's theory are mutually related, what their relationship is based on and how empirical research on reflexive responsibility is carried out. How can we identify the values in question, and in what way are they related to principles, purposes, policy goals and regulations? Regarding the analysis of values, Selznick states that they are aspects of moral experience. Does this mean that he bases all philosophical discussions on observable reality? In view of his remarks on the 'core values' of the community we feel that is not the case. More questions arise when we try to operationalize Selznick's ideas on a continuum of procedures and substance. Selznick does not make clear how these ideas should be specified within ethical standards. Also, his terminology is rather vague. For example, what does he mean by 'institutions'? When introducing this concept he speaks of social patterns, attitudes, relations, and practices without giving any clear definition. Selznick's moral theory provides inspiring guidelines for a new ethics of public administration. However, it does not present a method of evaluation. In view of our objective as stated above, further elaboration of Selznick's theory is certainly called for.

3. Standards of Legitimacy

3.1. General Remarks

To obtain standards for the ethical evaluation of decision-making in public administration we depart from the notion of legitimacy. Referring to Selznick's concept of in-depth legitimacy, we may say that moral justification has to do with effectiveness and efficiency. It includes aspects of legality which imply a legitimisation of administrative decision-making on the base of positive law. Legitimacy in depth is associated with the ideal of reflexive responsibility. This means that standards for ethical assessment refer to the autonomy of institutions, self-defining principles and self-correcting measures, responsiveness, and extended accountability. Following Selznick, we may state that ethical standards are based on principles of legitimacy of the democratic state, which in turn are based on certain 'core values'. Here principles are regarded as authoritative starting-points for justification (Pound, 1959:292). Ethical standards imply the operationalization of principles; they can be seen as a means to achieve certain purposes of the democratic state (De Jong & Dorbeck-Jung, 1997). As 'core values' of the democratic state we may identify freedom, equality, democracy, legal security and reason. Principles of legitimacy are: the rule of law, constitutional rights, checks and balances, judicial review and reasonable decision-making. Responsibility can be regarded as the unifying concept of the principles of the democratic state (Saladin, 1984).

The relation between basic values, principles and standards of the democratic state is depicted in figure 2.

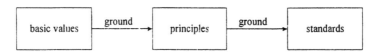

Figure 2. Relations between basic values, principles and standards

3.2. Principles and Standards

Following Selznick's ideas, we shall try to interpret the *rule of law* from a 'responsive' point of view. This means that we see the self-regulation approach as being more legitimate than legislation, if it responds to the social problem at stake in a more appropriate way. In assessing the 'appropriateness' of a form of governance, we shall discuss policy goals from the perspective of social objectives and principles. From this point of view the subject of regulation cannot be established merely by self-regulation when a right or duty is formulated by a Constitution; at the very least, legislation should provide a structure and some fundamental conditions. The legal framework can then be specified by means of self-regulatory rules. This is the model of legally structured and conditioned self-regulation (Dorbeck-Jung, 1993; Eijlander, 1993). Other regulation models are *state control* and pure *self-regulation*. From the perspective of responsiveness, the model of legally structured and conditioned self-regulation seems to be the most adequate approach (Dorbeck-Jung, 1997c). According to Selznick's ideas on institutionalisation and responsive law, the rule of law should cover both formal and informal law and also deal with the effects of rule-making. In the light of legal security, the rules must be clear and understandable.

Constitutional rights and duties are interpreted from the point of view of their social function and their social context. Thus, for example, a constitutional right to academic freedom is balanced with a social need for quality controls and accountability.

In the responsive approach, the classic concept of a separation of powers has been abandoned. To respond to social needs and problems, regulating powers were combined. For this reason standards of *checks and balances* were given high priority so as to minimise the risk of an abuse of power. According to Selznick, effective protection against arbitrariness can be achieved through self-correcting mechanisms and additional government control. This means that a sophisticated system of internal and external control should be set up. Considering the acceptance of internal control, self-correction mechanisms must be assessed on the basis of the institution's charter. Whether and how these standards are fulfilled will have to be assessed by means of external evaluation. Such an external evaluation should be carried out by an independent authority, and institutions must be obliged to submit information about their activities. To achieve transparency, activities must be reported regularly. If institutions do not observe the external rules and internal standards, sanctions may be imposed. In cases where harmful decisions are taken and the rights of the actors within institutions are involved, a *judicial review* should be granted.

According to Selznick's ideas on the basic value of reason, the standards of *reasonable decision-making* refer to consistent argumentation, effectiveness, dialogue, participation and the balancing of multiple interests. To enable an assessment of decision-making, this process must be made visible. If this is not the case and dialogue also fails, sanctions such as the ones mentioned above in the context of standards of checks and balances, may be imposed.

The standards of legitimacy are depicted in the figure 3.

Figure 3. Standards of legitimacy

principles	rule of law/ constitutional rights + duties	checks and balances judicial review	reasonable decision-making
standards	• rules (+ effects) • constitutional rights + duties • policy goals and purposes • regulation model • intelligibility of rules	• self-correcting mechanisms • impartial external control • transparency and reporting • sanctions • legal protection	• dialogue • democratic participation • balancing of interests • transparency of decision-making

4. Case-study

4.1. General Remarks

The standards of legitimacy we developed in the previous section are somewhat theoretical and abstract. To give a better idea of their advantages and disadvantages, we will apply them to regulations of higher education by exploring the legitimacy of Dutch quality evaluation regulations in higher education. Over the past few years, quality evaluation and quality assurance have been controversial issues in higher education discussions. In the Netherlands, a system of quality evaluation which covers curricula, research and quality management was set up by law four years ago. Since these Dutch regulations and their effects have already been investigated (Dorbeck-Jung, 1997b; Frederiks, Weusthof & Westerheijden, 1994; Wester-heijden, 1996), the case of quality evaluation of higher education in the Netherlands may serve as an interesting example to 'test' the value of our ethical standards.

Following Selznick's concept of 'thick' institutionalisation, our case-study focuses on formal and informal structures. Institutions are defined as distinct sets of rules (De Jong, 1992: 32; Hall & Taylor, 1994). Rules are seen as being part of the social practices in which the actor participates. 'Rule-guided behaviour' is an important concept in (socio-) legal theory (Griffiths, 1996:471; Loth, 1988: 51). We define rules as standards of individual or collective behaviour. Formal rules are based on formal authority. Formal rules can be written as well as unwritten ones (i.e. customs). Informal rules are defined as the actual standards of behaviour (De Jong & Dorbeck-Jung, 1997).

In our case-study, we will first give a survey of the formal and informal rules that govern the quality evaluation process in Dutch higher education. Wherever possible the effects of these rules will be described as well. Our survey distinguishes three stages of the quality evaluation process: self-evaluation, external evaluation and control (including reporting). In a second step we evaluate the legitimacy of the rules involved.

4.2. Evaluation of Quality Assessment in Dutch Higher Education

4.2.1. Rules

As far as *formal rules* are concerned, the Dutch Higher Education Act of 1992 (WHW) is the main legal source. This Act lays down the structure and basic conditions for the three stages of the quality evaluation process (art. 1.18). Article 1.18 of the WHW must be seen in light of Article 23 of the Dutch Constitution, which obligates the Dutch government to care for the quality of education. The provisions of Article 1.18 of the WHW stipulate that organisations of higher education are held to evaluate the quality of teaching, study programmes and research. Also, these organisations are legally required to cooperate as much as possible during the evaluation process. Independent experts must be involved in the evaluation. If external experts were involved in the evaluation process, evaluation reports have to be published. According to the legal rules, students must also participate in the evaluation of study programmes. The legal framework leaves room for self-regulation of the institutions as well. During an early stage of the discussion the Association of Dutch Universities (VSNU[1]) laid down formal rules pertaining to the processes of self-evaluation, external evaluation and reporting. These rules formulated commitments made by the Ministry of Education and the VSNU during negotiations at the end of the 1980s. The VSNU set out guidelines for the evaluations, which were later revised. The rules laid down by the VSNU also apply to the external evaluation and publication of the evaluation reports. The VSNU appoints the peers, who have to be independent national and international experts. Initially participation on the part of the students was limited to the self-evaluation stage, but during the last two years students have also participated in the external evaluation of education activities. Regarding government control, the Higher Education Act provides an ex-post approach. A Higher Education Inspectorate is legally authorised to investigate the impact of self-regulation on the evaluation of educational activities (art. 5.2). Their investigation focuses on the evaluation system (meta-evaluation). If the Inspectorate concludes that over the past few years the quality of a programme was too low, the Ministry of Education is authorised to terminate the programme (art. 6.5) The Minister also can stop public funding if institutions violate the provisions of the Higher Education Act (art. 15.1); for example, if they refuse to evaluate their education or research activities.

Recent studies which deal with the impact of the rules show that *informal rules* are emerging with respect to the three stages of quality evaluation (Frederiks, Westerheijden & Weusthof 1994; Westerheijden, 1996). The level of correspondence of the informal rules to the formal ones seems to be fairly high. Generally, institutions are taking measures to improve quality wherever shortcomings are found as a result of the internal or external evaluations. Due to the Dutch focus on self-regulation, rule-making has increased at the level of the individual institutions and their professional organisations. It is not clear whether rule-making has actually decreased at the central level. Permanent revisions of higher education legislation suggest that this is not the case. The above-mentioned studies indicate that informal rules may emerge regarding the publication behaviour of researchers. Due to the pressure to publish, researchers are behaving more and more in a consciously strategic manner.

4.2.2. Aspects of Legitimacy

Regarding the standards of the *rule of law*, the Dutch regulation approach can be characterised by the model of legally structured and conditioned self-regulation. In view of the government imposed obligation to care for the quality of education as stipulated by the Dutch Constitution, pure self-regulation would interfere with the constitutional conditions. Nor would pure state regulation be appropriate in the Dutch case. Therefore, in 1985 Dutch regulatory policy introduced the concept of 'steering from a distance' to improve the quality and effectiveness of higher education. Using Selznick's terminology, we may say that reflexive responsibility has been introduced into the Dutch regulation system of higher education. The 'steering' concept is based on the assumption that quality can be enhanced through non-governmental initiatives. Self-regulation, increasing autonomy and deregulation are regarded as appropriate strategies to achieve certain policy objectives. It is not clear, though, whether these strategies are used only to improve effectiveness and efficiency, or whether they are also intended to enhance the quality of higher education. It is worth noting that the tensions between efficiency and quality enhancement, and also between the core values of higher education (such as academic freedom and equality) are hardly mentioned in the relevant policy documents and debates. Regarding the intelligibility requirement, the Dutch standards do seem to be rather clear.

Considering the standards of *checks and balances*, the Dutch approach is aimed primarily at self-correcting measures. As a consequence of self-control, empirical research seems to indicate an increasing influence on the part of administrators. Self-regulation is controlled by peers and by the Higher Education Inspectorate. The rules with respect to the selection of the peers seem to indicate objectivity. The same cannot be said of the supervision by the Higher Education Inspectorate, which is a government organisation. The standards of transparency and reporting are met by the stipulations of Art. 1.18 of the WHW and by the guidelines of the VSNU. Empirical research shows that the informal rules comply with the formal ones. If self-regulation does not lead to any improvement in cases where the quality was found to be low, the Ministry is entitled to impose sanctions. In such cases a *judicial review* is provided. The institutions are entitled to an administrative review if the Minister stops funding. So far, no sanctions have been enforced yet.

Regarding the standards of *reasonable decision-making*, the participation of students and teachers is guaranteed by legal rules. The empirical studies indicate that the Dutch system has stimulated a dialogue between teachers, students and administrators. The conclusion is that a 'quality culture' has begun to put out roots in the Dutch organisations of higher education. However, the acceptance of the quality evaluation system may be undermined by the fact that the academic staff regards the evaluation process as a too heavy and too expensive burden. Since the organisations are not obliged to report on the self-evaluation process, it is not clear whether the interests at stake are represented in adequate proportion at this stage of the quality evaluation. Also it has not been empirically investigated, as far as the external evaluation and control stages are concerned, whether the various interests are evenly balanced.

5. Conclusion

Our case-study shows that the Dutch rules of higher education quality evaluation largely correspond to our standards of legitimacy. The standards of impartiality of external control and transparency of self-evaluation are not met, however. Our case-study also indicates that the evaluation system may result in:

- increasing rule-making at the decentralised level,
- strategic behaviour by researchers and teachers,
- a one-sided focus on efficiency and effectiveness,
- increasing power of administrators,
- an evaluation overload, and
- extensive evaluation costs.

Of course, our assessment standards are insufficiently refined to cover all the rules that govern legitimacy. Their value lies in the fact that they give an idea of the legitimacy of regulations. Our case-study also indicates that these standards may serve as a basis for taking a critical look at decision-making in public administration. If this would result in a higher awareness of moral restraints, moral commitments and social objectives, as well as more far-reaching effects, the ideal of reflexive responsibility would be realised and organisations of public administration would indeed become 'moral institutions', in Philip Selznick's terminology.

Note

[1] Vereniging van Samenwerkende Nederlandse Universiteiten

Bibliography

Bovens, M. (1996) "The Integrity of the Managerial States", *Journal of Contingencies and Crisis Management*, Vol. 4, No. 3, pp. 125-132.

DiMaggio, P.J., and Powell, W.W. (1991) "Introduction", in Powell and DiMaggio, Eds., *The New Institutionalism in Organization Analysis*, Chicago: University of Chicago Press, pp. 63-83.

Dorbeck-Jung, B.R. (1993) "Wettelijk geconditioneerde zelfregulering; symbolisch concept of instrument met gevolgen?", in Ph. Eijlander, P.C. Gilhuis and J.A.F. Peters (red.) *Overheid en zelfregulering*, Zwolle: Tjeenk Willink, pp. 141-154.

Dorbeck-Jung, B.R. *Conceptualizing Legisprudence, From legislation to responsive regulation*, Paper for the Annual Conference of EGPA, Rotterdam, September 1995.

Dorbeck-Jung, B.R. (1997a) *Philip Selznick and the Art of Legislating*, Contribution to the 24th Annual Conference of the UK Association for Legal and Social Philosophy, Edinburgh, April 1997.

Dorbeck-Jung, B.R. (1997b) *Comparing Regulations of Higher Education Quality Evaluation* (will be published in no. 1 of the European Journal for Education Law and Policy).

Dorbeck-Jung, B.R. (1997c) *Setting Priorities in Dutch Legislative Policies*, in Boorsma, P.B., Aarts, K., Steenge, A.E. Eds., *Public Priority Setting Rules and Costs*, Dordrecht-London: Kluwer, pp. 201-216.

Eijlander, Ph. (1993) *De wet stellen*, Zwolle: Tjeenk Willink.

Etzioni, A. (1994) *The Spirit of Community; The reinvention of American society*, New York: Touchstone.

Frederiks, M.M.H., Westerheijden, D.F. and Weusthof, P.J.M. (1994) "Effects of Quality Assessment in Dutch Higher Education", in *European Journal of Education*, Vol. 29, No. 2, pp. 181-199.

Griffiths, J. , Eds., (1996) *De sociale werking van recht: Een kennismaking met de rechtssociologie en rechtsantropologie*, Nijmegen: Ars Aequi Libri.

Habermas, J. (1992) *Faktizitat und Geltung*, Frankfurt am Main: Suhrkamp.

Hall, P.A. and Taylor, R.C.R. (1994) *Political Science and the Four New Institutionalisms*, Cambridge· paper for the Annual Meeting of the American Political Science Associaton.

Jansen, Th. and Klink, A (1993) "The moral commonwealth van Ph. Selznick", in *Beleid & Maatschappij*, 1993, No. 3, pp. 157-161.

Jong, H.M. de (1992) *Twijfel en verantwoordelijkheid in het recht*, (Enschede).

Jong, H.M. de and Dorbeck-Jung, B.R. (1997) *Juridische Staatsleer*, Baarn: Coutinho (1997).

Loth, M.A. (1988) *Handeling en aansprakelijkheid in het recht*, Arnhem: Gouda Quint.

Nonet, P. and Selznick, P. (1978) *Law and Society in Transition, Towards responsive law*, New York: Harper & Row.

Pound, R. (1959) *Jurisprudence*, St Paul, West Publishing Company, Vol.1, part 1, p.292.

Rawls, J. (1980) "Kantian Constructivism in Moral Theory", in *Journal of Philosophy*, Vol. 77, September.

Saladin, P. (1984) *Verantwortung als Staatsprinzip Ein neuer Schlussel zur Lehre vom modernen Rechtsstaat*, Stuttgart: Haupt.

Selznick, P. (1985) "Focusing Organizational Research on Regulation", in R.G. Noll (ed.) *Regulatory Policy and the Social Sciences*, Berkeley: University of California Press.

Selznick, P. (1992) *The Moral Commonwealth. Social theory and the promise of community*, Berkeley, Oxford: The University of California Press.

Westerheijden, D.F. (1996) *A Solid Base for Decisions*, Enschede: CHEPS.

WHW (1992) "Wet op het Hoger Onderwijs en Wetenschappelijk Onderzoek", (Act on Higher Education and Scientific Research), *Staatsblad 593*.

Wiethölter, R. (1985) "Materialization and Proceduralization in Modern Law", in G. Teubner, Eds., *Dilemmas of Law in the Welfare State*, Berlin: De Gruyter, (1986), pp. 221-249.

*Ethics and Accountability in a Context
of Governance and New Public Management*
EGPA Annual Conference, Leuven 1997
IOS Press, 1998

Les réformes comptables et budgétaires et la responsabilisation des agents de l'État en France et en Grande-Bretagne

R. Fabre[*]

Une question posée par le Groupe de Travail du G.E.A.P. sur la responsabilité était celle de déterminer comment les outils comptables et budgétaires pouvaient soutenir une action de responsabilisation des agents de l'État. Je souhaiterais tenter d'y répondre, en m'appuyant pour ce faire sur une analyse comparée des expériences française et britannique. Le choix de ces pays, qui traditionnellement avaient élaboré des systèmes très différents l'un de l'autre, permet de souligner des convergences tant au niveau des besoins comptables identifiés (meilleure lisibilité, outil de prévision), que des choix budgétaires réalisés (globalisation des crédits, plus grande fongibilité et reports).

1. L'adaptation des mesures comptables aux besoins des gestionnaires

1.1. Des constructions comptables aux principes fondateurs très divergents

Il existe de grandes différences entre les systèmes de comptabilisation britannique et français, à la fois dans leur présentation et dans leur finalité. S'agissant de leur présentation, jusqu'à une période récente - les modifications sont en cours actuellement -, les systèmes comptables britanniques apparaissaient beaucoup plus simples, dans la mesure où ils ne faisaient pas l'objet d'une écriture double, comme c'est le cas en France du fait du principe de la séparation de l'ordonnateur et du comptable. Leur lecture était plus facile et les difficultés d'établissement moindres, mais les indications qu'ils fournissaient étaient plus limitées. La finalité poursuivie était celle d'apprécier les écarts entre les divers postes, et non d'opérer un contrôle reposant sur une confrontation entre deux séries d'écriture, comme c'est le cas en France.

Le système de comptabilité de caisse qui s'appliquait jusque récemment en Grande-Bretagne ne prenait en compte que les entrées et les sorties en numéraire. Le résultat final n'était ni plus ni moins que le livre de caisse. Il n'y avait pas de bilan, car il n'y avait ni actif, ni passif. Les ventes n'étaient prises en compte que lorsque les sommes avaient été encaissées - il n'y avait donc pas de débiteur - et les achats que lorsque les sommes avaient été décaissées - il n'y avait donc pas non plus de créditeur -. Il n'y avait pas de prise en compte des stocks, puisqu'aucun enregistrement comptable n'était prévu, en dehors des sommes versées pour les achats. Il n'y avait pas non plus de charges fixes pour les mêmes raisons[1].

En France, en revanche, le principe fondateur de la comptabilité administrative repose sur la vérification de la concordance entre les décisions des ordonnateurs et les opérations des comptables:

---

[*] Raphaëlle Fabre, CRAPS - Université de Lille II, France.

> "Les procédures originaires de la comptabilité publique, beaucoup plus rigides que les règles actuelles, faisaient de la caisse publique une sorte de coffre à double serrure, dont l'une des clés appartenait à l'ordonnateur et l'autre au comptable, mais qui ne pouvait pas s'ouvrir sans leur intervention conjointe, assurant ainsi l'effectivité d'un auto-contrôle de l'Administration."
> (Montagnier, 1981. 91)

C'est en 1808, par le décret du 4 janvier, que le système de la partie double fut introduit en comptabilité publique. L'objectif principal du décret de 1808 était de s'assurer, par l'équilibre des débits et des crédits, qu'aucune rétention de recettes ne soit pratiquée par un comptable public. Ce sont ces observations qui ont amené MM. Rowan JONES et Maurice PENDLEBURY à conclure que les pratiques anglo-saxonnes donnaient la priorité aux faits, alors que les pratiques continentales s'attachaient davantage à la règle (Jones, Pendlebury, 1992: 186).

Mais au fur et à mesure de la remise en cause du concept traditionnel de service public et de l'extension du rôle de l'État dans l'économie, la pertinence de l'analyse classique a été progressivement amenée à évoluer. L'exigence de rendement, du fait d'une aggravation continue de la pression fiscale et de l'ouverture sur l'extérieur, est devenue une contrainte réelle et forte dans tous les pays industrialisés. Il est devenu nécessaire d'anticiper sur l'avenir pour réaliser les choix les meilleurs en termes d'efficacité.

1.2. Des adaptations aux finalités convergentes

À la fin des années 1980, les gouvernements ont remis en cause les schémas comptables traditionnels afin d'offrir aux chefs de service un outil de gestion pertinent et fiable, qui leur permette d'optimiser leurs choix.

En Grande-Bretagne, c'est dans le cadre de l'expérience des "Étapes Suivantes" que le système de la comptabilité budgétaire d'engagement *(accrual accounting)* a été retenu, puis élargi par la suite aux autres services. Contrairement au précédent, ce mode de comptabilisation tient compte des créances acquises et des dépenses engagées. La reconnaissance des dettes et des créances a donc lieu avant l'encaissement ou le décaissement et les mouvements de capitaux sont rattachés à l'exercice financier de leur émission.

De la même manière, en France, depuis 1988, le deuxième plan comptable de l'État est entré en application[2]. Conformément à l'article 133 du décret du 29 décembre 1962, ce plan applique les grands principes de même que les techniques de la comptabilité privée comme la partie double et le classement décimal des opérations. Mais, et c'est là son originalité, la comptabilité de l'État doit d'abord décrire l'exécution de la loi de finances conformément à l'autorisation donnée par le législateur. De cette double exigence, le système comptable de l'État tire sa double vocation qui consiste à décrire les opérations à la fois dans une optique patrimoniale, au sens du plan comptable privé, et dans une optique budgétaire, au sens de l'article 16 de l'ordonnance du 2 janvier 1959[3]. C'est ce qui explique que le système comptable de l'État en France comporte deux sous-systèmes complémentaires et interactifs. Il comprend d'abord une comptabilité générale, qui décrit de façon synthétique l'ensemble des opérations de nature budgétaire et patrimoniale dans dix classes de comptes comparables, sous réserve des adaptations nécessaires à la spécificité de l'État, à celles du plan comptable général. Il comprend également des comptabilités auxiliaires, qui développent et détaillent les opérations de la comptabilité générale, notamment l'exécution du budget de l'État conformément à la loi de finances.

Dans les deux pays, les pouvoirs publics ont éprouvé le besoin d'améliorer la mise à disposition d'informations utiles pour la prise de décision. La Grande-Bretagne a opté pour une logique commerciale de la gestion de ses services et les formules comptables retenues sont calquées sur celles du secteur privé. Cela n'est pas sans poser problème, eu égard à la difficulté de mesurer les coûts d'exploitation et les bénéfices réalisés. La France a gardé une approche plus traditionnelle: la loi de finances étant structurée comme un budget de moyens, elle dresse la liste des dépenses à réaliser en distinguant les différentes catégories de moyens mis en oeuvre sans faire apparaître le lien avec les fonctions poursuivies. Seul le développement de la capacité des matériels informatique et microinformatique devrait à terme permettre d'apporter une réponse satisfaisante à ce problème que représente le développement des comptabilités analytiques, en établissant des correspondances entre les deux schémas comptables. Des difficultés communes aux deux pays persistent cependant dans le domaine de l'appréciation quantitative des prestations de l'administration.

1.3. Des difficultés communes

La comptabilité publique occulte bien souvent les aspects patrimoniaux des actifs de l'État: la gestion des stocks et des biens immobiliers, notamment, ne sont pas pris en compte, alors qu'ils constituent une donnée importante dans la prise de décisions pour l'avenir. Pour offrir aux gestionnaires une vue d'ensemble qui soit le plus proche possible de la réalité, il conviendrait de prendre en compte tous les avoirs de l'État et de leur imputer, quand il y a lieu, un amortissement correspondant.

1.3.1. L'amortissement dans les comptes publics

Il n'existe pas plus en Grande-Bretagne qu'en France de politique générale de prise en compte systématique des amortissements dans les comptes publics, comme cela existe dans le secteur privé. L'amortissement pour dépréciation est la constatation comptable d'un amoindrissement de la valeur d'un élément d'actif résultant de l'usage, du temps, du changement de technique ou de toute autre cause. C'est en raison des difficultés de mesure de cet amoindrissement que l'amortissement consiste généralement dans l'étalement, sur une durée probable de vie, de la valeur des biens amortissables. Au bilan, les amortissements sont présentés en déduction des valeurs d'origine de façon à faire apparaître la valeur nette comptable des immobilisations[4].

En Grande-Bretagne, dans le cadre de l'initiative des "Étapes suivantes", il n'existe pas de schéma comptable obligatoire[5]. Certes, il est préconisé la publication de comptes qui s'apparentent à ceux de type commercial. Une proposition de présentation et de calcul des amortissements figure dans le guide gouvernemental sur les comptes de commerce publics[6]. Mais cette pratique n'est pas obligatoire et elle n'est pas réalisée dans tous les ministères.

En France, dans le plan comptable de 1970, les investissements de l'année étaient inclus dans les comptes de charges en classe 6, ce qui dénaturait profondément le résultat comptable ainsi dégagé. Depuis la mise en place du plan comptable de 1988, les immobilisations sont comptabilisées en classe 2, avec un système d'amortissement annuel. Il s'agissait là d'un progrès puisque les dotations aux amortissements sont des charges qui ne donnent pas lieu à des décaissements. Mais le dispositif retenu en 1988 ne donne pas pleinement satisfaction, dans la mesure où les immobilisations sont intégralement amorties dès la première année, à l'exception des terrains, qui seuls apparaissent donc dans le bilan de l'État. Cette option va à l'encontre de la réalité économique, l'amortissement étant censé enregistrer une dépréciation réelle de l'actif.

Les bâtiments et les équipements ont été mis en place pour servir à la production de services publics durant plusieurs années: ils se déprécient en remplissant cette fonction. Pour rendre compte de la "consommation" étalée de ce moyen de production, on pourrait inscrire une dotation annuelle correspondant à sa dépréciation. De cette manière, le total des charges de fonctionnement mesurerait le coût total des prestations de la collectivité. Les amortissements seraient répartis entre les services de l'administration publique en fonction du capital que chacun utilise: cela permettrait les comparaisons entre les services qui utilisent relativement beaucoup de capital et ceux qui encourent plutôt des charges de personnel.

Cependant, ainsi que le fait remarquer M. Philippe THALMANN (Thalmann, 1994: 53-74), la pratique des amortissements n'est qu' "un emplâtre sur une jambe de bois" si l'État ne se dote pas d'un projet plus vaste de comptabilité analytique des coûts et des bénéfices des opérations de la collectivité. Même si l'on comptabilise de façon idéale la dépréciation du patrimoine, le compte de fonctionnement ne pourra jamais constituer à lui seul un indicateur de l'efficacité de la gestion publique.

1.3.2. La comptabilité patrimoniale de l'État

Les États français et britanniques possèdent chacun un patrimoine très important, multiforme et mal évalué. Dans un contexte où la situation des finances publiques est marquée par l'importance du passif (la dette publique), et où les services sont gérés de manière plus autonome et responsable, il est légitime de chercher à mieux connaître et à exploiter l'actif de l'État, qu'il s'agisse de ses immeubles, de ses terrains, de ses équipements, de ses participations, de ses créances ou de ses droits incorporels.

En Grande-Bretagne, le système retenu est calqué sur celui du privé dans la mesure où cela est possible (la valorisation des immobilisations ne peut concerner que des biens qui sont dans le commerce; une telle opération ne présenterait aucun intérêt pour des biens inaliénables, comme, par exemple, un palais national). Les mesures comptables en vigueur sont directement inspirées du *Companies Act*[7] (loi sur les sociétés commerciales ou industrielles) de 1985 qui prévoit la mise en place d'un compte de pertes et profits et d'un bilan d'inventaire. À la différence de la France[8], les stocks sont pris en compte dans le bilan. Par ailleurs, la Grande-Bretagne a opté pour un rattachement des terrains et des immeubles aux agences autonomes qui sont gérées sous la forme d'un fonds commercial[9]. En contrepartie, les agences d'exécution sont tenues de procéder aux frais d'entretien et de réparation. C'est un choix qui a parfois été contesté car le risque est grand de voir certains directeurs d'agence se focaliser sur les indicateurs de performance aux dépens des investissements nécessaires à long terme.

En France, la comptabilisation des immobilisations se heurte à une connaissance insuffisante des flux d'entrées et de sorties. Avant l'entrée en vigueur du nouveau plan comptable, les flux d'immobilisations étaient inclus dans les comptes de charges et leur individualisation n'a été réalisée qu'à partir de 1981. Le bilan de l'État ne recense donc que les investissements réalisés depuis une bonne quinzaine d'années. L'État français dispose certes d'une comptabilité budgétaire élaborée, mais ses systèmes de comptabilité patrimoniale et analytique restent embryonnaires par rapport aux entreprises privées. Bien que le décret du 29 décembre 1962 portant règlement général sur la comptabilité publique[10] assigne à cette dernière, entre autres finalités, "la connaissance de la situation du patrimoine" et la "détermination des résultats annuels", la publication par l'État d'un compte de résultat digne de ce nom n'est intervenue qu'en 1988.

Il est vrai que l'ordonnance organique du 2 janvier 1959[11] et le règlement général sur la comptabilité publique[12] limitent la marge d'innovation possible. Une contrainte majeure est la règle de l'annualité budgétaire[13], en vertu de laquelle l'autorisation conférée par le Parlement de percevoir des recettes et d'engager des dépenses n'est valable que pour un an et surtout que les crédits ouverts au titre d'un budget ne créent aucun droit au titre du budget suivant[14]. Les achats de l'année sont supposés être consommés dans la même période et il n'est donc pas possible de prendre en compte les stocks restants dans les comptes de l'année suivante, comme c'est le cas en Grande-Bretagne où s'applique pourtant également le principe de l'annualité budgétaire. En France, tout système de comptabilité en droits constatés nécessite un retraitement *a posteriori*, complexe et nécessairement imparfait, de la comptabilité budgétaire de l'État.

Le système de réflexion en fin d'année a été conservé. Celui-ci permet de décrire l'exécution de la loi de finances (recettes et dépenses du budget) selon les classements de la loi organique et de dégager de manière distincte, en fin d'année, un résultat de nature patrimoniale. En pratique, au jour le jour, les comptes de charges et produits ne sont pas utilisés par les comptables publics. Ceux-ci se servent des comptes de classe 9, qui sont des comptes de dépenses et de recettes, en contrepartie des comptes de bilan. La classe 9 reproduit les ventilations budgétaires retenues par la loi de finances et permet de suivre l'exécution du budget. En fin d'année, les opérations de la classe 9 sont reclassées par réflexion et retraitées, afin d'obtenir une présentation dans une optique de comptabilité patrimoniale en droits constatés. La complexité de ces opérations résulte du choix du maintien d'une dualité de comptabilités (budgétaire et patrimoniale).

Enfin, la comptabilité de l'État ignore le mécanisme des provisions. En comptabilité privée, et c'est ce mécanisme qui a été repris par les agences britanniques établies sous forme de fonds commercial, les provisions permettent de constater une diminution potentielle de valeur liée à des événements survenus au cours de l'exercice, mais dont les effets ne sont pas jugés irréversibles. Les provisions les plus courantes sont les provisions pour dépréciation d'éléments d'actif (telles que les immobilisations, ou les stocks) et les provisions pour risques et charges (comme les provisions pour litiges ou pour grosses réparations). L'introduction de ce dispositif dans la comptabilité de l'État, en France, permettrait par exemple de provisionner des créances douteuses. Certaines de ces créances sont déjà identifiées, puisque les comptables publics peuvent dégager leur responsabilité personnelle pour des créances irrécouvrables, par la procédure dite d' "admission en non-valeur".[15]

Finalement, la comptabilité patrimoniale de l'État reste en France, aujourd'hui, un outil encore imprécis et embryonnaire. Les notions d'enrichissement ou d'appauvrissement commencent seulement à trouver leur traduction dans les comptes. Le résultat d'exécution des lois de finances, simple soustraction des recettes et des dépenses de l'année, ne tient compte que de l'activité financière de l'État. Pourtant, la comptabilité patrimoniale pourrait constituer, une fois rénovée, une source d'informations appréciable en faveur de la responsabilisation des agents.

2. Une évolution des règles budgétaires en faveur d'une gestion plus responsable des dépenses

Le reproche essentiel adressé au budget traditionnel en tant que budget de moyens est qu'il tend à cloisonner l'affectation des deniers publics entre les divers services de l'État dans un cadre annuel. Des outils solides existent dans le domaine de la gestion du budget de l'État, que ce soit pour préparer le budget, pour en suivre l'exécution, ou pour encadrer et contrôler la dépense publique, mais les procédures actuelles comportent de graves défauts qui tiennent à ce que les gestionnaires ne sont pas assez responsabilisés. Ils sont à la fois insuffisamment sensibilisés aux contraintes financières de l'État et dépourvus de véritables marges de manœuvre. Pour permettre une gestion plus responsable des dépenses, comme le préconisent les pouvoirs publics, il était nécessaire de mettre en place, en sus du recours accru au procédé de la globalisation des crédits, certains aménagements en ce qui concerne les règles budgétaires classiques.

2.1. La formule des crédits globaux

De manière générale, de part et d'autre de la Manche, le financement gouvernemental pour tous les services autonomes est autorisé et contrôlé par le Parlement, par la fixation d'allocations ministérielles dans les prévisions de dépenses de l'année pour chaque département. Mais l'autorisation des dépenses peut s'opérer de différentes manières: par le biais de votes séparés ou par le biais d'un budget global. Il est clair que la dotation d'une enveloppe unique en vue de pourvoir aux dépenses et aux frais de fonctionnement permet au service de se doter de modalités de gestion plus souples et mieux adaptées à ses besoins. Cela s'est traduit en France par la création de chapitres globalisés[16]; en Grande-Bretagne par l'application de la loi de 1973 sur les fonds commerciaux[17].

Un "fonds commercial" fournit un cadre de financement qui couvre les coûts d'exploitation et les bénéfices, la mise de fonds, et les liquidités disponibles nettes et empruntées. Il peut emprunter pour couvrir sa mise de fonds, pour établir son roulement de trésorerie, ou pour établir des réserves. Il peut également honorer ses dépenses sans que les mouvements détaillés de son budget aient fait l'objet d'un vote parlementaire. Le gouvernement britannique a exprimé sa détermination à faire de ce mode de répartition et de gestion des crédits le mode de droit commun pour les agences qui relèvent de l'expérience des "Étapes Suivantes".[18]

En France, c'est dans le cadre de la circulaire sur le "Renouveau du Service Public" de février 1989[19] qu'ont été initiées et mises en œuvre dans tous les ministères des modifications de nomenclature conduisant à la création de chapitres globalisés. Outre la création de centres de responsabilité, cette circulaire traite de la gestion budgétaire en appelant à un "assouplissement des règles budgétaires" à travers "la globalisation de certains crédits de fonctionnement dont les reports annuels seraient facilités". Le regroupement des chapitres concernant les dépenses de fonctionnement doit permettre la notification et la délégation d'une enveloppe globale de crédits pour un service. Il s'agit techniquement d'une modification de la nomenclature budgétaire qui va conduire à regrouper différents chapitres de dépenses par nature en un chapitre unique de dépenses de fonctionnement. Les crédits ainsi regroupés sont notifiés et délégués sous forme d'une dotation globale à un chef de service qui les gère en assurant la répartition entre les différentes dépenses dans le cadre d'une nomenclature de paragraphe par nature de dépenses.

Les modifications de nomenclature se sont effectuées progressivement et elles auraient dû s'achever au 1er janvier 1995. Mais les travaux de la Cour des comptes[20] ont fait apparaître des procédures de notification et de délégation de crédits très éloignées des instructions du ministre. Dans certains départements, la procédure de répartition n'aboutit pas à une seule enveloppe de crédits pour un service mais à plusieurs (une dotation pour le fonctionnement courant, une autre pour les travaux d'entretien immobilier, une troisième pour financer des projets correspondant à des grandes priorités nationales, par exemple). Par ailleurs, certaines enveloppes de crédits globalisés font l'objet de prescriptions quant à leur emploi. C'est le cas notamment lorsqu'il y a des normes impliquant le recours à certains types d'achats. Ces normes créent une forte limitation à l'autonomie de gestion des crédits globalisés. En outre, les critères de répartition des crédits sont très différents. Dans certains ministères, la répartition est négociée, c'est-à-dire précédée par un dialogue à travers lequel les services déconcentrés expriment des demandes de crédits, basées sur des projets de budget élaborés dans le cadre d'orientations annuelles ou pluriannuelles. Dans d'autres, l'administration centrale décide de manière unilatérale la répartition entre services en utilisant des critères "objectifs" tels que le nombre de fonctionnaires, ou des indicateurs sommaires sur les missions (comme le nombre d'habitants dans le département, ou le nombre d'établissements sous tutelle, par exemple). Parfois, la répartition des crédits est faite essentiellement sur une base historique avec des corrections limitées (la "péréquation"). De manière générale, les dispositifs qui conduisent à une répartition unilatérale ne prennent pas en compte la performance dans l'accomplissement des missions.

Au total cependant, le mouvement de regroupement des chapitres de fonctionnement du titre III (frais de fonctionnement) est pratiquement achevé. Le nombre des chapitres a diminué année après année et est passé de 1823 en 1984 à 1147 dans le projet de loi de finances pour 1994. Il n'en va pas de même pour les dépenses d'investissement et les crédits salariaux de rémunérations et d'indemnités. En ce qui concerne les crédits d'investissement du titre V, il existe depuis 1970 un classement des investissements distinguant les crédits de catégorie 1 gérés au niveau central et ceux de catégorie 2 et 3 gérés au niveau déconcentré; mais dans la pratique, il s'agit surtout d'une déconcentration de la gestion administrative et comptable, la programmation restant très centralisée. À l'occasion du premier séminaire gouvernemental d'application de la politique du "Renouveau du Service Public", il a été fixé un objectif de déconcentration de 30 % des crédits d'investissements; celui-ci n'a pas encore été atteint. Sur le plan théorique, il est certain qu'il y a des limites à la déconcentration des opérations d'investissement, car la gestion des investissements traduit des choix stratégiques qui doivent être cohérents sur l'ensemble de l'organisation concernée. Les investissements engagent l'avenir, supposent des ressources importantes et requièrent des compétences spécialisées pour leur mise en œuvre.

Pourtant, les Britanniques ont fait le choix d'inclure les opérations d'investissement dans les comptes des agences gérées sous la forme de fonds commercial. Dans un premier temps, cette solution avait été écartée par crainte de voir les agences gonfler leurs crédits de fonctionnement par la possibilité qui leur serait donnée de rendre le fonctionnement et l'investissement fongibles, mais finalement le gouvernement a opté pour une autonomie complète des agences en terme de gestion budgétaire. Bien entendu, toutes les agences ne sont pas concernées: seules le sont celles qui bénéficient du statut de fonds commercial.

Les réformes financières ne sont pas achevées; plusieurs pistes sont envisagées par le ministère des Finances pour les consolider[21]. Le gouvernement souhaiterait étendre le statut de fond commercial de l'administration à l'ensemble des agences, y compris à celles qui n'ont pas de recettes externes[22]. Dans ce cas, les facturations internes de services à l'administration seraient considérées comme des recettes fictives. Ce statut permettrait d'avoir des comptes plus lisibles et des mécanismes de gestion plus clairs. Des détails sur l'exemption d'un contrôle approfondi des dépenses ont été donnés dans le Livre Blanc sur la dépense publique de 1987 et dans ceux qui ont suivi. À mesure que l'initiative des "Étapes Suivantes" progresse, le gouvernement souhaite que la proportion des budgets globaux augmente[23]. Cette orientation va de pair avec un allègement de l'application stricte des principes traditionnels de droit budgétaire.

2.2. Des dérogations aux règles budgétaires classiques

Le principal avantage de la formule des crédits globaux est de permettre une plus grande fongibilité des crédits, ce qui accroît considérablement les marges de manœuvre des directeurs de services autonomes. Mais cette autonomie se trouve encadrée par les limites de la gestion annuelle des budgets. À titre dérogatoire, il a donc été prévu un recours accru aux possibilités de reports de crédits.

2.2.1. Des mesures en faveur d'une plus grande fongibilité des crédits

La fongibilité des crédits favorise l'autonomie et la responsabilisation des services, et elle est présentée à ce titre comme un vecteur de modernisation; mais elle diminue *a priori* les possibilités de contrôle parlementaire. C'est une véritable conflit qui s'exerce entre ces deux impératifs.

Les Britanniques attachent une très grande importance au contrôle parlementaire sur les dépenses. C'est ce qui explique que la plupart des budgets de dépense des agences soit encore autorisée par le vote au Parlement d'une comptabilité provisionnelle. Tout changement par rapport aux prévisions initiales fait l'objet d'une approbation parlementaire. À la fin de l'année, les comptes sont vérifiés par le *Comptroller and Auditor General*[24], et peuvent être examinés par la Commission parlementaire de vérification des comptes publiques *(Public Accounts Committee - P.A.C.*[25]*)*. Les encaissements (en tant que rémunération pour service rendu, par exemple) sont normalement restitués au Fonds d'amortissement de la dette publique; ils peuvent également être intégrés au bénéfice du budget, mais dans ce dernier cas seulement après autorisation parlementaire.

À l'intérieur des limites des crédits disponibles, les dépenses des services publics figurent dans les frais d'exploitation de chaque département ministériel. Ces derniers sont généralement contrôlés dans leur totalité, ce qui signifie que les encaissements ne permettent pas d'augmenter les dépenses (méthode des coûts bruts de fonctionnement). Dans certains cas, toutefois, lorsque les frais sont recouverts par les droits correspondants, d'autres mécanismes de contrôle comme des indicateurs de performance, ont été mis en place. Les agences sont alors exemptées d'un contrôle détaillé de la gestion des comptes (méthode des coûts nets de fonctionnement), mais leurs dépenses nettes sont toujours sujettes à des limites de liquidités *(Cash Limits)*[26]. Ce mode de gestion permet d'introduire une certaine fongibilité des crédits, mais celle-ci reste limitée.

Le principal reproche adressé à ces formules traditionnelles était de restreindre la marge de manœuvre des agences, ce qui allait à l'encontre des objectifs poursuivis. C'est finalement grâce à la formule du "fonds commercial" dont nous avons parlé dans le paragraphe précédent que le gouvernement est parvenu à introduire une plus grande fongibilité des crédits. Selon cette formule, le détail des mouvements financiers est retiré du contrôle traditionnel du Parlement. En contrepartie, ce dernier doit donner son approbation pour l'institution de chacun des fonds, et pour la limite générale de ses emprunts. Une autorisation parlementaire reste également nécessaire pour toute allocation du ministère envers le fonds (y compris les paiements pour des biens ou services en provenance du fonds), et pour les prêts issus du ministère de tutelle[27].

En France, de la même manière, le principe de spécialité a pour objet de permettre aux assemblées délibérantes de connaître de façon précise comment vont être utilisés les crédits budgétairement autorisés, puisque ces derniers sont spécialisés en fonction de leur nature ou de leur destination. Mais l'application stricte de ce principe réduit très fortement l'autonomie des gestionnaires qui ne peuvent avoir d'initiatives personnelles dans la répartition de dépenses de leurs budgets que dans d'étroites limites.

Certes, la Cour des comptes avait signalé en 1987[28] la difficulté de concilier la tendance à l'ouverture de dotations globales et la règle de spécialité telle qu'elle est posée par la loi organique, estimant que la protection des droits du Parlement pose des limites à la globalisation. Elle a cependant admis que l'article 7 de l'ordonnance organique relative aux lois de finances, qui oblige à grouper les dépenses par nature ou par destination, n'interdit pas de considérer les dépenses de fonctionnement, autres que de personnel, comme des dépenses de même nature. Ainsi, les orientations retenues privilégient une simplification et un allégement du contrôle sur les moyens de fonctionnement courant des administrations: le service qui décide de se transformer en centre de responsabilité n'est plus contraint de gérer des enveloppes morcelées, il dispose d'un chapitre unique pour ses dépenses de fonctionnement [29]. Dans le cadre de l'expérimentation des contrats de service[30], il est même prévu une certaine fongibilité des crédits de fonctionnement et des crédits de personnel. Six directions départementales de l'Équipement sont concernées cette année. Alors que le ministère du Budget prévoyait la possibilité d'un accroissement des crédits de fonctionnement en contrepartie de crédits de personnel, le ministère de l'Équipement a demandé que cette fongibilité puisse s'établir dans les deux sens: il a donc été mis en place un forfait à déduire des crédits de fonctionnement par agent supplémentaire, et ce pour une durée de trois ans - soit la durée de vie du contrat.

Dans chacun des deux pays, l'objectif poursuivi est double: il s'agit de recentrer le contrôle financier sur les enjeux budgétaires importants et d'alléger le contrôle sur les actes courants ou répétitifs, grâce à un élargissement de l'engagement provisionnel. Pour compléter ce dispositif, des mesures ont été prises par ailleurs, dans le but de multiplier les possibilités de reports de crédits.

2.2.2. Un recours accru aux possibilités de reports de crédits

Des dispositions générales concernant la flexibilité des dépenses d'une année sur l'autre ont été mises en place dès 1983 en Grande-Bretagne. Ces dispositions introduisent une plus grande flexibilité, tout en maintenant le principe du contrôle parlementaire des crédits budgétaires accordés. À la fin de l'année, il y a reddition des comptes et les reports d'une année sur l'autre doivent être décidés par le vote au Parlement de crédits supplémentaires.[31]

Depuis 1989, dans le cadre notamment de l'initiative des "Étapes suivantes", de nouvelles mesures ont été mises en place. Alors que, théoriquement, les budgets prévisionnels supplémentaires sont votés par le Parlement avant que les crédits d'une année puissent être reportés sur l'année suivante, des crédits peuvent désormais être redéployés entre différents chapitres sans qu'un nouveau vote du Parlement soit nécessaire. Il est opéré dans ce cas un virement avec l'approbation du Ministère des Finances.[32]

En France également, de nouvelles possibilités de report de crédits sont avancées par le gouvernement comme un facteur de mobilisation et de responsabilisation des services déconcentrés. Les directives gouvernementales sur le "Renouveau du Service Public" laissaient entendre aux services qu'une gestion raisonnable conduisant à des économies conduirait à autoriser une pratique des reports plus libérale, de façon à les récompenser en quelque sorte d'un effort de bonne gestion; mais les nécessités de régulation budgétaire et de resserrement du déficit ont amené le gouvernement à prendre des mesures tout à fait contraires aux objectifs qu'il s'était fixés[33]. Il semble que la France ait des difficultés à concilier la nécessaire stabilité des engagements financiers à l'égard des services qui se modernisent et les fluctuations dues à la situation économique du pays. Comment établir des prévisions à long terme dans ces conditions? L'effet direct d'un tel phénomène est la démotivation des agents qui ne voient pas leurs efforts pris en compte et qui préfèrent se cantonner à un comportement peu innovateur, quitte à perdre en efficacité.

3. Conclusion

Les réformes budgétaires et comptables qui s'opèrent actuellement dans les deux pays expriment une volonté profonde des gouvernements de voir les deniers publics gérés de manière plus responsable, et donc plus économe. Dans un contexte où les services bénéficient d'une autonomie de gestion renforcée, les mesures qui ont pour objet d'introduire une comptabilité plus opérationnelle et de rendre le budget plus souple doivent permettre d'éclairer les choix des décisionnaires, et faciliter leur mise en œuvre.

Les réformes sont en cours; des progrès sont encore à réaliser, notamment dans le domaine de la prise en compte du patrimoine et des amortissements. En France, ces questions sont évoquées dans le document de travail de M. Dominique PERBEN sur la "réflexion préparatoire à la réforme de l'État"[34]; il est peu probable que le nouveau gouvernement souhaite inverser cette tendance pérenne vers une plus grande responsabilisation des services. En Grande-Bretagne, dans le prolongement de l'expérience des "Étapes Suivantes", le gouvernement préconise, pour l'ensemble des services de l'État, la mise en place d'une comptabilité qui prenne en compte les charges fixes - y compris les frais salariaux et les éléments du patrimoine -, l'amortissement, et des provisions pour créances douteuses[35]. Il faudra sans doute encore attendre quelques années pour que ces dispositions soient opérationnelles. Elles nécessitent un certain apprentissage de la part des gestionnaires, et les résistances à leur encontre sont encore nombreuses du côté des administrations centrales. Néanmoins, leur application paraît indispensable si l'on veut conférer aux services une réelle autonomie de gestion.

Notes

[1] Pour une analyse plus détaillée, voir H.M. Treasury, *"Trading Accounts. A Guide for Government Departments and Non-Departmental Public Bodies"*, Londres, H.M.S.O., (1989), pp. 41-51.
[2] Il fait l'objet de l'instruction n° 87-128 P.R. du 28 octobre 1987 (modifiée à plusieurs reprises).
[3] Ordonnance n° 59-2 du 2 janvier 1959 portant loi organique relative aux lois de finances, *J.O. du 3 janvier 1959*, p. 180, rectif. *J.O. du 11 janvier 1959*, p. 756.
[4] Instruction budgétaire et comptable M.14 concernant les collectivités locales, Édition des documents administratifs, *J.O. du 3 janvier 1997*, vol. I, p. 29.
[5] H.M. Treasury, *"The Financing and Accountability of the Next Steps Agencies"*, White Paper, Londres, H.M.S.O, Cm 914, (1989), §5.15.
[6] H.M. Treasury, *"Trading Accounts: A Guide for Government Departments and Non-Departmental Public Bodies"*, op. cit., p. 34.
[7] Companies Act 1985, Law reports, Statutes, 1985.
[8] Conformément au principe d'annualité budgétaire, les achats de l'année sont supposés être consommés dans la même période.
[9] H.M. Treasury, *"Trading Accounts: A Guide for Government Departments and Non-Departmental Public Bodies"*, op. cit., pp. 25-26.
[10] Décret n° 62-1587 du 29 décembre 1962, op. cit.
[11] Ordonnance n° 59-2, op. cit.
[12] Décret n° 62-1587, op. cit.
[13] Article 16 de l'ordonnance organique.
[14] Article 17 de l'ordonnance organique.
[15] Voir à ce propos l'article de M. GLIMET Emmanuel, "La comptabilité patrimoniale de l'Etat: une image fidèle?", *R.F.F.P.*, n° 40, 1992, pp 48-66.
[16] La création de chapitres uniques, propres aux centres de responsabilité, en est la principale illustration.
[17] Government Trading Funds Act 1973, chapter 63, pp. 1887-1893, (amendé en 1990).
[18] Notes internes du ministère des Finances pour la préparation du budget 1994.
[19] Circulaire du 23 février 1989 relative au renouveau du service public, *J.O. du 24 février 1989*, pp. 2 526-2 529.
[20] Cf Cour des comptes, *"La globalisation des crédits, les centres de responsabilité et la déconcentration"*, dossier préparé en vue de la réponse à la question n° 7 de la Commission des Finances de l'Assemblée Nationale, posée par M. Auberger le 16 décembre 1993, dans Assemblée nationale, *"Rapport sur le projet de loi (n° 914) portant règlement définitif du budget de 1992"*, 1993-1994, n° 1070, pp. 246-265.
[21] Notes internes du *Treasury* pour la préparation du budget 1994.
[22] Jusque très récemment, la règle était qu'une agence ne pouvait revêtir la forme d'un fonds commercial que si la moitié de son budget au moins provenait de recettes externes.
[23] H.M. Treasury, *"The Financing and Accountability of the Next Steps Agencies"*, op. cit., pp. 8-9
[24] Il n'existe pas en France d'équivalent à cette fonction sur le plan institutionnel, qui consiste à procéder à la vérification de la bonne tenue des comptes publics.
[25] Commission parlementaire de vérification des comptes publics; il s'agit d'une commission spéciale de la Chambre des Communes qui s'intéresse à la mise en œuvre des politiques publiques, sans discuter les politiques elles-mêmes. Sa compétence s'étend à tous les départements ministériels. Depuis quelques temps,

la commission procède essentiellement à des vérification de la bonne utilisation des crédits en termes de rendement *(Value for Money Audit)* .

[26] Cf notamment Cabinet Office - Training Development Division, "*Public Expenditure Management*", 6 vol., London, H.M.S.O., 1989.

[27] H.M. Treasury, *"The Financing and Accountability of the Next Steps Agencies"*, op. cit., pp 12-13.

[28] Cour des comptes - Formation interchambres, "Réponse à la question n° 7 posée par l'Assemblée nationale: globalisation des crédits et centres de responsabilité", op. cit.

[29] Direction du Budget - Direction de la comptabilité publique, "*Réforme du contrôle financier des dépenses déconcentrées*", Cahier des charges du ministère du Budget, (1994), p. 13.

[30] Circulaire n° 1B-96-337 du 12 juillet 1996 du ministère de la Fonction publique, de la réforme de l'État et de la décentralisation et du ministère de l'Économie et des Finances relative à la mise en œuvre de la démarche expérimentale des contrats de service, non publiée au J.O.

[31] H M. Treasury, *"The Financing and Accountability of the Next Steps Agencies"*, op. cit., p. 10.

[32] Mc ELDOWNEY John F., *"The Budgetary system of the United Kingdom"*, Commission Européenne, Direction générale du contrôle financier, Rapport national, (1996), pp. 13-14

[33] Comme par exemple en 1991 où l'on a décidé en mai qu'il n'y aurait pas de report. Finalement 56 milliards de reports ont été ouverts en octobre, c'est-à-dire plus que l'année précédente, mais ils ont été gelés, c'est-à-dire reportés en fait à l'exercice 1992 !

[34] PERBEN Dominique (Dir.), *"Réflexion préparatoire à la réforme de l'État"*, Document de travail non publié, 1996, p. 71.

[35] H.M. Treasury, *"Better Accounting for the Taxpayer's Money. Resource Accounting and Budgeting in Government"*, op. cit., pp. 32-38.

Bibliographie

En langue française

Ouvrages et rapports

Conseil d'État, "*Les centres de décision et de responsabilité dans l'administration*", Section du rapport et des études, Paris, ronéotypé, (1973), 137 p.

MONTAGNIER Gabriel, "*Principes de comptabilité publique*", Dalloz, 2ème éd., (1981), 412 p.

DE CLOSETS François (Dir.), Commissariat Général au plan, "*Le pari de la responsabilité*", Rapport de la Commission Efficacité de l'Etat, La Documentation Française, Éditions Payot, Paris, (1989), 259 p.

Direction du Budget - Direction de la comptabilité publique, "*Réforme du contrôle financier des dépenses déconcentrées*", Cahier des charges du ministère du Budget, (1994), 30 p.

PERBEN Dominique (Dir.), "*Réflexion préparatoire à la réforme de l'État*", Document de travail non publié, (1996), 73 p.

Articles et contributions

GLIMET Emmanuel, "La comptabilité patrimoniale de l'Etat: une image fidèle?", *R.F.F.P.*, n° 40, (1992), pp 48-66.

HARDY Vincent, TOWHILL Brian, WOLF Adam, "La responsabilisation comme stratégie de modernisation", *P.M.P.*, volume 8, n° 3, (1990), pp. 86-123.

LOGEROT François, "L'évolution des instruments traditionnels de la pluriannualité: la gestion des autorisations de programme et le problème des reports de crédits", *R.F.F.P*, n° 39, (1992), pp. 33-37.

THALMANN Philippe, "L'amortissement dans les comptes publics", *P.M.P.*, vol. 12, n° 1, (1994), pp. 53-74.

Cour des comptes, "La globalisation des crédits, les centres de responsabilité et la déconcentration", dossier préparé en vue de la réponse à la question n° 7 de la Commission des Finances de l'Assemblée Nationale, posée par M. Auberger le 16 décembre 1993, dans Assemblée nationale, "*Rapport sur le projet de loi (n° 914) portant règlement définitif du budget de 1992*", n° 1070, (1993-1994), pp. 246-265

Textes officiels

Circulaire du 23 février 1989 relative au renouveau du service public, *J O du 24 février 1989*, pp. 2526-2529.

Circulaire n° 1B-96-337 du 12 juillet 1996 du ministère de la Fonction publique, de la réforme de l'État et de la décentralisation et du ministère de l'Économie et des Finances relative à la mise en œuvre de la démarche expérimentale des contrats de service, non publiée au J O.

Décret n° 62-1587 du 29 décembre 1962 portant règlement sur la comptabilité publique, *J O. du 30 décembre 1962*; modifié par 1. Décret n° 74-246 du 11 mars 1974, *J.O du 17 mars 1974*, 2. Décret n° 76-1027 du 10 novembre 1976, *J O du 13 novembre 1976*, 3. Décret n° 86-620 du 14 mars 1986, *J O. du 20 mars 1986*.

Ordonnance n° 59-2 du 2 janvier 1959 portant loi organique relative aux lois de finances, *J.O du 3 janvier 1959*, p. 180, rectif. *J O. du 11 janvier 1959*, p. 756

Instruction budgétaire et comptable M.14, Édition des documents administratifs, *J O du 3 janvier 1997*, 2 vol., 643 p. et 1 279 p

En langue anglaise

Ouvrages et rapports

JONES Rowan, PENDLEBURY Maurice, "*Public Sector Accounting*", Pitman, 3ème éd., (1992), 236 p.

Mc ELDOWNEY John F., "*The Budgetary system of the United Kingdom*", Commission Européenne, Direction générale du contrôle financier, Rapport national, (1996), 58 p.

Publications gouvernementales

Cabinet Office - Training Development Division, "*Public Expenditure Management*", 6 vol., London, H.M.S.O., (1989).

HM Treasury, "*Trading Accounts: A Guide for Government Departments and Non-Departmental Public Bodies*", Londres, H.M.S.O., (1989), 53 p.

HM Treasury, "*The Financing and Accountability of the Next Steps Agencies*", White Paper, Londres, H.M.S O, Cm. 914, (1989), 29 p.

Textes de loi

Companies Act 1985, Law reports, Statutes, 1985.

Government Trading Funds Act 1973, chapter 63, pp. 1887-1893, (amendé en 1990).

Ethics and Accountability in a Context
of Governance and New Public Management
EGPA Annual Conference, Leuven 1997
IOS Press, 1998

Vers une refonte du régime de la responsabilité des fonctionnaires en Belgique ?

O. Daurmont[*]

1. Introduction

La problématique de la responsabilité des pouvoirs publics, spécialement de l'administration, et des fonctionnaires est riche. En attestent le foisonnement de décisions de justice en la matière, la densité et la variété des thèses et des idées défendues par la doctrine. Si la présente communication dépasse l'analyse juridique, celle-ci la nourrit cependant en grande partie. La responsabilité personnelle des agents à l'égard du citoyen peut exister seule ou coexister avec la responsabilité de l'Etat[1], la responsabilité des personnes publiques peut aussi être engagée seule. Les conditions de mise en oeuvre de ces responsabilités révèlent l'évolution des rôles respectifs des pouvoirs publics et des fonctionnaires ainsi que des droits et obligations de chacun de ces acteurs de la vie publique.

Sous l'influence d'événements souvent tragiques, une refonte de la responsabilité personnelle des fonctionnaires se dessine. Elle est souhaitable dans l'intérêt des victimes et des fonctionnaires et d'une manière plus générale, afin de mieux assurer le respect de l'égalité, de l'équité, d'une éthique politique et d'une déontologie des fonctionnaires.

2. L'extension au droit commun de la responsabilité des pouvoirs publics

Conceptuellement et schématiquement, le régime de la responsabilité civile des pouvoirs publics en vigueur en Belgique peut paraître simple, cohérent, satisfaisant. Aujourd'hui en effet, ce régime est identique à celui qui s'applique à toute personne privée. Comme tout particulier, l'Etat et les autres autorités publiques doivent respecter "le devoir général de la prudence" prévu par les articles 1382 et 1383 du Code civil.

Les pouvoirs publics engagent leur responsabilité lorsqu'ils commettent une faute, une négligence ou une imprudence et que celle-ci cause un dommage à autrui. Ils devront réparer le dommage le plus souvent en payant des dommages et intérêts à la victime. Parfois même, ils seront tenus à réparer en nature. Ils s'exposent au paiement d'une astreinte s'ils n'exécutent pas la condamnation principale. Leurs biens, en tout cas ceux qui ne sont pas utiles pour la continuité du service public, peuvent faire l'objet d'une saisie en vue de désintéresser leurs créanciers.

En un siècle et demi, un changement radical du régime de la responsabilité des pouvoirs publics s'est opéré. En effet, après avoir été jugée inapplicable aux pouvoirs publics, la faute, si légère soit-elle, peut leur être imputée. Des réformes récentes garantissant l'indemnisation

---

[*] Odile Daurmont, Conseiller d'Etat, Chargée de cours à l'U.L.B., Belgique.

de la victime réduisent des prérogatives de puissance publique pourtant tenaces, telle l'immunité d'exécution forcée contre les autorités publiques.

Ce revirement n'a pu se produire qu'en raison de l'émergence d'une nouvelle philosophie politique. Le développement des exigences de démocratie a produit une organisation politique dans laquelle les citoyens ont un rôle à jouer et des intérêts légitimes auxquels doivent veiller les pouvoirs publics. Parallèlement, l'idée selon laquelle les autorités publiques ont des obligations vis-à-vis des citoyens, notamment le respect du droit, s'est affirmée. La conception quasi sacrale de l'État a ainsi fait place à celle d'un État au service du citoyen. L'action administrative s'est prodigieusement développée et diversifiée, engendrant un accroissement des litiges et rendant plus impérieuse la nécessité de sanctionner les cas d'arbitraire administratif. Le pouvoir judiciaire a adapté sa jurisprudence, c'est-à-dire ses moyens d'action, à ces nécessités et a considérablement étendu son pouvoir de contrôle. De nouvelles autorités juridictionnelles - Conseil d'État et Cour d'arbitrage - ont été créées et ont renforcé le pouvoir juridictionnel.

Dans ce contexte, l'appréciation de la séparation des pouvoirs s'est modifiée. La conception absolue de la séparation des pouvoirs soutenue par le pouvoir judiciaire est abandonnée. Chacun des trois pouvoirs dont le pouvoir législatif, qui a perdu sa suprématie au profit d'un pouvoir exécutif hypertrophié, tente de développer les contrôles qu'il exerce en "contrepoids" sur les deux autres pouvoirs. Contrôler dans le respect de l'indépendance des pouvoirs; voilà bien un exercice difficile. L'actualité toute récente en illustre les risques. L'échec tragique des enquêtes sur l'enlèvement de cinq fillettes a provoqué l'institution au sein du parlement d'une commission spéciale d'enquête aux pouvoirs très étendus. Déjà, des affaires ayant suscité une émotion collective profonde - comme les "tueries du Brabant wallon" et l'assassinat du Ministre d'État André Cools - avaient occasionné un recours plus fréquent à l'enquête parlementaire, ultime moyen en quelque sorte face aux "dysfonctionnements" des deux autres pouvoirs. La commission d'enquête, couramment désignée par le nom du principal pédophile mis en cause dans l'enlèvement des fillettes, Dutroux, a été dotée du pouvoir de procéder à l'audition de magistrats chargés de l'instruction de dossiers en cours. Les travaux de la commission - notamment de nombreuses auditions de magistrats, de gendarmes et de policiers - ont été largement retransmis en direct par la télévision. Dans ses conclusions, la Commission "Dutroux" a relevé des "manquements individuels". Ces procédés - même si la loi les autorisait - ont exacerbé les tensions entre le pouvoir législatif, d'une part, et les pouvoirs exécutif et judiciaire, d'autre part. Des voix se sont élevées pour les critiquer. Ainsi, un ancien bâtonnier, concepteur d'un nouveau code de procédure pénale, a mis en exergue la responsabilité collective des trois pouvoirs dans ces dysfonctionnements et l'indifférence longtemps manifestée par le pouvoir politique à l'égard de la justice. Il estime que le rapport en lui-même constitue une sanction qui est contraire à la présomption d'innocence et risque de constituer une pression considérable sur les autorités disciplinaires des agents dont les manquements ont été révélés parce que relayée par l'opinion publique (Franchimont, 1997).

De leur côté, les autorités juridictionnelles contrôlent de plus en plus étroitement l'activité du pouvoir exécutif et du pouvoir législatif. Commencé en 1920, le mouvement d'extension de la responsabilité civile des pouvoirs publics au droit commun connaît des étapes décisives à partir des années 60. Par un arrêt du 23 avril 1971, la Cour de cassation a considéré "qu'aucune disposition constitutionnelle ou légale ne soustrait le pouvoir exécutif, dans l'exercice de ses missions et de ses activités réglementaires, à l'obligation, résultant des articles 1382 et 1383 du Code civil, de réparer le dommage qu'il cause à autrui par sa faute, notamment par son imprudence ou par négligence; que, même dans les cas où aucun délai n'est prescrit au pouvoir exécutif par une disposition légale pour prendre un règlement, l'abstention de prendre celui-ci peut, en application des articles 1382 et 1383 du Code civil, donner lieu à réparation si un dommage en est résulté"[2]. Elle affirme ainsi de manière très nette que l'obligation générale de prudence s'impose aux autorités administratives dans tous les cas, même lorsqu'elles exercent la fonction réglementaire. La Cour étend son contrôle au pouvoir discrétionnaire de l'autorité publique puisque même lorsqu'aucun délai n'est légalement prévu et que l'autorité publique dispose donc du pouvoir d'apprécier l'opportunité d'agir, la Cour suprême décide si le délai écoulé est ou non raisonnable et le cas échéant, constitutif de faute. La preuve de la faute d'une administration résulte notamment, mais pas seulement[3] d'un arrêt d'annulation du Conseil d'État. Celui-ci peut annuler l'acte litigieux pour violation de la loi comprise au sens large, quelle que soit la norme écrite ou non écrite en cause, pour violation de certaines formes, pour incompétence de l'auteur de l'acte et même pour détournement de pouvoir. Au rang des règles non écrites dont le Conseil d'État assure le respect figurent le principe de proportionnalité et le principe de bonne administration. Dans les cas où de telles violations sont alléguées, le contrôle du Conseil d'État s'exerce aux confins de l'opportunité. Mais quels que soient la norme dont la violation est constatée par le Conseil d'État et le motif de l'annulation, celle-ci est toujours prononcée pour violation de la loi, pour illégalité. Dès lors, l'acte illégal étant en principe fautif[4], la faute civile de l'autorité publique sera automatiquement prouvée dès qu'un arrêt d'annulation a été prononcé par le Conseil d'État. Le Conseil d'État et la Cour de cassation sont cependant attentifs à ne pas s'immiscer dans le domaine de l'opportunité. La Cour de cassation a récemment répété que l'appréciation de l'opportunité d'un acte administratif n'appartient pas au pouvoir judiciaire mais relève de l'appréciation discrétionnaire de l'autorité administrative[5]. "Les limites respectives du contrôle d'opportunité et de la vérification de la légalité restent (cependant) dans une large mesure incertaines et évolutives" (Lewalle, 1997: 255).

La responsabilité de l'administration joue que le dommage consiste dans la lésion d'un droit civil ou d'un droit politique ou dans la lésion d'un intérêt.

Un arrêt de la Cour suprême du 26 juin 1980 condamne une autorité publique à la réparation en nature lorsqu'elle est possible[6]. Il fait donc fi de la prohibition faite au pouvoir judiciaire d'adresser des injonctions à l'administration. L'opinion selon laquelle le juge exerce seulement un pouvoir de commandement inhérent aux fonctions du pouvoir judiciaire lorsqu'il ordonne à l'administration de faire cesser ce qui cause le préjudice, a prévalu.

L'extension de la responsabilité des pouvoirs publics concerne non seulement la fonction exécutive mais aussi la fonction judiciaire, voire à l'avenir la fonction législative[7].

Dans bon nombre de cas, les pouvoirs publics sont tenus, même sans faute de leur part, de prendre en charge la réparation de certains dommages comme ceux subis par les victimes d'actes intentionnels de violence.

Ce rapide état des lieux permet certainement de comprendre qu'un auteur, spécialiste du droit de la responsabilité et des assurances, ait écrit que la responsabilité civile "donne d'elle-même une image aussi angoissante qu'une mer sans rivages" (Fagnart, 1994: 303).

3. L'inadéquation de la théorie classique de la responsabilité personnelle des fonctionnaires aux mutations de l'organisation politico-aministrative

Comme les autorités publiques, les fonctionnaires sont, en principe, soumis au droit commun de la responsabilité. Ils sont responsables vis-à-vis des tiers et de l'administration de leur faute même la plus légère. Celle-ci doit s'apprécier concrètement par rapport au comportement du fonctionnaire normalement prudent et diligent. Au pénal cependant, le Code prévoit un régime spécifique de répression des crimes et délits contre l'ordre public lorsqu'ils sont commis par des fonctionnaires dans l'exercice de leurs fonctions. Divers textes normatifs portent encore des peines pénales pour certains faits reprochés à des fonctionnaires. Pour un même délit, des peines plus lourdes que celles applicables aux particuliers sont parfois fixées lorsqu'il est commis par un fonctionnaire public. Cette sévérité est justifiée par le fait que certaines pratiques, comme des actes racistes ou xénophobes, apparaissent particulièrement odieux lorsqu'elles sont le fait de fonctionnaires[8].

La mise en oeuvre de la responsabilité personnelle des fonctionnaires devrait, en bon sens, être parfaitement corrélée avec celle des pouvoirs publics. N'est-ce pas le fonctionnaire qui agit au nom de l'État, entité purement abstraite ? Cette façon de voir a été suivie par des juridictions de fond. Il a été ainsi décidé que l'État ne pouvait être responsable lorsque la responsabilité personnelle de l'agent n'était pas retenue[9]. Il a aussi été admis que lorsque la responsabilité directe de l'État était engagée, celle de l'agent devait être exclue[10]. Par son arrêt du 19 décembre 1980, la Cour de cassation s'écarte de cette conception. Elle a jugé que "la seule constatation que tout fonctionnaire placé dans la même situation aurait donné la même interprétation erronée que celle du fonctionnaire en cause n'exonère pas l'administration de sa responsabilité pour l'excès de pouvoir qu'elle a commis"[11]. Elle a ensuite, dans un arrêt du 17 juin 1982, consacré le principe de la possibilité de coexistence des responsabilités de l'État et des fonctionnaires[12]. Trois hypothèses en matière d'imputabilité des responsabilités peuvent donc se présenter en droit belge: soit l'État seul ou le fonctionnaire seul est responsable soit, l'un et l'autre sont responsables solidairement.

La dissociation des responsabilités des personnes publiques et des fonctionnaires trouve son origine dans une conception particulière de la qualité de fonctionnaire. Cette conception est appelée la "théorie de l'organe". En vertu de celle-ci, les fonctionnaires sont qualifiés soit d'organe soit de préposé selon la mission qu'ils exercent. "Sont organes de l'État ceux qui, en vertu de la loi ou des décisions prises ou des délégations données dans le cadre de la loi, disposent d'une parcelle, si minime soit-elle, de la puissance publique exercée par lui ou qui ont le pouvoir de l'engager vis-à-vis des tiers"[13]. A contrario, les agents qui n'exercent pas la puissance publique ou qui n'ont pas le pouvoir d'engager l'État vis-à-vis des tiers, sont des préposés. L'organe s'identifie à l'État; il en exprime la volonté, il agit pour lui. Il s'ensuit qu'il engage directement la responsabilité de l'État lorsqu'il commet un acte fautif dommageable dans l'exercice de ses attributions. La responsabilité de l'État et celle de l'organe sont régies par les articles 1382 et 1383 du Code civil[14]. Selon les conceptions paternalistes et patriciennes du 19ème siècle, les préposés, assimilés à des "tâcherons vulgaires"[15], ne peuvent occasionner la responsabilité des pouvoirs publics qu'indirectement sur la base de l'article 1384, alinéa 3, du Code civil[16]. La personne publique est de plein droit, de manière automatique, présumée responsable des fautes dommageables de son préposé. Le commettant a en effet le devoir de bien choisir ses préposés et de les surveiller. Peu importe dès lors que le fonctionnaire-préposé, à l'inverse du fonctionnaire-organe, ait agi intentionnellement ou seulement à l'occasion de l'exercice de ses fonctions, l'État sera responsable. La responsabilité du préposé entraîne toujours celle de l'État; le fait fautif de l'organe ne provoque la responsabilité de l'État que si l'organe a agi dans l'exercice strictement normal de ses missions. Les abus commis par l'organe dans l'accomplissement de ses attributions, alors qu'ils peuvent pourtant consister dans des agissements graves, comme l'atteinte volontaire et injustifiée par un policier à l'intégrité physique d'une personne, ne donnent pas lieu à la condamnation solidaire de l'autorité publique. Du point de vue de l'éthique politique, cette conséquence de la théorie traditionnelle de la responsabilité est heurtante, même si la responsabilité politique du mandataire public concerné joue et qu'il doive démissionner de ses fonctions. Dans bien des cas d'abus de fonctions, le fonctionnaire est non seulement contraint, en raison de sa responsabilité civile, d'indemniser la victime mais aussi de renoncer à son emploi. En effet, la personne publique même pour qui il a agi l'aura parfois révoqué à l'issue d'une procédure disciplinaire. N'est-elle pas pourtant responsable du bon fonctionnement des services quelle que soit la qualité de l'agent ? Ne doit-elle pas dès lors être également responsable - à tout le moins civilement - à l'égard de la victime même en cas d'abus de fonctions ?

Comment ne pas comprendre que tant la victime que l'organe et finalement la société civile ressentent ce système comme inéquitable.

L'organe, dont par hypothèse le patrimoine est plus limité que celui de l'autorité publique, supportera seul l'indemnisation. Du point de vue moral et déontologique, l'organe - qui a peut-être agi conformément aux instructions de l'autorité ou ce qui n'est pas nécessairement une cause de justification pour l'autorité, sans instructions -sera confronté à un sentiment d'incompréhension, d'acrimonie voire de défection de sa hiérarchie politico-administrative. L'inertie, l'indifférence, l'incapacité de l'autorité publique à concevoir des politiques et les moyens de les appliquer sont fréquemment et quasi-unanimement dénoncées. Plus particulièrement, il leur est reproché, tant à l'intérieur de l'appareil administratif qu'à l'extérieur, de ne pouvoir contrôler les services administratifs. Lors de ces dix dernières années, des ministres de toute tendance politique ont avoué publiquement ne pas être au courant de décisions importantes prises par leur administration. Récemment, interpellé sur un traitement de faveur octroyé à une banque, le ministre des Finances a déclaré devant la commission des finances de la Chambre ne pas avoir été mis en possession du dossier complet par son administration[17]. Les pouvoirs publics ne doivent-ils pas par le recrutement, la formation continue, l'évaluation permanente et les mesures disciplinaires prévenir de telles situations ? En tout état de cause, il apparaît indispensable de définir plus précisément les rôles et responsabilités respectifs du politique et de l'administration. L'élaboration d'un code de déontologie des fonctionnaires et une généralisation des analyses des fonctions administratives pourraient contribuer à la réalisation de cet objectif. Le recours aux analyses de fonctions se développe depuis 1987 mais les responsables politiques n'en sont généralement pas informés et ne s'y réfèrent donc pas dans les rapports qu'ils ont avec leurs fonctionnaires. Quant à la déontologie, un arrêté royal du 26 septembre 1994 fixant les principes généraux de la fonction publique fédérale, communautaire et régionale rappelle les grands devoirs auxquels les fonctionnaires sont tenus - devoir de réserve, loyauté, intégrité, devoir d'obéissance, compréhension des usagers et non-discrimination notamment - et consacre, pour la première fois, les droits des agents - liberté d'expression et droit à l'information et à la formation continue. Cette réglementation ne constitue cependant pas un code de déontologie. En effet, les droits et devoirs des fonctionnaires sont énoncés en termes extrêmement généraux. Les règles de conduite plus précises doivent être dégagées de la jurisprudence du Conseil d'État en matière disciplinaire; ce travail n'est actuellement accompli que par la doctrine ainsi que par certaines universités.

Quant à la victime et aux citoyens en général, eux non plus, ne comprendront pas que l'indemnisation ne soit, le cas échéant, pas possible ou fort réduite ni que le pouvoir politique puisse éventuellement échapper à toute responsabilité juridique.

En 1947 déjà, la Cour de cassation avait tempéré la rigueur des exigences légales quant à la nécessité d'agir dans les limites de ses attributions pour que la responsabilité de l'État puisse être engagée du fait d'une faute d'un organe. Elle a admis en effet "l'apparence de fonctionnalité" lorsque l'organe pouvait avoir été "tenu comme agissant dans les limites de ses attributions légales par tout homme raisonnable et prudent"[18], spécialement s'il s'agit d'organes subalternes[19].

Un autre effet pervers de la théorie de l'organe consiste dans l'impossibilité d'intenter une action civile contre les personnes publiques devant les tribunaux répressifs alors que dans de nombreux cas, la faute aquilienne constitue aussi une infraction pénale, comme par exemple, le défaut de prévoyance. Cette conséquence résulte d'une autre impossibilité, celle d'intenter une action pénale contre les autorités publiques. Dès lors, la responsabilité civile directe de l'État est exclue dès que la victime d'une faute pénale commise par un organe se porte partie civile devant un tribunal répressif[20]. Un auteur a résumé de la manière suivante les inconvénients que ce système engendre pour la victime et pour l'État: "La victime est lésée, qui, après avoir épuisé tous les degrés de juridiction où l'aura entraîné le prévenu contre qui elle se sera constituée partie civile, aura, pour prendre jugement contre l'État (et, souvent, pour obtenir ainsi vraiment, réparation) à repasser devant toutes les juridictions civiles où l'Administration organisera sa défense. L'État, lui-même, voit par ce système sa défense compromise devant le juge civil, pour n'avoir pu faire valoir des moyens au moment où les faits qui engendrent sa responsabilité étaient soumis à l'appréciation du tribunal répressif. Comment pourra-t-il, au cours de l'action civile, dénier ce que les décisions judiciaires devenues définitives auront déjà déclaré acquis" (Glansdorff, 1988: 78). Une fois de plus, l'iniquité et l'incohérence du système légal sont critiquées.

Une autre conséquence de la théorie de l'organe aggrave encore ce constat. Lorsque l'État a indemnisé la victime d'une faute, même légère commise par un organe, il peut en règle générale se retourner contre celui-ci en exerçant l'action récursoire et exiger de l'organe une contribution au dédommagement. Toutefois, lorsque l'agent - qu'il soit organe ou préposé - est contractuel, ce recours n'est possible que si le dommage a été causé par une faute légère "habituelle". En effet, l'article 18 de la loi du 3 juillet 1978 relative aux contrats de travail, qui s'applique aux travailleurs du secteur privé mais aussi aux travailleurs occupés contractuellement par les pouvoirs publics, limite la responsabilité du travailleur aux seuls cas de dol, de faute lourde et de faute légère "habituelle". Dans la pratique, l'autorité s'abstiendrait généralement d'exercer son recours contre l'agent en cas de faute légère.

Enfin, last but not least, une critique fondamentale doit encore être adressée à la théorie de l'organe. Elle consiste dans la difficulté même de qualifier un agent ou une catégorie d'agents d'organe plutôt que de préposé et inversement, et de faire coïncider cette qualification avec la réalité de l'organisation administrative.

Certaines fonctions ne donnent pas lieu à discussion. Ainsi, la qualité d'organe des magistrats judiciaires a été réaffirmée récemment par la Cour suprême. L'appréciation de la faute du fait d'une juridiction se fait conformément au droit commun de la responsabilité. La faute s'apprécie concrètement suivant le critère du magistrat normalement soigneux et prudent, placé dans les mêmes circonstances de temps. Elle peut consister dans la violation d'une norme imposant au magistrat de s'abstenir ou d'agir de manière déterminée, sous réserve d'une erreur invincible ou d'une autre cause de justification[21]. La particularité consiste ici dans le fait que la responsabilité personnelle du magistrat ne peut être engagée, sauf prise à partie. Le magistrat jouit en effet dans l'exercice de la mission de juger d'une immunité justifiée par le souci de préserver son indépendance. Seul, l'État est responsable.

Pour qualifier l'agent d'organe ou de préposé, les juridictions de fond se fondent parfois sur la nature statutaire ou contractuelle de l'engagement de l'agent. Selon cette jurisprudence, l'agent recruté à la suite d'un appel public et de la réussite d'épreuves de recrutement et ensuite nommé selon la procédure fixée par le statut auquel il est soumis est un organe. L'agent engagé sur la base d'un contrat de travail est un préposé. Cette conception patricienne et dichotomique de la fonction publique ne correspond plus à notre organisation administrative. A l'heure actuelle, le critère de la nature de l'engagement de l'agent et par conséquent du régime juridique auquel il est soumis, statutaire ou contractuel, ne situe nullement le fonctionnaire ni dans la hiérarchie des grades ni dans celle des fonctions. Un agent contractuel peut être titulaire d'un grade élevé dans la hiérarchie administrative et exercer une parcelle de la puissance publique. Dans la pratique, il est courant que des agents contractuels engagent l'autorité publique vis-à-vis des tiers sans que cela suscite la moindre réserve ni de la hiérarchie administrative et politique, contrainte à rechercher efficacité et efficience, ni du citoyen, soucieux d'obtenir le meilleur service. Un exemple illustre clairement l'inadéquation du critère de distinction aux réalités fonctionnelles. Un jugement a qualifié de préposé un directeur d'enseignement, engagé par contrat[22], mais l'huissier de l'immeuble où sont donnés les cours est un agent statutaire et doit donc être considéré comme un organe de l'État alors qu'il n'exerce sans doute aucune parcelle de la puissance publique. Les statistiques attestent de l'augmentation du nombre de contractuels dans la fonction publique, notamment dans la fonction publique locale où leur nombre peut dépasser celui des statutaires. La contractualisation croissante de la fonction publique, malgré la réaffirmation du principe du recrutement sous statut, accentue l'inadéquation du critère de distinction et d'une manière plus générale, de la responsabilité personnelle des fonctionnaires, telle qu'elle est conçue sur la base de la théorie de l'organe.

4. Abandon de la "théorie de l'organe" et évolution vers une "privatisation" ou une "contractualisation" du régime de la responsabilité personnelle des fonctionnaires ?

Des modifications du régime de la responsabilité personnelle des fonctionnaires sont intervenues récemment dans deux secteurs de la fonction publique: celui de l'enseignement libre subventionné et celui des forces de sécurité.

Un décret du 1er février 1993 de la Communauté française a fixé le statut des membres du personnel subsidiés de l'enseignement libre subventionné. Statut et régime privé de la loi sur le contrat de travail constituent normalement des régimes juridiques des relations de travail diamétralement opposés, l'un excluant l'autre[23]. Le décret emprunte cependant aux deux régimes pour régler les relations professionnelles des enseignants, subsidiés, de l'enseignement libre subventionné. L'engagement de l'enseignant a lieu sur la base d'un contrat de travail régi par la loi du 3 juillet 1978 mais le reste des relations de travail et notamment le régime disciplinaire est réglé, à quelques exceptions près[24], selon les dispositions statutaires classiques. Quant à la responsabilité de l'enseignant, le décret limite la faute légère, comme fait générateur de la responsabilité, à la faute légère "habituelle". Conçue comme une conséquence de l'engagement contractuel, cette réduction des faits générateurs de la responsabilité est calquée sur l'article 18 de la loi du 3 juillet 1978 relative aux contrats de travail[25]. L'enseignant, subsidié, de l'enseignement libre subventionné ne répond, en cas de dommage causé au pouvoir organisateur ou à des tiers, que de son dol et de sa faute lourde; il ne répond de sa faute légère que si celle-ci présente dans son chef un caractère habituel plutôt qu'accidentel. Ce régime n'est pas applicable aux autres réseaux de l'enseignement dans la Communauté française.

C'est un événement dramatique qui est à l'origine de la réforme des responsabilités des autorités de police et des fonctionnaires de police. Dans la foulée, deux ans plus tard, la réforme à été étendue aux militaires.

A l'occasion d'un match de football, opposant au stade du Heysel un club italien et un club anglais, des supporters anglais provoquèrent des incidents qui causèrent la mort de trente-neuf spectateurs italiens. La commission parlementaire, qui fut instituée pour enquêter sur cet événement, conclut que si les responsabilités administratives étaient réelles, les responsabilités politiques existaient également et que ce serait "faire oeuvre de mauvais discernement que de tenter de dissocier les unes des autres tant elles étaient intimement liées"[26]. Elle met notamment en cause le ministre de l'Intérieur en tant que responsable final du maintien de l'ordre. Il incombe dès lors au ministre de l'Intérieur, selon la commission, d'apprécier "sous sa responsabilité politique la nature et l'importance (des) manifestation(s)" et de prendre les initiatives nécessaires pour assurer le maintien de l'ordre[27]. Malgré ces conclusions et l'émoi général de la population, le ministre de l'Intérieur ne présenta pas sa démission; les ministres libéraux offrirent leur démission mais le gouvernement resta finalement en place[28]. Pour ce qui concerne les autorités publiques, seul le comportement du commandant du service d'ordre sur place fut sanctionné par les juridictions. La cour jugea que l'absence de réaction du commandant en présence d'une situation qui aurait dû l'alerter constitue une faute; qu'en effet, en n'agissant pas, il n'a pas eu le comportement normalement prudent et avisé de tout officier de gendarmerie placé dans les mêmes circonstances[29]. La loi du 5 août 1992 sur la fonction de police qui fut ensuite adoptée est animée de la préoccupation de délimiter les responsabilités du pouvoir politique et des fonctionnaires ainsi que par le souci de préciser les droits et obligations des fonctionnaires de police à l'égard des citoyens. Aux termes de cette loi, l'État et la commune sont respectivement responsables du dommage causé par les fonctionnaires de la gendarmerie et de la police judiciaire, d'une part, et par les fonctionnaires de la police communale, d'autre part, dans les fonctions dans lesquelles ils les ont employés, "comme les commettants sont responsables du dommage causé par le fait de leurs préposés".

Le pouvoir politique est donc juridiquement responsable en toutes circonstances. Le fonctionnaire de police, quant à lui, n'est responsable vis-à-vis de l'autorité publique et des tiers que de sa faute lourde, de sa faute intentionnelle et de sa faute légère si elle présente dans son chef un caractère habituel[30]. Enfin, les fonctionnaires de police, qui font l'objet d'une action en dommages et intérêts, peuvent appeler à la cause l'État ou la commune devant la juridiction civile ou répressive; l'autorité publique peut intervenir volontairement. La responsabilité juridique des autorités publiques est engagée en toute hypothèse, même lorsque la faute commise par le fonctionnaire de police est la plus légère, et devant toute juridiction qu'elle soit civile ou pénale. Du fait même, la responsabilité politique de ces autorités est proclamée. Elles ont failli dans l'exécution de la politique qu'elles avaient à mener. Le titulaire du mandat politique concerné, ministre par exemple, devra en tirer les conséquences. Quant au fonctionnaire de police, non seulement il ne sera plus seul devant les juges et les victimes, mais encore sa responsabilité personnelle est limitée par le jeu de la réduction des faits générateurs de responsabilité: la faute légère occasionnelle ou accidentelle ne figure plus au nombre de ceux-ci. La modification législative est aussi révélatrice de l'inadéquation de la théorie de l'organe. Alors que sa mission fondamentale de maintien de l'ordre public et de la sécurité n'a pas sensiblement varié, et participe manifestement de l'exercice de la puissance publique, le gendarme est qualifié de préposé. Cette combinaison des règles contenues dans l'article 1384 du Code civil et dans l'article 18 de la loi du 3 juillet 1978 relative aux contrats de travail réalise un meilleur équilibre entre la responsabilité des pouvoirs publics et la responsabilité personnelle des fonctionnaires, entre l'éthique politique et la déontologie administrative. La situation de la victime est confortée.

Cette réforme déjà encouragée par le Conseil d'État dans l'avis qu'il a donné sur le projet de loi sur les fonctions de police[31] se révèle encore plus impérative à la suite d'un arrêt du 18 décembre 1996 de la Cour d'arbitrage. En réponse à une question préjudicielle, la Cour d'arbitrage a dit pour droit que le principe constitutionnel d'égalité est violé en ce que, en matière de responsabilité civile, d'une part, les articles 1382 et 1251, 3°, du Code civil permettent aux pouvoirs publics d'intenter une action récursoire contre l'agent statutaire lorsqu'à la suite d'une faute légère occasionnelle commise par celui-ci dans le cadre de ses fonctions, lesdits pouvoirs ont indemnisé la victime du dommage dont cet agent a été déclaré responsable et, d'autre part, l'article 18 de la loi du 3 juillet 1978 relative aux contrats de travail limite la responsabilité civile du travailleur, lié par un contrat de travail, aux seuls cas de dol, de faute lourde et de faute légère habituelle[32].

Le ministre fédéral de la Fonction publique a déposé en comité de négociation syndicale commun à l'ensemble des services publics un projet de loi relatif au régime de responsabilité d'une grande partie des fonctionnaires qu'ils soient fédéraux, communautaires, régionaux ou locaux. Seules certaines catégories de fonctionnaires, soumis à des régimes juridiques particuliers, comme les magistrats, sont exclues.

La responsabilité personnelle des fonctionnaires tant à l'égard de l'administration qu'à l'égard des tiers n'est mise en oeuvre qu'en cas de faute intentionnelle, de faute lourde ou de faute légère habituelle. Les fonctionnaires sont responsables du dommage causé en violant "les obligations liées à l'exercice de leurs fonctions". Par ces termes, il est fait référence à l'article 1384, alinéa 3, du Code civil qui prévoit que le commettant est responsable du dommage causé par le fait de son préposé. L'agent contre lequel une action en dommages et intérêts est intentée devant une juridiction civile ou pénale peut appeler à la cause l'administration dont il dépend; celle-ci peut intervenir volontairement. La réduction des faits générateurs de la responsabilité civile personnelle des fonctionnaires répond à l'objection soulevée par la Cour d'arbitrage. Les règles prévues par le projet reproduisent, de manière parfois moins explicite, des réformes déjà opérées par le législateur pour les fonctionnaires de police et pour les militaires. Si le projet devait être adopté, la théorie de l'organe, dont l'inadéquation aux réalités administratives et l'incohérence ont été dénoncées, serait abandonnée.

5. Conclusion

En guise de conclusion, quelques considérations sur l'apport de l'élaboration d'une déontologie des fonctionnaires à la détermination d'un régime de responsabilité personnelle des fonctionnaires seront faites.

L'intérêt légitime, voire le droit, du citoyen au bon fonctionnement des services publics devient une composante de l'intérêt public. L'appréciation de celui-ci n'est plus du domaine exclusif des gouvernants. Les exigences de démocratie participative font émerger des rapports nouveaux entre les trois acteurs de la vie publique, l'autorité publique, le citoyen et le fonctionnaire. Le citoyen revendique une relation plus égalitaire avec l'autorité et ses agents et un rôle de partenaire dans le processus de décision publique. Il exige d'eux une capacité à décider et à agir dans son intérêt. Il réclame une information claire et objective sur leurs décisions et leurs actions. Des relations commutatives de partenariat se nouent entre eux. Celles-ci modifient profondément l'organisation et le fonctionnement des institutions et des administrations ainsi que la gestion de la fonction publique, et la conception des normes de conduite des fonctionnaires.

Le citoyen et l'autorité publique veulent des fonctionnaires compétents, efficaces et ouverts au public. Le fonctionnaire ne doit pas seulement être "normalement attentif, diligent et prudent", il a aussi l'obligation de réaliser la convergence de l'intérêt public et de l'intérêt du citoyen. Des textes épars et de valeurs normatives diverses, fixent ces obligations. Une réglementation récente du 26 septembre 1994 arrête les principes généraux en cette matière notamment. Elle rappelle que le fonctionnaire doit traiter les usagers des services publics avec compréhension et sans discrimination. Une charte de l'utilisateur des services publics, adoptée le 4 décembre 1992, indique comment mettre en oeuvre ces principes généraux, dégagés dès 1991.

De son côté, le fonctionnaire, rendu attentif dans l'accomplissement de ses fonctions au respect des droits des citoyens, exige de sa hiérarchie administrative et politique le respect de ces droits dans les relations de travail qu'ils entretiennent. La hiérarchie politique et administrative est contrainte de se démocratiser. L'autorité publique doit rechercher un plus juste équilibre entre ses intérêts et les revendications des fonctionnaires visant à acquérir à la fois indépendance et association au processus décisionnel. Il importe donc de permettre légalement à l'autorité publique et politique d'être présente au côté de l'agent devant les tribunaux en cas de dysfonctionnements de l'administration. Le législateur est déjà intervenu en ce sens pour les fonctionnaires de police et les militaires; un projet de loi vise à étendre ces réformes à l'ensemble de la fonction publique, sauf exceptions. La confusion de plus en plus importante du secteur public et du secteur privé et plus particulièrement le phénomène de contractualisation de la fonction publique incitent le législateur à limiter la responsabilité des fonctionnaires, pour ce qui concerne la faute légère, à la faute habituelle. Le fonctionnaire ne serait plus responsable du dommage causé par sa faute purement accidentelle, occasionnelle. Cette conception concorde avec les règles de déontologie dégagées par le Conseil d'État en matière disciplinaire. Selon la jurisprudence du Conseil d'État, le caractère "répété" ou "systématique" d'un manquement aux obligations professionnelles est un élément constitutif du fait disciplinaire. Une attitude persistante de non-coopération, un refus systématique d'obéissance, des critiques systématiques de l'autorité sont des fautes de service[33]; c'est à juste titre que l'autorité les sanctionne disciplinairement. Pour exercer son contrôle, le juge administratif analyse la nature des fonctions exercées par le fonctionnaire sanctionné disciplinairement et les responsabilités qu'il assume ou la place qu'il occupe dans la hiérarchie. Ces éléments contribuent à l'appréciation du fait disciplinaire et de la peine infligée ainsi qu'à l'évaluation du rapport de proportionnalité qui doit exister entre ces deux éléments. De cette manière, le Conseil d'État trace des normes minimales de conduite auxquelles le fonctionnaire doit se conformer. La détermination d'un code de déontologie, rassemblant les différents textes fixant des droits et devoirs des fonctionnaires et les normes minimales de conduite dégagées de la jurisprudence du Conseil d'État, serait certainement de nature à permettre aux fonctionnaires de mieux situer leurs responsabilités.

Notes

[1] Le terme "Etat" indique, dans cette communication, aussi bien l'autorité étatique que les démembrements de celle-ci (Communautés, Régions, Provinces et Communes).
[2] *Pas*, 1971, I, 752.
[3] La victime d'un dommage causé par une autorité administrative peut agir directement devant les tribunaux judiciaires. Mais le recours préalable au Conseil d'Etat permet à la victime d'avoir accès au dossier de l'administration et par là, d'établir plus aisément l'illégalité.
[4] Des arrêts de la Cour de cassation du 19 décembre 1980 (*Pas.*, 1981, I, 453) et du 13 mai 1982 (*Pas.*, 1983, I, 297) ont précisé les limites dans lesquelles une illégalité est constitutive de faute et réservé le cas de l'erreur invincible ou d'une autre cause de justification.
[5] Voy. notamment Cass., 19 avril 1991, *Pas.*, 1991, I, 751; Cass., 10 juin 1996, *J.T.*, 1997, p. 197, avec concl. Avocat général Leclercq, J.-F.
[6] *Pas*, 1980, I, 1341 et s., concl. Velu, J. Cette position a été prise à nouveau par la Cour dans un arrêt du 21 avril 1994 (*Pas.*, 1994, I, 388)
[7] Des signes d'évolution sont perceptibles en ce sens dans quelques décisions de juridictions de fond.
[8] Batselé, D., Hanotiau, M., et Daurmont, O. *La lutte contre le racisme et la xénophobie*, Bruxelles: Nemesis, (1992), spéc. pp. 76 et 77.
[9] Voy. par exemple, Civ. Bruxelles, 24 décembre 1987, *J.L.M.B.*, 1988, p. 236 et *J.T.*, 1988, p. 159, Bruxelles, 21 novembre 1989, *J.T.*, 1990, p. 759 (confirmation de la décision susvisée).
[10] Bruxelles, 21 octobre 1981, *J.T.*, 1981, p. 758.
[11] *Pas*, I, 1981, 453.
[12] *Pas.*, 1982, I, 1221.
[13] Cass., 27 mai 1963, *Pas*, 1963, I, 1034.
[14] Les articles 1382 et 1383 du Code civil disposent comme suit :
"*1382 - Tout fait quelconque de l'homme, qui cause à autrui un dommage, oblige celui par la faute duquel il est arrivé, à le réparer.
1383 - Chacun est responsable du dommage qu'il a causé non seulement par son fait, mais encore par sa négligence ou par son imprudence*"
[15] Cass. 30 mars 1893, *Pas.*, 1893, I, 148, concl. de Mesdach de Ter Kiele.
[16] Aux termes de l'article 1384 :
"(...) On est responsable non seulement du dommage que l'on cause par son propre fait, mais encore de celui qui est causé par le fait des personnes dont on doit répondre, ou des choses que l'on a sous sa garde.
(...) Les maîtres et les commettants, du dommage causé par leurs domestiques et préposés dans les fonctions auxquelles ils les ont employés;
(...)".
[17] Il s'agit de l'affaire dite de la "K.B. luxembourgeoise" (Voy. le journal "La Libre Belgique" du 9 juillet 1997 et la presse récente en général).
[18] Cass., 29 mai 1947, *Pas.*, 1947, I, 216.
[19] Dalcq, R. O., "Les causes de responsabilité" in *Les Novelles*, Bruxelles: Larcier (1967), n° 1370.

[20] Sauf lorsque la loi déroge expressément à ce système comme la loi du 1er juillet 1956 relative à l'assurance obligatoire de la responsabilité civile en matière de véhicules automoteurs.
[21] Cass., 19 décembre 1991, *Pas*, 1992, I, 215, concl. Premier avocat général Velu, J.; Cass.. 8 décembre 1994, *J T.*, 1995, p.497.
[22] Trib. trav. Bruxelles, 11 octobre 1972, *J T.*, 1974, p. 317; Obs. J. Salmon, p. 319
[23] Voy. l'article 1er de la loi du 3 juillet 1978 relative aux contrats de travail.
[24] Le licenciement notamment.
[25] L'article 18 de la loi du 3 juillet 1978 sur le contrat d'emploi dispose comme suit :
"En cas de dommages causés par le travailleur à l'employeur ou à des tiers dans l'exécution de son contrat, le travailleur ne répond que de son dol et de sa faute lourde
Il ne répond de sa faute légère que si celle-ci présente dans son chef un caractère habituel plutôt qu'accidentel.
A peine de nullité, il ne peut être dérogé à la responsabilité fixée aux alinéas 1er et 2 que par une convention collective de travail rendue obligatoire par le Roi, et ce uniquement en ce qui concerne la responsabilité à l'égard de l'employeur
( )"
[26] Doc. parl., Ch., sess. 1984-1985, 1232, n° 2, p. 86.
[27] Ibid , p. 84
[28] Uyttendaele, M., "L'enquête parlementaire sur les événements tragiques qui se sont déroulés le 29 mai 1985 au stade du Heysel", *J.T*, 1986, p. 364
[29] Bruxelles, 26 juin 1990, *R G A R*, 1991, 11.757, 11.758, 11.759, 11.762.
[30] Les fonctionnaires de police peuvent aussi être exonérés, par une disposition réglementaire générale, de leur responsabilité à l'égard de l'Etat
[31] Doc. parl., Ch., sess. 1990-1991, n° 1637/1, p. 125.
[32] C.A., arrêt n° 77/96 du 18 décembre 1996, *Mon b* du 8 février 1997, p. 2.539.
[33] Batselé, D., Daurmont, O., et Quertainmont, P., *Le contentieux de la fonction publique*, Bruxelles: Nemesis (1992), spéc. p. 204; Gillet, E., "Les droits et les obligations des agents", in *Précis de fonction publique,* Bruxelles: Bruylant (1994), spéc. p. 223.

Bibliographie

Batselé, D., Daurmont, O., et Quertainmont, P., *Le contentieux de la Fonction publique*, Bruxelles: Nemesis (1992).

Daurmont, O., "Les principes généraux du droit de la Fonction publique"; J. Sarot et autres in *Précis de fonction publique,* Bruxelles: Bruylant, (1994), pp. 83-102.

Daurmont O., "Profil de la fonction publique locale" in *La fonction publique locale en mutation,* Bruxelles: la Charte, (1994), pp. 13-25.

Dony, M., "La responsabilité de l'Etat pour faute du pouvoir judiciaire" in *La responsabilité des pouvoirs publics,* Bruxelles: Bruylant, (1991), pp. 363-382.

Fagnart, J.-L., "Les communes dans la tourmente de la responsabilité civile", *Revue dr commun, (1994)*, pp. 301-322.

Flamme, M.-A., "La responsabilité personnelle des fonctionnaires", *Rev adm ,* (1968), pp. 85-103.

Franchimont, M., "Point de vue", *La Libre Belgique,* 24 avril 1997.

Gillet, E., "Les droits et les obligations des agents"; J Sarot et autres in *Précis de fonction publique*, Bruxelles: Bruylant, (1994), pp. 215-258.

Glansdorff, F., obs. sous Liège, 26 mars 1987, *Droit de la circulation,* mars 1988, pp. 78-82.

Lewalle, P., "La responsabilité délictuelle de l'administration et la responsabilité personnelle de ses agents: un système ?", *A P T*, (1989), pp. 6-29

Fuzzy in Theory and Getting Fuzzier in Practice: post-modern reflections on responsibility in public administration and management

W. Parsons[*]

1. The Problem: modernist discourse and post-modern governance

In this text I want to argue that the issue of responsibility can be illuminated by the critical turn in public administration and policy analysis. The intention here is to simply reflect (in a playful way) on some of the questions raised in this literature rather than attempt any kind of systematic appraisal of the post-modern and argumentative contribution [1] and to suggest that students of public administration ought to take more account of such ideas in discussing the topic of responsibility. In the context of this literature the problem may be seen in terms of a growing tension between the legitimising modernist discourse of responsibility and accountability getting more and more out of phase with the challenges of governance in contemporary Europe. We can express this tension in terms of the shift from the 'modernist' paradigm of public administration towards the 'post-modern' or 'high modern' paradigm of new (sic) public management.

The archetype of modernist notions of administration is the Weberian notion of bureaucracy. In this model rational organisation is held to be about clearly defined hierarchical levels and zones of responsibility. However, of late *hierarchy,* as defined by the classical (Weberian/Wilsonian) paradigm, is giving way to *heterarchy* and talk of market and network structures. The language of control has become translated into the language of 'steering'. Whereas once upon a time the language of business was considered to be inappropriate to 'public administration', the drift towards NPM -'new public management' - is indicative of an ever fuzzier relationship between 'management' in McDonalds and management in schools and hospitals. The relationship between the public and private spheres becomes, therefore, ever more indistinct as we employ the same modes of discourse to understand, explain and reform public administration.

Since the 1960s governments have been seeking to tackle the problems of improving public management. At first this was expressed in the belief that the solution lie in the direction of doing something (anything) to make policy making and administration more *rational.* This was the hey-day of 'policy analysis' whose failure brought in its wake the idea that the old problems needed 'new' public management which was less about getting more wizz kids to think clever thoughts, than learning from the biz kids how to make government more effective, efficient and economic. But, of course, *plus ça change,* back in 1887 Woodrow Wilson had also been optimistic that public administration could learn from business without injury to politics and democracy. He argued that:

---

[*] Professor, Dr Wayne Parsons, Queen Mary and Westfield College, University of London.

> "If I see a murderous fellow sharpening a knife cleverly, I can borrow his way of sharpening the knife without borrowing his probable intention to commit murder with it; and so, if I see a monarchist dyed in the wool managing a public business well, I can learn from his methods without changing one of my republican spots." (Wilson: 1887: 198)

This dubious notion of being able to borrow techniques from murderous fellows is central to the discourse of modernist public administration. It was, apparently, possible to learn from these knife sharpeners without doing any damage to the boundaries which marked out politics and administration. In this sense NPM is far more continuous with Wilsonian public administration than it looks at first sight. The main difference, perhaps, is that the liberal concept of responsibility in the Wilsonian discourse was pretty straightforward in theory, if not always in practice. Essentially it involved the idea that the government of a country should be so arranged that citizens and their representatives should be able to know where to fix blame, or who to hold to account. There was a strong linkage between layers and levels of authority and layers and levels of responsibility. The Weberian model of bureaucracy and the Wilsonian distinction between policy and administration provided a framework for thinking about responsibility which, one could argue, served liberal democracy very well. In this world we knew where things were: there was a sense that responsibility existed in time and space. In this modernist sense responsibility had location and transparency. Politicians made policy, and were responsible to the people for this policy, and civil servants carried it out and were responsible to the politicians for how they carried it out. But over the last decade or so we have become concerned that Wilson's 'murderous fellows' sharpening their knives to improve efficiency, economy, effectiveness and (of late) make managers more 'entrepreneurial', have actually cut deep into the ethics of the body politic.

It appears to me that this sense of having lost the certainty of the past, and the desire to somehow regain a sense of control and shared meaning over a system which is ever more unclear and fuzzy is part and parcel of *la vie postmoderne*. Or is it? Personally I tend to sympathise with the criticism of the post-modern school(s) by the likes of Giddens and Habermas. It may well be that what we are seeing are the symptoms of high modernity rather than 'postmodernity' as such. MacDonalds, for example, which is often characterised as the ultimate symbol of postmodernity, may equally be read as the triumph of Taylorism[2]. This issue of high modernity versus postmodernity should be a debate which students of public administration address rather than ignore [3]. However, the present paper is not going to get involved in this question, but suggest that the fuzziness surrounding the theory and practice of responsibility is a question which can be profitably be investigated in the light of the debate on modernity. In this context the confusion surrounding responsibility in public administration / management is all too typical of *la malaise postmoderne*. The world is increasingly less and less clearly defined a place: time and space are being compressed whilst the world appears to be ever fuzzier and fragmented and we are all desperately seeking something to bring it into focus and pull it all together again. I think that this is not a vain hope, but if we are to make progress we have to think differently about the issues. As we enter the millennium we must turn and bid farewell to the liberal idea of responsible representative government as the best way to hold our rulers to account. We have, in short, to devise fuzzy systems of democracy to ensure that our fuzzy forms of responsibility work. We have to come to terms with the fact that, as Dynes and Walker put it: 'something has been lost' and face up to the questions of how 'we recover a sense of identity and purpose?' and 'where is the irreducible core?' (Dynes and Walker, 1995: 340).

It may well be, however, that if we are to recover our sense of identity and purpose we have to confront the terrible (well for some) reality that there is no irreducible core anymore and that identity and purpose are fast disintegrating. This is especially relevant for us in the European Union. The nation state is no longer the focus of responsibility as in the time when Weber mused on bureaucratic rationality. So much of what happens is no longer simply the responsibility of national government. In contemporary Europe responsibility is spread out and shared between a multiplicity of organisations. Citizens see their national governments as responsible, but this notion hardly fits well alongside Europeanification and globalisation. Thus, not only is there a growing fuzziness of responsibility in the nation state, there is a ever increasing fuzziness in what the nation state and its elected government is responsible for. Responsibility is thinning. One could argue that in the good old days the grand narrative worked: it was real. Representative and responsible government may have had its defects and inadequacies, but it was 'authentic' enough. People felt - or perhaps had the illusion - that they knew where things were. The world was, apparently, pretty predictable and reasonably certain. However, today there is a growing gap between the rhetoric of responsible government and the reality in which politicians and public servants get away with things and appear to be less and less accountable to the people. Sensing this Joe and Josephine citizen may be quite in order to vote with their feet, and exit from the political process on the grounds that it is all a sham and a waste of time. It may be that the feeling that constitutional responsibility is more virtual than real is all too symptomatic of the post-modern condition. What you see is what you see. Responsibility is something which is played out for the benefit of the media: it is just a spectacle. In which case what passes for responsible government is (to use the jargon) mere simulacra of constitutionalism. The 'real thing' has long since gone and what we now have is an increasingly fuzzy photocopy. Nothing is clear anymore, everything is a fake and voting only encourages and legitimates it. After all, says the disillusioned post-modern citizen/consumer as he sits flicking through his TV channels whilst eating Chinese food and a pizza, you only have to look at sleaze and corruption in high places to realise that responsible government is a farce.

And yet alongside this fuzziness where responsibility is spread more widely, and is more indefinite, and heterarchial than ever before is the trend for ever more definition and precision as a way of coping with the complexities of managing fuzzy, loosely coupled organisations. This is particularly noticeable in terms of the bias towards quantificationism and measurement. Postmodernists sometimes refer to this as the concern with the language of 'performativity'. At the heart of so much of modern public management is the belief that the key to improving accountability, control and efficiency is to improve measurability. Thus although responsibility is getting fuzzier, management is getting more preoccupied with performance and calculating inputs and outputs. New modes of accountability have therefore taken place in the context of the policy core seeking to distribute or download responsibility into a complex network, grid or matrix of relationships. A cynic might point out that by so doing policy makers can thereby distribute blame to those out of the policy loop and in the management network. Sir Francis Bacon once observed that money, like muck, was no good to policy unless it was 'spread' around. Perhaps the same dictum might be held to be true in the case of responsibility in the modern (if not post-modern) state.

The wise politician ensures that responsibility is spread out so that when things go awry, and the bovine excrement hits the fan, then he or she remains as clean as the driven snow and comes out smelling of *eau de toilette*. And, of course, the more the muck is spread around the more indistinct becomes the line between the policy of those elected to govern us and the actions of those appointed to manage us. The term NPM therefore could also be held to stand for 'New Public Machiavellianism': a strategy by which politicians deploy the discourse of managerial reform to deal with complexity by making policy and administration fuzzier. 'Look', says the politician with one hand behind his back, 'I'm not rowing I'm just steering. It's not my fault if the people rowing are not up to it!' Of course, not being a cynic, but a political scientist, I would prefer to use another, less colourful language. What we can say is that the notion of responsibility is becoming ever more complex, and the sources of this complexity might be located in wider socio-economic and political trends towards decentering, disembedding and delocation which we face in the late twentieth century.

In practice, not unsurprisingly, we find that there is considerable diversity between European countries. It is clear that the experience of NPM is vastly different between countries which possess such contrasting political and administrative systems and structures. Thus it is a fair argument to say that the UK experience has been off the curve when compared to other EU countries, and that developments in public management vary between centralised unitary states and federal systems, or between those where local governments enjoy high levels of autonomy and those where they do not, or between countries where public administration is highly legalistic and others where it is not. But what is more important is that there is growing diversity between departments, cities, localities and regions within countries. Globalisation, it seems, is producing ever more localisation, and it may be that it is this issue of diversity within nation states which is the important question. If there are 'post-modern' forces shaping responsibility then it does not mean that we are heading towards convergence, so much as ever more divergence between government departments, cities, forms of local government and the rest. To resort to some jargon here: the grand narratives of the nation state are giving way to micro, mini and local narratives. This divergence in practice may well take place alongside a convergence of legitimating discourse: that is although the modes of management may vary the discourse employed to account and argue for public management reform may be increasingly similar. Although divided by many languages in Europe and by diversities of practice we may be united in the *lingua franca* of management speak. Nation shall speak management unto nation and revere the same gurus and a thousand flowers will bloom.

2. Oppositions, tensions and trends

The complexity of late twentieth century government poses a number of oppositions and tensions. Here I have selected a dozen, in no particular order of significance. But I would argue that it is in the context of these kind of trends in which we have to find a new, or should I say perhaps, post-new public management approach, to the issue of responsibility. These dozen issues are significant for what postmodernists might describe as their 'intertextuality', that is, they are issues which are enfolded in and interwoven with each other. If there is a theme which knits them altogether it is that we are shifting from the kind of clear and well demarcated world of modernist administrative discourse where public and private, policy and administration were believed to be reasonably well defined in theory and practice to one in which we don't know quite what we are seeing, and in which we don't know quite what we are getting. (Related to this theme, not explored here, is the way in which public administration itself as a discipline is becoming ever more problematic as a separate or distinct field of teaching and research.)

2.1. Weberian hierarchy versus networks, markets and communities

Let us begin at the beginning. The Weberian ideal type provided public administration with a way of thinking about responsibility which saw responsibility in terms which involved the notion that administration of the state could be so organised in a hierarchical way that you knew where to find it. You might have difficulty in holding bureaucratic expertise to account, but you knew where it *was*. The beauty of hierarchy was that it provided a rationale for the efficacy of representative politics. Civil servants were expected to have a sense of common purpose and responsibility as servants of their political masters and parliament could keep tabs on the activities of the state functionaries. Liberal democracy was therefore held to be a representative *and* responsible form of government. Indeed, for Weber the 'iron cage' of bureaucracy could be kept in check by a combination of charismatic leadership and parliamentary oversight. In this Weberian world there was a place for everything and everything was in its place. Civil servants knew their place and parliaments knew where things were and who was responsible for them. However, matters become far more complex when these hierarchical forms of organisation begin to give way to new patterns of inter-organisational relationships. That is when iron cages give way to plastic nets or, to do great injury to the French language, when *bureaucratisation* gives way to what we might term *filetisation* and bureau*cracy* gives way to filet*archy*. (From 'filet' or net.) Whereas the modernist forms of organisation and its accompanying discourse was about levels and tiers of responsibility, the network forms which have evolved in recent decades involves lines of demarcation which are no longer well delineated. In network forms of organisation responsibility is something that is *shared*, rather than *shouldered*. At a micro level, for example, this may be seen in the notion of the 'team' and of the need for 'team building' as advocated by NPM. In the modernist - if not downright Taylorist - view of bureaucracy, responsibility was bundled out to Tom, Dick, or Harry. The idea of the 'team' is that responsibility is something which is 'owned' (sic) by the team. In turn this team shares responsibility with other teams and other organisations. So, whereas in the past we could identify who did what, when and how, it becomes far more problematic when we move further and further away from the Weberian ideal type. The image which comes to mind is that of Agatha Christie's *Murder on the Orient Express*. In the normal course of events Poirot gathers everyone together in the drawing room and announces that it was 'you Milord who killed Sir Abraham in the library with the pipe of lead'. (Let us take this as some kind of paradigm for the modernist version of responsibility, but let us not take it too far.) However, in *Murder on the Orient Express* our erstwhile moustachioed Belgian says that they all did it, no individual blame can be attached, and so as Richard Rodney Bennett's evocative music swells we learn that, as no-one did it, they *all* get off. Teams and networks organised around the 'ownership' of 'tasks' may be all very well for improving efficiency and effectiveness, but they are inherently less responsible forms in the context of the old modernist concepts of responsibility as something which you can pin down and pin on. Hence, it seems to be the case that, in so many instances of poor judgement and incompetence as well as conspiracy, we are on the *Orient Express*: (if not on the *Eurostar*) where responsibility is shared and spread and culprits go free.

Another key feature of the modernism embedded in the notion of 'public administration' and which is challenged by NPM is that there is a clear distinction between state bureaucracy and market modes of organisation. The arguments are well known and do not have to be rehearsed here: in essence it was held that public bureaucracies were different to private bureaucracies. Many who advocated the application of public choice economics and business methods in government went along with this, but posited that it was this very difference which had to go. The introduction of market type mechanism, contracting out, agencification, privatisation *etc.*, means that bureaucracies no longer share common forms or structures of responsibility. Thus what we increasingly see is the emergence of highly diverse patterns of responsibility (and values) operating in different parts of the apparatus of policy formulation and delivery. Different agencies, departments, or quangos relate to one another and share responsibility, but they do not share the same kind of responsibility. Some will be located in a hierarchy, others will be in more network forms, and others will be operating as kinds of business organisation. In a sense they are all responsible, but not in the same languages. (As in an advertisement for *Barclaycard* wherein the comedian Rowan Atkinson impresses his young assistant in negotiating to buy a carpet from a 'Twareg' market vendor. 'I didn't know you were fluent Sir', says Boff. To which the poor man's James Bond replies that :'both of us are fluent, but in different languages!') The language of responsibility for an organisation operating in accordance with 'business' values or 'mission' (sic) is very different to that of the classic department located in a hierarchy. Both are fluent but in different languages: bureaucracy and filetarchy.

2.2. Clear/located versus fuzzy/dislocated responsibility

This takes us to another point. The key thing about the modernist organisation was, to coin a phrase often on the lips of estate agents, location, location, location. As noted above, the classic Weberian model was about being able to locate responsibility for a given task in a definite time and space. In a hierarchy one has a better chance of knowing who was responsible for what, when and how. Responsibility could be located in time, place and person. One could locate where policy took place and where administration took place, and furthermore which actors were responsible for what. However, as so much of the literature on public policy now amply attests, the location of policy and administration or policy making and implementation is so very unclear that many in the field of public policy advocate new models which abandon the old 'stagist' approach wherein there are well defined steps and phases in the policy process. Perhaps the most famous, or most infamous is that developed by Sabatier, the so called 'advocacy coalition' framework. The emphasis in such 'policy design' literature is to show how policy implementation and policy formulation are (in the present author's sense) 'enfolded' into one another. As an approach the design school has much to offer the study of public policy, but one of the big issues which has not been confronted in this literature is : what are the consequences for liberal democratic governance in a world in which there are no longer hard and fast divisions between policy formulation and implementation. When is a civil servant carrying out policy, and when is she making it? When is a minister responsible for the way in which policy is being implemented by her civil servants? In the (good) old days (in Britain leastwise) if there was a serious mistake a minister would resign and claim that it was his responsibility that such and such happened. However, in the dislocated forms of responsibility which now pertains, politicians can all to often claim that what happened in this agency, or that quango or where-ever and had nothing to do with him. So saying he will then offer up to the baying opposition and media a scapegoat to take the rap. Fuzziness in the relationship between policy and implementation can and does have serious consequences for the way in which politicians and civil servants are held responsible for their decisions. But, once again, the further we travel from Weberian bureaucracy towards filetarcy, the more we are adrift from the 'mechanisms' which were devised to keep the 'iron cage' responsible to the elected representatives of the people. Liberal democracy, it seems, abhors fuzziness, as nature does a vacuum.

2.3. Hierarchical discipline versus regulation

Nothing is more fuzzier, of course, than regulation. Whereas modernist forms of organisation functioned through clear and unequivocal discipline, the post-modern state has a growing preference for regulating. The thesaurus on my Mackintosh tells me that synonyms for discipline include punishment and control; whereas regulation encompasses such words as aligning and fixing. Hierarchical discipline involves the idea that there are clear sets of rules which control you: step over the mark and you will be punished. Regulation on the other hand has to do with allowing independent choices which are subject to realignment and adjustment. Regulation in this sense is about 'fixing' rather than control. Now again there are obvious dangers in shifting towards more regulative than directive relationships. Regulation comes with trust. An organisation which is subject to regulation is also subject to the privilege of trust. The state says that it will trust an organisation to make decisions, but that it retains the right to hold its decisions to account. So this takes us to another sense of 'responsibility': one is given responsibility because of trust. And, as even the most ignorant students of human history are all too well aware, trust is oftentimes more honoured in the breach than in the observance. In regulating the state is actually handing out responsibility on trust. What seems to me to be alarming is that given the very fuzziness of (post) modern organisations the breaking of trust is, of its nature, very difficult to nail down. Where organisations share or pool responsibility it is likely that they will claim that they were not responsible for breaking this trust, so much as they themselves were let down by another organisation whom they trusted. Regulation here is to do with fixing plausible stories rather than fixing responsibility. We are once again in the carriage of the *Orient Express:* 'we all did it, so nobody did it, more Bucks-Fizz anyone?'

2.4. Bucks stop, heads roll versus bucks never stop and heads never, well hardly ever, roll

And so, speaking of bucks, we come to what is the *sine qua non* of responsibility in liberal democracy: the stopping of bucks and the rolling of heads. As responsibility becomes ever more fuzzier we tend to see an increasing tendency for bucks never to stop, and heads to remain firmly attached to necks. Where they do stop, and where they do rock and sometimes roll, it is frequently to do with scapegoating rather than responsibility. A characteristic of the post-modern organisation is that, as they are more fragmented and decentralised, responsibility is not something which gravitates upwards, so much as permeates downwards. The emphasis in MBO of bringing responsibility close to the tasks involved means that effectively, whereas in the old public administration blame tended to go up to the most powerful, nowadays responsibility for (inevitable) failure is a buck that stops at the street level, rather than in the ministerial office. In the 1970s there was much talk of 'overloading' government with too many responsibilities. One could say this was a manifestation of a deepening crisis of modernist government. However, in the 1990s the strategy seems to be one of downloading as much responsibility as possible to lower levels, thus taking the heat off the policy making core. A good instance of this in the British context is education. For over a decade British educational policy makers have focused primarily on the responsibility of teachers for 'failing' schools. The policy making core has (and this has remained the case in spades with the new Labour government) effectively downloaded the 'blame' for failure to 'poor' teachers. In which case it is Mrs Brown, of class 3b who gets it in the neck rather than the ministers and civil servants who have overseen education 'policy'. Or, to give another example of this logic, it is the prisoner governor who takes the rap for escaping prisoners rather than the minister responsible for prisons 'policy'.

2.5. Centralised (Fordist) versus decentralised (post-Fordist) organisations

The downloading of responsibility in new public management might be explained as an outcome of the shift away from Fordist structures. In the Fordist organisation you can have any colour you like as long as it is black, and that black car is the product of a pattern of responsibility in which managers manage and take decisions and workers work and do what they are told when they are told to do it. Responsibility in this model moved in an upwards direction: managers are responsible for making sure that people do what they are supposed to do. In this model control takes place through externally enforced disciplines and modes of surveillance. The post-modern organisation is characterised by strategies which are far more invasive. Using the techniques of 'HRM' people are now subjected to techniques of assessment and appraisal in which the aim is to make individuals more responsible for their 'career development'. This is because the key to success resides in the capacity of organisations to produce individuals and teams who are flexible, 'enterprising' and responsive to (if not welcome and embrace) change. The demands of flexibility and (multi-tasked) adaptiveness mean that the post-Fordist organisation is one in which responsibility spreads through the organisation rather than remains in one particular or definite location. This cuts many ways. It may well be that decentralisation produces greater flexibility and responsiveness, but this may bring with it an inevitable increase in the diversity of procedures, protocols and ways of doing things. In the Fordist organisation there was only one way to skin a cat, but in the post-Fordist organisation there are many types of cat, many kinds of skin, and many ways to remove one from the other. Post-Fordism will encourage variation and difference in customs and practices. There will be fewer shared norms and great differences in contractual status between people in the public service even though they supposedly share a common 'mission'. Keeping track of such developments may be immensely difficult for existing modes of democratic accountability which were designed for a time when organisations were more stable, regular, predictable and subject to hierarchical controls and fixed rules and procedures.

2.6. Focus on control versus focus on steering

Many of these difficulties are to do with the way in which public management is moving away from (modernist) notions of controlling towards a more flexible (post-modern) desire to 'steer'. The notion of steering recognises that the old control model is no longer appropriate to the situation in which there exists such diversity and complexity. Public management in this sense is seen to be an activity of guiding through signals rather than through control or direction. Such signals might, for example, be setting targets for agencies and evaluating them in terms of how they have met specific targets over time. This model means that management is far more hands-off than in the modernist strategy of being very hands-on and seeking to control in a direct way how things are done. From the point of view of responsibility the discourse has shifted to a focus on performance rather than following procedures. The aim of steering is to improve the delivery of the goods, rather than the day-to-day accountability of those agencies involved. The focus is on output as opposed to process. But, in the modernist discourse process *does* matter. This involved making sure that a common process was adhered to and divergences from a given administrative norm were minimised. Modernist public administration was / is very hands-on and concerned with control, and process whereas post-modern public management is concerned with hands-offness, steering and output. Responsibility in these two modes of organisation are consequently two very different language games. Responsibility in the control model is straightforward hands-on direction of process, whereas in steering models responsibility is embedded in the success or failure to meet given targets. Steering is about freeing up relationships. As Christian Pracher notes in the case of the German model.

« According to the new model of guidance and steering, the ideal employee should be independent, initiatory, responsible, prepared to take risks, enterprising, oriented towards citizens, conscious of the quality as well as the costs, flexible, communicative, committed, willing to commit and to admit mistakes for the sake of progress, able and ready to learn, full of confidence and self-assurance, willing to achieve something and able to co-operate with his or her colleagues and superiors...The specialised departments, which are now responsible for their results and resources will -like the administrative leaders- be freed from unnecessary and troublesome interference and can take decisions on the use of resources and completion of works independently. Staff members have a wider latitude for creativity and will become more independent and responsible in fulfilling their tasks...Citizens will get information about what is achieved with their tax money, what the different administrational services really cost, and they can confidently expect as efficient a performance as possible. Due to the increased orientation of administration towards the citizens they can rely on the administration to take their wishes and needs into account in a better way than they did before ». (Pracher, 1996: 154-5)

Here we are a long way from the Weberian ideal type and modernist organisations which were largely framed in accordance to practically the mirror image set of conditions. Responsibility in the steering model seems to be all over the place: everywhere and nowhere. How this fits with the rather less flexible modes of political accountability is somewhat hazy. Liberal democracy evolved out of the need to hold a well defined bureaucratic hierarchy to account for itself. The big question is how well equipped are our political institutions to adapt to these new forms of filetised administration? We shall look at this in section three below.

2.7. Rigid structures versus flexible, *ad hoc* structures

The notion of steering is, as we have seen, predicated on the idea that the old rigid structures have to be replaced by organisational forms which are more flexible and able to adapt. In place of permanent structures we have a situation in which organisations are seen as essentially more *ad hoc* than in the past. They may and will change and mutate into something else. The iron cage of bureaucracy has given way to plastic and rubber cages. What was once a virtue (permanence) is now perceived as a vice. The name of the game is flexibility. Departments, agencies, quangos and the rest are expected to evolve and adapt: the fittest survive and thrive. If ultimately the criteria is performance, rather than process, the arrangement and location of tasks can move around so as to attain more effectiveness. No institution is safe. In the long run (as Keynes might have put it) they are all dead. *Institutions in the post-modern world are no longer immortal: the art is not in being, but becoming. Change is all.*

This is all very well, but from the point of view of 'responsible government' there are problems. Political institutions are (as Weber argued) disadvantaged enough when it comes to dealing with bureaucracy. Adhocracy makes the issue of making the bureaucracy accountable to the elected representatives of the people ever more problematic. If organisations keep reinventing themselves it demands that society has to learn pretty damn quick. What was the responsibility of one agency/department/quango is now the responsibility of another acronym - and that bit is now part of the private sector! Accountability in liberal democracy works best when organisations stay still: a sitting duck makes a much easier target than a flying duck. Representative government was designed for a world in which ducks remained reasonably still. They are ill-equipped for dealing with (and 'managing') rapid change and flux.

2.8. Uniform and predictable versus diverse and uncertain organisations

The emphasis on decentralisation and being close to the 'customer' in the discourse of public management gives rise to a profound shift in organisational patterns. The Weberian model was about uniformity and predictability. The system was so organised that the various components of the 'machinery' of government were like one another. Each bit of the machine was like another bit, and because they were it meant that bureaucracies were very predictable in how they worked. However, NPM and its variants argues that uniformity and predictability do not lend themselves to performance and customer oriented organisation. Thus public management reforms have tended towards creating ever more diverse forms of organisation and relationships in which there are higher levels of uncertainty. This is inevitable if we accept the logic of using heterarchies and markets in preference to hierarchies as ways of improving public management. Markets, so it is argued, can better improve the responsibility and accountability of bureaucracies by subjecting them to the discipline of less uniformity (competition in and between organisations) and more uncertainty (in pay, contracts, rewards, organisational continuity *etc.*). Indeed, it is this increase in diversity and uncertainty that is an essential method of keeping bureaucrats and service providers 'on their toes'. The strategy is evidently to keep changing the goal posts. You may be top of the league table this year, but next year - who knows?

2.9. Organisations fixed over time and space versus contingency

Related to the question of diversity and uncertainty is the way in which the drift away from modernist forms of administration involves the destruction of time and space. One of the most notable aspects of modernist organisations was that they remained continuous over time and space. That is to say they tended to stay the same for long periods of time. This is not so say that no change occurred, but that it usually occurred in phases which punctuated a long term equilibrium. Institutions were, if not immortal, very difficult to kill off. So every now and again there would be a burst of change which would be followed by a long period of continuity. Furthermore, organisations reproduced themselves in spatial or territorial terms in such a way that whereever they were they resembled one another. From the point of view of accountability and responsibility this was all to the good. However, the trend which may be discerned in many countries, even those which have not fully embraced NPM discourse, is that organisations are now becoming more contingent. The demands of performance means that organisations have to *constantly reinvent themselves* (over time) and adapt to local conditions. Hence decentralisation promotes a more contingent strategy in organisational design so as to ensure that there is enough flexibility to facilitate the 'management of change' (sic).

2.10. Discourse of liberal constitutionalism versus failure of grand narrative

The consequence of this destruction of modernist time and space in public administration is that, to use the jargon of postmodernism, we lack a grand narrative. As responsibility and accountability become more fragmented and fuzzy we no longer have one account of what these concepts mean. In practice we have varieties of administrative responsibility and accountability. Some forms remain in the context of a hierarchical story, whilst others are couched in the language of markets, and others in terms of networks and community. The citizen therefore no longer operates in one frame of discourse, but he or she has to learn to understand a number of languages. The closer a system is to the kind of models we find in the US, UK, and other Anglo-Saxon countries, the more do we find that the reinventing and re-engineering of government is creating a complex picture of responsibility. Thus for some public services the language spoken is 'market' or 'consumer' for others it is 'voter' or citizen', and for others it may be 'community'. In many situations the language of filetarchy is the political equivalent of 'Spanglish': a curious hybrid mix of metaphors. In part the uncertainty of post-modern public administration stems from the fact that we do not know oftentimes what language we are supposed to be using, and that the language we used last year is no longer appropriate for this year. Buzz words are now the language of democracy as of business. The penchant in Britain for appointing business people to deal with a variety of problems relating to 'public management' well illustrates that you might as well appoint someone who is fluent in Buzz to do the Biz. Thus it may be that, as the liberal constitutional narrative declines, it is being replaced by the plausible stories told by Wilson's knife sharpeners. In this brave new world everything is business. And business is business.

2.11. Overloading versus downloading

As we noted earlier, the overload debate in the 1970s marked a significant turning point in the politics of the late twentieth century. The argument was that liberal democracies were facing a crisis of taking on too much: political systems such as Britain were seen to be overburdened with demands and responsibilities. The response to this theory in practice came in the form of the 'Thatcherite' project to cut back the state and get government off the backs of the taxpayer. The reply to overload was, therefore, one of what we termed a 'downloading' of a whole range of problems from the state to markets and individuals. Mr Blair has essentially accepted the challenge of managing or steering the 'downloaded' state. This involves the recognition that the state cannot take more responsibility, so much as 'empower' or 'facilitate' communities, individuals and markets. The question is one of how the state can be managed so as to socially 'enable' rather than socially engineer. But the real problem is that in so downloading and hollowing the state NPM may simply prompt another bout of overloading. Evidently this overloading through downloading is very different to that of the 1970s. Governance via NPM involves managing complex filetarchial relationships rather than directing or controlling hierarchies. This may manifest itself in terms of both an overloaded centre and an increasingly overloaded network. As responsibility is more diffuse and spread out so the costs of managing rise. Indeed, one of the main consequences of NPM is that we are all managers now. Public policy takes place in an ever more complex grid of inter-organisational dependency, inter-organisational co-ordination and inter-governmental management. *When you replace hierarchies with heterarchies and bureaucracy with filetarchy that is precisely what you get.* It means that doing anything requires the co-operation of a range of other organisations. The more we move away from well marked Weberian structures and Wilsonian policy/ administration divides, the more too we face a world in which policy making/implementation/delivery requires us to become enmeshed in power and resource dependencies. The response to this may be that the state actually seeks to centralise more power so that as the process of public management becomes looser and fuzzier, the core decisions become increasingly more tight knit. The result of this may be that there is a growing gap between the (downloading) rhetoric of 'enabling' and the reality of (centralising) decision making. As society becomes more de-centred, the state may respond by becoming more centred. Having apparently killed the wicked dragon called 'Overload' in the 1980s we may find that it has but slept. Rule by the net may simply mean that we are all overloaded.

2.12. Clear, shared public service values, versus unclear, fragmenting values

One of the most important aspects of a bureaucratic structure which is uniform and hierarchical is that it is possible for common values to permeate the public service. Amongst the values which lay at the core of the Wilsonian view of public administration was that civil servants should be free from corruption and bias. In the Whitehall model it meant that civil servants had a responsibility to be impartial and able to offer advice free from partisan bias. Theoretically, of course, public choice approaches have put paid to this notion. Civil servants, it turned out, were basically self-interested people who operated to get bigger budgets and bigger bureaux rather than in the 'public interest'. In place therefore of the civil servant as motivated by honesty, integrity, and a capacity to give balanced advice and analysis, the 1980s was to see the emergence of a view of civil servants as a needing to be tamed by market and management rather than old fashioned political accountability. We are all familiar with the result: the reform of civil services on more 'business-like' lines. The consequence of such reforms however have been that the new style organisations are different from one another. They no longer have the kind of shared values of the Weberian type bureaucracy. Diversity of organisational forms also means diversity in the values which inform and shape departments, agencies quangos and the rest. This means that the standards which may operate at one level or kind of organisation concerned with 'policy' may be very different to that of 'units' which have more to do with government 'business". Holding all these components of the (postmodern) state to account therefore is not an easy matter when there is a declining sense of common public service values. Indeed, the very term now has an increasingly Victorian smell about it when set alongside the measurable data on economy, efficiency and VFM (value for money). 'Business culture' and the culture of public service may well be as incommensurate in practice as they appear in theory. Civil servants may have less and less in common with one another in terms of pay, location, status, prospects, power, recruitment than they did in the past. To what extent is it possible to make loosely coupled organisational *structures* responsible when the *values* and cultures of public administration and management are fragmenting? As we shall discuss below, one response to this is to argue that we need to enforce common codes of conduct so as to permit organisational diversity whilst ensuring that there are shared standards of conduct. However this renewal of public service ethics may not be sufficient to counteract the centrifugal effects of *filetisation* on the loyalty of stakeholders. The situation where values are fragmenting is reflective of the way in which *filetarchy* is conducive to promoting loyalty to parts rather than to the system as a whole. Public servants may become prone to be loyal to their 'team', 'unit' or organisation rather than to the common mission or goal. An example of this in the UK is education. Under LMS (Local Management of Schools) and the regime of performance league tables schools have inevitably come to see themselves in intensely competitive relationships. In place of shared loyalty to a public service may evolve a more Balkanised system of public management. Balkanised loyalties *may* prove to be more efficient, effective and economical, but then again, they may prove to be deeply problematic from the point of view of responsibility. Responsibility may become something which exists in the context of administrative clans for whom loyalty involves putting their tribe first. *Tribalisation* may therefore be the inevitable outcome of *filetisation*.

3. What can be done? Prospects for revolution and renewal

I do not accept that postmodernity (or high modernity) necessarily leads us into a *cul de sac*. What we have examined above are, in many respects, more the shape of things that might be, than of the things that are. The danger is that these trends we have noted above continue apace without any attempt to remedy the deficiencies of late twentieth century public administration. There are some lights at the end of the tunnel. These may be considered under two headings: the need for a revolution in the way we think and the possibilities of renewing responsibility in democratic societies through what I term the four 'Cs'. In terms of the former I want to argue (section four, below) that we need to move on from a highly Newtonian conceptualisation of responsibility towards a more 'quantum' realisation of responsibility as something which is more probabilistic, spread-out, uncertain and indefinite. This shift in the way we think about administration has many implications for the kind of strategies which may be deployed to improve responsibility. These strategies of renewal (set out in section five below) may be summed up in terms of four 'Cs': the use of constitutional methods; the use of community forms of accountability; the development of critical policy analysis for public policy; and the renewal of common public service values.

4. Towards a revolution in the way we think

Modernism has its roots in that period of European history which was shaped and formed by the Newtonian revolution. The development of constitutional discourse itself, for example, was greatly influenced by the language of Newtonian mechanics as were the emerging social sciences in general. In place of a mysterious notion of power, the liberal (Newtonian) revolution disclosed how power and authority could be analysed and how it was necessary to secure a 'balance' in political 'forces' in conformity to the great natural laws which kept the universe running like clockwork. The notion of responsible government came out of this Newtonian infused discourse: constitutionalism was about defining clear levels and domains of responsibility and ensuring that causes and consequences could be known. Hence the language of mechanics was central to the development of constitutional democracy. Government could be responsible if it was so organised that the machine functioned so that responsibilities were precise and unequivocal. That this metaphor is still with us today is evidenced by the (doubtful) notion that one can 'reinvent' and 're-engineer' government. Weberian notions of rationality derive from the idea that the rationality of the machine had its analogue in bureaucratic organisation. Taylorism was little more than the amplification of the idea that human organisations could become most efficient if they approximated to how machines worked.

In one sense, therefore, one could argue that NPM is less to do with postmodernism than (in Giddens's sense) *high* modernity because in so many respects it represents the consummation of the mechanistic metaphor. The strategy variously employed is essentially predicated on the use of 'performance' as the way to render the complexities of government more 'manageable' and 'controllable'. To do this much reliance is placed on the price 'mechanism' as the way to achieve a new relationship between the state and society, and between policy and administration. But ironically, the more we push in this direction the more do we enter into a world in which the old mechanical metaphor is not sustainable. What I want to suggest is that we are shifting away from a Newtonian towards what we might term a 'quantum' polity. The implications of this are somewhat too big to be dealt with here [4], but what we can say is that we have to get away from thinking in terms of responsibility in a mechanical or atomistic and causal sense to one which comprehends it as involving considerable interminancy, uncertainty and multi-causality. That is to say, responsibility is no longer just something which is clearly defined and located but also spread out throughout the system in waves which defy being pinned down. In this fuzzy quantum polity the old command and control structures are being eroded. The social sciences are still, for the greater part, rooted in the Newtonian positivist world view. If we are to fully get to grips with the profound changes which have taken place to the theory and practice of responsible government we have to make something of a quantum leap. We have to confront the fact that our ways of thinking are no longer adequate to understand what to do about the uncertain and indeterministic nature of organisations in conditions of postmodernity/high modernity. If we are to renew democracy we first have to revolutionise the way we think and the discourse and metaphors that we use. The nineteenth and twentieth centuries were framed by Newtonianism and I believe that the twenty-first will be framed by a post-Newtonian social science which takes account of complexity, indeterminacy, uncertainty, and non-linear causality. This is a theme set out in the work of Lincoln and Guba, Fox and Miller and Farmer [5], amongst others. It is a literature worth exploring by students of public administration.

5. Renewal through the four Cs

What this analysis means in practical terms may be considered under four broad headings or strategies.

5.1. Renewal of constitutionalism

The first part of the strategy must deal with the Newtonian side: the *mechanics* of liberal democracy. Certain values must be rediscovered. The chief amongst these is that audit is no substitute for accountability and performance does not mean the sacrifice of process. Legislatures of elected representatives exist to hold government to account and to make government responsible. NPM has placed considerable emphasis on making government more efficient and effective, but there has not been a sufficient response from NDA: New Democratic Accountability. Legislatures have lagged behind in the reforms which have taken place and if they are to regain the central place in liberal democracy they have to be made more effective and more efficient in the way they work. As a policy analyst I naturally think that part of the answer to this is in making legislative investigation and monitoring better able to use knowledge. There is a widespread failure of government programmes and polices to be subjected to adequate and rigorous evaluation. My plea is therefore for our representatives to make greater use of knowledge in society. In particular universities and the policy and problem specialists they contain should have a far more important role in providing backup and support to legislative and societal scrutiny. But, and this is a very big but, the role of the expert must be very different in the future than it sought to be in the past. The idea that experts 'know things' is somewhat anachronistic. What we have to realise is that democracies need to improve the ways in which they make sense of and use policy arguments. Hence the significance of the ideas advanced by the so called 'argumentative turn' school which focuses on the need to address the way in which societies produce and construct meaning. Allied to the strengthening of political accountability by improving the argumentative capacities of the political process is the problem of time and space. The fuzzier government becomes over time and space the more do we need to downsize, decentralise and devolve government and democratic processes. In other words, let democracy go with the flow. In the case of Britain, for example, the need for reforming the territorial dimension of our political system is a matter of real urgency. The centralised nature of the British state leaves Wales, Scotland and the English regions - as well as Westminster and Whitehall - poorly equipped for the future. We in Britain desperately need to move forward with setting up democratic institutions which make governance responsible and transparent to the people. Democracy and public learning is, I believe, the greatest remedy for *la malaise postmoderne / haute moderne*. The fact that most EU countries have considerably more political decentralisation than Britain suggests to me that, from the point of view of the architecture of the post-modern state, continental Europe is, in this respect, far better equipped to institute the kind of constitutional reforms necessary to make responsible government more attainable. With the election of the Blair government we live in hope: but as Burns once observed, the best laid plans of mice and men have a habit of going 'aft a-gley'. At the European level we now have far more regional involvement and it is to be hoped that the 'regionalisation' of the EU will, in time, help to create more avenues for democratic control and participation. Territorial devolution is, I would argue, a vitally important way in which we can begin to improve the capacity of government to manage the downloaded 'hollowed' state of the 1990s.

5.2. Renewal through community

But it is not enough to renew representative government. We need to realise that representative democracy is reaching its limits. If we are to develop a responsible society we must look towards extending the possibilities of dialogue and participation. Here I might just note the importance of citizen panels, juries and forums as ways of enlarging the potentialities of responsible government. Again the policy sciences must have a key role in this process. If we are to create a society in which there is more of an active dialogue taking place, then social scientists must develop more participative research strategies. This will involve thinking more in terms of direct rather than representative democracy. As the writings of people like Etzioni make clear, a central aspect of improving democracy for the future involves renewing community and empowering people in their communities. One idea here which seems to be of great importance is the role of new communications technologies. The internet offers the prospect of a far more direct kind of relationship with government, administration and management than in the past. As we move towards organisational structures which are network based, it makes sense to develop more network forms of democracy. Citizens and communities in the future may increasingly relate to policy making and service delivery through electronic means rather than in traditional political and administrative ways. Through the internet it may (and no doubt will) be possible for citizens to have a far better grasp of who is responsible for what by the use of the new engines of cyber-democracy: the various search tools such as *Yahoo* and *Alta Vista*. Such search facilities enable people to explore highly complex networks of information and links in ways which may help to tame the complexity of modern governance. Web sites which are exploring the impact of the internet on democracy and government should be followed closely by students of public administration as offering the possibilities of new ways of citizens interacting with each other and with the 'network' of contemporary government.

5.3. Renewal through critical analysis

Linked to the renewal of community is the need to shift away from instrumentalist rationality to communicative rationality. Here the work of people such as Frank Fischer and others in the argumentative school are of special relevance. Fox and Miller, for instance, in their book on post-modern public administration, put the case for a more critical and more communicative form of public policy making and evaluation. In these approaches public policy becomes a means of public learning, rather than of problem solving. Relating back to the previous section, the use of 'Cyberspace' may, as some commentators argue, point towards the possibilities of new kinds of dialogue and communications which may move us much closer to the Habermasian ideal[6]. Such ideas have wide-ranging repercussions for redefining what we mean by responsibility and the relationship between the public and private spheres. Of its nature public administration *qua* management is fundamentally erosive and destructive of the public sphere. If the discourse of democratic responsibility is framed by the language of business then we are altering what democracy means to us. Thus far NPM speak has permeated and eaten away at the line between what is public and what is private. If we are to renew democratic responsibility we have to subject this discourse to a more open and challenging argument than has taken place in the last decade or so. Language changes meaning and transmutes values. We have to be very careful that marketisation, consumerisation and managerialism do not erode the very values which have been, for so long, a bulwark of democratic government.

5.4. Renewal of common public service values

Finally, therefore, but no means the least, is the vital need for the renewal of a sense of common public service values. That is, we must place the ethical dimension of public administration/management at the heart of democratic renewal. With the fragmentation of public management through the use of NPM there is a real danger that we destroy values which are absolutely central to the possibilities of democracy. Politicians and civil servants must be honest, and free of corruption. Civil servants must be able to give advice and analysis in an impartial manner. They must be motivated by a genuine sense of public service. The ethics of public service are not those of the market or business. As my colleague Peter Hennessy notes in his Manion lecture for 1997:

« The public service impulse - the desire to join a disciplined profession with its own ethic for the purpose, under democratically legitimated political guidance, of shaping or implementing public policy for the wider public good - remains one of the most powerful motivators for those who seek a career in the public service ».(Hennessy, 1997)

To which I say a loud *Amen*. But we need to apply to the problem of renewing the public service ethic the same kind of energy that has gone into reinventing performance driven government. From a post-modern perspective, however, this may be just another symptom of the loss of certainty and centre. It may well be that returning to the kind of world which Peter Hennessy has in mind is hopelessly out of place in the brave new Balkanised tribalised world of NPM. Some might think that he is being wildly optimistic and rather nostalgic in believing that it is possible to reinvigorate the old ethic to strengthen responsible government for the next century. But, if ways and means are not found to ensure the continuity of the public service ethic then the future for public administration is bleak indeed. Public administration free from corruption and dishonesty is an absolute *sine qua non* for both democracy *and* efficient government. There is enough empirical evidence to illustrate the sad fact that when integrity and honesty go fuzzy and tribalism breaks out then things do indeed fall apart, centres do not hold and anarchy is loosed.

Notes

[1] See Farmer, D.J., *The Language of Public Administration*, The University of Alabama Press, Tuscaloosa and London 1995 ; Fox, C.J and T. Miller *Postmodern Public Administration: Towards Discourse*, Sage Thousand Oaks, California,1995; and Frank Fischer's latest book *Evaluating Public Policy,* Nelson Hall, Chicago 1995.

[2] See G. Ritzer, *The McDonaldization of Society*, Pine Forest Press, Thousand Oaks, California,1993.
[3] See in this regard R.A.W. Rhodes, *Understanding Governance*, Open University Press, Buckingham, 1997.
[4] See the author's forthcoming book *Redesigning Public Policy*, Edward Elgar 1998.
[5] Y.S Lincoln, (ed) *Organisational Theory and Inquiry. The Paradigm Revolution*, Sage Beverly Hills, 1985, E.G. Guba and Y.S. Lincoln, *Naturalistic Inquiry*,Sage Beverly Hills, 1985, Fox and Miller, op cit, *passim* and pp 100 - 1:Farmer, op cit, pp212.
[6] See for example: D.B. Whittle, *Cyberspace The Human Dimension*, Freeman and Co, New York 1997

Bibliography

M. Dynes M and D. Walker, *The Times Guide to the New British State*, Times Books, London, 1995

Pracher, C, 'New Models of guidance and steering in public administration.' in N. Flynn and F. Strehl (eds) *Public Sector Management in Europe,* Prentice Hall, London 1996, pp154-5.

Hennessy, P 'The Essence of Public Service', *The Manion Lecture* 1997.

Wilson,W, 'The study of Administration', *Political Science Quarterly*, 1887, 2: 197-222.

Working Group on Transparency, Openness and Service to the Public

Report of the Working Group on Transparency, Openness and Service to the Public

W. Jann and B. Hubeau[*]

The Working Group 2 "Transparency, Openness and Service to the Public" was co-chaired by Dr. Bernard Hubeau, Ombudsman of the City of Antwerp and Prof. Dr. Werner Jann, Chair of Political Science, Administration and Organisation at the University of Potsdam, Germany.

Starting from the general theme of the conference the Working Group set itself the task to help clarify the concepts of transparency, openness and service to the public within the framework of a modern, democratic polity. In doing this the workshop decided to look at these concepts both from a number of different disciplinary backgrounds and practical experiences, and, of course, tried to include as many different national viewpoints and practices as possible. All in all ten papers from eight different countries were presented, starting from questions like

- is the relationship between public administration/civil servants and the public really changing?
- what is the impact of new steering mechanisms (contract management, autonomous agencies etc.) on transparency, openness and bureaucratic ethics?
- are traditional bureaucratic ethics too narrow for modern government?
- what are negative and positive side effects of transparency and openness and what is the proper role of the citizen?
- do we need new concepts of neutrality, objectivity and new ethical attitudes?
- and, finally, do we need a new public sector ethos?

The workshop organised its deliberations under three headlines, looking in session one first at a possible "New Framework" for transparency, openness and public service, dealing in session two with particular "Practical Experiences" in different countries and concluding in session three with a general discussion of "Ethical Aspects" of the traditional and future public service.

In session I The New Framework papers dealing with the changing context of modern governance and modern public administration started with Torben Beck Jorgensen from the University of Copenhagen (Denmark). In his paper "The Public Sector in an In-Between Time" Beck Jorgensen asked whether the public sector in modern democracies is moving away from old principles and traditional institutional arrangements, but at the same time is heading in no specific direction. He argued, taking the case of Denmark as a starting point, that we face serious displacements in the deep structures of the public sector, between politics and administration, between public and private, and between national and

---

[*] Prof. Werner Jann, Postdam University, Faculty of Social Sciences and Economics, Germany
Dr. Bernard Hubeau, Ombudsman of the city of Antwerpen, Belgium.

international. Therefore professional autonomy and functional democracy may be in conflict with classical territorial democracy and thus political responsibility may gradually disappear.

In the second paper Torbjörn Larsson from EIPA (the European Institute of Public Administration in Maastricht) dealt with the question "How Openness and Transparency can create new Secrets and an Artificial Government". Starting from the "strange Swedish case" of a well established open government he claimed that certain forms of openness and transparency may create inaccurate pictures of how government actually works. He therefore challenged conventional ideas of openness and transparency and especially the traditional methods to achieve these purposes. Finally Rudolf Maes from the Katholieke Universiteit Leuven (Belgium) in his paper "Political and Administrative Innovation as Social Project: The Belgian Case" argued strongly that openness and transparency cannot be discussed and cannot even be understood without a proper understanding of the traditional and future role of citizens in the democratic polity. As possible starting points he presented three different models of participation and empowerment of citizens, the represented, calculating and producing citizens, or, in other words, citizens as subjects, consumers and partners of government and public administration.

Session II Practical Experiences asked whether concepts of New Public Management actually led to greater transparency and accountability, who is expected to benefit from increased transparency (top or line managers, politicians, citizens etc.) and what lessons can be drawn from existing empirical data on the use of performance management instruments and concepts. It started with a paper from Christoph Reichard (now University of Potsdam, Germany) dealing - from the German case - with practical experiences concerning "The Impact of Performance Management on Transparency and Accountability in the Public Sector". Reichard discussed impacts with regard to efficiency, effectiveness, quality, responsiveness and customer orientation, legality and finally legitimacy and democratic decision making and concluded that there are certain positive impacts but that they vary and that we have to take the "demand side" of performance data (from politicians and citizens) into account when advocating specific instruments of performance measurement.

Patrick Staes from the Ministry of the Public Service in Belgium showed in his paper "Baromètre de qualité dans le Cadre de la Charte Belge des utilisateurs des Services Public" how new instruments of quality measurement of public services have been developed with the help of central government in Belgium, how these instruments are supposed to work, how they can be applied, and how their application is implemented in a complex decentralised process. Stefan Sjöblom from the University of Helsinki (Finland) in his paper "Citizen Participation and Effectiveness: On the relationship between participation and policy formation" showed that citizen attitudes towards effective, open and transparent government differ, and that even if government is trying to be open and transparent this openness and transparency is not used in the same way by all citizens, i.e. that there are important social biases. The empirical findings in Finland show furthermore that the most critical dimension to explain citizen participation in government is size (e.g. of the respective local community).

From the position of a practitioner Rita Passemier, Ombudswoman of the City of Gent (Belgium) in her presentation "Transparency, Openness and the Ombudsman/woman" looked at the experiences with ombudsmen/women and how transparent and open these institutions really are? She showed how ombudsmen/women can help to increase transparency and openness of government, but also how far away from universal standards of openness and transparency the current practice in Belgium still is. Finally Teresa Gorzinska from the Institute of Judicial Research at the Polish Academy of Science in Warsaw (Poland) discussed in her paper "Le Droit d'information et la Transparence Administrative en Pologne" the recent developments of current legal regulation of openness and transparency in the Polish government. She stressed that legal and structural changes are not sufficient, even though they are of the utmost importance and a crucial prerequisite of openness and transparency. Necessary is an accompanying cultural shift towards more openness and transparency in the society as whole.

Session III Ethical Aspects dealt first with the British experience, both its long standing ideology and its recent development, in a paper presented by David Richards (University of Birmingham) and Martin Smith (University of Sheffield) "The Gatekeepers of the 'Common Good' - Power and the Public Service Ethos". Richards/Smith argue that the traditional public service ethos is, in fact, a power/knowledge system which has legitimised the rule of a particular elite by presenting public service as a worthy occupation and, thereby, authorising a system of power which is relatively closed and secretive. Even though the introduction of managerialism in British government in recent years has affected the balance of power away from civil servants and in favour of ministers, they argue that there has been no explicit attempt to redefine the public sector ethos. Thus public service ethos continues to exist as a rhetorical device, but there is a clear dissonance between the rhetoric used and the reality of the balance of power between civil servants and politicians. Finally, in a paper called "Is There a Typical Public Service Orientation" Tarja Saarelainen from the University of Lapland in Rovaniemi (Finland) reviewed the relationship between scientific and practical knowledge, starting from a 'translation model' inspired by the new French sociology of actor networks and power. Organising New Public Management and governance is in her view a process of ongoing interaction whereby both a construction and reconstruction of knowledge and reality takes place. In her view it is therefore important that social science, as one important actor, reflects its own role in the power relationships and in the actor-networks of public service reform.

Discussions in all three sections of the Working Group centred around two different sets of questions. Transparency, openness and a new understanding of service to the public were both treated as 'dependent variables' and it was asked whether different developments in administrative reform (performance measures, managerialism, participation, ombudsmen/women etc.) causes alterations in these concepts. On the other hand they were looked upon as 'independent variables', thus asking whether new concepts of transparency, openness and service to the public are causing something, i.e. are enhancing or restricting new levels of efficiency, effectiveness, responsiveness, equality, legality and legitimacy. During the examinations of these questions it became more and more obvious that 'culture' and 'ethos' are important intermediary variables.

In the end there was widespread agreement that we do need a new discussion and definition of public sector values and that we at the same time need a value-based theory of public organisations. It became also quite clear that the politics/administration dichotomy is still a central departing point of these important controversies. The workshop was able to clarify some important relationships and to show some areas for a future common understanding, but in the end it was obvious that the scientific discussion of a new public service ethos is just starting.

Political and Administrative Innovations as a Social Project
The Belgian Case

R. Maes[*]

1. Introduction

In a democratic system citizens always have been entitled to participate. Yet, this could not prevent that their scepticism about the operation of government and about democratic institutions in general has increased. From the perspective of the citizen, the welfare state has become an 'administrative' or 'bureaucratic' state. For countless activities the citizen depends on governmental regulations, permissions, grant systems, homologations or conditions. They catch him like an octopus-like fishing net, that seems to operate along other principles than citizen-orientation.

Several political and administrative innovations intend to counter this scepticism. More precisely, political innovations aim at meeting the demand of both unorganised and organised citizen for a more qualitative interpretation of his democratic involvement. Administrative innovations explicitly want to recognise the citizen as client or consumer of public services and provisions.

Yet, these innovations look upon the citizen as an object of policy and steering. They do not question if the citizen deserves more recognition as social responsible co-producer of social surpluses and as a subject of policy. The political and administrative innovations should be supplemented with social innovations that recognise the citizen explicitly in his role as opponent or partner of government and administration.

The first part of this text focuses on the complexity of the relation between citizens and politics, government and public administration. Participation of citizens in this respect can be described in three models, models which have a different historic background, but gradually have become more and more intertwined. For the sake of clarity, they are individually described and afterwards their interrelations are treated. This is the second part. It is especially this interrelation that seems to resist fragmented reforms that are not a part of a global social, social-democratic project. This project should consider the fact that the relation government-citizen is developing in a multiple perspective and takes different shapes. Each of these perspectives is important since cleavages can develop inside and the 'gap with the citizen' is a complex issue as well. This is studied in a third part.

---

[*] Prof.dr Rudolf. Maes, Katholieke Universiteit Leuven, Faculty of Social Sciences, Department of Political Sciences, Belgium.

2. Three Models of Participation and Empowerment of Citizens

Three models describe the relation with the citizen. These models complement each other and their cohesion indicates that the relation with the citizen has become extremely complex and has different perspectives.

The first model, the classical model, focuses on the citizen as a voter and an object of law.
The second model is grounded in the public choice approach of the public sector. This model originates from the fifties. It considers the citizen as a tax-payer and a client or consumer of public provisions. Moreover, this model pointed at the need for fundamental political and administrative innovations in order to give the public apparatus a more accessible and citizen-controlled nature.

Both models depict the citizen as object of governmental policy and want to increase the power/control of the citizen for this reason. The third model focuses on the role of the citizen within civil society and on the contribution the citizen as subject of policy can make to the development of his collectivity.

2.1. The Citizen as Voter and Subordinate of Law in a Representative Democracy

The traditional line of thought about legitimacy of governmental action and democratic accountability within the political and administrative system starts from the following premises.

Firstly, the enfranchised citizens elect their representatives to the different elective bodies. Depending on the values they defend and on which they were elected, these representatives decide on the general policy. During elections citizens can decide to renew or not the term of office of their representatives. This implies that the representatives are accountable to the citizens.

Secondly, it is important that the politically composed governments or executive bodies are trusted by and accountable to the representative bodies. The governments or executive bodies have bureaucratic organisations at their disposal. These organisations assist them in the preparation and implementation of their policy. They are accountable to the political level and hierarchically organised. In Max Webers ideal type the administration is neutral, subordinate and loyal to the political level.

Thirdly, we find the citizen who is entitled to certain provisions, but also an obedient object of law. A conflict about concrete governmental regulations can only be settled by an independent judging body.

It is clear that this picture needs some refinement. Citizens have used their freedom of organisation to create political parties. These play an important role in the relation between citizen and government. On the one hand they are a platform for opinion-shaping and development of visions, on the other hand they function as integrator and communicator in society. The parliamentary democracy has been transformed in a party democracy (van Houten & von Meijenfeldt, 1942:53) The main political parties have become crucial actors in political decision-making. Moreover, through politicisation they managed to infiltrate the public administration and judicial organisation. Economic, social and cultural organisations linked to the political parties mushroomed in a pillared environment. From governmental side, especially after the second world war official advisory powers in national or high councils, and sometimes even rights of co-government were granted.

From the sixties onwards the idea that more possibilities for participation at the local level were needed gained ground. Municipal culture councils, youth councils, family councils and councils for the aged date from this time. They soon were followed by advice councils for land use, environment etc. Yet, what is depicted here as direct participation was shaped within narrow politically defined margins, such as the culture pact law of July 16th, 1973. In the seventies this law could be considered as the expression of a new political culture, because it wanted to abolish discrimination of political minorities. Nowadays, however, it can be described as an expression of old political culture. Indeed: the cultural organisations and associations are stimulated to join political or philosophical tendencies to use effectively their right of participation in the cultural policy and co-management in the cultural infrastructure.

The core argument of the first model is that the citizen not only is represented by the persons he elected as representatives, but also by political parties and pillared organisations, to whom he does not belong necessarily. These parties and organisations more and more identified themselves with government, because they managed to permeate the government so deeply. The citizen mainly is an object of policy, despite the fact that sometimes his opinion is asked free of obligations. Yet, only political parties and attached organisations manage to place less informal issues on the governmental agenda.

2.2. The Calculating Citizen and the Citizen as a Customer

From the fifties onwards, particularly economic studies of decision-making outside the market sector criticised the political formulation of demand and the provision of public goods and services in the welfare state by politically guided and bureaucratically organised public organisations. (Downs, 1957, 1967: Buchanan & Tollison, 1972,1984; Mueller, 1979,1989; Dunleavy, 1991).

Elections do not decide on content or direction of policy programs, nor do they allow for evaluation of public services. At best, some programs are highlighted in elections, but most of the time elections are slogan-based. The desires of the citizens or their evaluation of concrete governmental actions remain too obscure. Empirical research shows that there is a big gap between the ideas and desires of the electorate and their representatives. The latter are closer to the elite or semi-elite in society then to the mass. (Daemen & Thomassen, 1993, 217-237)

Politicians do not unconditionally defend the general interest, but also party interests. They attempt to maximise votes and try to enlarge the public sector for reasons of political power.

Neither do bureaucratic organisations care for a socially relevant supply. They can attempt to maximise their budgets for reasons of bureaucratic power, prestige or more simply because a growing organisation allows for more career opportunities. Problems are solved at the top, far away from the operational level where the problems are situated. Changes meet fierce resistance because they counter vested interests and positions. The citizen is dependent anyway because of the monopoly these organisations enjoy.

Neither is the citizen free of utility maximisation and political mechanisms sometimes lead to a situation where interest groups force the government to intervene or to provide services whose cost is devolved to others.

This is only a selection of conclusions, that shine a sharp light on democratic decision making and the operation of bureaucratic organisations. Neither is the democratic system alone confronted with alienation and a gap with the citizen. The same is true for the intermediate political parties and pillared organisations that were created in the name of the citizen and which aim to influence governmental organisation.

In this respect certain people advocate a reduction of the political system to core duties, mainly the correction of market failures within the social system. This would limit governmental action to better manageable and controllable proportions. More room would be available for market sensitive and more efficient private actions. The programs of the Reagan administration and the different Thatcher administrations were clearly inspired by this thought (Metcalfe & Richards, 1990). Other approaches aimed to create new relations between government and citizen (Berry, Poortney & Thomson, 1990:208-221; Ringeling, 1993). A start of this can be found in the numerous administrative and political innovations that were initiated in most western countries. To avoid maximisation of votes or budgets and to assure the citizen of an adequate governmental action, better adapted information, communication and control mechanisms must be created. Within the governmental organisation more accountability has to be introduced. Referenda are deemed useful, because they limit the margins of decisions of the politicians, but they can not be held on a regular basis. Moreover, it is necessary to think about new instruments to affirm the position of the citizen. And, even without voting powers a citizen can have justifiable demands. The government needs to become more transparent and should function as a glass house. The same goes for the relationship between decision makers and administrative services. The latter will be imposed contractual accountability and will have to respect stricter performance levels. This model considers the citizen as funding the governmental machinery with his fiscal efforts. This was also inherent in the first model, because elections were organised at those levels of government that could levy taxes.

Yet, to this was added the connotation that the citizen was entitled to a good price-quality relation for the services in exchange for his financial contribution. The citizen is a calculating citizen and a customer and consumer of public services. As a customer he is entitled to adequate and effective returns on investment. Services are specified in users charters and for policy making increasingly in policy contracts or covenants. In this respect one can think about the famous 'contract with the citizen' which was presented by the Belgian Federal government after the elections of November 24th, 1991.

Similar perspectives were developed towards political parties and all other intermediary organisations. In the first model they had become too much identified with governmental organisation. Social evolutions did not leave traditional parties and pillarisation unaffected. A lot of interest communities could not affiliate with these. Proponents of a 'green' ideology managed to organise in a new political party, but this was not the case for the increasing number of unemployed, dumped older employees, daily users public transport, migrants, inhabitants of derelict areas and neighbourhoods etc.

The traditional party-organisation, based on the conflicts between Flemish and Walloons, between labour and capital and between Church and laity, lacked the flexibility to react without endangering vested interests. The extreme right could proliferate against this by making the discontent and self-interests of mainly certain categories of urban population a new, but contestable political issue.

2.3. The Citizen as Producer of a Social Surplus

Despite the fact that the image of the calculating citizen coincides with this of an increasingly individualistic society, an important feature of a human society is that the citizen is part of a network of social relations and that he needs this for his self-development. Shortly, he cannot do without family, labour community, local community and municipal organisation nor without a state organisation. And the reverse is also true.

If in current governmental policy the term empowerment is used, then it is in this meaning. In labour policy, in environmental policy or mobility policy, the government cannot act alone and will have to conclude agreements with the parts of society involved, organisations or even private households or users of roads if it wants to succeed. The contracts for the future on employment which are to be concluded between government, trade unions and employers' organisations can be seen in this perspective. As a matter of fact, in the official education the parents were already given the right of co-government via elected school boards. These are examples of shared responsibility for developments in society, in which emancipated citizens are recognised directly or indirectly as producers of a social surplus, and where they organise themselves to act as opponents or partners of government in the organisation of society (Barber, 1984; Van Houten & von Meyenfeldt, 1992; Rawls, 1984, 1993).

When parents of murdered or missing children are since October 1996 at the origin of the "white marches", then this is from their and other people's wish to avoid this plague in future and of their desire for a government and judicial apparatus that manages to prevent this adequately. Which motives from the first or second model that are influential are only of marginal importance. They manifest themselves as mature and responsible citizens and opponents of government, to force the latter to restore order for the sake of the collectivity. This social innovation places the political and administrative innovations in a new perspective. In the same fashion the trade unions are expected to stop focusing exclusively on those who are employed. They should share responsibility with the employers to create new job opportunities. Yet, this will be impossible when actors calculate exclusively in terms of utility maximisation. The health of the social fabric that supports society can be measured in these terms (van Houten & von Meijenfeldt, 1992:13-35; Rosanvallon, 1995; Schlachter, 1995: 530-537; Wright 1996: 13-16).

The present policy of social innovations is legitimate, but in our country it has remained too much focused on specific target groups and backward or poor areas. Social innovations must be enlarged to the whole society. It is a duty for society to make sure that everybody is able to participate and develop. As such, it is irrelevant if this is realised by government, private initiative or public-private partnerships. A healthy society is tied together by fundamental values which are shared by all people, despite divergent material interests that can be a source of conflict. Solidarity and shared responsibility are in this the cornerstone. Government should be an enabling authority, enabling citizens to participate in social production processes and thus stimulating political participation. Those who are deprived of this, risk to take an extreme position or to turn their back on politics or lose every interest in it. (Idenburg & Kensen, 1996:43-61)

The next table summarises the essential characteristics of the three models:

The citizen as:	voter and subject of law	tax payer and client or consumer	opponent and partner
premises	• citizens elect political leadership • neutral bureaucrats are executing policy and are politically controlled • citizens are obliged to be obedient and subservient	• relative impact of elections • maximisation of votes • maximisation of utility • citizens want value for money	• solidarity and responsibilised society as civil society • citizens are co-responsible
applications	• party democracy • pillared democracy • participation of the citizen through political parties and pillared organisations	• core duties and privatisations • fragmented political and administrative innovations, strengthening the position of the calculating citizen. transparency-duties of justification- users charters-sporadic referenda	• political, administrative and social innovations as a social project • citizens not only are voters or customers, but first of all members of a civil society they support. • the government facilitates and stimulates
results	• the voter is represented and object of law	• the calculating citizen is object (and only sometimes subject) of policy and service delivery	• the citizen is subject and object of policy and service delivery

3. Political, Administrative and Social Innovations as Social Project

The fact that in theory three different models can be distinguished does not preclude that they are jointly important to illuminate the relation between citizen and government. In fact, they can be considered to be cumulative. The citizen is voter and object of law. He is taxpayer and client and he is opponent and partner of government. The present political and administrative innovations want to accommodate the citizen as voter, object of law, tax payer and client, but they are not founded in an all-encompassing project of social innovation. The result is that the citizen's frustration persists.

3.1. Fragmented, Political, Administrative and Social Innovations

The already pursued changes aim at more transparency of government and public administration. Examples are the constitutionally guaranteed openness of government, the duties of information and active information dissemination[1]. More transparency is also to be obtained by the alteration of traditional secrecy of civil servants in a right to speak, yet this option does not include the policy that is only in a state of preparation[2].

At the local level the (at this moment only consultative) referendum has been introduced[3]. At all levels of government expressions of institutionalised participation are existing. Yet, initiatives for citizen's participation that want to involve the citizen in the most direct way can only be developed properly at the local or sublocal level. Rightfully, a couple of months ago the Constitution was amended to allow for the creation of directly elected district councils in the cities with more than 100.000 inhabitants[4].

Customer-orientation is stimulated by the use of charters for users of public services [5] and by participation of citizens. Important impulses to improve the legal protection of the citizen confronted with illegal, unjust or inadequate -including careless- governmental action were already given [6]. Ombudsman services now can defend the citizen where he is harmed by capricious or unreasonable governmental action [7]. Yet, the judicial organisation remained too long outside this context of innovations. Priority must be given to multiple innovations in this sector. This will be impossible without adapting the present old-fashioned visions to the needs of the law-seeking citizen.

Numerous irresponsible privileges of the public sector have been cut. Individual acts of justice have to be motivated [8]. Unjust administrative decisions can be suspended [9], some goods can be sequestered and the administration can be condemned to pay damages[10]. Besides, not only legal and proper action of the administration are a matter of political and social dispute. Today, the question rises if parliaments should act as legisprudent legislative bodies. If not, the citizens should be able to claim recognisance.

Social innovations aim to integrate the deprived in society and already created several projects targeting at specific groups -at neighbourhood or other level[11].

3.2. A Social Project?

The citizens thus can be assured that the administration does not decide from its own bureaucratic rationality and that the interests and rights of the citizen are taken into account. "Die Hoheit der Verwaltung " got a more human face, but... the work is not yet finished. It is impossible to claim that the innovations, whose origin is rather fragmented, are part of a social project supported by politicians and incorporated by the citizen. The innovations originate from the fear to lag behind -at least at the legal or "paper" level- the social developments. They lack vision and are carried on without much publicity, possibly hoping that the citizen does not use too much the services that can cope hardly or not at all with the demand. The citizen remains frustrated because he can not grasp the complex public administration that resulted from the judicial high-tech used in this country. The educational system fails to transfer its main principles (Dewachter & Maddens, 1997:12-13). The citizen remains frustrated because of the inaccessible jungle of legislation, in which even specialists get lost. And despite the existing examples of simpler or less bureaucratic language, the officialese creates intellectual barriers, useless obscurities and confusion. The citizen is frustrated because different parts of society are not given a chance. Neither is he made aware of the relation price /quality in government. Frustration is his fate as well because of the fact that so many decisions that affect him so directly remain the monopoly of unapproachable sanhedrins and procedures. Finally, he is frustrated because he hardly manages to become a real opponent or partner of government. If the innovations are to succeed, then the whole social culture and relation between the government and the citizens must be the object of more drastic actions and a global social-democratic project.

4. The Relation between Government, Administration and Citizens in a Multiple Perspective

The relation between the government and the citizen is developing in multiple ways and takes different shapes. Each of these perspectives is important because cleavages can develop inside. The so-called "gap with the citizen" is a multiple one. Oversimplified we can frame this relation in a policy perspective, in a perspective of a government close to the citizen, in administrative-organisational and service perspective and in ethical and social perspective. (Korsten, 1988).

4.1. The citizen in the Policy Perspective

The citizen expects that the elected councils are the fora where well-documented debates lead to clear choices on the main issues. They expect fora where prudent legislation is made and the daily management of executive bodies is controlled. This is self-evident, but too often neglected.

How can a population be convinced that regional planning is balancing economic and ecological interests, if these are decisions made by the government, far away from the public debate? We are already one step ahead now that the Flemish Parliament at least must ratify the binding part of urban plans, yet the term 'ratify' creates suspicion, since too often it is explained in terms of 'take it or leave it'. How can a population be convinced that regional visions are developed if they are decided upon in regional platforms or regional development corporations while the directly elected provincial councils are kept out of the debate?

Yet, even if we manage to inform and value the public debate in representative bodies -and some good initiatives such as policy letters and whitebooks have emerged the last years- it is a matter of fact that the citizen does not accept any longer that everything is decided over his head. This presupposes a qualitative interpretation of citizens' initiatives, empowerment, referenda, hearings etc...

4.2. The Citizen from the Perspective of the Citizen-oriented Administration

It is clear that direct involvement of the citizen is only feasible at the local or municipal level. Despite the fact that the tasks of municipalities and social welfare centres have grown in the near past, in comparison to our neighbouring countries the real impact of these administrations on the total governmental budget is limited. This is the case both in terms of Gross National Product and in terms of share in total expenditure. (Maes, 1997:8). When the UK is focusing on reinventing democracy, this implies, besides devolution to Scotland and Wales, also the strengthening of local self-government (Stewart, 1966: 39-56).

At the regional or supralocal level democratic values represented by the provincial organisation must be carefully fostered. Those looking down on meso levels of government go too far. They neglect the reality of supralocal interests in the economic, social, spatial, ecological and cultural sector. Correct choices can only be made where the supralocal level can discuss with the local and central level. Moreover, isn't it a matter of fact that a citizen not only acts in the local political sphere but also in the supralocal or regional sphere?

This does not mean that subject of the operation of local and meso levels of government and their relation with the citizen has to be left untouched. On the contrary. The debate about political and administrative innovations and new political culture should be expanded to these levels. Everybody knows that also at these levels of government big efforts are required to arrive at just, democratic and effective policy-making. Besides, isn't it the case that the image of the citizen about the political level is as much or even more influenced by his local experiences than by things he learns about other levels of government? de Tocqueville already stated last century that local government means for democracy what primary education means for academic training.

We miss a giant opportunity offered by the municipality as government closest to the citizen, if we do not make the municipality the gate or counter of the whole governmental organisation, as is already mostly the case in Scandinavia. In this case, it is not the citizen but the local government that has to be familiar with the complex public administration. The local government is responsible to make sure that the demands of the citizen reach the correct administration -inasmuch the local government itself cannot deal with the problem. Municipalities are not very eager to accept this duty -sometimes described belittlingly 'as maiden for all duties'. The exercise of power is more attractive, but isn't it an achievement of the present service-society that in this respect more services can be rendered for the citizen?

4.3. The Citizen in Administrative-organisational and Administrative Service Perspective

The image of the municipality as sole counter answers to the desire to eliminate as much as possible obstacles for an effective client-oriented service provision. More generally, this concern would come down to a citizen-effect report for every organisational and operational decision of government.

Government often develops its own rationality, procedures, forms and hopes that the citizen will fit in. This is impossible without conflict with the citizen or the social reality. In this respect one can think about the fragmented and numerous ombudsmen services that mushroom nowadays and create a new jungle for the citizen.

4.4. The Citizen in Ethical Perspective

On the other hand, a citizen can be so much emancipated that he manages to extract more from government then he is entitled to. The citizen not only is voter, client, partner and opponent, he also is a fraud. And his irresponsible acts affect everyone. Services have to be organised partly as inspections or controlling administrations. New regulations and procedures have to be devised and enlarge the bureaucratic distance.

Public services must be more citizen-oriented but should not be benevolent towards unethical citizens. Citizen-orientation is wrongly interpreted if also illegal or unreasonable demands are accepted.

4.5. The Citizen in Social Perspective

Not only is the government expected to arm itself against possible negative effects of unethical acts of citizens, it also is expected to give a good example. Numerous illustrations show that this is not the case. We can refer to the registration abroad of Belgian planes and boats, not to mention more striking scandals. Moreover, the government is expected to allow the citizen to be a self- and co-responsible member of society, a partner or opponent of government. This means: stimulating self- and co-responsibility. This also offers a framework for social innovations.

5. Conclusion

Political, administrative and social innovations intend to restore the trust of the citizen and give legitimacy to governmental policy. This however, does not happen with a bit of new political culture and some fragmented reforms. It will only be possible if the innovations are framed in a new vision on the operation of society, a vision developed together with the citizen. Numerous reforms - and we still are in the primary phase- are not yet framed in a new global culture in which the citizen is valued as self- and co-responsible opponent or partner. Yet, democracy is only possible to the extent to which it is supported by a responsible democratic reflex in the population.

Legitimacy is not attained by new regulations alone. Some public services, particularly the judicial system, suppose it is possible to regain their legitimacy by a defensive position. This has the reverse effect. Only convincing examples of effective and democratic public action can provide a base for the desired renewed legitimacy for government.

Notes

[1] Since January 1st, 1995 Article 35 of the Belgian Constitution which stipulates that everybody has the right to consult governmental documents and even is entitled to receive a transcript, with the exception of the cases and under the conditions stipulated by Law, or for the regions and language communities, decree or ordinance, is in vigour. The legislation also aims at active publicity, by the imposition of the obligation to inform the citizen, e.g. by the publication of documents describing the competencies and duties of different governmental organisations.

[2] Article 3 of the Royal Decree of September 26th, 1994 which contains the general principles on the administrative position of civil servants of federal, regional or community governments stipulates:
* civil servants are entitled to express their own opinion on the facts which they know due to their position;
* they are only forbidden to make issues public which concern: the safety of the country, the protection of the public order, financial interests of the government, the prevention and punishment of illegal activities, medical issues, rights and liberties of the citizens and especially the right and respect for privacy. This ban is also applicable for facts related to the preparation of all decisions.
This stipulation has also to be regarded from the general context of the loyalty of civil servants, who have to avoid each action which might endanger the trust of the public in their service.

[3] The law of April 10,1995 introduced the municipal (consultative) referendum. The municipal council can, on its own initiative or on demand of at least 10 % of the voters, decide to organise a consultation on municipal issues. However, budgetary and tax issues, accounts, the admission, residence and expulsion of foreigners are excluded. Votes are only counted if at least 40 % of the electorate participated in the consultation.

[4] The change of Art. 41 of the Belgian Constitution (March 11, 1997) enables the creation of intramunicipal decentralised organisations. These can decide on issues of municipal importance. These organisations can only be created by the municipal council of municipalities with more than 100.000 inhabitants and the councillors of the new bodies have to be elected directly. Yet, in order to create these organisations in fact more legal and decretal initiatives are needed.
[5] Besides the "charter of users of public services", elaborated by the Federal government, which dates from January 12,1993 , we can also refer to the "charter of the social insured", dating from April 11,1995 and in vigour since January 1, 1997
[6] The Belgian Council of State assesses administrative decisions from the perspective of decent government
[7] Cfr Law of March 22,1995 on the creation of federal ombudsmen. Already earlier ombudsmen were created by regional governments and by some autonomous public companies such as the Railways (Nationale Maatschappij der Belgische Spoorwegen), Post and Belgacom.
[8] Law of July 19, 1991 This law obliges every administrative authority to motivate each individual act which aims at influencing one or more citizens or another authority. This duty only expires if this motivation would endanger the external security of the state, the public order or would endanger the respect for private life or stipulations on professional secrecy or secrecy.
[9] The law of July 17,1991 introduced the administrative summary procedure allowing the Council of State to suspend the execution of governmental acts and regulations if serious arguments can be brought forward and on the condition that the immediate execution creates important damages which are not easy to repair. The suspension then lasts till the final settlement of the conflict. Earlier already, the law of October 17,1990 granted the Council of State the competency to impose fines to ensure the effective execution of its provisions.
[10] Due to legislation of June 30,1994 it is possible to sequester public goods, if these are not necessary for the mission of the government or the continuity of the public service
[11] We think especially about decisions at the regional level to finance projects against poverty and initiatives for backward areas and neighbourhoods.

Bibliography

Barber, B.R., Srong Democracy. Participatory Politics for a New Age, Berkeley: University of California Press, 1984.

Berry, J.M., Poortney, K.E. and K. Thomson, "Empowering and Involving Citizens" in Perry, J.M., Ed., Handbook of Public Administration, San Francisco: Jossey-Bass Publishers, 1990, pp. 208-221.

Buchanan, J M. and R.D. Tollison, Eds., Theory of Public Choice, Ann Arbor: University of Michigan Press, Vol. I, 1972; Vol II, 1984.

Daemen, N.H.F.M. and J.J.A. Thomassen, "Afstand tussen burgers en overheid", in Hoogerwerf A., Red., Overheidsbeleid, Alphen aan den Rijn: Samson H.D. Tjeenk Willink, 1993, pp. 217-237

Dewachter, W and B. Maddens, " Het begint nog voor de verkiezingen", in Maes R. (Red.) Democratie, legitimiteit en nieuwe politieke cultuur, Leuven: Acco, 1997, pp. 11-24

Downs, A., An Economic Theory of Democracy, New York: Harper & Row, 1957.

Downs, A. Inside Bureaucracy, Boston: Little Brown & Co, 1967.

Dunleavy, P., Democracy, Bureaucracy and Public Choice, New York: Harvester Wheatsheaf, 1991.

Idenburg, Ph. A., and S. Kensen, "Sociale vernieuwing: een belangrijk leermoment", in Nelissen N.J.M., Iking T. and A.W. van de Ven, In staat van vernieuwing. Maatschappelijke vernieuwingsprocessen in veelvoud, Bussem: Dick Coutinho, 1996, pp. 43-64.

Korsten, A., Bestuurskunde als avontuur. Een beschouwing over bestuurskundige heuristiek: perspectieven op de toekomst van de gemeenten, Deventer: Kluwer, 1988.

Maes, R., "Het profiel van de lokale politiek" in: Res Publica, 1997, nr. 1, pp. 3-26.

Metcalfe L. and S. Richards, Improving Public Management, London: Sage, 1990

Mueller, D., Public Choice I, Cambridge: Cambridge University Press, 1979.

Mueller, D. Public Choice II, Cambride: Cambridge University Press, 1989.

Rawls, J. Political Liberalism, New York: Columbia University Press, 1984.

Rawls, J. A Theory of Justice, Oxford: Oxford University Press, 1993.

Ringeling, A., Het imago van de overheid, 's Gravenhage: Vuga, 1993.

Rosanvallon, P., La nouvelle question sociale Repenser l'Etat-providence, Paris: Editions du Seuil, 1955.

- Schlachter, H.L., "Reinventing Government or Reinventing Ourselves", in Public Administration Review, 1995, nr. 6, pp. 530-537.

Stewart, J., "Democracy and Local Government", in Hirst P. and S. Khilhani, Ed., Reinventing Democracy, The Political Quaterly Publishing Co., 1996, pp. 39-56.

van Houten H.J. and F.D. von Meijenfeldt, Integraal Participatiemanagement. Een strategische herdefinitie van democratie en burgerschap, 's Gravenhage: Vuga, 1992.

Wright, T., "Reinventing Democracy", in Hirst P. and S. Khilhani, Ed., Reinventing Democracy, The Political Quaterly Publishing Co., 1996, pp. 13-16

The Impact of Performance Management on Transparency and Accountability in the Public Sector

C. Reichard[*]

1. Issues and instruments of performance management

1.1. Introduction

Output or performance orientation is one of the most important elements of the new public management concepts. It plays a major role in almost all countries which are reforming their public sector. It means that organisations in the public sector are shifting their whole steering concept from traditional input control to an explicit output or outcome focus. Furthermore, most countries have begun to hold their public managers individually accountable for achieving certain output or performance targets, like key performance indicators in the UK or like key result areas in New Zealand. Thus, output or performance orientation is considered to be a major prerequisite for increasing transparency and accountability in public sector organisations (Pollitt/Summa 1997, 11)[1].

Performance measurement is the logical prerequisite of performance management. Public organisations are using several concepts and instruments for performance measurement. Among them are:

- performance indicator systems
- accrual cost accounting concepts
- performance budgeting
- performance monitoring/controlling
- benchmarking procedures
- quality assessments and awards
- general performance awards and competitions (like Citizen Charter Award, Malcolm Baldridge Award, Speyer Quality Award)

It is not the main idea of performance measurement to determine the absolutely accurate output or outcome of a public service but to support the management of a public organisation to follow a certain vision and strategy. Key questions to be answered by performance measurement are (Hailstones 1994, 192f.):

- to what extent have given targets been reached?
- where does an organisation's performance stay compared with others?
- how large are deviations from a given target or a benchmark?

---
[*] Prof. Dr. Christoph Reichard, University of Potsdam, Faculty of Economics and Social Sciences - Public Management - Germany.

- what are reasons of possible deviations?
- what actions are necessary to correct a deviation and to reach a given target?

Performance measurement data has several addressees. At first there are several recipients within the respective organisation: the politicians (e.g. councillors), the top management, line managers, employees and their representatives, and also citizens or customers, tax payers etc. Possible target groups are also competing authorities, supervisory bodies or other governmental institutions. Finally, the general public (press media etc.) is increasingly interested in performance data. All these different target groups need or expect data for their specific requirements regarding the scope and details of performance.

Performance measurement generally plays an important role in all states which are undertaking administrative reforms in the NPM style. In some states central government forces the regular collection of performance data, for instance in the UK (local government performance data comparisons of the Audit Commission; see Audit Commission 1995). In the U.S. according to Ammons more than half of all cities are collecting performance data. "In most cases, however, the vast majority of the measures collected by a given municipality merely reflects workload. ... Only few US local governments systematically assess quality and efficiency. ... An even smaller cadre measures effectiveness and efficiency for more than a handful of departments" (Ammons 1996, 2). It can be assumed that this description of the US situation is somehow typical also for other states. Efficiency or effectiveness measures and quality assessments are generally not the rule but the exception[2].

1.2. Performance measurement in Germany

A recent empirical study comparing the use of performance indicators in the U.S., the U.K. and in Germany comes to the result that the intensity of using performance indicators is much weaker in Germany than in the two other countries (Loeffler 1997, 108ff). The intensity of using indicators for budgeting or for reporting is twice as large in the U.S. or U.K. as in Germany. This finding seems to be quite realistic (see also Hill/Klages 1996). Since a couple of years performance indicators begin to play a limited role particularly at local level where the implementation of the "Neues Steuerungsmodell" - the German variant of NPM - has successfully been started since the early 90s (for more details of the German NPM see Reichard 1997). Municipalities have begun to define and to describe their services in the form of "products", expecting to increase the transparency of their services, particularly of the costs. Some of these product descriptions are following a common masterplan, developed by the KGST, an association of German municipalities to improve local government management. The "product catalogues" of the different cities are expected to serve as an instrument for performance measurement. However, up to present only few product descriptions are including output or outcome measures; most of them concentrate primarily on cost aspects.

One example to promote performance measurement in the German public sector is the "Speyer Quality Award" (Speyerer Qualitätswettbewerb). Since 1992 the Postgraduate School for Administrative Sciences in Speyer is organising every two years a nation-wide competition for well-performing public sector organisations. Ministries, state agencies, local governments and all other kinds of public organisations are invited to participate.

Candidates describe their innovations and their reform plan in a self-assessment by way of a comprehensive questionnaire, supplemented by some external inspections. Applicants are asked to describe their management by using several structural and performance indicators (for more details see Klages 1995). Since 1996 the Speyer Award is also open to public sector organisations in Austria and in Switzerland. About 70-80 different organisations, as an average, participate in one competition.

Another example is the so-called "inter-communal indicator network" ("IKO-Netz") which was founded in 1996 by the KGST. This network is continuing with the preceding performance comparison program of the German Bertelsmann Foundation (see next chapter). Several municipalities voluntarily join an indicator circle to exchange performance data with other members, to compare the data and to learn how to solve certain problems and how to organise better service processes. KGST is responsible for the logistical infrastructure and it moderates the exchange processes. At present there are already a number of these circles at work, most of them with about 20-30 member-communes, usually concentrating on a limited number of policy fields.

1.3. Case Study: The Bertelsmann Performance Comparison

An interesting experience has taken place in the last 7 years with a performance measurement program initiated and organised by the Bertelsmann Foundation: The *"local services benchmarking system"*[3] (Interkommunaler Leistungsvergleich; for more details see Adamaschek/Banner 1997), which took place from 1990 to 1997 and which has recently been integrated into the above-mentioned IKO-network. The Bertelsmann Foundation supported the development of a comprehensive methodology to define, collect and compare performance data from different local authorities. The comparison started with 7 medium-sized cities, concentrating on the areas of public order, residents' registration, immigration, social welfare, parks and recreation, local taxes and charges. Later on several additional circles of cities have been organised where similar comparisons took place. Meanwhile around 150 municipalities are still co-operating in such performance indicator circles. In a parallel program several cities with support from the Bertelsmann Foundation are undertaking indicator comparisons concerning different fields of local culture (adult education, music schools, libraries, theatres, museums etc.).

The basic idea of this comparative performance measurement program is to collect data from similar local authorities referring to four basic goals of local government:

- the service mission (task fulfilment)
- efficiency
- client satisfaction
- employee satisfaction

It may be interesting to note that the program has elaborated more than 50 indicators for each of the two goals, namely efficiency and employee satisfaction. On the other hand, indicators related to service mission as well as to client satisfaction are - in quantitative terms - underrepresented.

The indicators and the procedures and standards for data collection have been elaborated by different expert teams from the member cities. The indicators are the basis of a management reporting system, and they are regularly (quarterly) exchanged between the participating municipalities. Observed weaknesses are the subject of discussion in different quality circles within each city. Numerous seminars and workshops to train public managers and politicians of the participating municipalities have been held. The Bertelsmann Foundation paid during the first phase of the comparison (1992-1997) all expenses for infrastructure including training and consultancy. In future the participating municipalities are expected to continue the network at their own expense.

Reported results of the Bertelsmann program are (Adamaschek/Banner 1997):

- certain improvements in different local services, e.g. increasing the open hours of citizen offices, reduction of waiting times of phone calls to offices, introduction of one-stop-offices, etc.
- cost reduction as a result of intercommunal learning, but also because pressure to justify costs of certain services against the council or the top management rose as an effect of intercommunal comparisons
- increases of revenues because of utilising new sources or of higher motivation of staff to collect taxes or charges
- streamlining and simplification of processes as a consequence of learning from others but also as an effect of decentralising responsibilities

In assessing the intermediate results of the Bertelsmann comparison one can say that at first it is a great success to develop a functioning performance measurement infrastructure and methodology and to convince a large number of municipalities that regular performance comparisons are valuable. To some extent an "olympic spirit" of quasi-competition can be observed. Furthermore it can be assumed that such a performance comparison is promoting a more entrepreneurial or at least managerial ethos within the public sector.

The Bertelsmann Foundation in their evaluation of the first experiences mentions several advantages of performance comparisons (Adamaschek/Banner 1997, 202ff):

- the comparison promotes synergy through inter-communal co-operation
- the comparison initiates a process of continuous learning and improvement; every participant of a indicator network is benefiting from learning, even the "lame ducks"
- the comparison concentrates the focus on the whole organisation and on the organisational and motivational conditions of service delivery
- the comparison offers a chance to increase public interest in local services and to strengthen public accountability.

First empirical findings from practising the Bertelsmann comparison come to mixed results: The participating cities, without any doubt, have had success with regard to the efficiency of several services. Even more, the comparison has had positive impact on employee motivation and satisfaction. The available performance data in fact provides an opportunity for decision makers to have more transparency in their decisions.

However, several problems and deficits can be observed:

- the extremely high effort (personnel capacities) to elaborate the indicator system, to co-ordinate the network, but also to collect regularly the data for more than 700 different indicators raises the "value for money" question. It can be assumed that an average-sized city has to pay about 2 Mio DM per year only for the time consuming data collection which is reducing the personnel capacities.

- municipalities do sometimes misunderstand the aim of the comparison: they expect "100%-comparability" of services between different communes which is not feasible, despite the efforts to co-ordinate data sources and procedures.

- some municipalities have not found the right balance between the necessary homogeneity and comparability of the performance indicator system and the individuality of their own communal reporting system. These municipalities did not use the collected data for their own monitoring and reporting purposes. Consequently, they became frustrated collecting masses of data only for the performance comparison program without having a benefit from it.

- the network changed frequently their data collection standards which made periodic comparisons difficult or impossible

- the program concentrated to a large extent on data collection; according to the opinion of some participants the opportunity to discuss causes of deviations and to learn from "the best of class" was limited

- the quality and outcome orientation of the comparison seems to be limited; several participants regret that quality indicators are underrepresented within the system

Although it may be too early to sum up experiences with the Bertelsmann comparison and despite the existing lack of empirical data, some lessons can be drawn:

1. The way from a performance indicator network to a substantial increase of performance and to a change of structures and behaviour is long and difficult. There is some evidence that the Bertelsmann comparison had some positive effects on the efficiency of the participating municipalities, but substantial structural changes could not be observed up to present.

2. A successful performance measurement system needs realisation of certain framework conditions (Adamaschek/Banner 1997, 204ff.):

- *"performance boosters"*: the citizens, the market with its competition, and the local politicians are necessary factors to motivate the bureaucrats to undertake efforts for measuring performance. Some first empirical impressions show that none of the three factors played a significant role during the program. This is particularly true with market competition. Marketization is, however, not a major reform issue in the German case.

- results of performance measurement need publicity: they should be published in the local media to inform the citizens and other interest groups, as is the case in the UK with the charter results. It can be assumed that publicity of results only played a marginal role in the German program.

- performance measurement needs an adequate managerial infrastructure, i.e. quasi-autonomous, decentralised units which are responsible for the results of their work and which have the "freedom to manage"; furthermore adequate management tools (cost accounting, information technology, personnel management etc.) are required. Some examples of participating cities show that performance comparisons had only poor impact because the managers could not take the necessary decisions to increase performance.

- performance measurement needs "meta organisations" like city/county associations, foundations, consultancy, academic institutions to assist the municipalities in introducing and carrying out performance comparisons. This condition has been fulfilled to a large extent in the German case.

3. The politicians must be included: The sustainability of an indicator network can only be expected if the council and the politically appointed leaders of a public organisation are regularly involved in the interpretation of the results of performance comparisons, and if they take the consequent actions. Some German cities complain about poor impact of the comparisons due to resistance of politicians to react with adequate decisions on the produced data.

4. The citizens or more precisely the customers of a public organisation should be involved in the performance measurement process. They should be interviewed in customer panels and they should have the opportunity to tell their own demands concerning public services. Within a limited scope customer demands are included in performance comparisons. However, strengthening citizen participation is not an aim of the program.

5. The employees should actively participate in the performance comparison. They must have fair opportunities that job contents and working conditions are improving as a consequence of the comparison. Furthermore, employees will only follow the rules of the game if they do not expect their workplaces to be in danger. The massive financial crisis of German local authorities and the consequent cutback of workplaces in most offices appears as a severe danger for the performance comparison program with regard to employee participation. Experience from several cities with heavy cutback problems shows that some employees are forging the data.

6. In cities with heavy financial stress, performance measurement programs tend to get the image of being a mere cost reduction instrument. "Economy" seems to be the ultimate goal in several cities. Other criteria of the comparison, like client satisfaction or quality, only play a subordinated role.

2. Effects of performance management on transparency

Increased transparency is one of the major goals of NPM reforms (Jann 1997, 98). The whole NPM logic of output-oriented and decentralised steering is expected to increase transparency of public activities. Contributions to transparency are particularly resulting from NPM elements like the following:

- output (or product) oriented organisational structure (result centers etc.)
- units with clear cut result-oriented responsibilities
- council committees organised along the same product structures as administration
- council and top management concentrate on formulating clear strategic goals and financial targets and controlling the performance
- a regular reporting is based on performance indicators, it evaluates goal achievement and possible deviations.

Transparency is a *meta-goal*: Rational decisions and actions are possible, if goals and/or means are adequately transparent. However, due to imperfect information one can never reach complete transparency. In this sense transparency is also a condition of political and administrative action: It means that strategies and activities of a public organisation are lucid and distinct with regard to their goals, alternatives and effects. Transparency can be related to different goals:

- transparency with regard to efficiency
- transparency with regard to effectiveness
- transparency with regard to the quality of services
- transparency with regard to responsiveness and customer orientation
- transparency with regard to legality
- transparency with regard to legitimacy and democratic decision making

Higher transparency of performance of public organisations primarily means more and better information about efficiency and effectiveness. However, in a broader sense of "performance" the other aspects mentioned above would also be included. Transparency can be seen as a *dependent* or as an *independent variable* (e.g. transparency as precondition for practising performance management). In this article transparency is used as a dependent variable: depending on the effects of performance management.

Transparency can be viewed under two aspects: It is a question of *communication* between different actors. If the politicians are setting goals and the administration tries to break down the goals in concrete targets and budgets, the transparency of goals, targets and budgets is based on the social relations, power structures, and trust among the communicating actors. Transparency is also a *technical and instrumental topic*: How to make goals, targets and budgets clear and distinct. Performance management tackles both dimensions of transparency: It is at first a technical instrument to enlarge the lucidity and clearness of goals or actions. But it is secondly a topic of the social relations and organisational culture: To what extent are actors really demanding higher transparency and to what extent are they used to thinking and behaving in a "performance culture"?

Organisational studies are showing that actors within an organisation are interested in producing uncertainty and intransparency. Actors in hierarchies - both at the top and at bottom - tend to create *desinformation* as a means of securing autonomy, power and prestige. The *Principal Agent theory* for example explains that the agent tends to increase his information advantages against the principal agent to gain sufficient autonomy for his actions. Thus, intransparency to some extent also has a protective function in organisations. It is therefore important to find the right balance between transparency and intransparency.

It seems that most of the actual discussion about increasing transparency by using performance management is dealing with the technical dimension and is neglecting the social-communicative dimensions.

Transparency of administrative performance can be viewed from a *supply side* and from a *demand side* (table 1): From the supply perspective the main argument is to deliver meaningful, easy understandable, actual, and target-group-oriented data. From the demand side one has to consider that managers - as well as politicians and other addressees - must accept and use the tools and the data. That means that they must be motivated towards transparency and that they must be able to work with such tools and concepts. There is evidence that existing performance management concepts do not reflect adequately the demand-side of transparency.

Table 1. Supply and demand side of transparency

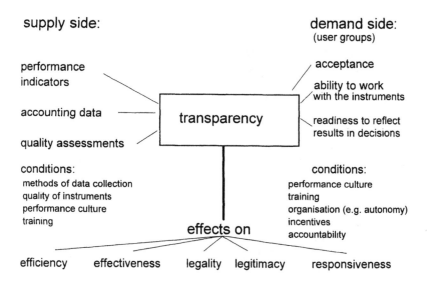

What contributions to transparency can be expected from performance measurement? Performance data

- informs about the efficiency and effectiveness of particular services
- informs about particular performance in relation to the performance of other comparable organisations
- is an instrument for monitoring, controlling and evaluation
- helps to distribute resources with more justice (e.g. to support underfunded policy areas)
- is a prerequisite for competition

Is there a substantial increase of transparency because of performance measurement activities in public sector organisations? According to the - highly limited! - empirical data available the effects on transparency of providing performance data for administrative decisions are mixed. Of course there are several empirical findings that increased transparency of performance data has had positive effects. Several municipalities in Germany are reporting increasing cost-consciousness among managers caused by the introduction of cost accounting. On the other side a study from 1996 about performance measurement in U.K. agencies is showing that although the amount of data has grown remarkably there is still a lack of meaningful information about "performance" (Talbot 1996). The study reports that no clear interrelations between objectives and performance indicators could be identified, and that no clear links between inputs, outputs and objectives could be observed. "While the amount of data available about government has increased, in many ways its comprehensiveness and utility have decreased" (Talbot 1996, 29). Furthermore, the originally simple framework of performance measurement "has resulted in a complex web of controls and reporting regimes which has little of the clarity originally envisaged" (ibid).

Other studies also report on the counter-productivity problem of performance measurement: A non-manageable data overkill can lead to decreasing transparency and therefore to a limited acceptance of the addressees.

Some additional reported difficulties with performance measurement among others are:

- difficulties with measuring performance can lead to systematic deviations or distortions. There is "a danger that performance will be skewed towards what is being measured" (Likierman 1994, 130)

- decision-makers may tend to prefer facts which are easily measurable. There is a tendency "for monetary to push out non-monetary indicators" (ibid).

- there are particularly problems to measure quality and to include quality indicators within an indicator system. Experience from product catalogues in Germany shows that most indicators provide information about the costs of a certain product but only few of them are covering the quality of the service.

- performance measurement is concentrating in most cases on the measurement of outputs. Although the outcomes of administrative activities are much more important than immediate outputs, evidence from different countries shows that outcome or effectiveness indicators are extremely rare and mostly not very informative (Jackson 1995).

- the increasing competition among public sector organisations also can have a counterproductive effect on transparency: competitive pressure can lead to informational isolation of single organisations or of competing units and thus can lead to lower transparency (Hepworth 1994, 141). Thus, performance orientation can cause the following *dilemma*: on the one hand, it promotes transparency. But on the other hand, it encourages competition, and competition can reduce transparency because of increasing partial interests of the competitors.

- there are reports from some cities in Germany about destructive behaviour of employees: some of them are forging data to present positive results, particularly in cities under strong financial stress (KGSt 1996, 46ff.).

- we experience a growing interest of citizens for "value for money" also within the public sector. They become increasingly interested in comparing the services and costs of different public authorities. But the results must touch their very individual demands and experiences. Very general publications of performance data in so-called "league tables" do not have much effect on the general public, the public response on such publications is limited, as we know from U.K. experiences (see Bowerman 1995, 174ff.).

One of the crucial questions of performance measurement is whether politicians are willing to *accept greater transparency* and to make more "rational" decisions based on transparent data. On the one hand, it can be argued that politicians cannot escape increased transparency. If they are sufficiently provided with performance data, it is difficult for them to neglect this data. Thus, higher transparency is a "new rule of the game", and politicians have to observe this rule. On the other hand, there is evidence that politicians tend to avoid clear and transparent decisions because transparency can also be (mis)used by their political enemies. The answer on this question remains open.

Following evidence from OECD (Trosa 1997, 7) there is a tendency for politicians to avoid the publication of evaluations which include negative results. "There is in general perhaps a natural reluctance for politicians to embrace performance measure willingly. Being too specific about political intentions, and in particular given the difficulties of doing so in a time of severe financial constraint, leaves politicians exposed to a subsequent charge of non-delivery if they do not achieve 100% of planned targets" (Hailstones 1994, 195).

Transparency is depending to some extent also on the *role of the citizens*: If a citizen is participating actively in the planning or production of a certain service, he or she will be more interested in the structures and conditions of the whole service as if he/she is only playing a passive role as consumer of certain services.

Vincent Wright (1997, 10f.) refers to another problematic aspect of transparency: If (social etc.) disparities which were hidden in the past due to poor data are becoming transparent this may cause political problems. The rationing of scarce resources, as he points out, has been managed in the past "by a combination of ignorance, obfuscation and legitimation" (ibid.). But now obfuscation is replaced by transparency and this can lead to *delegitimation* of the whole process of service delivery.

3. Impact on accountability

"Public accountability rests both on giving an account and on being held to account" (Stewart 1994, 75). Public accountability is the responsibility for exercising public power. The question is whether public accountability can be strengthened by introducing performance management into public sector organisations.

At first is has to be stated that neither the parliamentary chain of command nor the executive (or: bureaucratic) chain of command are functioning well in the present situation. Both traditional concepts of maintaining public accountability are more fiction than reality (Jann 1997, 97f.). Thus, the issue of strengthening public accountability emerged during the recent reform debate. Several governments experience that strengthening accountability is a necessary countermeasure against the decentralisation and devolution of power (OECD 1997b, 19ff.).

If we distinguish between *political and administrative accountability* (Uusikylä 1997) it can be said that performance measurement primarily contributes to administrative accountability and only secondarily to political accountability. The impact on administrative accountability is expected to be positive. The argument is the same as in the case of transparency. But there may be in future a shift of administrative accountability: If performance measures are addressed to citizens it can be expected that public managers will be held directly answerable to the users of certain services instead to political representatives.

We can observe that most performance measurement concepts are relatively weak to provide information about effectiveness and responsiveness. The impact on political accountability is therefore limited. Some critics are even more sceptical that performance data does not necessarily lead to a higher accountability but could reduce the accountability of politicians (Bowerman 1995, Klein/Carter 1988). The data supply from performance measurement sharpens the old dilemma: a minister cannot be held responsible and accountable for everything that is going on in his organisation. The distinction between strategic and politically sensitive issues and "the rest" becomes more obvious than before. Thus, performance management forces the government to redefine the political accountability of politicians (ministers, mayors etc.) towards responsibility for strategic goal achievement (Boston et al. 1996, 321, with reference to experiences from New Zealand). There may be a danger, however, that ministers may escape from their political accountability because of the new distinction between politics and administration. They will tend to make their chief executives responsible. Several actual cases in the U.K. (e.g. prison administration) show that such an attitude seems to be realistic.

Generally, many observers of the actual administrative reforms fear that political accountability - at least in their traditional forms - could be diminished or weakened. One major argument is the *fragmentation* of the politico-administrative system caused by decentralisation and autonomisation (Stewart 1994, Moe 1994). Whether alternative forms of accountability - the "market accountability" or the "contractual accountability" can replace the traditional public accountability, remains at least doubtful (Stewart 1994, 75ff.). Linda deLeon (in her EGPA-statement from 1995; see: DeLeon 1997) asks for a new and different concept of public accountability which should concentrate on results instead of strict rule observation and which should use professional control mechanisms rather than bureaucratic ones. However, the detailed elements of such a new concept of accountability appear to be unclear up to present.

4. Conclusions

Obviously, performance measurement and management do have positive impact on transparency and on accountability of and in public sector organisations. Generally, it can be expected that decision makers on the political as well as on the administrative level are interested in a higher transparency of goals, actions and consequences, i.e. in a higher degree of available information. It can also be expected that accountability - particularly on the administrative level - will be strengthened if accountable actors will be provided with relevant performance data. However, some limitations of these positive expectations ought to be observed (see above). Generally, we have to keep in mind the potential danger that sophisticated performance measurement systems can replace the necessary political debate with technical managerialism (Bowerman 1995, 180).

One important condition for success is the *"personal factor"*. The values, attitudes and behaviour of politicians and executives are a major prerequisite. Both groups of actors have to accept the results of performance measurement. They must have the ability to interpret the results, to undertake the necessary actions and to "translate" the results to their subordinates. This is a question of the *incentive structures*: a performance-related behaviour of executives is only to be expected if positive or negative deviations from targets - as long as they are caused by the management - have individualised consequences, i.e. consequences on salaries (performance-related pay) and/or on promotion.

The above mentioned personal factor which is essential for the development of transparency and of accountability can only grow within an appropriate *performance culture*. Research about administrative culture is showing that opportunities for developing performance culture are higher in civic societies with a high individuality orientation and consequently with greater acceptance of executives to work with individual responsibility and self-accountability. Pollitt/Summa (1997, 11f.) present findings from an international comparative NPM study that administrators in the Nordic states (Sweden and Finland) are more collective and egalitarian oriented than their Anglo-Saxon counterparts and therefore more reluctant to take over individual responsibility. Following the authors it seems to be suitable to distinguish between the performance orientation of an entire organisation and of individual actors. In countries with a high individuality orientation it can be advisable to motivate and to reward individual employees with regard to their personal performance. In other countries it may be more suitable to design incentive systems which are related to groups or to larger organisational units.

Finally it must be stated that we are still missing a sound and empirically valid theory to explain the effects and interrelations of NPM-related reforms on the state and on public sector organisations. This is also the fact with effects of performance measurement and management on transparency and on accountability. NPM "offers a lot of prescriptions which have a certain common sense appeal, but their basis in theory is often unclear or eclectic" (Jann 1997, 100).

Notes

[1] This article concentrates on the effects of performance management on transparency and on accountability. It does not reflect other NPM-related effects on transparency and accountability, e.g.

marketization or organisational decentralisation, which also may have remarkable impact on transparency and accountability.
[2] The introduction of performance indicator systems in several states during the last years has been critically assessed from numerous authors. For detailed experiences in Australia, the U.K., the U.S. etc. see for example: Ammons 1996, Alford/Baird 1997, Bowerman 1995, Buschor/Schedler 1994, Guthrie 1994, Hailstones 1994, Jackson 1995, OECD 1997a, Stewart/Walsh 1994.
[3] A more detailed summary of experiences with the Bertelsmann performance comparison program is available in German: see Adamaschek 1997 (about 150 pages). The structure of the Bertelsmann comparison seems to be to some extent comparable with the performance measurement program initiated in 1995 by the *International City/County Management Association (ICMA)* in the U.S

Bibliography

Adamaschek, B., Interkommunaler Leistungsvergleich. Leistung und Innovation durch Wettbewerb. Bertelsmann Stiftung, Gütersloh 1997.

Adamaschek, B., G. Banner, Bertelsmann Foundation: Comparative performance measurement - a new type of competition between local governments. In: M. Pröhl (Ed.), International strategies and techniques for future local government. Bertelsmann Foundation, Gütersloh 1997, 183-208.

Alford, J., J. Baird, Performance Monitoring in the Australian Public Service: a Government-wide Analysis. In: Public Money & Management April/June 1997, S. 49-58.

Audit Commission, Performance Indicators for the Financial Year 1996/97. London 1995.

Ammons, D. N., Municipal Benchmarks. Thousand Oaks etc. 1996.

Boston, J. et al, Public Management - The New Zealand Model. Auckland etc. 1996.

Bowerman, M., Auditing Performance Indicators: The role of the Audit Commission in the Citizen's Charter Initiative. In: Financial Accountability and Management 1995, 171-183.

Buschor, E., K. Schedler (Hrsg.), Perspectives on Performance Measurement and Public Sector Accounting. Bern, Stuttgart, Wien 1994.

Carter, N., Learning to Measure Performance: The Use of Indicators in Organizations. In: Public Administration 1991, S. 85-101.

Cave, M., M. Kogan, R. Smith (Hrsg.), Output and Performance Measurement in Government. London 1990.

DeLeon, L., Administrative Reform and Democratic Accountability. In: W. Kickert (Ed.), Public Management and Administrative Reform in Western Europe. Papers from the 1995 EGPA conference. Cheltenham, UK 1997, 237-252.

Guthrie, J., Performance Indicators in the Australian Public Sector. In: E: Buschor, K. Schedler (Eds.), Perspectives on Performance Measurement and Public Sector Accounting. Bern, Stuttgart, Wien 1994, 259-277.

Hailstones, F., Performance Measures - a practitioner's perspective. In: E. Buschor, K. Schedler (Eds.), Perspectives on performance measurement and public sector accounting. Bern et al 1994, 189-195.

Hepworth, N. P., Performance Measurement in Local Government in the United Kingdom. In: E. Buschor, K. Schedler (Eds.), Perspectives on Performance Measurement and Public Sector Accounting. Bern et al 1994, 137-162.

Hill, H., H. Klages (Eds.), Quality, Innovation and Measurement in the Public Sector. Frankfurt a.M.-Berlin-Bern-New York 1996.

Holloway, J. (Eds.), Performance Measurement and Evaluation. London 1995.

Jackson, P. M. (Ed.), Measures for Success in the Public Sector. London 1995.

Jann, W., Public Management Reform in Germany: a revolution without a theory? In: W. Kickert (Ed.), Public Management and Administrative Reform in Western Europe. Papers from the 1995 EGPA conference. Cheltenham, UK 1997, p. 83-102.

KGSt, IKO-Netz. Dokumentation des Gründungssymposiums am 16. Oktober 1996 in Hannover. KGSt-Sonderinformation Nr. 24S vom 31.12.1996.

Klages, H., Strategic Choices in the Process of Planning and Persuing a Quality Award. In: H. Hill, H. Klages (Eds.), Trends in Public Sector Renewal. Frankfurt etc. 1995, 279-292.

Klages, H., K. Masser, Ratios and Indicators as a New and Essential Part of Present Administrative Reform. In: Hill, H. u.a. (Hrsg.), Quality, Innovation and Measurement in the Public Sector, Frankfurt am Main 1996, S.107-136.

Klein, R., N. Carter, Performance Measurement: A review of concepts and issues. In: D. Beeton (Ed.), Performance Measurement: Getting the concepts right. CIPFA paper London 1988, 5-20

Likierman, A., Performance Indicators in the United Kingdom Public Sector: early lessons from managerial use. In: E. Buschor, K. Schedler (Eds.), Perspectives on Performance Measurement and Public Sector Accounting. Bern et al 1994, 129-135.

Loeffler, E., The Modernisation of the Public Sector in an International Comparative Perspective. Speyerer Forschungsberichte 174. Speyer (Germany) 1997.

McKevitt, D., A Lawton, The Manager, the Citizen, the Politician and Performance Measures. In Public Money & Management July-September 1996, S. 49-54.

Meekings, A., Unlocking the Potential of Performance Measurement. a practical implementation guide. In: Public Money &Management Oct/Dez 1995, S. 5-12.

Moe, R. C., The 'Reinventing Government' Exercise: misinterpreting the problem, misjudging the consequences. In: PAR 1994,111-122.

OECD, Benchmarking, Evaluation and Strategic Management in the Public Sector. Paris 1997. [1997a]

OECD, Issues and Developments in Public Management; survey 1996-97. Paris 1997. [1997b]

OECD, Performance Management in Government: performance measurement and results-oriented management. Paris 1994.

Pollitt, C., H. Summa, Trajectories of Reform: public management change in four countries. In: Public Money and Management 1997, 7-18.

Reichard, C., "Neues Steuerungsmodell": local government reforms in Germany. In: W. Kickert (Ed.), Public Management and Administrative Reform in Western Europe. Papers from the 1995 EGPA conference Cheltenham, UK 1997, p. 61-82.

Stewart, J., The Rebuilding of Public Accountability. In: N. Flynn (Ed.), Change in the Civil Service. CIPFA reader, London 1994, 75-79.

Stewart, J., K. Walsh, Performance Measurement: when performance can never be finally defined. In: Public Money & Management April-June 1994, S. 45-49.

Talbot, C., Ministers and Agencies: control, performance and accountability. CIPFA paper, London 1996.

Trosa, S., Chairman's summary. In: OECD, Benchmarking, Evaluation and Strategic Management in the Public Sector. OECD PUMA paper, Paris 1997, 5-9.

Uusikylä, P., Agency Discretion and Public Accountability. In: EGPA, New Trends in Public Administration and Public Law; EGPA yearbook 1996, Budapest 1997, 195-224.

Wright, V., The Paradoxes of Administrative Reform. In: W. Kickert (Ed.), Public Management and Administrative Reform in Western Europe. Papers from the 1995 EGPA conference. Cheltenham, UK 1997, 7-13.

Baromètre de qualité dans le cadre de la Charte Belge des Utilisateurs des Services Publics

P. Staes[*]

1. Origine de la mission, objectifs et définition

1.1. Origine de la mission

La Charte de l'utilisateur des services publics, approuvée le 4 décembre 1992 par le gouvernement et publiée le 22 janvier 1993 au Moniteur belge en même temps que la circulaire n° 370 y afférente, peut se définir le mieux comme un programme politique, destiné à tous les services publics, visant principalement à offrir aux utilisateurs un service public adapté et de qualité.

Afin de concrétiser ces principes, le Ministre de la Fonction publique présente au Gouvernement un rapport global biennal relatif à l'exécution de la Charte. Il y propose un certain nombre de recommandations en vue du développement ultérieur.

Dans le premier rapport présenté en juillet 1994, on a souligné la nécessité de mieux prendre en compte l'utilisateur et ses besoins et de développer un baromètre qui permette de mesurer la satisfaction des utilisateurs par rapport au service offert. En effet: "ce qui est connu peut être offert comme service de qualité et en temps utile selon une nouvelle perspective, tandis que les évaluations émanant des utilisateurs constituent la forme d'information idéale pour parvenir à des améliorations axées sur l'utilisateur et pour valoriser l'existant de manière optimale". Un service défini peut être offert selon une perspective nouvelle en respectant la qualité et les délais.

1.2. Objectifs et définition

Faire appel aux utilisateurs pour évaluer la qualité du service et mesurer leur degré de satisfaction afin de développer des actions d'amélioration sont dès lors les objectifs du projet "baromètre de qualité".

Le baromètre de qualité doit donner une image objective - étayée par des chiffres et évaluations "rigoureuses" - de l'opinion de l'utilisateur.

Le baromètre de qualité doit toutefois éviter de "culpabiliser" l'administration.

L'utilisateur des services publics doit être abordé d'une manière adulte: la Charte déclare en effet à juste titre que "la relation entre les services publics et l'utilisateur ne pourra

---

[*] Patrick Staes, Advies Bureau Conseil, Ministère de la Fonction publique, Belgique.

s'améliorer que si celui-ci ne fait pas seulement valoir ses droits, mais reconnaît également qu'il a certaines obligations ..."

L'apport du citoyen doit avant tout être envisagé de manière positive - en termes d'amélioration - et servir à situer la "responsabilité" et non la "faute".

Définir une image objective à l'aide de chiffres, dans le but d'établir la responsabilité et non la faute, tel est l'objet de l'instrument baromètre. Cela du reste est d'autant plus indispensable lorsque lesdits "utilisateurs" qui seront interrogés ne sont pas les "bénéficiaires" proprement dit et lorsque l'intervention de l'État dont ils profitent implique davantage un aspect de contrôle ou "d'obligation" qu'un aspect de service offert. Par exemple, les divers cas dans lesquels un producteur est contrôlé en ce qui concerne le respect de divers devoirs et conditions, en vue de protéger le consommateur final du bien (par ex. aliments).

2. Méthode

Bien que le secteur privé ait déjà fait de nombreuses recherches au sujet de la mesure de la satisfaction des clients - objet du baromètre de qualité -, il n'était pas possible d'adapter, dans le cas des services publics, un système d'évaluation "prêt à l'emploi".

Des recherches sur le terrain, sous forme de projets-pilotes, dans lesquels des idées théoriques ont été confrontées à la réalité, ont permis la création d'un instrument axé sur les besoins des services publics et adaptés à leur contexte. La faisabilité, autrement dit la "praticabilité" de l'instrument, était aussi une première exigence imposée à l'instrument.

Une caractéristique propre au système est notamment l'introduction de "variables d'environnement" qui permettent d'expliquer pourquoi les utilisateurs ont une telle perception et pas une autre.

Ainsi que nous l'avons déjà dit, la responsabilisation des services publics exige, afin d'éviter d'engendrer une culpabilisation improductive et suscitant des résistances, de tenir compte d'éléments qui constituent l'environnement des services publics mais dont ces derniers n'ont pas toujours le contrôle: l'utilisateur lui-même avec ses connaissances préalables et ses préjugés vis-à-vis de l'autorité, la réglementation parfois complexe et donc difficile à exposer, etc.

3. Le baromètre de qualité: l'instrument

3.1. Aperçu général de la méthode

L'utilisation du baromètre de qualité - qui doit être adapté spécifiquement aux nécessités de chaque service en particulier - comprend 5 étapes:

- L'identification des services ou "produits" fournis au sujet desquels on désire connaître l'appréciation de l'utilisateur.

- La détermination des caractéristiques ou "attributs" des services ou produits que l'on désire évaluer.
- L'identification des "variables d'environnement" au sujet desquelles on recherche de l'information sur l'utilisateur et qui donnent une idée du contexte général au sein duquel l'administration fonctionne.
- L'établissement des formulaires d'enquête, en adaptant les formulaires standard déjà formulés au départ selon diverses "familles de produits". L'enquête par écrit se fait lorsqu'il y a un nombre suffisant de personnes à interroger. S'il s'agit de groupes de personnes restreints ou de groupes fort professionnalisés, on peut élaborer des méthodes d'enquête alternatives, comme des interviews en profondeur.
- Détermination des modalités pratiques d'enquête: moment, public à interroger, ...

3.2. Étape 1: détermination des services ou produits au sujet desquels on désire connaître l'opinion de l'utilisateur

A propos de quelles prestations désire-t-on connaître l'opinion de l'utilisateur ? Pour répondre à cette question fondamentale, on peut s'inspirer de 2 sources:

- examiner ce qui retient déjà maintenant l'attention de l'utilisateur, en relevant les éléments du service offert qui provoquent déjà spontanément ses réactions (par ex. au sujet des réclamations et remarques qu'il émet);
- examiner à partir du "top" de l'organisation ce qui est d'une importance fondamentale pour l'organisation - du point de vue stratégique - et en fonction de quoi le point de vue de l'utilisateur serait apprécié.

Toute cette démarche est tendue vers l'identification de ce qui sera précisément soumis au jugement de l'utilisateur.

3.3. Étape 2: détermination des caractéristiques ou attributs des services sur lesquels on désire interroger l'utilisateur.

Ces attributs déterminent la qualité du service offert et peuvent être rangés sous les catégories suivantes qui reflètent l'accessibilité, l'efficience et l'efficacité:

- accessibilité et disponibilité du service et du prestataire de services;
- rapidité du service offert;
- prévenance dans les contacts avec l'utilisateur;
- exactitude et efficacité du service offert;
- qualité de l'information complémentaire éventuelle accompagnant le service;
- manière (rapidité, correction) de résoudre les problèmes éventuels (le service après-vente).

En d'autres termes: un service offert est qualitativement élevé s'il:

- est facile à atteindre et disponible;
- est fourni rapidement;
- est offert avec prévenance;
- aboutit à des résultats exacts qui satisfont aux besoins de l'utilisateur (est efficace);

- ne se limite pas simplement à ce qui a été demandé, mais donne également des informations complémentaires à l'utilisateur afin de l'aider davantage;
- offre la possibilité -en cas de problème imprévu- de résoudre celui-ci rapidement et correctement ("après-vente").

Dans cette étape, il s'agit d'estimer si toutes ces caractéristiques doivent être reprises dans l'enquête auprès de l'utilisateur, ou bien si l'on accordera plus d'importance à certains éléments.

3.4. Étape 3: détermination des "variables d'environnement" au sujet desquelles on désire recueillir des informations auprès de l'utilisateur et qui donnent une idée du contexte général au sein duquel l'administration fonctionne.

Le fait de savoir si un utilisateur sera ou non satisfait de l'ensemble ou d'un certain nombre d'aspects du service offert, dépend non seulement du prestataire de services lui-même mais également de facteurs sur lesquels il n'a pas toujours prise parce qu'ils ne se rapportent pas directement au prestataire de services lui-même mais à son environnement.

Sont principalement visés ici les facteurs propres à l'utilisateur lui-même, à savoir:

- sa connaissance préalable du prestataire de services et de la législation ou de la procédure que ce dernier applique: par ex. en matière d'information, il sera plus facile de satisfaire un utilisateur qui a déjà de bonnes connaissances préalables par rapport à celui qui n'en a aucune;
- ceci est en effet lié à l'attente de chaque utilisateur individuel: celui qui connaît la procédure sera peut-être plus compréhensif par ex. en matière de délais nécessaires que celui qui ne la connaît pas;
- son attitude a priori en ce qui concerne l'intervention de l'autorité et sa volonté de participer au fonctionnement du service;
- le résultat qu'il obtient: la personne qui obtient un résultat positif, sera sans doute plus indulgente que celle qui obtient un résultat négatif (amende, impôt, contrôle, ...)

Outre les éléments propres à l'utilisateur, on doit également tenir compte d'éléments structurels: la législation en vigueur, les exigences fixées par des organismes extérieurs. Les éléments structurels externes ne sont pas soumis à l'appréciation de l'utilisateur puisque ce dernier n'y intervient pas ou très peu et que son avis sera dés lors peu pertinent. Ces éléments doivent dès lors rester à l'écart de l'instrument actuel.

On peut enfin également insérer d'autres éléments encore dans le formulaire d'enquête qui ont par ex. traité un profil sociologique des divers utilisateurs.

La performance d'un prestataire de services du secteur public est en effet soumise à beaucoup plus de restrictions (externes) que celle d'un prestataire de services dans le secteur privé, de sorte qu'il n'est finalement possible de l'apprécier et de l'analyser qu'en tenant effectivement compte de l'environnement dans lequel le prestataire de services public doit travailler.

3.5. Étape 4.: établissement des formulaires d'enquête, en adaptant les formulaires standard déjà configurés selon diverses "familles de produits".

Dés que l'on connaît les aspects du service offert au sujet, à soumettre à l'appréciation de l'utilisateur, ainsi que les caractéristiques qui sont importantes et les éléments de l'environnement dont il faut tenir compte, on peut élaborer un formulaire d'enquête, sur base de formulaires types développés par le bureau ABC (Advies Bureau Conseil) compte tenu de l'expérience acquise dans les projets-pilotes.

Six formulaires types sont disponibles, représentant chacun une "famille de produits", à savoir:

- "prestations financières et allocations"
- "prestations non financières"
- "cotisations/impôts"
- "informations fournies par l'administration"
- "informations fournies à l'administration/statistiques"
- "contrôle"

Chacun de ces formulaires a ses propres caractéristiques, vu la nature du service offert. Il est possible en effet que certaines caractéristiques soient très pertinentes pour certains genres de produits, mais pas tellement pour d'autres (p. ex. la rapidité du service qui peut être très pertinente pour obtenir une allocation mais moins pertinente lors qu'on "obtient" une amende).

3.6. Étape 5: déterminer les modalités pratiques de l'enquête: moment, public à interroger, etc.

Ces éléments déterminent le déroulement pratique de l'enquête et se rapportent au choix d'un échantillon, au moment et à la périodicité éventuelle de l'enquête, aux modalités éventuelles de renvoi, etc.

4. Les possibilités pratiques de l'instrument.

L'application du baromètre de qualité offre les 3 possibilités suivantes :

- une description de l'appréciation du service par le public;
- un modèle explicatif des éléments qui seraient importants ou même décisifs en première instance pour l'image que se fait le public;
- entreprendre un développement d'actions et établir une fixation de normes de satisfaction du public.

4.1. Description de la façon dont le public apprécie le service.

Par "produit" et par aspect du service, on établit le bilan de la satisfaction des utilisateurs.

Un exemple (fictif mais basé sur des chiffres réels) nous montre les chiffres de satisfaction suivants :

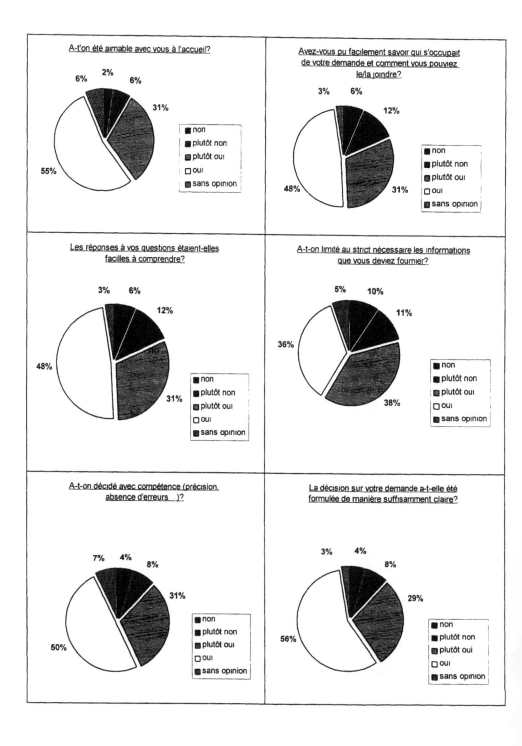

Au total, quelque 25 aspects différents peuvent être représentés ainsi (voir annexe: formulaires d'enquête). Ces données sont descriptives en ce sens qu'elles reflètent uniquement une réalité mais ne l'expliquent pas; on peut bien entendu établir un hit-parade de points forts et faibles, de façon à disposer déjà d'un premier ensemble de "lampes témoins", mais cela n'est pas suffisant en soi: après le "quoi" et le "combien" doit venir le "pourquoi".

4.2. Un modèle explicatif au sujet des éléments importants ou même décisifs pour l'image que se fait le public.

Il est important de savoir dans quelle mesure l'utilisateur est satisfait, mais il est tout aussi important de savoir pourquoi il réagit comme il le fait. Identifier certaines relations causales (ou des hypothèses les concernant) conduit à des actions pertinentes.

4.2.1. Qui est l'utilisateur ?

Le premier élément pour le modèle explicatif se trouve dans le portrait de l'utilisateur.

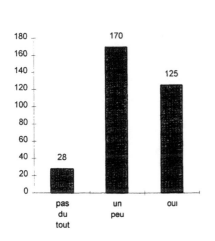
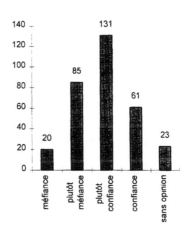

On peut déduire de ce portrait quelles sont les caractéristiques de l'utilisateur: a-t-il déjà été bien informé ou non, est-il positif envers le prestataire du service et envers l'intervention des pouvoirs publics en général ? Ces éléments doivent être pris en compte lors de l'interprétation de l'appréciation que porte l'utilisateur sur la performance du service.

Il serait toutefois erroné de ne pas exploiter ces éléments qui se situent dans le chef de l'utilisateur lui-même et donc en dehors du prestataire du service: l'information de l'utilisateur en général et les actions visant à inciter à plus de coopération et de confiance incombent de toute façon partiellement au prestataire du service, bien qu'il n'en soit évidemment pas le seul responsable.

En outre, il n'y a pas uniquement des éléments venant de l'extérieur qui déterminent l'appréciation de l'utilisateur, il y a également des éléments au sein de la prestation de services même qui - plus que d'autres - jouent un rôle important ou décisif pour l'image qui se fait l'utilisateur.

4.2.2. Y a-t-il certains éléments qui influencent la satisfaction de l'utilisateur plus que d'autres?

Deux questions peuvent se poser à ce sujet:

- quels sont les aspects "centraux" du service (ou de l'environnement) qui déterminent la façon dont l'utilisateur ressent la qualité, et qui peuvent donc être considérés comme **"leviers" dans cette formation d'image** ?
- quels sont les aspects influençant **un aspect spécifique** de l'estimation de la qualité ?

A l'aide de méthode statistiques (analyse de corrélation et grille de corrélations), on trouve en effet **des rapports** entre les divers éléments et variables de la satisfaction:

	Aspect de satisfaction 1 (p ex accessibilité)	Aspect de satisfaction 2 (p ex rapidité du service quant au fond)	Aspect de satisfaction n	Variable de l'environnement (p ex confiance de l'utilisateur dans le service)	Variable de l'environnement n
Aspect de satisfaction 3 (p ex heures d'ouverture)				*(B)*	
Aspect de satisfaction 4 (p ex rapidité de l'accueil)	*(A)*				→
Aspect de satisfaction n					
Variable de l'environnement 2 (p ex connaissance préalable de la part de l'utilisateur)				↓	
Variable de l'environnement n					

- Élément *(A)*: quel est l'élément influençant de façon générale transversalement (c.-à-d. dans un sens général) la façon globale dont l'utilisateur se forme une image ?
- Élément *(B)*: quels sont les éléments déterminants ou qui influencent au moins l'aspect "x" dans la façon dont l'utilisateur se forme une image ?

De l'exemple (fictif mais basé sur des chiffres réels), il apparaît que la rapidité de l'accueil influence - plus que d'autres éléments - transversalement (c.-à-d. globalement) l'appréciation de l'utilisateur: quand on est accueilli rapidement, on passe sur d'autres inconvénients, mais quand on doit attendre, il est difficile de rétablir de bonnes dispositions.

Dans ce cas, la rapidité de l'accueil est un des leviers pour effectuer une amélioration générale de la satisfaction (dans d'autres cas, d'autres facteurs peuvent éventuellement être décisifs).

La détection de pareils facteurs-clés est importante parce qu'elle présente éventuellement la possibilité d'effectuer une amélioration significative (plusieurs facteurs en sont influencés positivement) à coût réduit (un seul facteur est abordé).

4.2.3. Y a-t-il des groupes d'utilisateurs spécifiques faisant preuve chacun d'un "profil propre"?

Dans le cas où d'autres éléments ont été intégrés dans l'enquête, p.ex. des éléments du profil sociologique de l'utilisateur, on peut distinguer certains profils d'utilisateurs ou segments (de marché) sur base d'une comparaison statistique et mettre au point des mesures spécifiques à l'égard de ces groupes (segmentation).

4.3. Entreprendre des actions et établir des normes à l'égard de la satisfaction du public à poursuivre

La partie descriptive de l'analyse (point 4.1.) présente, comme dit ci-dessus, déjà naturellement quelques réflexions importantes en matière d'actions possibles: on peut établir un hit-parade de points forts et faibles.

La partie explicative offre en plus la possibilité de préciser le profil de l'utilisateur lui-même et d'y adapter spécifiquement l'intervention des pouvoirs publics; la segmentation est ici le mot-clé. Enfin, la détection de leviers et action au sein du service offre des possibilités supplémentaires d'intervenir efficacement et d'obtenir de bons résultats avec des moyens mesurés malgré tout.

Enfin, la définition de "segments d'utilisateurs" offre la possibilité d'orienter des actions vers certains groupes.

En ce qui concerne les normes elles-mêmes, il n'existe actuellement pas de normes a priori relatives au degré de satisfaction des utilisateurs.

Il faut évidemment viser une satisfaction 100%, mais en pratique cela est vraisemblablement hors d'atteinte.

C'est sans doute d'une part, par une comparaison entre services comparables et formes de prestation de services, et d'autre part, en suivant historiquement les résultats le long des années que des normes peuvent être créées.

Annexe 1.

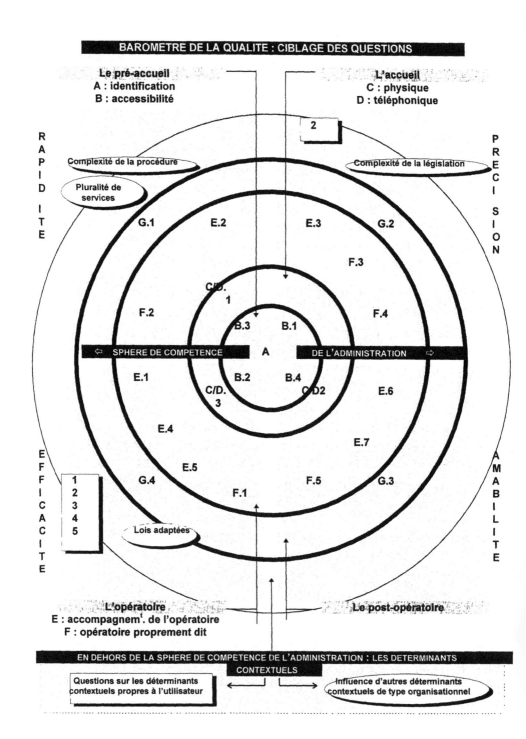

Annexe 2. Un exemple d'un des 6 formulaires: la famille des services financiers et allocations.

QUEL EST VOTRE DEGRE DE SATISFACTION (noircissez la case d'une des colonnes à droite des questions)	Oui ☺☺	Plutôt oui ☺	Plutôt non ☹	Non ☹☹	Sans opinion
A. Avez-vous pu facilement savoir à quel service vous devez vous adresser pour obtenir CETTE ALLOCATION ?	☐	☐	☐	☐	☐
B. Avez-vous dû vous rendre dans ce service ? Si non→ Passez aux questions D Si oui→ Comment atteindre le service ?					
1 Avez-vous pu facilement connaître son adresse et ses heures d'ouverture ?	☐	☐	☐	☐	☐
2 Les heures d'ouverture de ce service vous conviennent-elles ?	☐	☐	☐	☐	☐
3 Peut-on rejoindre facilement ce service (distances, transports publics utilisables, chemins d'accès, places de parking) ?	☐	☐	☐	☐	☐
4 Peut-on pénétrer facilement dans ses locaux (escaliers, ascenseurs, etc.) ?	☐	☐	☐	☐	☐
C. Comment vous a-t-on accueilli(e) à l'entrée des locaux ?					
1 Vous a-t-on accueilli(e) rapidement (file d'attente,) ?	☐	☐	☐	☐	☐
2 A-t-on été aimable avec vous à l'accueil ?	☐	☐	☐	☐	☐
3 L'accueil vous a-t-il orienté(e) vers le bon service ?	☐	☐	☐	☐	☐
D. Avez-vous dû téléphoner au service ? Si non→ Passez aux questions E Si oui→ Comment le/la téléphoniste vous a-t-il/elle répondu ?					
1 Le/la téléphoniste vous a-t-il/elle répondu rapidement ?	☐	☐	☐	☐	☐
2 A-t-il/elle été aimable avec vous ?	☐	☐	☐	☐	☐
3 Vous a-t-il/elle mis(e) en communication avec le bon service ?	☐	☐	☐	☐	☐
E. Comment a-t-on répondu à votre demande d'allocation ?					
1 Avez-vous pu facilement savoir quel agent s'occupait de votre allocation et comment vous pouviez le joindre (nom, n° de téléphone...) ?	☐	☐	☐	☐	☐
2 A-t-on répondu avec rapidité aux questions que vous avez posées en vue d'obtenir votre allocation ?	☐	☐	☐	☐	☐
3 A-t-on répondu avec précision à ces questions ?	☐	☐	☐	☐	☐
4 Les réponses à ces questions étaient-elles faciles à comprendre ?	☐	☐	☐	☐	☐
5 Ces réponses vous ont-elles aidé(e) ?	☐	☐	☐	☐	☐
6 Vous a-t-on aidé(e) à remplir les formalités ?	☐	☐	☐	☐	☐
7 A-t-on été aimable et attentif ?	☐	☐	☐	☐	☐

F. Comment-a-t-on décidé ?

1. A-t-on limité au strict nécessaire les informations que vous deviez fournir ? ☐ ☐
2. La décision sur votre demande d'allocation a-t-elle été rapide ? ☐ ☐ ☐
3. A-t-on décidé avec compétence (précision, absence d'erreurs) ? ☐ ☐ ☐
4. La décision sur votre demande d'allocation a-t-elle été formulée de manière suffisamment claire ? ☐ ☐ ☐
5. Vous a-t-on communiqué cette décision avec politesse ? ☐ ☐

G. Si vous avez posé des questions sur la décision prise, ou si vous l'avez contestée :

1. A-t-on répondu avec rapidité à ces questions ? ☐ ☐ ☐ ☐
2. A-t-on répondu avec précision à ces questions ? ☐ ☐ ☐ ☐
3. A-t-on répondu avec amabilité à ces questions ? ☐ ☐ ☐ ☐
4. Les réponses étaient-elles faciles à comprendre ? ☐ ☐ ☐

AUTRES QUESTIONS

	\multicolumn{4}{c}{RÉPONSES}
	Oui		Un peu	Pas du tout
1. Connaissez-vous la mission de ce service ?	☐		☐	☐
2. Connaissez-vous la législation qu'applique ce service ?	Oui ☐		Un peu ☐	Pas du tout ☐
3. Etes-vous disposé(e) à coopérer avec ce service ?	Oui ☐	Peut-être ☐	Un peu ☐	Non ☐ Sans opinion ☐
4. Avez-vous confiance dans les services publics ?	Confiance ☐	Plutôt confiance ☐	Plutôt méfiance ☐	Méfiance ☐ Sans opinion ☐
5. L'allocation que vous avez reçue est-elle satisfaisante c'est-à-dire suffisante et équitable ?	Oui ☐	Plutôt oui ☐	Plutôt non ☐	Non ☐ Sans opinion ☐

The Gatekeepers of the Common Good
Power and the Public Service Ethos[1]

D. Richards and M. J. Smith[*]

1. Introduction

The operation of Whitehall has been built on the notion of a public service ethos. Traditionally, this ethos has been defended by both conservative and liberal opinion as something fundamentally good. However, we wish to contend that, in reality, the public service ethos is a power/knowledge system which has legitimised the rule of a particular elite by presenting public service as a worthy occupation and, thereby, authorising a system of power which is relatively closed and secretive.

In this text, we first set out to provide a definition, or, in the very least, a description, of what has traditionally constituted a public service ethos. This, in itself, is no simple task, as, due to the nature of the British political system, there is an absence of any formal codification of the elements which, in part, go to make up such an ethos. We argue that during the last eighteen years, the Conservative Administration, suspicious of the public sector and drawing on elements of New Right ideology, introduced a series of long-term, managerial reforms which undermined a number of the key pillars of the public service ethos. However, while the Thatcher and Major Governments challenged a number of elements of the traditional post-war consensus, they remained constitutionally conservative. Thus, we argue that despite the introduction of managerialism into Whitehall in order change the balance in power relations, away from civil servants and in favour of ministers, there has been no explicit attempt made to redefine the public service ethos.

Instead, we contend that the reality of the public service ethos has, in the past, been as a form of power legitimisation for civil servants enabling them to act as a brake on ministerial excess. Nevertheless, managerialism has weakened the ability of civil servants to temper ministerial power. Therefore, we believe that, despite the broad attack on public service by the last Conservative Administration, it is ironic that, in the wake of the first Nolan Report (1996), the public service ethos has received a formal reaffirmation of both its health and vibrancy. We conclude by arguing that the public service ethos continues to exist as a rhetorical device which underpins minister/civil servant relations. However, there is a clear dissonance between the rhetoric used both by government and public servants and the reality of the balance of power in this crucial relationship. Finally, we believe this also highlights the discernible gap between an Administration which laid claim to being ideologically radical, yet, throughout its life span, remained constitutionally, conservative.

---

[*] Dr. David Richards, Lecturer, School of Politics and Communications Studies, University of Liverpool, United Kingdom. Dr. Martin J. Smith, Senior Lecturer, Department of Politics, University of Sheffield, United Kingdom

2. Defining a Public Service Ethos

Despite the many treatise available, it is difficult to conceptualise what constitutes a public service ethos. Indeed, when one former Cabinet Secretary was recently asked to provide his own definition of such an ethos he observed that, it is, at best, 'a portmanteau concept'. In fact, it is because of the very existence of the Haldane principle[2] which espouses the interdependent relationship between ministers and officials, that British public servants, along with their political masters, have consistently and successfully resisted outside pressure to introduce any statutory codification of ethics, in order to create a more formal definition of a public service ethos. Thus, without wishing to appear tendentious, the established line has been: 'we men *(sic)*, who make-up the senior ranks of the Civil Service, have been drawn from the *creme-de-la-creme* of society and, as such, by our very nature, have a sense of what is just, right, good and proper. These qualities we possess are both innate (in that we have inherited them from previous generations of our social class) and learnt (through the system of social and academic education to which we have privileged access). As such, it is almost impossible for us to provide, for outsiders, any form of practical codification of such qualities'. Again, the same former Cabinet Secretary provides a clear testimony of such a disposition:

> I think one can try to define it [a public service ethos], try to make it articulate...but in the end it is going to be example that carries it through. I do not believe one can rely solely...on codes or guidances to do so...I think it would be impossible to try to prescribe in too much detail what flows from the sense of public service or the public service ethos. (Armstrong 1997: 7)

Despite the absence of any formal ethical code, it is possible, through the testimonies of public servants and academic writings and, by a series of conventions which inform the (un)written Constitution, to compile some evidence of the various elements which constitute a British public service ethos. In 1996, the summary section of the Nolan Committee's First Report on Standards in Public Life, pronounced that there was seven principles of public life; selflessness, integrity, objectivity, accountability, openness, honesty and leadership. These could have been the very same principles espoused by Northcote-Trevelyan one hundred and fifty years earlier and, later, reiterated by Haldane, Hankey and Fisher. More particularly, civil servants, through their social status, education, training and a process of socialisation, have been implicitly trusted to maintain and uphold these principles. This set of principles has been shaped and informed by the various cultures of Whitehall and underpinned by a framework of ethics. The ethics which shaped Whitehall were based upon the Victorian Idealist, T.H.Green (1879, 1883). O'Toole contends that, in the same way that the organisational framework of Whitehall was constructed by Northcote-Trevelyan, similarly, it was T.H.Green who provided the ethical framework within which civil servants developed integrity in their work. Concomitantly, this led to their ministerial masters tacitly accepting them as being politically neutral.

What is interesting is that, because of the nature of the British Constitution, not one official statement exists which can be seen as a binding, legal document formally outlining the duties and responsibilities of officials. Nor do any explicitly state what ethical and professional considerations an official should make. Quite clearly, the readily accepted view in Westminster/Whitehall circles has been that the distinctive character of the British

Civil Service has been based on a general code or ethos, which, although unwritten, almost mystical in character is, nevertheless, very real and powerful.

In trying to identify what constitutes a public service ethos, we believe that officials have traditionally been perceived, by their political masters, to have been conferred with integrity in their work. This, in turn, has enabled public servants to be regarded as politically, neutral, actors. Although, the public service ethos has never been formally codified, indeed, due to its intangible nature it cannot be, it has, until recently, established and re-confirmed the three mantras on which the modern day Civil Service was established - neutrality, anonymity and permanence. In so doing, the public service ethos has enabled officials to act in such a way as to provide an effective check on ministerial power. This has been one of their most fundamental roles and is at the heart of the Whitehall/Westminster system.

Nevertheless in recent years a number of commentators have argued that the introduction of new public management has challenged the public sector ethos by introducing private sector values and practices (see Pratchett 1994; Sheaff and West 1997; Wrigley and McKevitt 1994). The apparent undermining of these values and practices appears to be empirically supported by the setting up and findings of the Scott, Nolan and Oughton reports and the Public Accounts Committee report of 1994 (O'Toole 1995; 1997; Efficiency Unit 1993)[3]. The almost unanimous defence of the traditional public service ethos by academics, politicians and officials suggests that the ethos is seen as intrinsically good. However, the central thesis of this paper is that the public service ethos is not a neutral set of values which ensures the ethical behaviour of officials but, a power/knowledge system which protects a particular elite. This is not to support the values of new public management but to highlight that the defence of a system of ethics is also protecting particular sets of power relationships.

2.1. Re-Defining the Public Sector Ethos: a Power/Knowledge Construct

Much of the discussion about the public service ethos has revolved around the notion that it is good to have officials who are committed to certain ethics and that managerialism is either challenging that ethos or improving on it. It is our contention that this position misses the point and the central element of the public service ethos is that it is a system of power which protects officials and ministers. What is clear is that this system of power has been tested by the reforms to the Civil Service and it raises the question of the extent to which the public service ethos remains an effective bulwark against ministerial power or, alternatively, whether it has now become simply a chimera.

It is a widespread assumption that the public service ethos is a good thing and the introduction of private sector values threatens the beneficial values which suffuse the British Civil Service. However, the public sector ethos is not a neutral set of values concerned with the public good, but an ideology aimed at protecting a particular conception of the Civil Service. The core of the public service ethos is built on two separate, but linked, ideas: the political neutrality of officials and their pecuniary and moral integrity. Officials do not go into public service for financial gain: those who are concerned with money making are seen as narrow and self interested (see Weiner 1981).

One former DTI official who spent most of his career in the private sector informed us: 'Officials are more rounded than average business people. People from the private sector are driven by a business ethic which is much narrower'.

The public service ethos is normatively good because it is built round a notion of integrity which is personal (not open to corruption), political (officials serve their ministers) and financial (they are not there to make money). Officials then are doing good: they are serving the public and ministers and they are doing it for the good of society, not for the good of themselves. Again, to quote Lord Armstrong:

> I think the sense of being in the service of the public, in the service of the state, if you like, of doing things that are worthwhile in that context and being able to make a personal contribution to the well-being of the public interest and the state is a very real consideration which we should be very greatly impoverished if we lost....that ethos is something of great value and strength to this country (Armstrong 1997: 7).

Such a position has a strong resonance with the British Civil Service because it reaffirms their political neutrality - they serve the elected politicians. The public sector ethos underpins the whole ethos of the Civil Service because it is concerned with demonstrating officials' lack of self interest and reinforcing the view that they serve ministers and the public.

The problem with these values is that they have been constructed as independent, normatively good and politically neutral. Of course, the reality is that they are a set of socially constructed values which protect the interests of officials and to some extent politicians. The public sector ethos is about maintaining a particular perception of the Civil Service which both identifies and hides the nature of their power. It identifies the power of officials because it places the determination of the public good in their hands and it hides it by presuming their neutrality and the purity of their motives. Officials are working for the public good and, therefore, they have no interest in power for its own sake. At the same time, the ethos identifies politicians as the decision-makers.

The central value and one which is continually repeated is the notion of integrity. As the Armstrong Memorandum states: 'It is the duty of civil servants to serve their ministers with integrity'. This integrity is important because it provides officials with power in a number of ways. First, if officials have integrity they can be trusted. Therefore, when a minister tells officials to do something they do it. However, more importantly, ministers cannot continually relay their wishes to officials and, thus, they have to trust officials to do what they want without any explicit instructions.

Second, it means that officials can define what is in the public good. This point links conceptions to the public sector ethos with secrecy. The decision making process in Britain is highly secret. Secrecy was permissible because officials could be trusted to make decisions in the right way and to do what was best for the public good. The Arms to Iraq affair is full of cases where decisions were made not to inform the public because it was believed adverse public reaction would disrupt the sales of arms and this was against the 'public interest'. It is interesting that with the publication of the Labour Government's White Paper on Freedom of Information in December 1997, Whitehall officials ensured that exemption will be guaranteed for: 'the integrity of the decision-making process in government' (*The Times*: 12 December 1997). In effect, this will ensure that any Freedom of Information Act will exclude the right to reveal discussions between ministers and civil servants concerning policy matters.

A crucial consequence of the public sector ethos is to provide officials with autonomy by denying they have autonomy. The integrity of officials is based on the idea that they serve the will of the minister. In this sense they lack decisional autonomy - it is the minister who makes the decision and it is left to the official to implement. This is a crucial value within Whitehall and in some ways accounts for the conflicts which occurred in the Home Office when Derek Lewis was Chief Executive of the Prison Service. Lewis believed that in switching from the private sector to operating in a semi-autonomous agency, he could make decisions independently. The Home Secretary, Michael Howard, believed that he was a civil servant who should do as he was told.

Nevertheless, there is a tendency for officials to see themselves as guardians of the public interest and to place themselves in a position to override ministers in exceptional cases. This concurs with the almost Platonic like status endowed on civil servants (see O'Toole: 1990; 1995). Perhaps the most famous example is Clive Ponting leaking documents relating to the sinking of the Belgrano because he believed it was in the public interest. As Ponting told a select committee: 'the Civil Service, as the one continuing institution in government, does see itself as the guardian of the way in which British government should work and as holding this in trust whilst the temporary occupants, the politicians, are in power' (Ponting 1985: 104). Similar examples occur in relation to Tony Benn, who officials believed was not always acting in the public interest. As one Industry official admitted: 'The department would brief him for a meeting with industrialists or trade unionists and he would then show them the brief...Of course it didn't do him any good because we immediately started writing different kinds of briefs'. This statement is revelatory in two senses. First, officials were clearly going against the wishes of the minister. Second, they determined that it was not in the public interest for official briefs to be revealed. The way this set of values reinforced the position of the Civil Service in the 1950s and 1960s is revealed by a former Home Office official:

> "It was a pretty self confident department when I first joined in 1959, still pretty elitist and exclusive in the administrative class and the people had a considerable confidence in their own judgement in the 1950s. Ministers were, I don't think its fair to say manipulated, but the department had their views that they would seek to impose on ministers and certainly attempt to persuade ministers to accept...So I think the main characteristics were confidence, sometimes bordering on simple arrogance, a sense that ministers were not terribly important, but a sense of professionalism and integrity which was immensely powerful and ministers were not, as it were, in the middle of things."

The crucial point here is that because officials had integrity, it was justifiable for them to 'persuade' ministers. They were acting in the public, not their own, interest.

This perception creates two related problems. It is clear that officials often do make decisions, either directly over executive matters, or indirectly, by persuading ministers to adopt a particular policy option. However, because the public sector ethos presupposes a lack of autonomy by officials, they are rarely held to account and even less often made responsible for decisions. Also, officials are doing what ministers want - and clearly ministers have a strong interest in maintaining that fiction - thus, it is ministers, not officials, who are held to account.

The importance of integrity defines what senior officials do and value. As officials are concerned with the smooth functioning of government in the public interest, their crucial role is to provide knowledge and experience. As they are neutral, they can provide 'the facts' and their experience of government empowers them to warn the minister off any plan which they consider may lack sufficient realism to be implemented.

The public sector ethos provides a framework for official influence. Through their integrity they can do the 'objective analysis' and advise the minister on the best course of action. However, if they fail to influence the minister, the ethos also justifies and legitimises their behaviour because it is for the minister to decide and the official to implement his or her wishes.

Officials are arbiters of what government and ministers should do but, curiously, the role of advising is viewed as separate from management. Management is something which occurs in the private sector or in the lower echelons of the public service. Senior officials are not managers but 'policy advisors' giving ministers the wealth of their experience and knowledge on how to deal with problems. As one senior official said, despite changes in management techniques: 'officials do not have the experience to manage change'. Another Home Office official confirms: 'Most of them will still, if you give them a budget, run a mile because they don't know what it is'. They want to be involved in policy formation in a cerebral, rather than managerial, way and this again accounts for some recent conflicts when ministers are clear what policy they want and are only concerned with officials delivering it.

Therefore, the public service ethos is a framework for Civil Service power which is not based on dominance of ministers but is concerned with protecting their position in the policy making process. A useful way of conceptualising Civil Service power is within Foucault's framework of power/knowledge:

> There is no power relation without the correlative constitutions of a field of knowledge, nor any knowledge that does not presuppose and constitute at the same time power relations...the subject who knows, the objects to be known and the modalities of knowledge must be regarded as so many effects of these fundamental implications of power knowledge (Foucault 1977: 27-28).

Civil servants have a clear epistemology and linked ethics which is based on the notion of integrity, objectivity and neutrality. It is this epistemology which is the basis of their power. Officials define and control objective knowledge - they define who knows and what is known and the modalities of the knowledge - and it is this control and indeed, construction of knowledge which empowers them. As it is based on 'fact', neutrality and integrity, it is very difficult for ministers to challenge this information without their being regarded as difficult or dogmatic. As much of it is secret and presented in terms of the public interest, it is hard for the public or outsiders to challenge (on issues of accountability see Flinders 1997).

A second important issue which reflects the position of officials is that their system of power/knowledge is effectively self-regulating. There is no Civil Service Act in Britain defining the duties of officials and, therefore, transgressions of Civil Service norms are adjudicated not by external actors but by the Head of the Home Civil Service - the Cabinet Secretary. There is some ambiguity concerning both when officials are acting. For example, is it acceptable to whistle blow to another department or to Parliament, if a Minister is acting improperly; many officials think it is (see Barker and Wilson 1997). Indeed, Chapman (1988: 305) uses the example of the Establishment's Officers Guide to highlight what he regards as the complacency of the official view of ethics and leads him to conclude that control is being exercised largely through a process of socialisation and the role of leading civil servants. It is perhaps indicative of these leaders that one of them, William Armstrong, could say without irony, that he was accountable to himself which was a great taskmaster: 'I am accountable to my own ideal of a civil servant' (quoted in Chapman 1988: 306).

2.2. Undermining the Public Sector Ethos

So far we have argued that the public service ethos can be more appropriately understood as a Foucaultian power/knowledge concept, than as, to return to the Robert Armstrong explanation - a portmanteau concept. Nevertheless, despite the existing problems of conceptualisation, we contend that the notion of a public service ethos has, traditionally, been a very real and powerful tool civil servants have relied on to empower themselves in relation to ministers. Despite this, we believe that in the last eighteen years, the public service ethos has been seriously undermined by the last Conservative administration's radical reforms of the central machinery of government. Yet, despite their broad attack on public service and, more particularly, on the foundations on which the public service ethos is grounded, we conclude, ironically, by arguing that it remains in the interests of both officials and ministers to maintain the myth that the public service ethos remains alive and vibrant.

The public service ethos operated smoothly in a particular, historical, context. It could work within the post-war era because of deference and consensus. Deference meant that people were, on the whole, prepared to accept closed Whitehall policy making without questioning policy makers. The consensus meant that officials had a relatively clear idea of what ministers from either party wanted to achieve. Hence, they were permitted a relatively large degree of autonomy in developing policy within that framework which was seen as essentially one of pragmatism rather than ideology. A number of officials reported how, in the 1950s - especially with fewer junior ministers - they were left very much to their own devices.

From the late 1960s, a number of factors have changed this context and to some extent began to challenge the public sector ethos. During that decade, government was seen to be failing. The elitist Whitehall machine was not regarded as providing either political or economic success. With political failure in Suez and increasing awareness of economic decline, respect for the *ancien regime* began to diminish. Many of the old institutions in Britain were questioned and the complacent continuation of the old ways was threatened. In response to these concerns, the Fulton Committee was established in 1966 to examine the 'structure, recruitment and management' of the Civil Service. The Fulton Report was critical of the amateurism of the Civil Service and called for professionalisation and the imposition of greater managerialism. Although many of the Fulton recommendations floundered on Civil Service resistance, they did indicate a questioning of many of the traditional values (see Hennessy 1991; Kellner and Crowther Hunt 1980; and Fry 1993 for a full account).

In the wake of the failure of Fulton to institutionalise radical reform, stress on the ethos was exacerbated in the 1970s, by what appeared to be 'Government overload' and the perceived inability of Administrations to meet the demands of its constituencies. This resulted in a loss of legitimacy and the decline of deference (Jessop 1974; King 1975; Beer 1982). Ministers in a number of Labour Governments were less enamoured of their officials and they were concerned that, through their autonomy, they were pursuing their own policies, rather than those of the government (see Crossman 1974; Benn 1980; Castle 1984). Whilst a number of academic, journalistic and political works pointed to the failures of the official machinery (Balogh 1959; Sampson 1962; Hennessy 1990).

Second, there was the challenge presented by the Thatcher Government (and Thatcherism) to the consensus and its lack of faith in the public sector. This was a reaction to what the new Government conceived as an elitist, 'world-weary' and defeatist view of politics festering away in the corridors of Whitehall. Thatcher did not value the public sector ethos, because that was associated with big government and ministers being dominated by officials (Fry 1995). She argued that officials would have an insidious affect on the radical policies her Government proposed. The solution was the introduction of market values as a way to reassert ministers' managerial control and to improve the efficiency of the Civil Service. Crucially, she explicitly wanted to 'deprivilege' the Civil Service, in order that it operated in a similar world as the private sector.

Thus, the Conservative Administration, driven by a strong anti-statist instinct, implemented a series of Whitehall reforms which have been widely referred to as New Public Management (NPM). Here, it is not our intention to chart the various reforms introduced by the Conservatives during their eighteen years in office; this is well documented elsewhere (see Campbell and Wilson 1995; Fry 1995; Foster and Plowden 1996; Theakston 1996; Richards 1997). However, it should be noted that the reforms of the Conservative Administration succeeded, where in the past, most notably under Fulton, they had failed, because of the enthusiasm and support displayed at the highest political levels (including both Prime Ministers Thatcher and Major). This ensured that the dynamism of the reforms was neither dissipated nor undermined by inside resistance. The outcome was that throughout the Conservative's time in office, Whitehall underwent a dynamic evolution which transformed much of the structure, personnel and culture of the central bureaucracy.

Thus, eighteen years of Conservative Administration brought about the imposition on Whitehall of: private sector work practises; performance-related pay; the contracting out of officials to semi-autonomous agencies; a change in the demands placed on senior officials; and the corroding effect of serving the same Government for such an extended period of time. Despite these changes, the intransigent senior mandarin cadre continued to support the notion that the public service ethos remained unaffected. Despite the continual reassertions that the public service is still strong (O'Toole 1995: 91), there is little doubt that the values system which underpins the civil service is in flux. For the first time since Northcote Trevellyan, the edifice which has legitimised the role of officials is under severe threat and there are competing notions of the ethics of the public service.

2.3. Competing Conceptions of the Public Sector Ethos

The notion of the public sector ethos as power/knowledge suggests that there could be competing power/knowledge frameworks intended to reformulate the balance of power within the core executive. The New Right's critique of bureaucracy is based on a direct challenge to the notion of public service: individuals are utility maximisers and, therefore, they are motivated by self-interest. The basis of the public sector ethos is idealist not utilitarian and officials subsume private interests to the state (see O'Toole 1990). New Right ideology is a direct counterpoint to the public service ethos. These two ideologies are based on contrasting ontologies; altruistism and egotism. Thus, from the New Right perspective, officials are not neutral; they will try to subvert ministers' intentions to protect their own interests. Therefore, they cannot be self-regulating; they have to be subject to external audit whether from ministers or performance indicators.

The last Conservative administration partially drew on the New Right critique of bureaucracy, in order to challenge the existing public sector ethos. They were broadly critical of the ethos because it placed a high value on public service, legitimised the role of a relatively closed and privileged elite, and it provided a significant role for officials in the policy process. Consequently, much of the Thatcherite reforms were concerned with imposing managerial accountability and reasserting ministerial prerogative. In so doing, they challenged the existing ethics of the Civil Service (O'Toole 1990). At the same time, wider economic and social changes have resulted in a questioning of the privileged position of the Whitehall mandarinate legitimising the criticisms of politicians. Thus, the Thatcher years did see some changes in the relationship between Ministers and officials with a shift away from the traditions of the Haldane model (Richards 1997). Instead of officials being partners, they increasingly became 'implementors rather than policy analysts' (Campbell and Wilson 1995: 61). For example, one permanent secretary we interviewed was very explicit about how he conceptualised his role. He was there to transform the department into one which saw its role primarily as servicing the minister rather than developing its independent expertise.

Moreover, the problem for the defenders of the public sector ethos is that it is a fragile structure. It is built on a set of interlinked concepts; neutrality, integrity, self-regulation; and public non-pecuniary, service. Without neutrality it is difficult to maintain integrity. Without integrity there cannot be self-regulation. Whilst, the introduction of pecuniary interests, more broadly, raises questions of neutrality, integrity and self-regulation. However, while challenges to various pillars of the public sector ethos seem many, Conservative and Labour politicians and senior civil servants have been vociferous in their defence of the public service ethos. Both argue that although there have been many changes to the organisation of government, the values which underpin the public sector ethos remain very much in place. As Robin Mountfield (1997), Permanent Secretary at the Office of Public Services said in a recent speech:

> One thing - a crucial element of the British Civil Service for well over a century - has not changed: the commitment to a non-political, and politically neutral, service. This commitment allowed us, with some confidence, to respond to a long predicted change of government in the belief that we would quickly be able to demonstrate, if there were a change, not only our professionalism and experience, but our genuine and deeply-rooted political neutrality. This [Labour]Government has a deep commitment to public service as an honourable profession...We will do all we can to support the ethos of the public service'.

So, despite 18 years of structural reform and ideological challenge, and the development of a new relationships between ministers and officials, the public sector ethos is still, apparently, firmly in place. However, what this paper shows is the extent to which dissonance exists between the structure of power within government and the ideology of the public sector ethos. This view is symptomatic of the British political system: a tendency to deny that structural changes have any constitutional implication.

3. Conclusion: The Public Service Ethos and the Persistence of Barmecidal Power

There can be little doubt that, at present, there is confusion within the Civil Service concerning its identity and its role. On one side, New Right influenced governments have challenged the post-war conception of the Civil Service and have attempted to reassert the dominance of ministers over officials (see Foster and Plowden 1996). But at the same time all the key actors have rejected any notion that there has been an attempt to undermine the public sector ethos or its traditional values. It is perhaps ironic that the Nolan Committee, set up to examine standards in public life, ended up, more or less, reasserting the traditional public sector ethos (as defined in the first section of this article). The attack on the Civil Service during eighteen years of Conservative Administration has, paradoxically, also provided an opportunity for Whitehall to reassert, rather than allow their political masters to rethink, the ethos. There can be little question that whilst the public sector ethos has become increasingly fragile, there is a lack of a coherent alternative.

How do we explain this paradox of structural reform but ideological conservatism? First, the Conservative Administration was never solely dominated by the New Right. Many of their perceptions of the state were influenced by traditional conservatism and, therefore, they retain the commitment to Parliamentary Sovereignty, an unwritten constitution and a neutral Civil Service (Smith 1996). Consequently, their attitude to the Civil Service was always confused and ambiguous and there was never an attempt to create a pure New Right model of bureaucracy. Even Thatcher, when speaking about civil servants as individuals, rather than Whitehall as an institution, was keen to praise their commitment and professionalism (Richards 1997).

As such, whilst there have been critics of the Whitehall model and the public sector ethos (see Hoskyns 1983), no coherent alternative to the public sector ethos developed within the context of the Conservative's reforms of the state. Moreover, if such a replacement to the traditional model had existed, it would have challenged not only the Civil Service, but the whole edifice of the British Parliamentary state. By changing the role of officials, the nature of the constitution, the role of parliament and ministerial accountability would also have been brought into question. Therefore, both officials and politicians have a strong interest in maintaining the existing system, partly because it is self-regulating and partly because it maintains the fiction that officials are only the advisors and politicians are responsible for making decisions. By asserting the dominance of ministers, developing alternative sources of policy advice, making officials managers rather than policy advisers and through imposing managerial accountability, officials and ministers now live in a hybrid world. There has been a considerable challenge to the professional ethic, but the illusion persists that the traditional ethos still governs behaviour and that officials remain, more than capable of performing their role as gate-keepers of the common good.

Bibliography

Armstrong, R. (1997) 'Minutes of Evidence, 12 November 1996' *House of Lords Select Committee on the Public Service Session 1996-97* London: HMSO.

Balogh, T. (1959) 'The Apotheosis of the Dilettante: the Establishment of Mandarins' in H. Thomas (ed) *The Establishment: a Symposium*, London: Anthony Blond.

Barker, A. and Wilson, G. (1997) 'Whitehall's Disobedient Servants? Senior Officials' Potential Resistance to Ministers in British Government Departments', *British Journal of Political Science*, 27, 223-246.

Beer, S. (1982) *Britain Against Itself*, London: Faber.

Benn, T. (1980) *Arguments for Democracy*, London: Jonathan Cape.

Brecht, A. (1959) *Political Theory* Princeton: Princeton University Press.

Cabinet Office (1996) *The Civil Service Code* London: HMSO.

Campbell, C. and Wilson, G. (1995) *The End of Whitehall Death of a Paradigm*, Oxford: Blackwell.

Castle, B. (1984) *The Castle Diaries 1964-70*, London Weidenfeld,

Chapman, R.A.. (1988) *Ethics in the British Civil Service*, London: Routledge.

Cmnd.3909, (1931) *Royal Commission on the Civil Service 1929-31* [Tomlin Report] London: HMSO.

Crossman, R. (1972) *Inside View*, London: Jonathon Cape

Dowding, K (1995) *The Civil Service* London: Routledge.

FDA News, (1984) *The Establishment Officers' Guide* December 1984.

Flinders, M. (1997) *Forms of Accountability*, University of Sheffield.

Foster, C. and Plowden, F. (1996) *The State Under Stress*, Milton Keynes: Open University Press

Foucault, M. (1977) *Discipline and Punish. Birth of the Prison*, New York: Random House.

Fry, G. (1993) *Reforming the Civil Service The Fulton Committee in the British Home Civil Service 1966-68*, Edinburgh: Edinburgh University Press.

Fry, G. (1995) *Policy and Management in the British Civil Service*, Hemel Hempstead: Harvester Wheatsheaf.

Gilmour, I. (1992) *Dancing with Dogma*, London: Simon and Schuster

Gray, A. & Jenkins, B. (1996) 'Public Administration and Government 1994-96' *Parliamentary Affairs*, 49, 235-55

Green, T.H. (1879) *Lectures on the Principles of Political Obligation* London: Longmans

Green, T.H. (1883) *Prologemena to Ethics,* New York: Cromwell.

Haldane, R.B. (1918) *Report of the Machinery of Government Committee Ministry of Reconstruction,* Cmnd.9230. London:HMSO.

Hennessy, P. (1990) *Whitehall,* London: Fontana

HM Treasury (1996) *1995-96 Fraud Report: An Analysis of Reported Fraud in Government Departments* London:HMSO

Hoskyns, J. (1983) Whitehall and Westminster: An Outsider's View, *Parliamentary Affairs*, 36, 137-147.

Jessop, B. (1974) *Traditionalism Conservatism and British Political Culture*, London: Allen and Unwin.

Kellner, P. and Crowther Hunt, N. (1980) *The Civil Service An Enquiry into Britain's Ruling Class,* London: Macdonald.

King, A. (1975) 'Overload: problems of governing in the 1970s', *Political Studies*, 23, 289-96

Lane, J-E. (1993) *The Public Sector: Concepts, Models and Approaches* London: Sage.

Massey, A (1993), *Managing the Public Sector: A Comparative Analysis of the United Kingdom and the United States,* Cambridge: Cambridge University Press.

Mellon E. (1997) 'Managerial Values: Executives in Transition'

Mountfield, R. (1997) 'The British Public Management Reform Experience', *Paper to the IDPM Public Management for the 21st Century Conference*, 1 July, University of Manchester.

Northcote-Trevelyan (1854) *Report on the Organisation of the Permanent Civil Service* Cmnd.1713 London:HMSO.

O'Toole, B. (1990), 'T.H.Green and the Ethics of Senior Officials in British Central Government', *Public Administration*, Vol.68/3. London:Blackwell.

O'Toole, B. (1995) 'The Concept of Public Duty' in Barberis, P. (ed) *The Civil Service in an Era of Change,* Aldershot: Dartmouth.

O'Toole, B. (1997) 'Ethics in Government', Parliamentary Affairs, 50, 130-142.

Ponting, C. (1985) 'Memorandum' Treasury and Civil Service Committee, *Ministers and Civil Servants: Duties and Responsibilities, Vol II: Minutes of Evidence* (HC 92-II), London: HMSO.

Pratchett, L. (1994) *The Public Service Ethos in Local Government: A Research Report*, London: ICSA.

Richards, D. (1997) *The Civil Service under the Conservatives 1979-97: Whitehall's Political Poodles* Brighton:Sussex Academic Press.

Richards, D. and Smith, M J (1997) 'The Gatekeepers of the 'Common Good' - Power and the Public Service Ethos' *Paper present to the EGPA conferences*, University of Leuven, September.

RIPA (1987), *Top Jobs in Whitehall Appointments and Promotions in the Senior Civil Servcice*, London: RIPA.

Sampson, A. (1962) *Anatomy of Britain,* London: Hodder and Stoughton.

Scott, R. (1996) *Report of the Inquiry into the Export of Defence Equipment and Dual Use Goods to Iraq and Related Prosecutions,* London: HMSO.

Smith, M.J. (1996) 'Reforming the State' in S. Ludlam and M.J. Smith (eds) *Contemporary British Conservatism,* London: Macmillan.

Sheaf, R. and West, M. (1997) 'Marketization, Managers and Moral Strain: Chairmen, Directors and Public Sector Ethos in the National Health Service', *Public Administration,* 75, 189-206.

Thatcher, M. (1992) *The Downing Street Years*, London: Harper Collins.

The Times, (1979) *The Times Guide to the House of Commons* London: Times Books

The Times (12/12/1997) *So far so Good, but Labour's Commitment has yet to be Tested*

Theakston, K. (1995) *The Civil Service since 1945* Oxford: Blackwell.

Weber, M (1949) *The Methodology of the Social Sciences* New York: Free Press

Weiner, M. (1981) *English Culture and the Decline of the Industrial Spirit 1850-1980,* Cambridge: Cambridge University Press.

Wrigley, L. and McKevitt, D. (1994) 'Professional Ethics, Government Information and Differential Information' in McKevitt, D and Lawton A. (eds) *Public Sector Management: Theory, Critique and Practice,* London: Sage.

---

[1] We would like to thank Dave Marsh for his input and Peter Kopecky for his comments and the ESRC, award n° L 124251023 for financial assistance.

[2] The Haldane principle is derived from the 1918 Report conducted by Lord Haldane, entiteled « the Haldane Committee Report on the Machinery of Government ».

[3] There is also some suggestion of a rising trend of fraud although the evidence is limited (see HM Treasury 1996). For further evidence of the decline of « public ethics » see Richard and Smith 1997.

Working Group on Integrity

Report of the Working Group on Integrity

B. De Clercq & G. Gulyàs[*]

Working group III had a relatively small number of participants and not so many papers to discuss. As a consequence, the participants had the opportunity - and they took it - to devote much of their time and intellectual energy to a discussion in depth of the content of each paper after it was presented by its author/authors. This was to the benefit of all the participants.

At first sight it may seem surprising that none of the papers attacked directly the issue of integrity. But on further reflection this is quite normal. There are good reasons for what one could call an indirect approach. Integrity, or lack of integrity, is a result of many factors and circumstances. So one has to focus on the elements and components of the sphere of the public service that are relevant and crucial for the promotion of integrity and the prevention of unethical, morally unacceptable behaviour of public servants (and politicians). Let me try to describe in a few sentences the main angles of view that were adopted and discussed.

1. *The point of view from within*: How do civil servants see themselves, how do they perceive their actual situation and the impact on it of the recent changes and evolutions toward (I summarise) less state and much more market (privatisation, deregulation, etc.)? The first impression is: they feel rather unhappy, in many respects. They feel themselves curtailed in the fulfilment of their tasks as servants of the *public*, i.e. the public interest.

A specific view that was explored is the situation of moral powerlessness in their position of subordination to the political authorities and their hierarchical superiors. They are often obliged or even forced to do or to omit things they can't agree with, for moral reasons. In this context, we discussed more particularly the hot issue of whistle-blowing (to be clearly and sharply distinguished from 'leaking') and the question of specific measures for protection of whistle-blowers.

A general and very interesting proposal explained by one of the participants is that of defining and concluding, in a new and systematically updated term, a double covenant:

a) an external covenant, between the civil servants, the political authority and (not to be forgotten!) the citizens. Inspiration can be drawn from the Citizens' Charter in the UK and similar initiatives, e.g. in Belgium and the Netherlands.

b) an internal covenant within the realm of the public service, comprising, among other elements, a workable ethical code, or probably several specific codes, in accurately

---

[*] Prof. dr. Bertrand De Clercq, Catholic University of Leuven, Department of Political Science, Belgium. Prof. Dr Gyula Gulyàs, Budapest University of Economic Sciences, Hungary

defined, measurable and valuable terms, and (a point to be emphasised) good programs for ethical training.

2. A second view is related to the question to what extent and in what sense can *economic models of thinking* be adopted - and adapted - in defining and judging moral and ethical problems that are typical for the public sector. Two models were discussed.

a) The so-called MLMB (market-led motivation behaviour). Put in general terms, a behaviour conditioned or determined by this sort of motivation, follows a line of 5 successive stages: learning (acquiring knowledge), creating (performing tasks), compromising (giving and taking), valuing (appreciating the outcome in term of costs and benefits) and, finally, improving (changes, readjustments). This abstract model can be applied in many different ways and in different fields of action. But concerning its applicability to the decision-making process in the sphere of the public service, there remained, after discussion, some disagreement by the participants.

b) A similar conclusion resulted from the discussion of a second conceptual model, defined by its advocates as a combination of two strategies, called respectively 'reducing the effects of bounded (i.e. limited), defective rationality and opportunism' and 'realising acceptable levels of public objectives'.

In short: in the reflection upon the required ethical qualities of civil servant behaviour and the improvement of these qualities, we are still in need of adequate and workable conceptual models. Much greater intellectual efforts must be made in this respect.

3. A third view is offered by, or can be borrowed from, the theories of *political corruption*. Three points, among others, became clear, or more clear and evident, after discussion.

a) We must carefully distinguish administrative from political corruption.

b) It is strongly recommended to work with accurate definitions of corruption. One thing is corruption defined in terms of the penal law of a country and comparing the definitions in different legal systems. Another thing is corruption as an ethic-political concept: a much larger concept, comprising all forms of morally defective behaviour, whether or not falling under the definitions of penal law.

c) We are inclined to warn against a tendency that asks for drastic measures that are too short-sighted, that have too much the character of panic reactions inspired by recent scandals, but could be dangerous and contra-productive in the long term.

4. The last view is a more specific one, related to the issue of the *conflicts of interests* resulting from the cumulating of a function, a position within the public sector with a function or position in the private sector. Here too, of course, one has to distinguish carefully, in order to avoid confusion, between civil servants and politicians. In both cases the situation and the problems are quite different, although the issues at stake from an ethical point of view are in both cases the same. In Belgium for instance the current discussion is mainly and explicitly about politicians' cumulation of functions; in the working group it was exclusively about civil servants. Basing themselves on a critical analysis of the recent experiences and controversies concerning the struggle against structural forms of conflict of interest in France, the working group defined a number of crucial points in this matter.

The Civil Servant, Society and the Citizen in Quest of Good Ethical Behaviour

P. Vermeulen[*]

1. Introduction

Unethical behaviour in general and corruption in particular have always existed. Man will always be eager to put into advantage his position of strength, be it willingly or forced by circumstances. Corruption, as one of the most visible and reprehensible aspects of unethical behaviour, can be defined as the obtaining/asking/proposing of advantages -in whatever form or size- to public officials which are not due or legally or legitimately permitted. It can be at the administrative level or at the political level.

We speak of an individual problem if it is confined to a small scale and to isolated cases of petty offences, even the proverbial tipping for rendered services. Dealing with it with severe and strict laws and punishments will only be partly effective, especially if the chance to be caught and punished is small. Socialisation of good ethics and a good human resources management could prove to be more effective.

When corruption becomes a wide-spread phenomenon and it starts to affect political and administrative legitimacy, it is a structural problem, calling for other and more diverse and even international approaches and solutions.

2. Ethics as a way of fighting corruption

This text starts from some basic assumptions.

1. *Ethics as a notion is to be preferred over deontology.* Deontology as concept only exists since the 19th century and can be defined as the science of what is correct and what is not. It evolved towards a strict code of professional conduct combining legal and technical (self-imposed or imposed by public authority) imperatives and regulations on internal and external relationships which became operational there where the courts, legal dispositions and criminal prosecutions were non existent. Furthermore, such a code reinforces the liberties, privileges and rights of the professional category in question. In this way, deontology easily becomes a conservative, protective, corporatistic and selfish instrument (Minon, 1997:39-48).

Nowadays these so-called established rights of self-protecting judicial-administrative constructions of all sorts are under attack. So is the concept of deontology. It is preferable

---

[*] PhilippeVermeulen, Advisor to the Civil Service, Ministry of the Federal Civil Service, Belgium.

to speak about ethics because ethics have a less legal and far more accessible and comprehensive connotation.

2. *There are different ways of fighting corruption, but to what extent can we prevent it?* A severe and strict criminal approach is one way, although it has never prevented corruption. Setting up special bodies for tracing and fighting corruption is another way. A third way is a global approach in setting up an **ethics infrastructure** in which both control and prevention of corruption are put on the same level. This paper will deal with this 3rd approach.

3. *Ethics cover more than corruption.* While codes of conduct and legal dispositions are about coercion in order to maintain or to enforce integrity and ethical behaviour, ethics may be used a non-coercive tool based upon values aiming at promoting integrity and ethical behaviour, but also on improving administrative functioning.

4. *There are many forms of unethical behaviour, each causing costs and each implying a different approach.* The following diagram tries to summarise the problem:

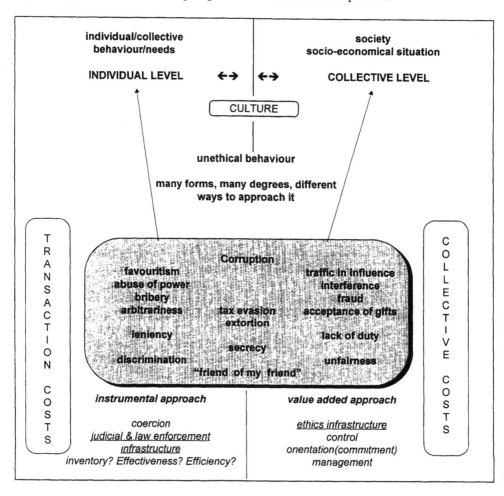

3. Ethics are what we make of our world

3.1. Why are ethics so important?

Ethical values, and among them integrity as a basic value, are key elements of every democratic society and the rule of law, and this in every domain. We must not forget that civil servants, most of the time, dispose, in their daily execution of their functions and in their daily management of public funding, of discretionary competencies. These values must not only protect the citizen against any arbitrary use of this public power, but also the public authority itself against any improper use of this power by its civil servants. Finally, the civil servants themselves must be protected against any abuse or diversion of law or authority on behalf of the public authority or its official bodies.

Furthermore, an ethical behaviour is essential to an effective and stable political-administrative authority and the social and economic structures. Corruption, whatever the size, can disturb economic competition, endanger free trade and stability on which is based the free market economy (Bially,1996:9). The eminent danger of corruption, extortion and all sorts of abuse or misuse of power is that it nourishes anti-political feelings, it promotes spilling of public funding, puts a stop to economic growth and disturbs normal social relations. It is in that perspective that an international institution like the OECD, itself one of the promoters of New Public Management, is looking for values and techniques which are nearer to traditional administrative values like stability, continuity, rule of law and procedural regularity.

3.2. Interaction between ethics and a good human resources management

In practice, both the public authority and private bodies use a number of tools and procedures in order to detect and to avoid deviant behaviour and to promote correct conduct. Such a code of conduct, how ever perfect it may be, is not the ultimate or the most effective answer. A good human resources management focuses on socialising essential ethical values. However, good ethical or moral conduct not only results from the existence or the acquisition of an 'irrefutable' code of conduct. Tools organising control and accountability can be elements pushing towards such behaviour. But nevertheless, corruption, extortion and abuse of power exist in spite of them. What is certain, is that a good human resources management, including a well elaborated legal status and good working and salary conditions which are competitive with those applicable in the private sector, have a positive effect.

We must examine all other possible causes of unethical behaviour. Insufficient means, downsizing, reorganisations, contracting out, an important input of external workers from the private sector in leading posts, changing relationships between civil servants and citizens, evolving or imposed standards or conducts, a bigger input from other social categories with a different cultural or ethnical background, ... all this can be a source of conflicts. Unfit behaviour must then be taken into account by every human resources management.

3.3. The dialectics of ethics

If corruption, like all the scandals emerging nowadays, how small they may seem, is only a symptom for a whole series of other problems and dysfunctions of which the origins can be found in the evolution of society itself, then ethics can not be seen as an isolate phenomenon. Furthermore, ethics are always evolving and are tributary to the changes in society. The last 20 years have been full of events for that matter. Every country admits having severe problems concerning public spending, management of the state (and the public debt...), institutional organisation and communications with the citizen, in addition to a democratic and political deficit, manifesting itself in all sorts of scandals to a point that the legitimacy of the system itself is put into question.

More and more there is a consensus at the supranational level on the decisive impact of public authority in the developing process[1] . The same is true of the influence of performing public services on democracy, the survival of the state and the rule of law, political stability, protection of human rights, and tprotection of fundamental freedoms.

The evolution in Central an Eastern Europe shows it clearly: changes at the institutional, political, social and economical level influence ethics. An economic liberalisation without a simultaneous reorganisation of the mechanisms of control and accountability, a huge devolution towards lower or external administrations or bodies, a bigger rotation and renewal amongst civil servants, poor working conditions and low pay have been very damaging (Sootla,1996:5). Poor equipment to fight corruption and other symptoms of unethical conduct, the absence of politics and social corrections, and the hesitating redefinition of the role of the public authority, lead to the undermining of political legitimacy. In such a context, ethics in general and integrity as its key element in particular, become a major problem.

The role and function of the civil servant becomes subordinate in a context of (imposed) reduction of state intervention and dismantlement of the Welfare State[2] . Furthermore, the growing complexity and the individualisation of society is the cradle for social structures which are difficult to control and which are based upon extremely diverse standards and values. This has its effect on the behaviour and the self-image of civil servants. One can speak of a sort of identity crisis in the mind of the civil servant: who will he be, what can he still do or more likely, what can he do no longer? What will be his place in an ever faster evolving society? Will he still be submitted to servitude, no longer or less needed by politicians, as also the citizen?

4. Terms of reference for a new code of ethics

4.1. Postulates

Improving services produced by public services is not only based upon a mercantile or strictly consumer orientated logic. Those services should meet far more basic necessities:

- keeping or promoting social cohesion;
- enhancement of the legitimacy of the State and/or its components;

- improvement of the citizens' - be they users, beneficiaries, consumers or clients - perception of the public service and public authority;
- stimulation of the concept of citizenship.

4.1.1. Keeping or promoting social cohesion

We find the same preoccupation for social cohesion in the new article 7D of the Final Act approved at the European Council on the 16th and 17th of June 1997.

Citizenship presumes that each citizen has civil, political, economical and social rights and obligations. This may seem evident as it seems also evident that the finality of the State lays first of all in the satisfaction of the needs of its citizens. Of course, it is up to each State to define those needs and to define who are the beneficiaries; so variations are more than likely. But to deduct from this that the management of public services should be submitted to the way those needs are satisfied is a completely different question. Furthermore, there is still the question of the representativeness of the group of beneficiaries. Representativeness supposes economic possibilities and economic possibilities suppose political impact or power to define and to determine those needs. The balance of power is very brittle in a coherent society. Once this social coherence is disturbed, situations are created like we see now in the former communist countries.

4.1.2. The role and nature of public authority, public services and civil servants

4.1.2.1. A new mission for the State?

The State at the service of all doesn't exist nor does the State exclusively exist to please citizens. Public action can contribute to the concept of citizenship. In any case, it is certain that, if the State does not live up to its promises, it surely cannot contribute in a constructive way to this conception. *The State, public action, the citizen: these are not neutral, uniform or unchangeable notions.* The primary function of the State is to govern. The way it governs is variable in accordance with the divisions of power and the politics which are promoted by certain interest groups.

Furthermore, the breakthrough of the *market state* leading to the dismantlement of the welfare state and public institutions, stimulates the fact that the State will manifest itself more and more as the advocate and the catalytic agent of the preservation of competitiveness.

The public services remain tools of the State, or tools of a certain State. When they no longer fulfil this function, they cease to be public services. They are privatised, if they represent an economic reality and a collective need. In all other cases, they are abolished or phased out.

4.1.2.2. A new definition for the civil servant?

Civil servants can be qualified in the same way. After all, civil servants are the personification of the public service. They act on behalf of the public. Or they execute the governments' policy, and then they belong to the public sector, or they act as real actors in the economical field and then they belong to the private sector.

Civil servants are also *full citizens* who have their own opinions and their own legitimate expectations. The actual tendency is to give them freedom of speech and to associate them with parliamentary political life so that their decisive impact -which is often unknown or underestimated- on management and State policy is crystallised and translated into concrete public actions likely to be sanctioned in a democratic way.

Civil servants are also *workers*: they execute their profession or their skills for the same fundamental economic reason: to work in order to live. If the civil servant must work to survive, then every effort on the ethical level will be submitted to this natural law.

Civil servants are also *men*. Each breach of whatever ethical code or rule or law is not due to the fact of being a civil servant, but due to the fact they -as men- dispose of the means - procured legally or on behalf of their function or prestige- to commit these infringements or to obtain certain advantages. A civil servant is no more or no less man than the man in the street. *Mutatis mutandis*, the same remark goes for *each* person holding or executing whatever authority and this regardless of the juridical quality of that person.

But the division between *core* and *non core business* has its effects as well. In the typology of the public authority and civil servants used in a study on working conditions in the public sector in a European perspective (Alessie,1996), civil servants - the study uses *employees* - are classified in two categories. The first group are those who are largely implicated in the public service and who don't or hardly exercise any merchant activities. This is the actual public sector of which the public enterprises are no part. The second group is the merchant sector which contains as well the public as the private enterprises. The 2 sectors are again divided into 2 or 3 subcategories.

This classification according to their industrial or economical activities leads to the conclusion that certain employees in the public sector are not civil servants *sensu stricto*, but nevertheless they can be classified in the actual public sector. This disappearance of clear cut limits between civil servant and employee is not a new phenomenon. Especially at a European level: such a sectorial classification possibly meets a need to compare, but it surely meets the will to harmonise these two categories.[3]

4.1.2.3. The new civil servant: manager or businessman?

Anyway, whatever model is chosen, it is a fact that traditional ethics cannot be grafted onto a modern society where the breakthrough of a State evolving towards a globalized free market will reposit the civil servants. It seems that they will become more and more public *entrepreneurs* next to the fact that they will be implicated more and more in general policies, decision making and evaluation of public action and that they will have to be even more at the disposal of the public.

On the other hand, in a society where only results at any cost count, the risk of abandoning honesty, equity and equality, even legality is eminent. If such values are not likely in the merchant sector where the regime of maximal profit and survival remain the primary rules, they will surely hardly survive in a market-orientated public sector. Recent scandals - bribes, hormones traffic, BSE,...- have proven it abundantly. Even if capitalism may have social appearances, capitalism remains capitalism. Civil servants nourished by a different ethics or moral code will hardly be able to resist the 'laws' and the 'habits' of a globalized economy.

Problems like corruption are but one of the most visible and the most reprehensible symptoms. When first of all the ethical or moral 'feeling' or awareness and secondly the impact and the number of ethical rules are reduced by adjusting or 'modernising' them to the shape of the 'big' world of commerce, corruption gets too easily a free hand. There lies the big danger of the *managerialisation* of the civil servant: that he becomes a businessman, with the emphasis on the less noble sense of the word 'business'... Especially when politics abdicate and policies and politics suffer from lack of legitimacy, confidence and credibility and when public action is hindered to play an important role in economical life.

4.1.3. The citizen: myths and realities

From a political theoretical point of view, it is feasible, even desirable to give more weight to the citizen in the management and decision making process, even to give him the role of the 'mother-in-law' in order to obtain a more effective and efficient management and an external non-partisan control on the respect of professional ethics and integrity. Nevertheless, it seems important to make some observations and some reserves which can also be made regarding the services rendered and the aids given by technocrats[4] :

a) *A citizen is not a civil servant*: being a civil servant necessitates, in spite of everything, a permanent effort and a permanent presence in the field, proper professional pride and honour and proper ethics which cannot be replaced *sito presto* by criteria or standards imported from the mercantile sector. Civil servants hold a position of force, sometimes more than politicians do, and a *de facto* monopoly of power through their knowledge of the terrain, their power of appraisal or their position in the decision making process or the execution of policies. They are a power factor. Citizens putting themselves in their place or at the same level will be as powerful.

b) *Who will control and evaluate the citizen? Who will protect the citizen against the citizen?*

c) The execution and the management of such a power must therefore remain submitted to special rules and particular sanctions in order to protect the community as a whole and the citizen as an individual against arbitrary abuses. Furthermore, a civil servant by nature and statute, serves the general interest. The *ordinary* citizen does not. Unless he is also subject to special rules and becomes a sort of semi-civil servant. But was it not one of the goals of citizen's participation to diminish bureaucracy, to relieve the structures and to broaden the basis of decision making and to reduce the State to a subsidiary state?

d) Taking into account this situation of exception, the possibility of sanctions, empowerment and delegation of competencies, how will the selection of candidates take place, what criteria will be used and who will perform the selection?

e) Even alerted citizens cannot function properly if they don't have the necessary means and delegations and if they are not also submitted to mechanisms of control and accountability and if they are not given the necessary time: *quick-fix* solutions are not the answer to the challenge to do more with less...

f) Therefore we must not give as such the laurels of objectivity and representativeness to "the" citizen, who by definition participates in his own interest in the decision making and political process. He has only a partial view, a temporary interest and reacts most of the time impulsively, motivated by a self-experienced feeling of injustice[5].

4.2. Which values?

4.2.1. Some practical examples

It's not easy to determine a effective framework. Most of the existing ethical rules are embedded in a series of texts which need to be co-ordinated and are so specific that it is almost impossible to graft onto other situations. An option is to start from what public authority should represent or should stand for in a society in full evolution and profound change.

The **United Nations** start from the principle that *'Public administration has to be based on the rule of law and democracy, with transparency and accountability...public administration should be adapted, not only to meet economic demands, but to promote the ideals of peace, equity and social justice '*[6]. The ethics of the perfect civil servant should be the emanation of these values.

The **European Union** has another concept. During the European Council of 16 and 17 June 1997 in Amsterdam a new Article 7D of the Final Act was approved and the following declaration was inserted : *"The dispositions of Article 7D relative to the public services are implemented in full respect of the jurisprudence of the Court of Justice for what it concerns, ..., the principles of equality in treatment, also on quality and the continuity of those services".*(Bauby,1997)

A member State of the European Union had another starting point. It sees itself more as the advocate and the catalytic agent of the preservation of competitiveness. A typical example was given during the presidency of the **Netherlands** of the European Union in the first half of 1997. In an inquiry aiming at examining the added value of public services for the competitiveness of the national economy, the quality of the functioning of the public services had to be compared on basis of the following criteria: the capacity to (re-)act rapidly to changing economic circumstances, transparency, reliability, proportionality (subsidiarity and reserves), and the possibility to respond to the needs and demands of society and more in particular to the economic sector.

4.2.2. A theoretical approach

Another approach could be to draw a theoretical construction. The evolution towards a *free market state* does influence the functioning and the role of the State and the way in which its civil servants work, and therefore their ethics, as it does in each living organisation.

The following scheme tries to systematise these 2 notions. It is a theoretical construction, so there is always the possibility of overlaps and mixing both notions:

	SOCIAL CONSTITUTIONAL STATE	FREE MARKET STATE
laws	equality in treatment continuity variability reasonable cost	efficiency effectiveness economy (*low cost, high output*) quality
executor	civil servant public body	civil servant - user - citizen public or private body
mechanism	regulation	auto-regulation
interest	collective interest general interest	individual interest group interest (only the strongest)
quality	political notion collective notion	individual notion quality is what the customer says it is
leitmotiv	balance between rights and obligations of the citizens and the authorities	economic power and "market-ability"
basic principles	umpiring & evaluation in function of general interest policy support policy execution policy correction	umpiring & evaluation in function of individual interest in search of a policy according to the laws of supply and demand
police	public power	public power market mechanisms
speed	planning in function of policies	real time
basic values	transparency suppleness, flexibility juridical protection confidence disinterested service general interest knowledge of the regulations contribution to and refinement of the regulations non-discrimination service is rendered regardless of the financial possibilities of the user	standards and criteria openness choice accessibility retribution in function of the possibilities and the cost price individual interest deregulation according to the appearance and the financial capacity of the client universal service next to service at market conditions

4.2.3. The shopping list method

Combining the values mentioned above by 3 institutions with 3 different visions - the United Nations, the European Union and a member State of that Union- we can compose a *shopping list* of basic values or basic attitudes:

- protection of the state of law
- democracy

- integrity
- participation
- transparency and publicity
- accountability and responsibility
- anticipation of economic imperatives whilst
- promoting internal and external security
- equality in treatment
- equity
- social justice
- continuity
- quality
- capacity to act swiftly in function of evolving needs and circumstances
- adaptability
- reliability
- proportionality
- professionalism
- pluralism
- competitiveness
- general interest

5. A framework for suitable ethics: conditions

The goal is not to develop a universal code. Such a code could exist in a situation where everything is measurable, but it gives no solution for practical ethical dilemmas which are the result of human action in different circumstances. In that case, pluralism and pragmatism should prevail. This means simple, comprehensive, less contestable but effective tools like laws and objective procedures on public tendering, public spending and criminal proceedings, corresponding to the necessities of maximal legibility, readability and exemplary simplicity; and this after doing an inventory, an evaluation and a shaping up of existing laws, rules and procedures before elaborating new ones.

The above mentioned elements can only be implemented if the material conditions are present or certain changes are made. The OECD has understood this. In its excellent report it indicates what necessary changes are to be made in order to obtain a real ethics infrastructure. These changes should involve 3 levels of functions:

a) an *orientation* function assured by a *real and coherent commitment* by the political leaders, codes of ethics expressing values, standards and norms and activities of professional socialisation (training and education) ;

b) a *control* function assured by a judicial framework providing independent means of proceedings and prosecution, effective mechanisms of accountability and the participation of and surveillance by the public;

c) a *management* function assured by an agency co-ordinating the infrastructure and good working conditions in the civil service based upon effective policies in human resources.

Onto which function the emphasis is to be put is a question to which no uniform answer can be given. Everything depends on the cultural and political-administrative context of each country[7].

5.1. Macropolitical conditions

Following conditions are to be mentioned:

- a legitimate, stable, independent and reliable political-administrative system;
- a legislative, judicial and institutional system capable of protecting social, industrial and relational stability between production and consumption forces and willing to take in charge the social burdens of the past and the present;
- a real political commitment and support;
- simple but effective and efficient laws;
- respect for the principle that no-one is above the law and that sanctions will be taken against anyone putting himself above the law (ministers, parliamentarians, civil servants);
- an internal (inspection, uniform and unambiguous administrative procedures) and external (courts, ombudsmen) control on the decision making process;
- a special service for the repression - and prevention - of corruption[8] and why not a media and information campaign (a supreme Council on prevention of corruption?)[9],
- adapted legislation related to active and passive corruption, illegitimate influencing on decision making (lobbying), illegal and illegitimate enrichment and coalition making in order to obtain such enrichment, not only as civil servants sensu stricto but also as politicians and citizens;
- a register of fortunes and possessions of politicians and senior civil servants;
- an active civil society with consistent transparency and citizens' participation;
- transparency of the administration and management[10];
- a cross border collaboration in order to fight and to identify the wheels of corruption; ...

5.2. Micropolitical conditions

For instance:

- effective mechanisms defining the responsibilities for public actions and the procedures for accountability;
- workable conduct codes settling both rights and obligations of the civil servants as well as the rules, settlements, rights and obligations valid for private merchant sector[11];
- mechanisms of professional socialisation[12],
- good working conditions in the civil service[13],
- pay in function of individual performances in those cases where individual work can be validly measured; in all other cases a system is to be used rewarding good group performances or using non financial rewards[14];
- the creation of a Corps of Senior Civil Servants who are well trained, well paid (like in the private sector), quality minded, incorruptible, capable, always available and easily integrated and very flexible[15],
- an effective evaluation of senior and of other leading and accountable civil servants;

- a body or institution performing control on ethics;
- a management whose intention it is to avoid meddling from or colluding with politics into daily management of the public services, so: a) a demarcation of attributions and missions between ministerial cabinets and administrations, b) a clear definition of the final political responsibility, c) an ethical code forbidding all forms of clientelism, interference or favouritism for every parliamentarian or public responsible.

5.3. Organisational conditions

Facing a rapidly changing society, public services and administrations must be capable to react swiftly and effectively: they must evolve from a simple and privileged knowledge organisation towards a service oriented organisation capable of learning, adapting and dynamising itself and passing on knowledge.

One of the basic conditions is that there is a good communication within the organisation and a minimum of common beliefs and priorities and a consensus on all these matters. Only in this way will the organisation be capable of (1) systematically solving its own problems, (2) experimenting, (3) taking into account new approaches, (4) learning from its own experiences and mistakes and (5) doing so from external experiences[16];

This needs some preconditions (Kayaert,1997):

- an internal and external legitimacy: the creation, emphasising and promotion of a legitimate and well-rooted basis for the organisation corresponding to the expectations of the civil society, the political responsibles and the organisation itself;
- the introduction of a culture where values occupy a central place;
- a living and communicative administration ;
- a particular attention for the human potential;
- enhancing and promoting the possibilities for change;
- inspiration and dynamisation of the civil society and the politically responsible.

The activities of the organisation or administration must be approved by the civil society which it represents. They must not only have a legal basis but also a legitimate one, living up to the expectations of society, politicians and the organisation itself. In this framework, citizens have a right to an open, neutral, objective, professional, reliable and representative administration where transparency of the decision making and managerial process, motivation, communication and information play a decisive role. Working together with politicians means having equal relations with different political 'families', having different political programmes and different political cultures. Developing a consistent, convincing and professional attitude is a key element in the ethics of the civil servant. This could lead to tensions with the politicians resulting in putting in 'offside' of the administration, which could lead to administrative chaos and confusion amongst citizens. Only mutual respect for the own responsibilities and trying to reach a consensus on the content and the implications of everybody's tasks can create legitimate relationships between politicians and the administration.

Internal legitimacy is equally important and can be obtained and enhanced by:

- clear and unbiased objectives;
- using a professional and moral code;

- keeping in touch with the human and the political aspect by dialogue;
- living up to the right and justifiable expectations of the target group and its collaborators;
- a constant evaluation of the policies and the collaborators; and
- a correct and consistent leadership.

The values of the organisation emerge from the objectives and the activities of the organisation. But values change, and different cultures have different criteria to judge those values. Even within a same so-called homogenous culture, there are differences on how these values are experienced.

A living administration can only survive if the smallest link also has its importance. Accountability, the distribution of functions based upon the skills of each collaborator, sufficient and appropriate means, real autonomy and delegation are essential tools.

A special interest in the human potential is needed to have a good and dynamic functioning of the organisation. This can be done by appropriate selection procedures based upon a thorough analysis of the functions, job descriptions, objective recruitment and permanent and appropriate training, motivation and evaluation of the collaborators.

The possibilities to adapt are enhanced and served by introducing an organisational structure which is flexible, simple, clear and dynamic and where the hierarchy is limited and importance is attached to cultural diversity. Another aspect are the possibilities given to the collaborators for meaningful work within the organisation, the creation of - formal and informal- networks and the promotion of the right to take individual and responsible initiatives.

6. Conclusion

6.1. An external alliance between civil servants, politicians and citizens

Such an alliance based upon the values that are to be the guidelines of public actions and its bodies and negotiated between the three parties is essential to restore confidence of the people in and the credibility and legitimacy of the institutions and public services.

Those values or guidelines must translate the social choices which have been made. It is up to each country, accordingly to its traditions and culture, whether the choice is made for a social constitutional state or a free market state, or whether there is a mixture of both. Nevertheless, some ethical values are universal and some, more recent, like citizens' participation, have taken on importance.

If the juridical status of the civil servant, or rather, the agent who represents public authority, no longer seems to play a dominant or decisive role in the execution of public tasks, there remain some reservations about the participation of the citizens in the preparation, the making, the execution, control and even rectification of decisions and the importance that one wants to give to those same citizens. Their participation can be enriching and can even be a contribution for the evaluation of the effectiveness, the universality and the pertinence of the proposed guidelines, values, conduct rules and performance standards upon which the action of the public authority and the civil servant is based.

The role of politicians is essential. They have to give a clear signal that the greater role they want to give to the citizen, the administration and private initiatives doesn't mean that politicians want to abdicate, but, on the contrary, that in this way they want to contribute to a lesser political implication and more democracy in order to restore legitimacy and confidence. Politicians have to acknowledge their own participation by a formal commitment to acknowledge the criteria that will serve as a basis for the action of the administration and the civil service in favour of the public rather than in favour of "the" citizen. And last but not least, politicians have to provide sufficient means so that this policy can work.

In the third place, there must also be a formal commitment by the administration to respect these guidelines.

Such a three party commitment which is close to a moral contract, exists in Belgium with the Charter of the User of Public Services where the rights and obligations of each party are stipulated. Similar charters exist in other countries although their starting point may differ. Other recent political measures in other domains - for instance justice- try to live up to the expectations of society.

6.2. An internal alliance for the public authority

6.2.1. An effective ethical code based upon values, attitudes and aptitudes that can be measured or evaluated

Some values are not (always) easy to measure, although this can be done, but from a negative point of view when scandals erupt. But they can surely be evaluated: pluralism, equity, integrity, transparency, quality, reliability,....

Other values which are derived from general basic ethical values and therefore nearer to the daily performance of civil servants - more likely to be evaluated on a continuous and general basis - can be introduced as *basic attitudes* on the one hand and *basic aptitudes* on the other hand.

These values must explicitly be part of an internal charter - *or the evaluation system* - which must obtain maximal publicity as is the case in Great Britain. But therefore, one must limit oneself to typical and well chosen values.

Furthermore, those values must correspond to the expectations of society and of politics and they must reflect the diversity of society so that these values can be as universal as possible and assimilated and approved by that same civil and political society.
The combination of a minimum package of values with the above mentioned attitudes and aptitudes, results in the following construction:

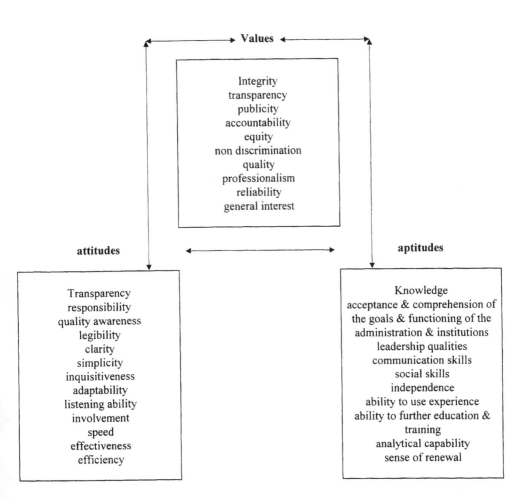

What about the control on the respect of those values? Must there be a special body and how must it be composed, organised,... or does this remain a prerogative of the courts? Must on the other hand the emphasis be put on the management of human resources? To what extent can we appeal to the public and to what extent can the public participate? There is no clear cut answer to these questions: everything depends on the cultural and political-administrative context of each country and the orientations one (wants to) follow(-s).

6.2.2. A socialisation preparing for the future

It is essential that ethical values are internalised by the civil servants. Therefore training is needed, both upon entrance into the civil service (introductory training) and during the career (permanent training).

6.2.3. Good working and pay conditions

If no attention is given to these conditions, the risk that the proposed values are not implemented, is great. The best way to encourage corruption and abuse of power is the non respect of expectations of civil servants concerning their legal statute, pay, stability of employment, union, working conditions and the means they esteem necessary to execute their duties and attributions.

6.2.4. Enhancement of political and civil consciousness of civil servants and citizens and the ability of expressing and committing one's self

There is a considerable advance in this field. For instance, in many countries, efforts are made to involve the civil servants more fully in political life by giving them more responsibilities, even by facilitating their access to legislative assemblies.

Much more importance is given to the freedom of speech and the right to be heard. But there is still lots to be done. Especially in the field of active communication on behalf of the administration and the civil servant. In spite of the duty of the first to inform and the right to speak up of the latter, the first still has a great tendency to remain quiet and the second still practices auto-censorship in fear of displeasing politicians and superiors and thus harming his the career prospects... In the field of external communication, the individual right to take initiatives and the responsibility of the civil servant in this matter, many more efforts have to be made. *Whistleblowing* should be acknowledged as a means to inspire, to incite and to preserve ethical behaviour.

Politicians enable citizens to participate more and better in the decision making process, e.g. by using tools like the referendum. One may ask however what importance is to be given to their wishes, contribution and even to their opposition.

Notes

[1] see the report of the 12th meeting of the group of experts on public administration A/50/525 of the 11th of October 1995 of ECOSOC of the general Assembly of the United Nations and resolution A/50/255 of the 19th of April 1996 on the occasion of the 50th session of the general Assembly of the United Nations on the problems of the public administration , see also the 19th French-African Summit of Ouagadougou on the 5th & 6th of December 1996 on good management and the *Assises francophones de l'Administration publique* held in Paris from the 12th until the 14th of December 1996 on the occasion of the 30th anniversary of the *Institut international d'Administration publique*.

[2] see the more and more restrictive interpretation of the conception of civil servants in the jurisprudence of the European Court of Justice; read· VERMEULEN, Philippe, "De toegang van niet-Belgen tot de overheidsdiensten. Het probleem van deelname aan de staatsmacht als beslissend criterium ", *Tijdschrift voor Vreemdelingenrecht*, 1996, n°4, (april 1997), p.303-316

[3] A process that already started in 1957 with the Treaty of Rome where only 2 categories of workers exist those who earn a salary and the independent workers. It's only in article 48,§4 en 51 that a reference is made to the existence of a "different" category. Nevertheless, as mentioned before, this notion is interpreted in a strict way by the Court of Justice, and, secondly, also in the special systems of social protection, the Commission remains advocate of a harmonisation with the normal regimes developed for the salary workers. For years there's a proposition to harmonise the special regimes with Ordinance 1408/71. For the moment without any result.

[4] Technocrats also only reason in function of their own vision of things and their specific skills. Thus the risk is great that the public service looses it primary function to be at the service of the whole of society (QUERTAINMONT, Ph., *Rôle et fonctionnement de l'administration*, in *L'administration en 7 questions*,

acts of the seminar of the 22nd of March 1996 of the *Institut Cooremans*, Bruylant, Brussels, 1996, 219 pp., p. 17-42, p.25)

[5] or as Halachmi calls it the Pharaoh Syndrome Citizens have sometimes a very dual view of public action. On the one hand, they consider themselves as a privileged beneficiary of every wanted for or thinkable service. On the other hand, they have a tendency to forget that public action serves the general interest and above all they don't like to have to deal much with taxes which finance those services and with rules that manage those services For them, public authority always costs too much and that authority should do more - or the same thing, as far as it concerns their own case - with less. (HALACHMI, A , *The Pharaoh Syndrome and the Challenge of Public-Sector Productivity*, National Productivity Review, winter 1994-1995, p.25-37)

[6] UN Press release GA/9065 of the 19th of April 1996

[7] In the US for instance, with its tradition of weights and counterweights much more importance is given to control, whilst in the Netherlands, with its tradition of confidence, the emphasis is put onto orientation and management (PUMA, *Infrastructure de l'éthique*, Optique, OCDE-PUMA, n°4, March 1997, p.4)

[8] In Belgium within the *Commissariat général de la police judiciaire* the *Office central pour la répression de la corruption* was created in which from the 1st of January 1998 the inquiry service of the *Comité supérieur de Contrôle*, which ceases to exist, will be integrated. In that same service exists also a special bureau dealing with the struggle against organised economic and financial crime (OCDEFO). Furthermore, in order to fight more effectively against corruption itself, a draft bill was approved by the Council of Ministers on the 14th of March 1997 which reviews the major dispositions of the Criminal Proceedings Code. There are 4 objectives·

1 to clarify basic conceptions and to modernise the terminology, taking into account actual jurisprudence and international conventions;

2. to amend the 'black holes' that exist in the current legislation on certain incriminations and it especially introduces incriminations such as attempt to passive corruption, abuse of influence, corruption of a candidate to a public promotion, the corruption of international and foreign civil servants and the private corruption;

3 to enhance sanctions and to establish a new gradation in penalties

4. to broaden the competencies of the judge on dealing with cross-border corruption, implicating international and foreign civil servants as well as the corruption committed abroad by persons exerting public functions in Belgium

[9] Like in Romania where a National Action Council against Corruption and Organised Crime was created on the initiative of the President of the Republic. This organism disposes of correspondents and of specially adapted means of collaboration and control. A great publicity was given to its results on television and in the written press (STOICA, Valeriu, *La Roumanie livre bataille contre la corruption*, TGP (Tribune de Gestion publique), SIGMA, vol. III, n°2, 1997, p.3)

[10] Like the publicity of administrative documents, of nominations and promotions, of management and appeal procedures, obligation to motivate administrative actions, responsibilisation and identification of the civil servants regardless of their ranks or level, an active policy on communication, *ombudsmen*,....

[11] F.i. not be part of the leadership or board of directors in a commercial private or public enterprise, or to be on the payroll of a company which has been under your supervision or at least wait a long period after the definitive dismissal of your functions. (see the French decree n°95-168 of the 17th of February 1995 regarding the transition of a civil servant to the private sector (X, "Le passage des fonctionnaires dans le secteur privé", *Service Public*, n° 46, February 1997, p.28)), an annual declaration of the mandates of economic interests (see the status of the Russian civil servants, art.12 of the law of the 5th July 1995)

[12] meaning the mechanisms and processes by which the civil servants learn and assimilate ethics, conduct rules and the values of the public service The training is based upon existing models and is an essential part of it.

[13] an appropriate salary level which is sufficient to avoid any cumulating and differs not too much from the salaries in the private sector, stability of employment, working hours,

[14] conclusion of the study by PUMA (n°15) de WOOD, Robert, *La rémunération liée à la performance pour les cadres du secteur public*, TGP, SIGMA, vol. III, n°2, 1997, p.7

[15] as recently in the Netherlands, Hungary and Poland (see the latest issue of *Tribune de la Gestion publique*, vol III, n°2, 1997)

[16] GARVIN, D A., *Building a Learning Organization*, Harvard Business Review, 1993, n°4 78-91 in HALACHMI, *o c* , p.30

Bibliography

ALESSIE,R.; DE VOS, K. & ZAIDI, A., *Terms of Employment in the Public Service in European Perspective Final Report*, Economisch Instituut Tilburg, juin 1996, 244 pp.

BIALLY, Sharon, *International Business Community Fosters Ethical Behaviour*, Public Management Forum, Sigma, vol II, n°.5, 1996, p.9

BAUBY, Pierre; BOUAL, J.-C., *Après Amsterdam*, Nouvelles-News-Europe, Comité européen de Liaison sur les Services d'Intérêt général, n°7,19/6/1997

HALACHMI, A., *The Pharaoh Syndrome and the Challenge of Public-Sector Productivity*, National Productivity Review, winter 1994-1995, p.25-37

HERMANS, Ron, "Het Britse mirakel. De herhaalde leugen", *Trends*, 24th April 1997, p.51

KAYAERT, M., *Omgaan met onvoorspelbaarheid. Kritische succesfactoren voor management in een inspirerende overheidsorganisatie*, © Marc Kayaert, 1997, 114 pp.

MINON, Paul, "Avatars et ambiguïtés de la déontologie", *Education-formation*, march 1997, p 39-48

PETRELLA, Ricardo· "Urgence: re-créer la citoyenneté dans L'Etat aux orties? Mondialisation de l'économie et rôle de l'Etat", *Ecosociété*, p.17-31, p.21

PUMA, *L'Ethique dans le service public Questions et pratiques actuelles*, Etudes hors série, n° 14, 1997, 72 pp.

QUERTAINMONT, Ph., "Rôle et fonctionnement de l'administration ",in *L'administration en 7 questions*, acts of the seminar of the 22nd of March 1996 of the *Institut Cooremans*, Bruylant, Brussels, 1996, 219 pp., 17-42

SOOTLA, Georg, "Estonia Aims to Promote Ethical Standards in the Public Service", *Public Management Forum*, Sigma, vol.II, n°5, 1996, p.5

STOICA, Valeriu, "La Roumanie livre bataille contre la corruption", *TGP*, SIGMA ,vol. III, n°2, 1997. p.3

VERMEULEN, Philippe, "De toegang van niet-Belgen tot de overheidsdiensten. Het probleem van deelname aan de staatsmacht als beslissend criterium ", *Tijdschrift voor Vreemdelingenrecht*, 1996, n°4, (april 1997), p.303-316

WALLIN, B.A., "The Need for a Privatization Process: Lessons from Development and Implementation", *Public Administration Review*, jan-feb..1997, vol.57, n°1, p.11-20, p.12

WOOD, Robert, "La rémunération liée à la performance pour les cadres du secteur public", *TGP*, SIGMA , vol. III, n°2, 1997, p.7

Searching for a Set of Values in the Ethical Behaviour of the Public Sector

L. Montanheiro[*]

1. Introduction

By many accounts the ethical behaviour within the private sector does not necessarily need to equal that of the public sector. The stakeholders' fulfilment in both of these sectors are somehow differentiated by financial objectives. The short- and long-term expectations of a set of values are not constant. Further still, certain conducts which are happily accepted in some regions or countries can have a total reverse effect in others. The foremost question challenging the critics is whether or not ethical stance should be similar throughout society or large group of individuals and/or countries, e.g. European Union, that is, should people have an identical and easy identifiable set of values? If so, then, how are we to pass this knowledge to others? With an increasing dominance of the free-market conditions in the world, any assessment of the need for and application of an ethical conduct must be subjected to the constraint of the market itself as a starting point. Based on a market-led approach to guide every day actions of those carrying out tasks for and on behalf of society as a public servant, then unethical conduct is tentatively defined as activities which one person or more can derive abnormal benefit at an adverse effect upon others and society. It is often the case that critics speak of a 'capitalist ethics' if ever there was one. However, many believe that it is about time that both public and private sectors operating in a capitalist kind of environment must develop and apply in everyday activity a clear set of ethical behaviour. Furthermore, one has to bear in mind that only few value-connotation concerns possess a cross-boundaries, perpetual, and universal scope such as: "*people are mortal*" or even "*people are born free*". In most cases, within a 'global village' market conditions, ethical conduct can be heavily disputed as not applicable, irrelevant, strong biased, and out-of-date. In a free market economy, one has to consider carefully whether or not a set of market-led principles are more likely to influence task performance and community relationship. So, from existence to non-existence, people either as part of a small group – family, business, or a region – or a large one – a country – are put under some constraints in relation to their social role and this can be depicted in terms of market-led behaviour stages as described in Table 1. In a dynamic process, it is perfectly desirable to reach 'Stage 5' at some point in time, then revert back to 'Stage 1' and continuously to follow the process so to bring improvements necessary to up-date existing concepts on 'ethical behaviour' as society improves its conduct by gathering a wider experience from a global market.

---

[*] Luiz Montanheiro, Sheffield Business School, United Kingdom.

Table 1: Market-led Motivation Behaviour (MLMB)

Stage 1	to learn (i.e. acquire knowledge or imitate each other's behaviour)
Stage 2	to create (i.e. to work, perform tasks)
Stage 3	to compromise (i.e. to exchange, to respect and/or give-take)
Stage 4	to value (i.e. to appreciate benefit/utility/cost)
Stage 5	to improve (i.e. to change, modify, make better)

The major limitation when society performs tasks related to one or more of these stages is undoubtedly the one which sets the conditions under what kind of system it operates. This can facilitate the absorption of a global value-led behaviour which can have, simultaneously at least, more of some issues and less of others taking place at different time [1]. So, once the full circle is complete, and in here it is perfectly feasible that some groups in society will be stuck somewhere before getting to the position 'to improve', the process will go back to its initial point, i.e. 'to learn' stage. As the understanding and performance of a nation's social, political, and economic values are constantly changing, in other words nothing remains still in society, then the need to have most of the activities in the public and private sector examined is of great importance for moving from the stage 'to improve' back to the 'to learn' stage, and to progress towards 'to improve' once again, from time-to-time. One important aspect, therefore, is to appreciate that the private sector has profit or money surplus as the motive to return to Stage 1, whilst the public sector is moved by duty-bound obligations on how to serve each stratum of the community. It is, therefore, in the interest of society that the public sector keeps updating the level and manner of conduct expectation so that grey areas are kept to a minimum.

2. Public Sector Administrators and Governance

Quite often it seems that some actions taken by members of the public sector are approved almost unanimously with a helping hand of the media, i.e. newspaper and television mainly, on creating a public awareness of the relevant issues, i.e. in terms of their promotion and dissemination. Although some analysts might judge this behaviour as unethical, the fact is that they exist and society overall gets to know them more frequently. Somehow, it seems then that some public servants are allowed to take the power in their own hands and decide the course of action which, in their opinion, reflects what the community wants to attain by itself. This is that aspect of the significance of ethics raised because public servants are required to have a personal conduct above reproach. Undoubtedly, this is the area in which political colours and corruption play a strong part within the set of values adopted by public administrators. Although, it must be the case that some public managers may not fully comprehend the intricacy of ethical conduct. In other words the 'I did not know' type of behaviour can appear rather too frequently. However, as not all issues are cut-and-dry decisions, many critics would allow some degree of justice, fairness, and equity, to be left in the hands of public servants. The difficulty in here is that all these three aspects are confined within a strong degree of dependence on past experience and they can be heavily influenced by family upbringing, belief, education, and social class [2]. In the absence of all these, unethical actions must be deemed as human error, if there is proven evidence of this being innocently performed.

People overall can act ethically as a response to the position they take as individuals when offered with a chance to express their feelings. This seems to be more the case when small, in significance, and less, financially bearing, dimensions exist at the decision-point when ethical discretion has to be observed. One thing is to be aware of or hold ethical values, another thing is to put them into practice when comes to action and decision that really matters. When people are put together to represent the works of the private sector enterprises or public sector institutions there exists a trade-off between one's ethics and the group and/or organisational ethics. It is possible that individuals can progress quite confidently from Stage 1 to Stage 5 on the MLMB table above, but the same does not happen, at the same extent at least, at corporate level. This might be related to the nature of individuals overall, on the one hand, as people primarily will look after oneself first [3]. People do not see the need to act as defending a large group such as their organisations or institutions, on the other hand [4]. Very often size, importance, and market position of a company or public institution will demand a greater awareness of ethical principles. It is, however, the case that the private sector is more advanced than the public institutions in terms of searching for a optimal level of ethical stance for companies. It is, therefore, equally right that institutions within the confine of the public sector begin the search for the best measurement of ethical performance despite the variation in individual commitment likely to be found among stakeholders in each area of the economy. In the public sector, at least, it must be of certain importance to have procedures to improve collective performance as well as that of each individual public servant.

3. Ethical Stance: Searching for an 'Organisational Style' for Public Sector Institutions

An attempt is carried out in here to advance a few points on each of the areas related to the MLMB table above with direct relevance to the public sector.

3.1 To Learn (i.e. acquire knowledge or imitate each other's behaviour)

As government activities becomes more intermingled with that of the private sector, it is important that public servants learn the best practice for the overall economy in terms of ethical behaviour. Stakeholders can, and often will, switch places when playing the free-market game especial as they can take part as either a member of the public or the private sector. It is important that certain areas such as power, leadership, and delivery are carefully taken care of so that the community can respond supportively to the needs and objectives of the work the government has to carry out either from central or local levels [5].

3.2 To Create (i.e. to work, perform tasks)

Once the learning stage has taken place, public servants need to perform daily tasks based on a new set of 'ethical stance' applicable to that particular area of public governance. Here is where individuals apply the institution's code of ethics, if there is a written one, or just observe the best practice to act as ethically as possible in today's world observing the requirements of the institution in relation to its stakeholders.

3.3 To compromise (i.e. to exchange, to respect and/or give-take)

This is the most difficult aspect of market-led ethical behaviour. Under this stage, individuals will have to give up some of each one's personal ethical position for the sake of applying the institution's recognised ethical values. Quite often, individuals, as plain humans like all of us, will conduct themselves as if they were 'correct' and the organisation or its management's instructions 'incorrect'. If there are occasions in which advancing a further stage in the MLMB process is impeded by this, then one has to return to Stage 1, and re-start the learning process into the best practice as far as the public institution is concerned. However, if Stage 4 can influence the course of action, all the more the better. However, a comparison between one's set of values against the institution's will have to provide positive results which has to be in terms of some tangible evidence.

3.4 To Value (i.e. to appreciate benefit/utility/cost)

Ethical actions must provide results which are appreciated by individuals and are fully recognised by the management of public institutions. Furthermore, the public sector governance position must be observed thoroughly. At this stage in the market-led ethical behaviour one has the right, not so much the duty or perhaps obligation, to question the importance of one's ethical action. Also, it is important that outcomes in this stage are either perceived as an Utilitarian measure – the highest benefit with the minimal consequences – or Pareto's optimal – at least one person is made better off without anyone being worse off.

3.5 To Improve (i.e. to change, modify, make better)

This is the stage in which past experiences are re-assessed and changes implemented. Perhaps, for today's world, this is the situation in which a set of values for the public sector must be applied in terms of a 'continuous improvement measure'. One has to accept that countries throughout the world are under continuous changes as far as their social, political, and economic system are concerned. A set of values based on ethical behaviour must account for this and necessary adjustments have regularly to be considered. Once these are implemented, the new concept must be shared, taught, understood, and applied by others. In other words, this means returning to Stage 1 in the MLMB pattern and re-starting the process all over again. It is significant, therefore, to shake off some of the old roots in order to create new ones which can provide improved benefits.

4. Ethical Issues in UK's Experience

The UK's public administrators have experienced, possibly like most of other European countries, a large number of 'unethical' mishappenings involving diverse areas of public governance and responsibility levels, i.e. from top government leaders down to a few municipal authorities. In terms of what were at the very top of several headlines in the press lately, the following are the ones which had quite a widespread consequence:

a) PUBLIC SERVANTS PASSING OFFICIAL GOVERNMENT INFORMATION TO THE PRESS: this is a clear case of Stage 3 and Stage 4 above. Public servants find themselves too often torn aside by their own political and/or financial constraints which can drive them into carrying out actions considered by many as unethical. It is feasible that public servants tend to hold, not generally perhaps, a strong 'right' or 'wrong' attitude when they wish to act on behalf of a larger group of individuals. In the UK, supporters of a more radical political line quite often try to ensure that editors of reputable newspapers are fully informed of what the government is up to. In many circumstances, this has caused some frustration and deep concern to government leaders. A code of ethics in this area would have to cover the essential aspects of a corporate group rather than just individuals. An ethical conduct has to be appreciated in terms of what is most significant to present and future maturity of public governance.

b) THE RESTRICTED INFORMATION ON MEDICAL CONSEQUENCES OF THE MAD-COW DISEASE ON HUMANS (i.e. BSE): in here, the UK government of the 1980s did not quite agree with medical evidence and judged it as being of little material significance to the farming sector, in particular, and to the beef industry, generally. Complaints to the European Union were made and financial losses affecting the British beef industry alone have been extremely heavy. So far, the government has taken a uncompromising position in accepting overall responsibility although some compensation to farmers, mainly, was provided for cattle which needed to be put down. This event can be associated with Stages 4 and 5 in the MLMB process. It is the case, clearly, that the authorities fail to recognise the potential explosion on the costing side along with consumers' reaction influencing the national economy and overseas markets. A code of ethics in here must include some sort of 'committee' approach to advise leading authorities on strategic matters.

c) THE DONCASTER CITY COUNCIL ALLEGED IRREGULARITY IN GRANTING BUILDING PLANNING PERMISSION IN OVER TWO HUNDRED CASES: this has culminated with the suspension of all members of the Labour Party leaders of the City Council. In here, there is little doubt that the Doncaster group did not observe the practices of other municipal authorities on ethical conduct. Lessons on how to manage local affairs without compromising a political line has got to be put along ethical stances. It is the case that such actions will have a certain price in terms of political allegiance on the part of public administrators. This will have to be fully appreciated as soon as their public career is about to begin. In terms of the MLMB table above, this category falls within areas of Stage 1, 2, and 3. A code of ethics would ensure that public leaders recognise fully the benefit to public institutions which operates well under a strict set of ethical principles. An ethical committee on public sector governance, at least at regional level, could highlight malpractices during their initial phase. Such a process would certainly increase, generally, community confidence on the management style of the public sector.

There exists well documented evidence on whether or not individuals can learn ethical conduct [6]. Assuming that it is possible to teach and learn corporate ethics, the next huddle is whether individuals are capable of applying ethical measures when it is in their time to act [7]. Perhaps, as a suggestion only, a certain financial penalty should exist to restrain actions deemed as unethical conduct. This should not be too heavy in total as to cause unnecessary hardship or too extreme, so to send waves of panic in the sector. The process of learning is slower than many can put up with. A sustainable progress towards a more ethical conduct must be a long-term objective. It is not appropriate to move fast so to penalise offenders. It is relevant to have a stage-by-stage approach on the ethical behaviour conduct of individuals and corporate performance to teach everyone good public administration practices. In terms of the learning aspect of ethical behaviour along with a gentle lead towards the level of conduct aimed at by the institution, the creation of a code of ethics for the institution can provide substantial long-term benefits primarily for the institution and later on for the individuals themselves.

5. Conclusion

It has been highlighted above that ethical conduct for each area of the economy need not be the same as stakeholders have different expectation on how they ought to conduct themselves in different circumstances. Quite often, this depends on which side of the fence people are placed. Critics must recognise the importance of market-led motivation which exists in guiding the behaviour of everyone and everything confined to a free-market system. Any code of 'ethical stance' has got to be subject to continuous and increasing influences related mainly to time, location, sector, progress and changes along with the social, political and economic stages of each region in the country. The public sector is, by nature, susceptible to external influences in setting up an ethical conduct path. Ethical stance when applied to the public administration area must provide for a condition which can be better described as a 'continuous improvement' process. The well known characteristics of business based decisions such as: cost cutting, staff reduction, speedy decisions, quick success, among the many in a free-market economy, must not be allowed to interfere with public governance as these can compromise too much the ethical principles so relevant for a smooth and caring public service delivery. When behaviour patterns fall within the realm of an expected ethical conduct, it is of extreme importance to allow for a certain amount of learning time. In here, it is suggested that shared-action promoted towards 'leading others to behave ethically' is the best punishment for incorrect actions. Acquiring an unique and workable ethical stance is a matter of long-term strategy. The earlier this process starts, the shorter the journey will be.

Notes

[1] An interesting account on how a system can influence structure-conduct-performance is given by Alexander Filatov in his article "Unethical Business Behaviour in Post-Communist Russia: Origins and Trends", *Business Ethics Quarterly*, V.4, N.1 (1994), pp.11-15.
[2] B.G. Mujtaba "Ethics and Morality in Business", *Journal of Global Competitiveness*, V.4, N.1(1996), pp.339-345. The author identified these points as influential in people's ethical behaviour. As far as gender

having no influence on affecting moral reasoning of individuals, the author did not give much evidence to substantiate this claim.

[3] R.C. Solomon *New world of Business. Ethics and free Enterprise in the Global 1990's.* (1994, 2nd. ed.) New York: Rowman and Littlefield Publishers, Inc. The author shows survey results in which the statement "Most people are not really honest by nature" went up by around 20% in the response rate under 'agree with' between 1980 and 1990.

[4] Mike Hunt "Ethics and Strategic Development", pp. 385-394, in S.Nwankwo and L.Montanheiro (editors) *Strategic Planning and Development. Developing Economies in Perspective*, Sheffield Hallam University Press: Sheffield (1997). The author examines several examples in developing economies where corruption and poor public sector management is the work of few however causing devastating effect nationally.

[5] Bruce Lloyd "Power, Responsibility, Leadership and Learning: An Integrated Approach at the Core of Ethics", *Journal of Global Competitiveness*, V.4, N.1(1996), pp.204-211. The author explains these aspects in terms of the performance of companies mainly. However, the points observed in his work are extremely significant to the public sector as well.

[6] K. Kerhaghan "Codes of Ethics and Public Administration: progress, problems and prospects", *Public Administration*, Summer (1980), pp.207-223.

[7] K. Denhardt *The Ethics of Public Service*, London Greenwood Press (1988).

Moral Powerlessness in Relations of Subordination
Moral Responsibility and Organisational Culture

K. Raes[*]

1. Introduction

Organisational ethics is one of the most developed parts of applied ethics. More and more firms are aware of their larger responsibilities vis à vis their stakeholders, apart from their responsibilities toward their shareholders. Simultaneously, it cannot be denied that an ethical approach to labour-relations is sometimes motivated by mere instrumental objectives, derived from the insight that purely coercive or remunerative means do no suffice as incentives to motivate employees or public servants.(Etzioni, 1988)

Recent flexibilisation of labour-relations within the private and the public sector confronts organisations with the question of how to maintain a certain loyalty of employees, if their own commitments become more conditional and limited in time and can at any moment be the object of renegotiation. No doubt the recent rise of all sorts of company magazines within firms, as well as new methods of internal marketing aim at stimulating a certain identification of employees with their organisation have and its products. In a similar vein, many organisations established ethical codes of conduct, committing themselves to standards of minimal ethical behaviour.

Such theoretical and practical evolutions imply a certain perspective on business and organisational ethics, e.g. a perspective from the point of view of managers and those in power. They take, as 'principal agents' initiatives to make their organisations and their personnel 'more ethically conscious'. From such a viewpoint, questions arise whether managers may control their personnel by means of cameras, the taping of telephone conversations, body searchs etc. This is the top-bottom point of view, assuming that unethical behaviour is a problem of managers regarding their personnel.

But we should also look from the point of view of the personnel. What means do they have at their disposal when they are confronted with manifest unethical behaviour - from sexual harassment to fraud or blackmail - of their superiors? This is, indeed, the question of 'who controls the controllers'. As Hirschman (1970) argued, employees and civil servants should have, next to 'loyalty' or 'exit' ('love us or leave us'), options to 'voice' as well, options to participate in establishing the terms of labour relations. Limiting their choices to the options of loyalty or exit - as is characteristic of market relations - would be very prejudiced, as work is for an employee or civil servant more than the fulfilment of contractual obligations: it is also their means to gain a living. Moreover, it is not evident at all that mechanisms whereby personnel may control their controllers are at odds with the interests of the organisation.

---

[*] Prof. Dr. Koen Raes, Faculty of Law, University of Gent, Belgium.

Anyway, it should be clear that managers and employees or ministers and civil servants have different assets at their disposal to respond to unethical behaviour. A boss can simply fire employees who are caught in immoral acts. But an employee can not fire his superior and has perhaps only the option to quit.

In this contribution, we focus on the problem of the moral powerlessness of employees when confronted with utterly unethical behaviour of their superiors.

This problem is not of mere theoretical interest. On the contrary, recent history in Belgium and elsewhere has shown a bulk of cases wherein virtuous employees and civil servants have done all they could to struggle against fraudulent practices within their organisations. Often, they were blamed for this and criticised for their 'lack of loyalty' with regard to their superiors. But even more often, subordinates simply keep their mouth shut, out of fear of reprisal.

2. Sources of Moral Powerlessness

2.1. A Moral Problem or a Problem of Morals ?

Everyone who is capable of indignation has, once in his life, already experienced moral powerlessness, the experience of being invited, stimulated or forced (not) to do something which one is convinced to be morally objectionable. This inspires feelings of helplessness. You have not done what you think you should have done.

One of the causes may be morality itself. If moral rules are utterly unreasonable or unrealistic, you may feel guilty for having trespassed rigid moral rules. Such may have been the experience of many Catholics when confronted with the official doctrine of the church concerning sexuality. The importance of such 'moral impotence' may not be underestimated, for it may give rise to cynicism and amoralism. If what is morally required is unrealistic and what is realistic immoral, then the moral system itself pushes people 'away from morality'. Moral absolutism and amoralism are two sides of the same coin.

Here, of course, moral powerlessness should be solved by changing moral codes, by adapting such codes to what people can do or be: ought implies, can.

2.2. A Question of Ignorance

A second possibility is that a person lacks information about available alternatives for action and feels, because of this, morally impotent. There may be situations wherein people know theoretically what they should do, but do not know how to bring it into practice. People may, for instance, decide to save up money or to invest in 'socially responsible business initiatives'. But how can they know that their money is really used that way? A civil servant may radically refuse to participate in fraudulent initiatives, but how can he be certain this will never happen? Society is very complex, and it is not only simple naïveté which may inspire us to behave contrary to our deeply felt convictions. People may even develop 'adaptive preferences' for certain choices by lack of reliable information.

Nevertheless, the only way to counter such powerlessness is to work for greater transparency within society as a whole and within organisations.

Although the preceding sources of moral powerlessness are without any doubt widely spread phenomena, we will not analyse these further here, but concentrate on the more specific cases where such powerlessness is a direct consequence of unequal power-relations within organisations.

2.3. The Power of 'Economic Rationality'

Exactly because our culture has, ever since Bernard Mandeville and Adam Smith proclaimed an unbridgeable gap between 'economic rationality' and 'morality', the problem of moral powerlessness of employees regarding their superiors is an important one. Is the sphere of economic activity indeed a morally 'black box', which can only be valued externally, by its results ? Is an ethical appraisal of 'market behaviour' utterly irrelevant ? We present here an example borrowed from Robert Bellah et.al.'s *The Good Society* (1992). It describes the case of Marian Metzger, a market manager in the colour business. She invested all of her energy to make her firm survive the recession of the eighties, by developing a new marketing strategy. She succeeded in motivating her salesmen for the new strategy which was, indeed, a great success. The more client-centred approach reached a much larger market. But exactly because the market of her firm widened, it became an interesting asset for a take-over. A larger company bought the firm, but was not interested in its production department. It was only interested in its sales market. The firm was thus closed, and Marian Metzger got, ironically, the mission to manage the take over of the firm and the dismissing of her salesmen. This 'successful marketer' had thus succeeded in closing her own firm. And she felt guilty for her collaborators; she had made them enthusiast for the new strategy which finally proved to be fatal for their employment. The take-over firm was only interested in profit, she said, its shareholders do not feel any commitment to the fact that so many people who had contributed to the firm's success, were put on the street. But what can you do about it?

This example illustrates the most global kind of moral powerlessness in capitalist society. And it is also the most problematic from the moral point of view. For who exactly is responsible ? No question here of fraud or blackmail. Here, the only relevant forces at work are the 'anonymous' (?) forces of the market, the 'logic of capital'. This is the kind of powerlessness the personnel must have felt in companies such as Renault-Vilvoorde or Forges de Clabecq, which were recently closed in Belgium. It is a powerlessness confronted with delocalisations and restructurating on a world scale in a globalizing economy. (Petrella, 1994). Moral indignation may be great, but to whom should it be addressed? What difference does it make whether one feels such indignation at all? If morality should inspire rules of action, what action should be taken?

It is no accident that many texts on business ethics focus - although from another perspective - on this problem. The concept of 'stakeholding' was exactly introduced to argue for more global responsibilities for business. (Preston & Sapienza, 1990; Brenner & Cochran, 1991; Donaldson & Preston, 1995). But the question remains open what this would have meant in the concrete case of Marian Metzgers' firm. From a similar perspective, civil servants are today more than ever trained and motivated for a client-centred approach to public services and administrations; their responsibility is thus widened from the classic hierarchical top-bottom model - the civil servant as executioner of political decisions - to a more horizontal model, where the civil servant is directly related to the citizens and should render an account of his decisions to them. This is the idea of 'publicity of government'.

2.4. Conflicts Between Interests and Ethical Norms

A rather different kind of moral powerlessness can be illustrated by the well known case of the engineer of Goodyear, a company producing, amongst other things, engines for the military. (Van Luijk, 1985) The American marine submitted a quotation for a new brake system for its fighting planes. Goodyear received the offer because its system was the cheapest and the lightest. However, when the company tested the system in its own laboratory, it appeared to fail. In all experiments, the brake system did not work well. A young engineer discovered the fault: the system had been made too light. But Goodyear had no more time to develop a new prototype, which would anyway be more expensive and heavier. Its shareholders are already nervous enough. Thus, the engineer was put under pressure to falsify the test reports. Which he did; after all, this was not his decision, and why should he reject attractive career expectations? The defective brake systems were delivered to the marine and after two test flights with almost deadly consequences, the fraud was brought to light. Goodyear losts an offer and a reputation and business had one more scandal to discuss.

The engineer argued that he was morally powerless. His superiors forced him to falsify the reports. If he did not do it, he would lose his job and the support of his colleagues, who were all dependent on the offer Goodyear had carried off. He was forced by the management which in its turn was forced by its shareholders.

This case was brought to light, but how often is this the case ? How often are smaller or larger responsibilities simply dismissed and a blind eye turned to immoral behaviour if it is considered 'good for the firm' ? How often is such ostrich-behaviour not an integral part of an organisation's 'culture' and even stimulated by the so-called requirement of 'loyalty', which made even Oliver North into a 'hero' (Wall Street Journal, 17 July 1987). As far as public services are concerned, similar scandals were brought to light in the case of the French health department, knowingly distributing HIV-infected blood to hemophilia patients, in the case of the Belgian Institute for Veterinary Inspection where some of its inspectors made a deal with hormone dealers or in the case of the Belgian Department for Development Aid in which some public servants were mainly interested in their own gains.

It is all too simple to interpret such cases from a rigid, categorical point of view, the point of view of good versus bad guys. Much more relevant is an approach in terms of organisational culture, professional ethics and personal relations. This involves research into the global context of an organisation which may foster or block virtuous behaviour. The examples are not only from private business organisations, but can be found in every institution: public administrations, the courts of justice, the police as well as organisations with a semi-public statute such as universities, (public) radio and television stations or hospitals. Both contexts become even more comparable as many public services are decentralised and made more autonomous and responsible for their decisions. As Etchegoyen (1995) has shown, decentralisation of responsibilities in public administration may either result in more reliable or more corrupt local services. Particularly public servants with a mission of control, inspection and surveillance are vulnerable to fraud, whilst it should be the least expected from them. But how to motivate them, when they are confronted with an organisational culture which plays fast and loose with moral responsibilities, either out of self interest, fear of reprisal from superiors or out of experiencing an absolute lack of interest from superiors.

3. Specifying Moral Powerlessness

The argument for moral powerlessness seems to be based on the general 'I know but I can't'. However, it should be distinguished from moral weakness, which refers to a similar kind of reasoning. (Charlton, 1988) Moral weakness is the psychic impotence to act in a way the actor nevertheless knows to be morally required. Moral powerlessness is the social impotence to do so, because of the unequal power-relations within which an actor stands. Moral weakness is thus rather a question of personal character, whilst moral powerlessness is question of social context. Whilst it may be very difficult to discriminate between both in certain situations, and whilst most situations will be characterised by combinations of (more or less) weakness vs. powerlessness, they have a quite different moral status. When a person is said to be morally weak, it is the person who is taken to be responsible for a moral failure. When a person is considered to be morally powerless, this responsibility is (mainly) attributed to his superiors or to institutional structures.

This distinction is clear from the reaction of the person. A morally weak person may have feelings of shame, remorse or guilt. A morally powerless person will feel indignation, anger or resentment.

Both should, in their turn, be distinguished from hypocrisy and indifference. Hypocrisy is the psychic unwillingness to act morally, although one is very well able to do so ('I know but I won't'). In most of the cases, this is accompanied by efforts to hide this for others. Indifference is the psychic incompetence to value the moral dimensions of situations, events or actions. A morally indifferent person lacks moral feeling.

In all of these ways of acting, a certain idea of a 'normally rational person' and of 'normal circumstances' will be used. Radically opposed to moral powerlessness and moral weakness is bravery and self-sacrifice, when a person chooses, from all available alternatives, the most difficult but morally required one. But when this has not the intended effects, one may speak of moral recklessness ('Don Quichottery'). On the other hand, both may slip into cowardice, when a person chooses, from all available alternatives, the easiest and least moral choice. A person who underestimates his available alternatives acts opportunistically. A person who overestimates the alternatives available to him acts presumptuous.

4. Avoidance Strategies

Opportunism and hypocrisy are strategies to avoid moral responsibilities, which are sometimes combined with cognitive dissonance: although one may have a morally better alternative at his disposal, this possibility - or the consciousness about it - is repressed. Avoiding moral responsibilities can take a variety of paths such as (Petit & Wempe, 1993, 42)

a) reducing the morally blameworthy to what is pragmatically necessary
b) uplifting the morally blameworthy into the morally required
c) toning down the morally required by reference to relativism
d) reducing ethics to what is legally required
e) de-ethicising the problem by making ethics into a mere 'theoretical viewpoint'

Everyone uses, one moment or the other such-like 'arguments', raised to make us feel more comfortable with the choices we make. But are they really intended as arguments, or rather as strategies to block further discussion?

Much will depend here on the general climate within an organisation. Uplifting a choice to a necessity ('I really had no choice') is the easiest way to avoid moral argumentation. But of course, the question should be asked whether indeed there were no other alternatives. Who will be prepared to raise the question? Is there, in general, room for such questioning within the organisation?

The tendency to avoid moral responsibilities is fostered in a culture wherein the credibility and authenticity of moral values is worn out, where moral indifference is, so the speak 'the cool way' to handle problems. The more superiors have such an attitude, the more their subordinates will imitate it.

Finally, one may also reject moral responsibilities by invoking 'bad luck': why should exactly I be confronted with this problem? Let it be solved by someone else! A culture which takes individual autonomy as its central creed is not by definition a culture where individuals are prepared to take their autonomy seriously when it matters really!

5. Coping with Moral Powerlessness in Relations of Subordination

What moral meaning has the relation of subordination for problems of moral responsibility? It has no doubt that subordination makes a difference. But it does not make the subordinate totally irresponsible for what he does, even though he acts under the authority, the guidance and the control of a superior. On the other hand, the fact of being a superior in a position of power does not imply that one may use this power in any possible way. If a principal agent would use his power exclusively for his own sake, and without any regard for the interests of others, one may speak of executive piracy.

A manager may have the power, but has not the right to force his subordinates into illegal or immoral acts and an employee has the moral right to refuse to be involved in such acts. But as the problem is that the latter's legal or moral right may be threatened by the risk of being fired or of not getting promotion, the moral responsibilities are not equally distributed.

Furthermore, the way a person is confronted with improper actions of superiors may be relevant also. Thus, it makes a difference whether a subordinate is:

- merely confronted with managerial decisions he cannot influence but which he considers to be morally objectionable
- by accident informed of morally objectionable acts of his superiors within the organisation
- intentionally invited to participate in morally objectionable acts by his superiors
- forced to participate in morally objectionable acts by his superiors (the threat being that if one refuses one will be either fired or lose attractive promotion chances)
- etc.

In all of these cases, the subordinate is confronted with a dilemma. He knows - let us assume this - perfectly well what is morally wrong and he has the possibility to object. However, he is unsure of the consequences of doing so, whilst he is asked to be 'loyal' to his superiors.

Group loyalty is, as Durkheim already emphasised, an important source of moral feelings. And for many people, such loyalty prevails over other moral values ('right or wrong, my company') or, more exactly, such loyalty is felt to be a moral value of its own. But it has twofold implications. On the one hand it may be a strong weapon to fight moral weakness but on the other it may inspire moral permissiveness as well, removing further the boundaries of what is morally acceptable. Loyalty is only a moral good in so far as it is solicited by a moral organisation.

However, things are not always that transparent and very often a person will be confronted both with the more or less moral appeal of loyalty to his organisation and/or his superiors and the moral appeal of values he knows to be trespassed by his organisation and/or his superiors. Exactly this makes the situation into a dilemma: either he has to betray his superiors or he has to betray certain moral values.

Undoubtedly, superiors may only expect strong ties of loyalty from their subordinates if these are embedded in a larger moral consciousness, which also defines its limits. Of particular importance is here the global culture of the organisation, wherein 'the place of ethics' may be larger or more limited. If an organisation cares for an ethical culture, it will establish clear rules for both superiors and subordinates to protect them against their eventual moral weakness and to avoid slippery slopes whereby smaller forms of illicit behaviour spread the way for ever greater immoralities. Moral powerlessness can be avoided by making clear that the organisation takes moral values seriously and does not easily step over conflicts of value, when they arise. Very often, compromises will have to be made, but then it must be clear what the compromise consists of and why exactly this compromise has been chosen. There is a fundamental distinction between an indifferent and a moral organisational culture, even if both inspire the same compromise.

In this context it should be emphasised that 'no one is an island' and that it is for most persons very difficult to remain moral on their own. It is the organisation as a whole that will inspire more or less ethical behaviour in it, and superiors play here an important exemplary role: every organisation has the moral consciousness it deserves, exactly as every country has the 'citizenship' its political leaders radiate. More often than not corruption at the bottom has found its inspiration in corruption at the top.

If conflicts of value arise, one should first ask whose interests are involved and to what degree these interests are at stake. Do these interests involve the general interest, the interest of the organisation, the interests of a group of personnel or an individual interest? Are the values or interests at stake necessary, useful, neutral, harmful or catastrophic? Are the expected (im)moral implications of particular acts possible, probable or certain ? It may thus be helpful to situate them within the following framework:

	general interest	organisational interest	group interest	individual interest
necessary				
useful				
neutral				
harmful				
catastrophic				

Not all moral choices have the same weight, not all interests are of similar importance. Nevertheless, it should be remembered that permissiveness toward small 'immoralities' - phone calls for private purposes, whilst using the organisation's telephone - may inspire indifference toward greater immoralities - stealing money from the organisation -, if it is not made clear where the boundaries of permissivism exactly are defined. This is the task of the organisation as whole. In Belgium, for instance, it is widely known that in firms and public services, the consumption of paper and pencils rises during September. This has nothing to do with a certain boom in the productivity of employees and public servants, but everything with the start of a new schoolyear. How to handle such a phenomenon? How to avoid that not only paper and pencils but more of the company's property is stolen ?To my knowledge, one firm decided to give its personnel, proportional to their school age children, a certain amount of paper and pencils, but then strongly sanctioned anyone who took objects from the firm home. This is a rather inane example. But it shows a way to handle unethical behaviour, as it makes clear what the boundaries of permissiveness are.

It is furthermore important for an organisation to present its personnel with clear and trustworthy procedures when it is confronted with immoral behaviour of superiors. Operational complaint procedures may avoid that personnel, confronted with their moral powerlessness, finally have to blow the whistle, because no one within the organisation was prepared to react against manifest immoral and perhaps very dangerous behaviour where the general interest or the interest of the organisation as a whole was at stake. (Nader, 1972) Transparent and reliable complaint procedures are the best means to 'control the controllers' from below and from within. They empower the personnel and strengthen reciprocal moral control.

6. Conclusion

Not all dimensions of moral powerlessness were discussed in this contribution. Nevertheless, they all point to the same problem e.g. the place of ethics within markets or bureaucracies where instrumentalism prevails. Exactly because markets and bureaucracies are characterised by anonymous interhuman relationships, they may foster immorality, as persons may have the illusion that no one in particular is affected by it.

However sophisticated economic models of 'enlightened self interest' may be, they do not by themselves inspire ethical behaviour if it is not assumed to be present beforehand and external to the models themselves. From homo oeconomicus, no ethics can be derived. But at the same time, no economic system and no organisation could even function if the participants were not inspired by certain moral values (Fox, 1974; Lane, 1991) Whilst the instrumental rationality of markets and bureaucracies *relies upon* moral values and norms, it is not in itself able to *inspire* such behaviour.

Social structures, institutions and organisations are not neutral vis à vis values. They can foster or disappoint ethical behaviour, they can be parasitic on them or they may stimulate their flourishing. Any discussion of moral weakness or moral powerlessness remains incomplete if it does not point at this more global context. But on the other hand, it is much too easy to explain anything in terms of contexts, without any reference to individual responsibilities. People have always some possibilities to take 'the moral point of view' and a moral choice is not yet unavailable, because it is difficult.

Managers sometimes complain about the growing norm-erosion and normlessness of their personnel or about their lack of loyalty to 'their' firm. As politicians complain about a lack of citizenship, public spirit and of civic virtues in the population. But they would perhaps do good by first looking into the mirror and ask themselves what sorts of examples they themselves spread in society.

Bibliography

Bellah R e.a., *The Good Society*, New York: Knopf, (1992)

Brenner S.N. & P. Cochran, 'The Stakeholder Theory of the Firm. Implications for Business and Society', in Mahon J.F. (ed.), *Proceedings of the International Association for Business and Society*, (1991), pp. 449-467

Charlton W. , *Weakness of Will A Philosophical Introduction*, Oxford: Oxford University Press, (1988)

Donaldson T. & L.E. Preston (1995), 'The Stakeholder Theory of the Corporation. Concepts, Evidence and Implications', *Academy of Management Review*, 20, (1995), pp. 65-95

Etchegoyen A., *Le Corrupteur et le Corrompu*, Paris: Julliard, (1995)

Etzioni A., *The Moral Dimension Toward a New Economics*, New York: The Free Press, (1988)

Fox A., *Beyond Contract Work, Power and Trust Relationships*, London: Harvester Press, (1974)

Nader R., *Whistle Blowing*, New York : The Free Press, (1972)

Petit M. & J. Wempe, 'Open Kaart. Een Speelse Inleiding tot de Bedrijfsethiek', *Filosofie en Praktijk*, 1, (1993), pp. 38-44

Preston L.E. & H.J. Sapienza, 'Stakeholder Management and Corporate Performance', *Journal of Behavioural Economics*, 19, (1990), pp. 361-375

Van Luijk H.J., *In het Belang van de Onderneming. Aantekeningen voor een Bedrijfsethiek*, Nijenrode: Hogeschool voor Bedrijfskunde Nijenrode, (1985)

Nouvelles perspectives de la lutte contre les conflits d'intérêts dans la fonction publique française

D. Jean-Pierre[*]

1. Introduction

Les rapports des fonctionnaires avec l'argent sont régulièrement évoqués par les médias et l'opinion publique comme autant de "liaisons dangereuses" de nature à nuire à la crédibilité et à la réputation de l'administration. En effet, l'actualité a mis sans cesse sur le devant de la scène les abus les plus criants commis par les agents de la fonction publique à un point tel que le pouvoir politique, ainsi interpellé, a dû réagir juridiquement aux scandales dénoncés. Indéniablement, le débat déontologique l'a aujourd'hui emporté, en France, sur le débat statutaire. Aussi paraît-il intéressant de s'attacher à l'étude de l'un des vices de moins en moins caché de la fonction publique française, celui des conflits d'intérêts.

En effet, tandis que des textes nouveaux et innovatoires ont été édictés, la jurisprudence administrative a confirmé cette tendance à la moralisation de la fonction publique en intervenant avec solennité. Les transformations du droit positif ont apporté deux types de solutions aux problèmes posés par les conflits d'intérêts: d'abord, une réponse purement normative en modifiant les règles de passage du secteur public au secteur privé, mais aussi une réponse de nature institutionnelle par la création de commissions de déontologie et d'un service central de prévention de la corruption.

2. La réglementation des conflits d'intérêts dans la fonction publique française

2.1. L'interdiction statutaire

Hormis la volonté de voir le fonctionnaire consacrer l'intégralité de son activité professionnelle au service, la finalité de l'interdiction, faite au fonctionnaire, d'exercer en marge de ses fonctions publiques, une activité privée lucrative ou de prendre des intérêts dans une entreprise privée s'explique surtout par le souci d'éviter les collusions et compromissions de l'agent.

2.1.1. L'interdiction d'exercer une activité privée lucrative

2.1.1.1. Le principe

L'article 25 alinéa 1 du statut général de la fonction publique française, issu de la loi du 13 juillet 1983 "interdit à tout fonctionnaire d'exercer à titre professionnel une activité privée

---

[*] Didier Jean-Pierre, Maître de conférences à l'Université de Toulon et du Var, France.

lucrative de quelque nature que ce soit". Il s'agit donc bien de préserver le fonctionnaire des possibles conflits d'intérêts auxquels il peut se trouver soumis.

Par exemple, un administrateur civil au service des enquêtes économiques commet une faute disciplinaire en exerçant une activité privée de consultation auprès d'un commerçant.

Le Conseil d'État a rappelé très clairement que l'objet de cette interdiction est "d'éviter les situations dans lesquelles les agents de l'Etat se trouveraient durablement liés par des liens de subordination ou d'intérêt à des organismes privés" et qu'en conséquence, un maître-assistant titulaire de l'Université ne peut cumuler sa fonction avec celle d'ingénieur dans un centre de recherche, constitué sous la forme d'une association de droit privé.

La question de l'indépendance du fonctionnaire se pose aussi avec acuité, lorsque celui-ci souhaite exercer des fonctions dans les organismes directeurs des sociétés commerciales. Saisi pour avis, le Conseil d'Etat a estimé qu'un fonctionnaire ne peut être membre du conseil d'administration d'une société anonyme. De même, il s'est déclaré favorable à l'interdiction faite à un fonctionnaire d'exercer la fonction de membre du conseil de surveillance d'une société à responsabilité limitée sauf si la société n'attache aucune rémunération ni aucun avantage matériel à cette participation. Mais, même en cas de participation licite, le juge administratif rappelle que "les principes généraux qui régissent le comportement des fonctionnaires" peuvent conduire l'administration à restreindre ou à supprimer, dans l'intérêt du service, la faculté d'exercer les fonctions en cause. Or, il ne fait aucun doute que l'indépendance constitue bien l'un de ces principes généraux.

Enfin, un fonctionnaire ne peut faire état de sa fonction pour faire de la publicité et créer sa propre entreprise. Il ne peut pas non plus écrire et éditer des ouvrages qui contiendraient de la publicité pour les entreprises qu'il contrôle dans l'exercice de ses fonctions.

2.1.1.2. L'indépendance du fonctionnaire au regard des exceptions apportées à l'interdiction de principe

En dehors de la libre production d'oeuvres scientifiques, littéraires ou artistiques, les fonctionnaires peuvent effectuer des expertises ou donner des consultations, sur la demande d'une autorité administrative, ou s'ils y sont autorisés par le ministre ou le chef de l'administration dont ils dépendent. Ils peuvent, dans les mêmes conditions, être appelés à donner des enseignements ressortissant à leur compétence. L'exercice de telles activités suppose donc l'autorisation écrite ou verbale du supérieur hiérarchique du fonctionnaire. En outre, cette activité privée ne doit pas être dirigée contre l'Etat ou une personne publique. Mais il faut bien reconnaître, malgré toutes ces restrictions, que la discrétion qui entoure ce genre d'activités, rend leur contrôle extrêmement difficile, voire impossible.

Certains fonctionnaires, notamment les membres du personnel enseignant, technique ou scientifique des établissements d'enseignement et de l'administration des beaux-arts peuvent exercer les professions libérales qui "découlent de la nature de leurs fonctions", sans devoir solliciter l'autorisation préalable de l'administration.

C'est par l'interprétation de cette disposition, qu'il a été permis aux professeurs des Facultés de Droit, d'exercer la profession d'avocat, à la condition cependant, qu'ils ne plaident pas contre l'administration. Il ne fait pas de doute qu'une telle limitation découle d'impératifs d'éthique professionnelle.

Enfin, il faut signaler que la loi du 27 janvier 1987, réintroduisant le secteur privé à l'hôpital supprimé en 1982, permet aux médecins des hôpitaux publics de déroger à l'interdiction d'exercer une activité privée lucrative.

Grâce à une interprétation assez stricte des exceptions apportées au principe de l'interdiction du cumul, la jurisprudence du Conseil d'Etat protège l'indépendance du fonctionnaire par rapport aux intérêts privés et limite, à chaque fois que l'occasion lui en est offerte, les risques de collusion et de compromission de l'agent. Mais il est vrai que le manque général d'informations dont souffre l'administration en matière de cumuls nuit gravement à l'efficacité de ce contrôle.

2.1.2. L'interdiction de prendre des intérêts dans une entreprise privée

L'honneur et la probité du fonctionnaire sont aujourd'hui maintenus par l'article 25 alinéa 2 de la loi du 13 juillet 1983 qui prévoit que "les fonctionnaires ne peuvent prendre, par eux-mêmes ou par personnes interposées, dans une entreprise soumise au contrôle de l'administration à laquelle ils appartiennent ou en relation avec cette dernière, des intérêts de nature à compromettre leur indépendance". Par ce texte, il s'agit d'assurer la neutralité et l'honnêteté de l'action administrative en évitant les conflits d'intérêts.

Cette obligation de probité est renforcée pour les membres de la fonction publique hospitalière, puisque l'article 209 bis du Code de la famille et de l'aide sociale, leur interdit de recevoir des dons de personnes hébergées dans les établissements. Il est impossible de tolérer, qu'un agent titulaire des services hospitaliers, détienne et manipule des fonds, appartenant à un pensionnaire de l'établissement, par le truchement d'un compte bancaire joint ouvert dans une banque.

Il arrive aussi au juge administratif de devoir interpréter la notion de "démission de l'agent public à prix d'argent" lors de l'application de l'article L. 59 du Code des pensions civiles et militaires de retraite. Cette disposition prévoit, en effet, la suspension du droit à l'obtention de la pension, à l'égard de tout agent qui aura été révoqué ou mis à la retraite d'office, pour s'être démis de ses fonctions à prix d'argent ou à des conditions équivalant à une rémunération en argent. A propos d'une sanction disciplinaire, le juge constate qu'un fonctionnaire des impôts "s'est rendu coupable d'une démission de fonctions à prix d'argent, a trahi les devoirs de sa fonction et a jeté le discrédit sur le corps auquel il appartenait".

Mais l'interdiction statutaire est complétée également par une interdiction pénale.

2.2. L'interdiction pénale

2.2.1. Le délit de prise illégale d'intérêts

2.2.1.1. L'application du code pénal par le juge administratif

Ce contrôle, exercé par le juge administratif, présente un caractère relativement original, puisqu'en la matière de délit d'ingérence le juge administratif fait directement application des dispositions du Code pénal.

Récemment, le Conseil d'Etat a annulé pour excès de pouvoir la nomination de M. Beaufret au poste de sous-gouverneur du Crédit foncier de France, au motif qu'il avait été auparavant chef du service des affaires monétaires et financières de la direction du Trésor, et qu'en tant que tel, il avait été amené à contrôler et surveiller les activités du Crédit foncier, violant ainsi les dispositions de l'article 432-13 du nouveau Code pénal. Celui-ci est ainsi rédigé: "Est puni de deux ans d'emprisonnement et de 200 000 F d'amende le fait, par une personne ayant été chargée, en tant que fonctionnaire public ou agent ou préposé d'une administration publique, à raison même de sa fonction, soit d'assurer la surveillance ou le contrôle d'une entreprise privée, soit de conclure des contrats de toute nature avec une entreprise privée, soit d'exprimer son avis sur les opérations effectuées par une entreprise privée, de prendre ou de recevoir une participation par travail, conseil ou capitaux dans l'une de ces entreprises avant l'expiration d'un délai de cinq ans suivant la cessation de cette fonction".

Ces dispositions du nouveau Code pénal s'adressent donc à tous les fonctionnaires, de l'Etat, des collectivités locales, des établissements publics hospitaliers, et la détermination de la sanction demeure, bien entendu, sous le contrôle exclusif du juge judiciaire répressif.

2.2.1.2. L'application du code pénal par le juge judiciaire

Le nouveau Code pénal distingue les délits de prises illégales d'intérêts selon qu'ils sont commis par un fonctionnaire en activité ou un ancien fonctionnaire. L'article 432-12 du nouveau Code pénal dispose: "Le fait, par une personne dépositaire de l'autorité publique ou chargée d'une mission de service public ou par une personne investie d'un mandat électif public, de prendre, recevoir ou conserver, directement ou indirectement, un intérêt quelconque dans une entreprise ou dans une opération dont elle a, au moment de l'acte, en tout ou partie, la charge d'assurer la surveillance, l'administration, la liquidation ou le paiement, est puni de cinq ans d'emprisonnement et de 500 000 F d'amende.

Cette prohibition est très large et vise autant les intérêts personnels pécuniaires du fonctionnaire que ses intérêts moraux. La preuve de la participation à la prise illégale d'intérêts est d'autant plus facilitée que le juge n'a pas à démontrer la participation directe du fonctionnaire mais doit seulement considérer le lien existant entre la mission dont était investi l'agent, sa qualité et la commission de l'infraction.

2.2.2. L'interdiction faite à l'autorité administrative de placer le fonctionnaire en situation d'infraction

Avec l'arrêt "Société Lambda", le Conseil d'Etat a doublement élargi le champ d'application de l'article 432-13 du nouveau Code pénal en l'étendant aux fonctionnaires en détachement et aux nominations à la décision du Gouvernement. Cet article dispose: "est puni de deux ans d'emprisonnement et de 200 000 F d'amende le fait, par une personne ayant été chargée, en tant que fonctionnaire public ou agent ou préposé d'une administration publique, à raison même de sa fonction, soit d'assurer la surveillance ou le contrôle d'une entreprise privée, soit de conclure des contrats de toute nature avec une entreprise privée, soit d'exprimer son avis sur les opérations effectuées par une entreprise privée, de prendre ou de recevoir une participation par le travail, conseil ou capitaux dans l'une de ces entreprises avant l'expiration d'un délai de cinq ans suivant la cessation de cette fonction".

En effet, le juge administratif a réalisé une interprétation extensive de l'article 432-13 du code pénal, dans le sens d'une plus grande rigueur, en étendant ses effets aux fonctionnaires placés en situation de détachement.

Il sera intéressant de savoir dans l'avenir si la Chambre criminelle de la Cour de cassation partagera la même vision du juge administratif et l'appliquera aux fonctionnaires détachés.

L'opposabilité de la prise illégale d'intérêts a également été étendue aux nominations aux emplois à la décision du Gouvernement. Il est vrai qu'il est difficile d'éradiquer le doute qui ne manquera pas de s'immiscer dans les esprits quant à la situation de conflit d'intérêts susceptible de découler d'une telle nomination. Aussi, il est apparu impossible au Conseil d'Etat de préserver la haute fonction publique des foudres du code pénal, et l'on ne peut que se réjouir du caractère audacieux de cette jurisprudence.

L'avertissement solennel ainsi lancé par le juge ne s'adresse pas uniquement aux fonctionnaires en quête d'activités dans le secteur privé, il tance aussi vertement le comportement des autorités administratives en matière de "pantouflage" et d'exercice de leur pouvoir de nomination.

L'apport le plus intéressant de cet arrêt "Société Lambda" réside probablement dans le nouveau principe dégagé par le Conseil selon lequel l'autorité administrative ne doit pas nommer un fonctionnaire dans une entreprise privée, quelle que soit sa position statutaire, s'il a, par ses précédentes fonctions, été chargé d'assurer la surveillance ou le contrôle de cette entreprise, et ce, pendant un délai de cinq ans. Mais sous couvert d'une formule quelque peu elliptique, le Conseil d'Etat a donné aux plus hautes autorités de l'Etat une double leçon de droit et de morale administrative.

Il appartient en effet à l'administration d'agir afin de garantir l'impartialité du service et le désintéressement du fonctionnaire. L'autorité administrative commet donc un excès de pouvoir si elle place le fonctionnaire en situation d'infraction. Elle trahit également la confiance des citoyens et ses fins d'intérêt général et remet en cause, à terme, sa légitimité. Son pouvoir de nomination ne peut donc s'exercer qu'en conformité avec l'intérêt du service.

Cette avancée jurisprudentielle constitue aussi un renforcement du contrôle juridictionnel, jusque-là quasi inexistant, des nominations aux emplois à la décision du Gouvernement.

3. La surveillance institutionnelle des conflits d'intérêts dans la fonction publique française

3.1. Les avis rendus par les commissions de déontologie du "pantouflage"

Le "pantouflage" peut se définir comme la situation trouvée dans le secteur privé, par un fonctionnaire, qui a ainsi renoncé, temporairement ou définitivement, aux autres services de l'Etat et des collectivités publiques. Cette pratique n'est certes pas, en elle-même, contraire à l'intérêt général, puisqu'elle permet à des entreprises privées de bénéficier des compétences et de l'expérience de fonctionnaires ayant souvent exercé des responsabilités importantes dans le secteur public. En contrepartie, le fonctionnaire jouit d'une rémunération nettement plus importante que celle que peut lui offrir la personne publique, et compense ainsi la dévalorisation matérielle de sa fonction, que ne semble pas rehausser le prestige de servir l'Etat.

Il est évident, toutefois, que ce "passage aux affaires" du fonctionnaire peut susciter un certain nombre d'abus. Dès lors, des textes édictés en matière pénale ont été adoptés afin de limiter cette pratique. Mais les sanctions prévues se sont révélées trop lourdes et ces dispositions sont alors, pour l'essentiel, restées lettre morte, les tribunaux n'étant jamais saisis. Les dispositions statutaires n'ont guère connu plus de succès. En effet, la loi a posé, à l'égard des trois fonctions publiques, le principe de l'interdiction, pour les fonctionnaires cessant leurs fonctions de façon temporaire ou définitive, d'exercer des activités dans le secteur privé qui seraient incompatibles avec leurs précédentes fonctions. Mais jusqu'en 1991, ces activités n'étaient définies par aucun texte.

La loi du 28 juin 1994 laisse cependant supposer que, désormais, va être institué un contrôle effectif du "pantouflage", notamment, grâce à la création de commissions de déontologie, destinées à rendre des avis qui, en l'absence de contentieux, tiennent lieu dans l'immédiat de "jurisprudence".

3.1.1. Organisation et fonctionnement de ces commissions

Le décret du 17 février 1995 dispose que les commissions, instituées au sein de chacune des trois fonctions publiques, sont placées auprès du Premier ministre auquel elles doivent remettre un rapport annuel d'activité.

Chaque commission doit être présidée par un conseiller d'Etat et comprend divers membres, parmi lesquels on compte un conseiller maître à la Cour des comptes, trois personnalités qualifiées, le directeur général de l'administration concernée et un membre représentant l'autorité dont relève l'agent. Il faut ajouter, pour la fonction publique territoriale, un représentant de l'association d'élus locaux concernée.

Le Président, le conseiller maître à la Cour des comptes et les personnalités qualifiées sont nommés par décret pour une durée de trois ans sur proposition des ministres concernés. De plus, chaque commission compte un rapporteur général nommé par arrêté ministériel et généralement choisi au sein des grands corps de l'Etat.

L'initiative de la procédure appartient, en définitive, au fonctionnaire lui-même, qui doit informer, par écrit, l'autorité dont il relève, lorsqu'il envisage d'exercer une activité privée et qu'il se trouve dans l'un des cas suivants :

- il demande à être placé en disponibilité ;
- ou bien étant déjà en disponibilité, il souhaite rester dans cette position ;
- il demande à bénéficier d'un congé sans rémunération ;
- ou bénéficiant déjà d'un congé sans rémunération, il souhaite continuer à en bénéficier ;
- il veut quitter définitivement la fonction publique ;
- il a quitté la fonction publique depuis moins de cinq ans ;
- ou déjà en position de disponibilité, ou ayant cessé définitivement ses fonctions depuis moins de cinq ans, il souhaite changer d'activité privée.

L'autorité administrative, qui a reçu la déclaration, a l'obligation de saisir, dans les quinze jours, la commission compétente au regard de la fonction publique concernée. Le fonctionnaire intéressé peut aussi de lui-même saisir la commission, ainsi que le préfet si l'agent appartient à la fonction publique territoriale. Mais tous deux doivent informer de cette saisine l'autorité dont relève l'agent.

La commission dispose alors d'un délai d'un mois pour rendre son avis, à compter de la date de réception du dossier complet au secrétariat de la commission, le silence valant avis favorable à l'égard de l'activité privée envisagée.

La commission détient un véritable pouvoir d'instruction et peut convoquer le fonctionnaire pour entendre ses explications, ou recueillir auprès des personnes publiques et privées les informations nécessaires à l'accomplissement de sa mission. Bien évidemment, les droits de la défense sont respectés. Ainsi, le fonctionnaire peut être entendu sur sa demande ou se faire assister par un conseil.

L'avis rendu par la commission est ensuite transmis à l'autorité dont relève le fonctionnaire, qui en informe l'intéressé.

Cet avis n'est cependant pas rendu public. Il faut reconnaître que sa publication au Journal officiel ne présenterait aucun intérêt particulier.

Par ailleurs, l'avis de la commission ne lie pas la décision de l'autorité administrative, qui peut refuser d'accorder, au fonctionnaire qui le lui demande, la disponibilité, en raison de l'incompatibilité avec les fonctions envisagées.

Mais afin d'inciter à la célérité de la prise de décision, le silence gardé par l'autorité administrative pendant un mois après l'avis de la commission vaut approbation du sens de l'avis rendu par la commission.

3.1.2. La "Jurisprudence" rendue par ces commissions

La commission de déontologie de l'Etat a été la première installée et a déjà rendu un certain nombre d'avis intéressants. Ces derniers font application de l'article premier du décret du 17 février 1995, qui distingue deux types d'activités professionnelles, incompatibles avec les fonctions antérieures exercées: d'une part, celles interdites en raison des liens ayant pu exister dans le passé entre le fonctionnaire et l'entreprise, et, d'autre part, celles prohibées en raison des liens futurs susceptibles de se nouer entre le fonctionnaire et l'entreprise qui souhaite le recruter.

3.1.2.1. Les incompatibilités en raison des liens passés avec l'entreprise

La première interdiction vise les liens qui ont pu exister, en raison des fonctions qu'il exerçait, entre le fonctionnaire et l'entreprise dans laquelle il envisage d'aller travailler. Cette catégorie d'activités, interdites aux fonctionnaires en disponibilité et aux fonctionnaires ayant cessé définitivement leurs fonctions depuis moins de cinq ans, est ainsi définie:

activités professionnelles dans une entreprise privée, lorsque l'intéressé a été, au cours des cinq dernières années précédant la cessation définitive de ses fonctions ou sa mise en disponibilité, chargé, à raison même de sa fonction:

a) soit de surveiller ou contrôler cette entreprise ;
b) soit de passer des marchés ou contrats avec cette entreprise ou d'exprimer un avis sur de tels marchés ou contrats.

Cette interdiction s'applique également aux activités exercées dans une entreprise:

- qui détient au moins 30% du capital de l'entreprise susmentionnée, ou dont le capital est, à hauteur de 30% au moins, détenu soit par l'entreprise susmentionnée, soit par une entreprise détenant aussi 30% au moins du capital de l'entreprise susmentionnée ;
- ou qui a conclu avec l'entreprise susmentionnée un contrat comportant une exclusivité de droit ou de fait.

Le champ d'application de ce texte apparaît relativement restreint, puisqu'il ne concerne expressément que les fonctionnaires au sens du droit administratif, et non l'ensemble des agents visés par le Code pénal. Mais il a, par la suite, été étendu aux agents non titulaires.

La commission de déontologie pour la fonction publique de l'Etat a décidé qu'il n'est pas nécessaire pour justifier l'interdiction que le fonctionnaire ait effectivement et personnellement contrôlé cette entreprise, il suffit qu'il ait seulement eu vocation à exercer ce contrôle. C'est ainsi qu'un sous-directeur à la direction de l'architecture de Paris, chargé de passer des marchés, n'a pas reçu d'avis favorable pour aller travailler dans une filiale d'une société concluant habituellement des marchés avec cette direction.

La notion de contrôle a donc été étendue et paraît indépendante du pouvoir de décision, que peut détenir le fonctionnaire. Il est indifférent, par exemple, que l'agent n'ait pas possédé de délégation de signature. Par conséquent, l'incompatibilité n'est pas réservée aux fonctionnaires situés sur les sommets de la hiérarchie administrative. Un simple avis donné à propos d'un contrat ou d'un marché peut justifier l'incompatibilité.

Mais une telle jurisprudence place dans une position délicate les membres des cabinets ministériels. En raison de leurs fonctions, ils auraient pu être considérés comme chargés de surveiller toutes les entreprises exerçant leur activité dans le domaine des attributions de leur ministre. Au nom d'une "interprétation raisonnable" des textes, il n'a pas été interdit à l'ancien directeur du cabinet du ministre de l'Economie, ou du Premier ministre, ou à l'ancien secrétaire général de la Présidence de la République d'aller travailler dans une banque.

3.1.2.2. Les incompatibilités en raison des liens futurs avec l'entreprise

Ces incompatibilités visent les activités lucratives, salariées ou non, dans un organisme ou dans une entreprise privés, ainsi que les activités libérales si, par leur nature ou leurs conditions d'exercice et, eu égard aux fonctions précédemment exercées par l'intéressé, ces activités portent atteinte à la dignité desdites fonctions ou risquent de compromettre ou de mettre en cause le fonctionnement normal, l'indépendance ou la neutralité du service.

L'atteinte à la dignité des fonctions n'a été retenue, pour l'instant, que dans un seul cas, au demeurant flagrant. En effet, le projet d'un agent des impôts, de créer un cabinet de soins des malades par imposition des mains, a été considéré comme portant atteinte à la dignité des fonctions exercées, cette activité constituant un exercice illégal de la médecine.

Les cas de mise en cause du fonctionnement normal, de l'indépendance ou de la neutralité du service ont été, au contraire, plus nombreux devant la commission. Celle-ci ne s'est pas engagée dans un essai de définition et considère ces trois notions comme étant indissociables. Aussi prend-elle un avis défavorable lorsque le fonctionnaire, qui souhaite partir, risque d'avoir dans sa nouvelle activité professionnelle des liens avec son ancien service et ses anciens collègues. La commission souhaite ainsi empêcher qu'une entreprise ne recrute un fonctionnaire, que pour son entregent et sa connaissance du milieu administratif. Il est donc essentiel aux yeux des membres de la commission qu'un agent n'exerce pas sa nouvelle profession dans le même secteur d'activité et dans le même ressort territorial que lors de ses fonctions antérieures.

Ainsi, un inspecteur des impôts ou un inspecteur du travail peuvent devenir avocats s'ils ne traitent pas d'affaires relatives à la circonscription territoriale de leur ancien service.

En revanche, un inspecteur des impôts ne peut pas devenir conseiller fiscal ou avocat fiscaliste dans le ressort territorial de son ancien service, tandis qu'un ingénieur des travaux ruraux ou un ingénieur des travaux publics de l'Etat ne peut exercer les fonctions d'ingénieur conseil auprès de collectivités locales ou d'entreprises soumissionnant à des marchés de travaux publics dans le département où il exerçait précédemment ses fonctions.

A l'égard des fonctionnaires ayant participé à des cabinets ministériels et ayant eu, à raison de leurs fonctions, une influence sur de nombreux services et agents, la jurisprudence des commissions est encline à l'indulgence et ne s'oppose qu'aux situations dans lesquelles les risques de collusion sont trop évidents. La position de la commission se comprend aisément, tant il ne s'agit pas de dresser entre la fonction publique et le secteur privé une barrière infranchissable, mais seulement de limiter les abus du "passage aux affaires" des fonctionnaires.

Le caractère récent de l'installation de ces commissions ne permet de dresser un premier bilan qu'à partir de la commission compétente pour la fonction publique de l'Etat. En une année d'activité, la commission a rendu 552 avis qui, si l'on exclut les 80 avis d'incompétence et d'irrecevabilité, étaient dans 93 % des cas favorables et dans 7 % des cas défavorables. Ce bilan permet aussi de relever que les "pantouflages" sont d'autant plus nombreux que l'on s'élève dans la hiérarchie administrative. Les grands corps de l'Etat les plus concernés par les demandes d'avis sont dans l'ordre décroissant: le corps des mines, celui des Ponts et Chaussées, la Cour des comptes, le génie rural, l'inspection générale des finances et le Conseil d'Etat. Sur les 82 avis rendus concernant les grands corps, un seul, relatif à un ingénieur des Ponts et Chaussées, a été défavorable.

Le succès du contrôle du pantouflage ne doit pas uniquement se mesurer à l'aune des avis défavorables rendus par les commissions de déontologie. Il faut aussi prendre en compte, mais sans évidemment pouvoir le mesurer, l'aspect préventif et dissuasif d'un tel contrôle.

3.2. Le service central de prévention de la corruption

3.2.1. Organisation et fonctionnement du service

La loi du 29 janvier 1993, relative à la prévention de la corruption et à la transparence de la vie économique et des procédures publiques, a instauré un Service central de prévention de la corruption, placé auprès du Ministre de la Justice, et chargé de centraliser les informations nécessaires à la détection et à la prévention des faits de corruption active ou passive, de trafic d'influence commis par des personnes exerçant une fonction publique ou par des particuliers, de concussion, de prise illégale d'intérêts ou d'atteinte à la liberté et à l'égalité des candidats dans les marchés publics.

Dirigé par un magistrat de l'ordre judiciaire et composé de magistrats et d'agents publics, son rôle consiste essentiellement à donner des avis à des autorités administratives qui le lui demandent sur les mesures susceptibles d'être prises pour prévenir de tels faits. Le Service peut aussi prêter son concours aux autorités judiciaires.

3.2.2. Les activités du service: premier bilan

Installé depuis le 9 mars 1993, le Service n'a commencé à réellement fonctionner qu'à partir d'octobre 1993. Lors de sa première année d'activité, il a reçu des informations provenant d'administrations et de particuliers portant sur une vingtaine d'affaires.

Dans son premier rapport annuel, le Service central de prévention de la corruption a mis l'accent, entre autres, sur la pratique du lobbying et sur la corruption par rapport aux collectivités locales et au contrôle de légalité.

L'influence des groupes de pression et le développement récent des actions de lobbying mettent de plus en plus en péril l'impartialité des décisions administratives.

En 1992, la commission de prévention de la corruption réclamait l'encadrement juridique des activités de lobbying à l'instar de la réglementation existante aux Etats-Unis. Le Service central de prévention de la corruption a d'ailleurs repris cette idée en constatant que "l'image du lobbyiste arpentant les couloirs du Parlement est sommaire, tant vis-à-vis du professionnel qu'à l'égard de l'Etat: la procédure législative n'est pas purement parlementaire et les lobbyistes ont compris qu'ils devaient intervenir en amont, auprès des fonctionnaires chargés de la rédaction du projet de texte".

Ces risques d'atteinte à l'impartialité et à l'indépendance des fonctionnaires ne menacent pas uniquement les agents de la fonction publique de l'Etat. Ils pèsent, de surcroît, très précisément sur les agents de la fonction publique territoriale qui disposent depuis la décentralisation de pouvoirs considérables. Faute de contre-pouvoirs réels et de contrôles efficaces, les fonctionnaires territoriaux constituent en fait des cibles de choix à de tels jeux d'influence.

Dès lors, deux orientations sont possibles. Il faut, soit, protéger plus sûrement le fonctionnaire des pressions exercées sur lui et sanctionner plus sévèrement le trafic d'influence, soit, réglementer l'activité de lobbying elle-même. Le Service central de prévention de la corruption envisage plutôt la seconde voie en demandant à ce que les lobbyistes soient enregistrés auprès d'un service interministériel représentant toutes les administrations. L'établissement d'une telle liste permettrait aux pouvoirs publics d'avoir une vision synthétique immédiate des sollicitations dont ils sont l'objet.

Bibliographie

Chambon, F. et GASPON, O., *La déontologie administrative*, Paris, LGDJ, (1997).

Jean-Pierre, D., *L'éthique du fonctionnaire civil Son contrôle dans les jurisprudences administrative et constitutionnelle françaises*, Aix-en-Provence, Thèse, (1996).

Jean-Pierre, D., "Le pantouflage et les commissions de déontologie des fonctions publiques", in J.-L. Bergel, *Droit et déontologies professionnelles*, Aix-en-Provence, Librairie de l'Université, (1997), pp. 229-248.

Vigouroux, C., *Déontologie des fonctions publiques*, Paris, Dalloz, (1995).

The Recent Debate on Curbing Political Corruption

K. Robben[*]

It is common knowledge that some politicians eagerly make use of their position to unlawfully enrich themselves or a third party. The opportunity thereto is created by the environment in which they work, since this allows for or even incites corruption. One of the main requirements of their job is to decide between alternatives. Afterwards it is very difficult to assess whether the decision was influenced, and, if it was, whether this happened in an unlawful and inadmissible way. Such an environment, receptive to political corruption, is brought about by defaults in the political-administrative system. However, of crucial importance to the issue is that these defaults are deliberately not remedied, or even kept secret to the outside world. A failure or even lack of control on the exercise of political power is what makes this possible. The eventual result is a deficient protection of citizens from corruption and its consequences, which in turn undermines democracy.

Ideally speaking, everyone should act with integrity and in a conscientious manner, certainly politicians. If they don't abide by the law themselves, they hardly have the authority to make citizens do so. But since every human being is fallible, so are politicians, and therefore political corruption will always persist. However, the impossibility to deal with this human characteristic does not mean that the social structures in which politics takes place should not be altered to stop them from being a breeding ground for and invitation to corruption. One may wonder where the moving force for such changes will come from, considering that those who have built up an entire network of relations thanks to corruption will not be removed from power easily. The right-minded politicians, on the other hand, lack the "political weight", and the citizens can only exercise influence through elections, which are in fact for a large part controlled by the same political parties that also lodge corrupt politicians. Most probably we will have to wait for an alliance of moral politicians and alert citizens who do possess the political weight and the moral characteristics to curb political corruption. Although corruption may give the impression that everything is running smoothly, no pains should be spared to curb it.

In this text I want to discuss some means to curb political corruption, applied in Belgium. The essential condition for these means to be successful is that political corruption is experienced as reprehensible, and that furthermore the political will exists to actually try to fight political corruption. First, however, it will be necessary to define corruption.

1. Toward a Definition of Political Corruption

Numerous essays, books and studies on corruption still have not resulted in a clear-cut definition of the phenomenon. According to An Deysine (Deysine, 1980:448), political scientists initially emphasised the importance of a correct definition, while since the

---
[*] Katrien Robben, Catholic University of Leuven, Belgium.

eighties they seem to admit implicitly that everybody knows what corruption is, which enables them to proceed beyond the question of definition. It is now generally accepted to include at least abuse of power: "any illegal or unethical use of governmental authority for personal or political gain." (Simon & Eitzen, 1990:209) If you consider this to be a rather narrow definition, as is the one in the Belgian Penal Code, the following broader definition, composed of several definitions to be found in the literature, allows us to bring together a larger number of relevant elements: political corruption is the purposeful and secretive violation of the standards of moral behaviour in a certain political community by public servants or politicians who act or neglect to act to the advantage of a certain person or group of persons, so that the action no longer answers up to its dictated purpose, and this person or group of persons gains access to a higher level of decision-making than in case of a public transaction, so that damage is done to other persons or groups of persons or so that at least these aren't protected from it; this behaviour may result in tangible benefits for one or all participants.

This definition covers a much wider variety of actions, which are equally corrupt compared to the actions covered by the notion of abuse of power. Capturing all the relevant actions in a law that will allow corruption to be fought successfully, is very difficult because they often constitute borderline cases between ethically right or wrong types of actions. We then need to be able to depend on the moral characteristics of the people involved. A politician of high morals will know which actions are permissible and which are not, but someone of rather low morals who is only interested in his own career will not bother with ethically right and wrong actions and try to gain as much as possible. Still, when we look at the earlier mentioned human fallibility, it becomes clear that enormous efforts will have to be made to curb political corruption effectively. The main effort must be focused on restructuring the political-administrative system.

2. Causes of Political Corruption

Before we can turn to the potential remedies for corruption, it is necessary to provide a brief outline of the possible causes. In this area significant disagreements exist among authors who have studied the phenomenon. There is unanimity on the fact that corruption is widespread, but the thesis that it is the result of some dishonest individuals has lost a lot of support. In Belgium, it has recently been argued that corruption is allowed to flourish by a caste of influential power holders who thereby protect their vested interests. And that is exactly what Yves Mény argues in his book "La corruption de la république" (Mény, 1992). He draws four scenarios (p. 243-248) for corruption going from bad to worse. It is only in the fourth case that he comes to what we would definitely call corruption, but which he calls direct corruption. Here the relevant actions pertain not only to obtaining a right or a favour, but to breaking the rules and laws that would under normal circumstances prevent someone from achieving the desired decision, or which would at least not guarantee the certain outcome of it. Therefore, according to Mény, corruption occurs more frequently in situations where an official has largely discretionary powers and furthermore when the costs of a decision going against the individual are high. Basically, such behaviour can be classified as an instance of unlawful exercise of authority. The corrupter and the corrupted gain advantage from such transactions at the cost of the state. Apart from these relations between administration and citizens, corruption also occurs in other sectors, namely where state and private enterprise temporarily enter into business with each other. Here again, it becomes clear how difficult it is to demonstrate corruption, since we usually tend to define as corruption only those actions that take a monetary form, while rather more informal and sociable forms of interaction are left aside. Yet in both cases the exercise of authority is diverted from its purpose. In Mény's view, it gets even worse when a few public decision makers are enabled, through the importance of the economic and financial decisions they take, to define the nature of the relations between the administration and the private sector. These public servants, few but well positioned as they are, take decisions and are thus able to set up a parallel system in which decisions will be made that are favourable to the political friends. This is a secret system, which is nevertheless being controlled perfectly by a circle of insiders. In the middle of the constitutional state a club, a mafia-like club, is thus set up, obeying its own rules and codes of conduct, salaries and sanctions, thereby safeguarding its own interests. The power holders that are members of this secret system, will abuse their granted authority to take decisions in their and their friends favour. And as I will next explain, it often is very difficult to find out which influences have played a role in the decisions politicians take, so that one can hardly control if it was made merely to benefit the insiders.

As Hoetjes (Hoetjes, 1979:7) put it, the ultimate foundation of corruption is obviously the fact that, in the political world many decisions have to be made on matters that are on the brink of the acceptable. Politicians take decisions about alternatives, with each alternative having its moral merits. But the future remains uncertain, even after the decision is made, which compels them to open their mind to other influences in society. Consequently a large grey area exists for the politician to take decisions in, in which it cannot be determined with certainty which influences and which interests are right and lawful and which are not. The problem for the politician will of course be that he can quite easily enlarge his power through corruption, but that a possible revelation constitutes a serious threat to his re-election. For democracy both actual corruption and the imputations that often go along with it are pernicious.

It seems undeniable that political corruption can only develop and flourish as a result of certain deficiencies in the political-administrative system of a country, in this case Belgium. More specifically, the causes summed up in the literature are in the first place the increased complexity of the functioning of the public administration due to unclear laws and indistinct prescriptions. The amount of regulations that have to be conformed to by public administrators has increased enormously to ensure the safeguarding of public interest. It is therefore no longer workable to take into account all these regulations, which does of course result in passing them by. So the final outcome constitutes nevertheless an increased risk to the preservation of public interest. This is connected with another evolution, namely bureaucratisation. Large areas of decision making have been relegated to public administration, which has seen its power expand together with its tasks, and at the same time these decisions have been withdrawn from the public view. Most important though is the fact that this shift in decision making power has resulted in private groups gaining access to public administration bodies, which once again gives rise to an increased risk for the public interest to be endangered.

A second possible cause is the lack of financial control on executive power. At bottom, this is due to the increased complexity and obscurity of the political-administrative system which makes the application of the principle of democratic control almost impossible. In theory, parliament has some means for control at its disposal, but the complexity and the scope of its task means that it does not have enough ways and that parliamentarians need specialised help. Apart from that, parliament's independence from the government has decreased, which is hardly surprising, given the fact that the government is made up from the ranks of the same political parties that dominate parliament.

Thirdly, there are the political appointments. Politicians can be suspected of using these to increase their power by means of appointing friends to important positions, so that they can guarantee their influence on policy, even if they will not be re-elected, through a web of relations (cf. Mény s mafia-like club).

And finally, there is the fact that the public and private sector have become intertwined. The bottleneck is obviously the concentration of power that goes with it, during the holding of office as well as afterwards. Leading figures in politics have to take into account that their participation in economic decisions goes hand in hand with political influence, and that eventually they do not owe this political influence to themselves but to their electorate. This makes one wonder whether political power holders are not using political influence for the advancement of private interests. The question becomes all the more compelling if they have their seats in companies which depend on state orders and contracts for their continued existence. It is clear that simply ignoring such conflicts of interests must not be allowed.

All together these deficiencies amount to what can be specified as an environment that invites corruption: it is the aggregate of elements in the political-administrative structure of a country and in the accepted political practice which makes possible or even encourages the promotion of one's private interests by way of public exercise of power. The development of such an environment rests on a constantly recurring, distressing lack of democratic control, which is due to a shortage of means for the authorised controlling bodies, and in the worst case even to the complete absence of such controlling bodies. So the persistence of political corruption is also determined by the social environment in which we find ourselves.

The following pages will deal with the possible adjustments of the social structures, which might allow for an environment inviting corruption to be remedied.

3. The Fight against Political Corruption

A condition imperative for the successful curbing of corruption, is the existence of the political will to restrain it. Otherwise many measures may be carried out, which will never be enforced rigorously since that would bring about too many victims in their own circle of political friends or damage their own interests. It is very likely that the extent of corruption in the western societies has become so large over the years, that the consequences of the disclosure of some scandals could not be properly estimated, neither for their own political party, nor for others. It might even bring about the end of democracy as we know it. Nevertheless, that cannot be an excuse for not fighting corruption at all. There is no justification for not trying to improve the functioning of the political-administrative system in order to prevent from happening the sort of things that now have to be kept secret for the sake of democracy.

The changes in the political-administrative system that will be discussed here, are in the first place the improvement of the environment, secondly the improvement of the work of the government, thirdly an improved control on the government and finally some potential changes in the law. All these elements can then be bundled in the notion of democratic transparency .

3.1. Improvement of the Environment

The fight against corruption can only succeed if the environment in which politicians and public servants work no longer invites them to act corruptly. Several changes can help to put a halt to government complacency. One of these is curtailing political appointments. They may guarantee an equilibrium, but their implications go far beyond that. If someone wants to get appointed for a certain job, they will be persuaded to become member of a party that will guarantee them the appointment. If it were to stop there, it would be tolerable. Unfortunately, it doesn't. The appointed party members will keep silent about abuses if the interests of their party might be damaged, or if other party members might be harmed by a breach of silence. Evidently, this amounts to an abuse of the trust the people need to put in their public servants: if one turns to the public administration these days, one really does not know if a request or a complaint is being rejected on legitimate grounds or because of party political interests.

A development that is not to be overlooked is the influence of private enterprise on political decisions. Many public servants take up a flexible position towards these enterprises in the hope of being employed there some time. However, the danger of excessive flexibility cannot be underestimated. Another aspect of these intertwined relations is the concentration of power as a result of the combination of offices. This leads to politicians participating in economic decisions, while they owe their political influence to their electorate and should in fact serve their interests. One wonders whether these politicians do not use this granted influence to achieve private goals instead of serving public interest. Voters no longer have the means of control on the representative here. True, accumulation of offices and combination of offices does not necessarily mean that corruption is involved, but they are often favourable conditions for its occurrence, not only because of the circumstances they create with regard to disputable situations, but also because they offer possibilities to those who dare or those who are least able to resist the temptation. And the same conflict of interest is likely to arise in the rendering of services. This can very easily go off the rails in the direction of misuse of office, which is definitely to be categorised as corruption.

Two sorts of solutions to these problems with conflicts of interest are suggested by Yves Mény (Mény, 1992:39-39), at least with regard to members of parliament, as in France ministers are since 1958 forbidden to simultaneously exercise any other professional activity. The first solution consists of not drawing up a restrictive list of incompatibilities, since every list inevitably is partial and unjust and not capable of taking into account all the numerous complexities of social reality. Mény therefore suggests an investigation into the situation of each separate member of parliament by a Bureau of the Chamber of

Representatives under the supervision of the Council of State. This suggestion could easily be implemented in Belgium as well.

A second solution, according to Mény, is the complete prohibition of the accumulation of any private function with a parliamentary mandate. Measures could then be taken to make sure that every member of parliament could easily return to his or her prior occupation, which would put an end to the web of authorities representatives combine. Usually the political class tries to depict this phenomenon as merely involving a few isolated and deviating cases. But the nature of most cases does not differ from a conflict of interest, it is merely the seriousness of the facts that changes, says Mény.

Equally alarming is the installation of pressure groups. The major concern here is with the fact that pressure groups represent only the interests of their members. The leaders of these groups are not elected by their members, although they defend their interests at the federal level. This means that they cannot be controlled or called back. Nevertheless, their democratic importance is not to be underestimated. It arises from an important ingredient of the type of political decision making that has evolved in Belgium, namely consultation. This means that an organised participation in the allocative power is guaranteed to those depending on this power. Pressure groups are an important tool for individual citizens to validate their capacity to influence the social and political policy. The key question however concerns the political efficiency of a system of pressure groups. They form a group around partial interests, which evidently evokes the question of the eventual realisation of what citizens find valuable. We may of course imagine that pressure groups representing interests deemed less important by the population as a whole are more powerful, especially politically speaking, than groups that represent more highly estimated interests, which will then obstruct the realisation of the more highly valued interests. A consultative system therefore only satisfies those needs which guarantee the continued existence of a pressure group. A solution may consist in neutralising pressure groups politically. Politicians would then not have to withstand so much pressure from these groups in the direction of partial interests that may not correspond to the public interest.

3.2. Improvement of the Work of the Government

Improving the work of the government can be achieved through a better definition of the government s responsibilities. Secondly, more publicity is required. Citizens must be given access to administrative files in order to enable them to optimally accomplish their controlling task if they wish to do so. And they must not only receive the data they ask for, they should also be given the data that public servants consider necessary for studying the matter citizens are interested in. In the US, many possible cases of flagrant abuse of power have been avoided thanks to such a Freedom of Information Act .

Above all increased visibility of the decision making processes and broader information as to who takes the decisions is necessary. Extensive bureaucratisation results in withdrawing major fields of decision making from the public eye. In this way, responsibilities can no longer be determined. Such a situation evidently encourages the development of an environment inviting corruption, since pressure groups find themselves in a position where it is very easy to force through their private interests, which in the end facilitates complying with requests from individuals. It is therefore of elementary importance to increase the visibility of the decision making processes and to provide the public with information on who takes decisions, because only in this way can corrupt politicians be prevented from hiding behind non-corrupt politicians as nobody knows who takes the decisions. In a transitional phase, however, awareness is needed from politicians as well as from citizens for the bringing out of scandals, merely to inflict damage on political opponents. If of course the structure of government were to be reformed so as to guarantee a more personal and less standardised treatment, citizens wouldn't need to address individual politicians in the first place, thereby damaging the public interest.

A third way to improve the work of the government is to establish a better financial control of executive power. Especially the control on the semi-autonomous government agencies needs to be expanded. And not to be neglected, of course, is the financial control on political parties. It is common practice amongst politicians to cause confusion between the practices of financing political parties in the seventies and eighties, and straightforward corruption. In Belgium the budget political parties can spend on an election has been restricted to 45 million franks (±1.2 mln. US$) per party and no more than 1 million franks (±26000 US$) per individual politician. Parties are also forced to keep records of all their expenses, and to make these expenses public. Expenditure records are overhauled every year to check their authenticity. Since 1989 political parties are given a yearly government allowance as a means for functioning in order to increase their independence. In 1993 donations from firms to political parties were prohibited. A next step would be a register of the property of politicians at the beginning and at the end of their term of office.

3.3. Increase of the Control on the Government

A third reform of the political-administrative system to be considered is the increase of control on the government. There are several ways to achieve this goal. Since the possibility for this form of control also rests with the representatives elected by the citizens, firstly the opportunities of these citizens to check the work carried out by their representatives and thus their ability to actually exercise their control through knowledgeable voting should be enhanced. At present, it is no longer obvious for a voter to find the promotion of all he deems important reflected in the program of one single political party. Further, the electorate rarely participates in political activity. It is therefore often suggested that voters should also be given the opportunity to vote on separate matters. In Belgium, the political "caste" tries to avoid such referenda, because they are well aware of the discordance that might be created between Flanders and Wallonia. This does not mean, however, that politicians should be allowed to hide behind this excuse, instead of trying to find out about voters' concerns and wishes. Politicians will maintain the authority to bundle these demands on a higher level and thereby exceed the inevitable self-centred nature of each voter's interest. But that is quite different from merely realising their own private interests, without even wanting to know what it is citizens have elected them to do.

A second way to improve the control on the government is suggested by Bouman (Bouman, 1978:216-218): do away with professional politicians. Bouman holds that professionals will try to increase their chances for reelection through every possible means, even the less high-principled ones: they will accumulate functions to increase their power and influence to make sure they will stand for a safe seat. The drawback of this accumulation of offices is obvious: politicians lack time to exercise each of their functions properly, because they are overloaded. Apart from that, professionals who accumulate will be less eager to bring charges against abuses, lest they ruin their chances of ever being eligible for a certain position. But citizens are not interested in the career of a politician; they seek to find someone who will defend their interests as best as possible on the higher levels of decision making. They trust the politician for doing what he is supposed to do. Bouman admits that it's only human to try and make a career for oneself. But if this is one's only aim, one should not want to be a politician in the first place. Bouman suggests we move toward a system with some sort of task forces. For example, the chamber of representatives would consist of people who resign after one year in function and go back to the work they used to do before.

A fourth way to improve control of executive power is to reverse the burden of proof. This would imply that a politician who is accused of a crime, in this case corruption, has to prove he didn't commit it, while at present whoever brings the charge against a politician has to prove the crime was indeed committed. It would mean that corrupt politicians can no longer hide away behind non-corrupt ones. Using this measure, we could tackle the secretiveness of corruption. The other side of the medal are the false accusations to try and eliminate an opponent. Still it is worthwhile to examine the possibilities of reversing the burden of proof and of working out a protection system against false accusations.

Last but not least there is "whistle blowing". Control of the government must not only be exercised by parliament; citizens can also play their part in it. Yet this requires alert citizens who are willing to pay attention to what goes on above their heads and who want to fight for it to happen in a correct and just way. In practice, these citizens will mostly be public servants or others who have access to the necessary information about the actions of the government. Even then it will not be easy for them to decide to blow the whistle, because they will always find themselves in a subordinate position. They turn to whistle blowing only as a last resort, when they have no more other means against the immoral actions of their superiors, that is, when all other ways to settle or solve the matter internally have been exhausted or simply do not exist. Whistle blowing is a power in the hands of those who suffer from moral powerlessness, but they need to be well aware of the fact that it can turn against them like a boomerang. It is evident that decision makers don't like to be rapped over the knuckles. They will cleverly divert the attention from the complaint to the lack of loyalty from the subordinate who, for instance, has always been an outsider in the department, which allows them to nip the matter in the bud. The alert citizen will evidently know what is going on, but he may not be able to keep it from happening. Nevertheless it will raise the question what the decision makers are trying to keep from the public eye.

3.4. Changes in Law

Finally, some potential changes in the law may help to curb political corruption. It is clear that the penal code needs to be repressive enough to deter people from turning towards corruption, but if they do it anyway, the punishment must be sufficiently heavy to keep them from ever even considering to do it again. At the moment, the Belgian legal system does not discourage political corruption. But, according to Mény, laws and repression will never suffice to root out corruption; we can only hope they will reduce the occasions on which to give in to the temptation so that the political world may find back its dignity. Of course, several problems will arise when laws need to be updated. The politicians who need to make the new law or vote on a change of the old one will try to disguise the problem, by claiming that it is only an individual who made a slip, and not at all the entire political system that is corrupt.

Another problem that occurs has to do with the severity of the punishment for different forms of political corruption. Decision makers don't seem to be able to reach an agreement on what is to be categorised as corruption and to what degree and what isn't, which makes it very difficult to determine the severity of punishment needed for different corrupt actions.

A final suggestion to be taken under consideration comes from Bouman (p. 218). He pleads for introducing a category of "Crimes against the population", besides the category of "Crimes against the State". Here penalties would have to be attached to threatening and damaging the environment and the interests and well-being of the population. He even suggests imprisonment, for crimes against the environment as well as for the bribing and for delivering false construction permits, or for allowing a firm to function without a permit.

4. Democratic Transparency

Taken together, the principles to be considered in the fight against political corruption converge in what can be defined as democratic transparency. This ethical principle is realised provided that the following measures are taken (De Clercq, 1980:652-654):

- The identification of the real powers: "of the groups and the structures in which they are embodied and of the interests of which they are the expression". Firstly, however, the recognition of such powers is needed, because if the political world does not want to recognise that the real power lies elsewhere than it will be very difficult to identify it. Only then can a new system of incompatibilities be designed.

- The formulation of rules concerning accumulation and combination of offices by politicians. A general consensus is growing on the fact that the legislator should intervene by establishing the incompatibility of political offices with additional jobs or at least by forcing such combinations of offices to be made public.

- A remedy for the appalling lack of objective standards for governmental decisions and of means for control on these decisions as well as on their implementation. Once again, it is imperative that the political will hereto exists. Apart from that, such remedy merely marks the application of the fundamental standard of political ethics: any power exerted that touches on public matters should be made to justify itself.

- A professional code for politicians, just as there is one for public servants, journalists, lawyers and doctors. Rules of conduct exist within political parties, but one wonders if they suffice, especially if we consider that the primary concern of a political party is the increase of its power. The difficulty about a code of conduct is that it should be workable, while at the same time guarantee the necessary freedom of action for politicians.

The real problem is that ethical behaviour may be accountable to two completely different and irreconcilable fundamental rules: it can on the one hand be oriented towards an ethic of ultimate ends or on the other hand towards an ethic of responsibility.

> " No ethics in the world can dodge the fact that in numerous instances the attainment of good ends is bound to the fact that one must be willing to pay the price of using morally dubious means or at least dangerous ones - and facing the possibility or even the probability of evil ramifications. From no ethics in the world can it be concluded when and to what extent the ethically good purpose justifies the ethically dangerous means and ramifications." (Weber, 1973:121)

In reality, ethical ideals are powerless, yet at the same time indispensable. A professional code would at the very least tell politicians what is expected of them, for as far as they do not already know that. And although they may not be able to attain the prescribed goal, they will know what to strive for, as opposed to their present struggle for power.

> "Its real political relevance consists of its indirect effects, through the constant pressure it can in many ways exert on the pragmatic ethics of the use of power, through the ethical resistance it keeps mobilising against the pure game of power. For politicians it is the criticism of outsiders, but to citizens it can only be helpful in their attempt not to be fooled." (De Clercq, 1980:655)

It is impossible to conclude otherwise than by pointing out that in the long term political corruption creates more difficulties than it solves, and that in the end it is the citizens who will be the major victims.

5. Conclusion

A corrupt act involves at least two people, corrupter and corrupted. For citizens to try and obtain a favour is irresponsible and shows little concern for the public interest. If politicians abuse the authority granted to them to the advantage of a third party or to enrich themselves, they will wrest the purpose of their function for private gain. This purpose is nowhere described clearly, but we may assume that politicians should at least look after the public interest and take decisions from that point of view, be it as interpreted by their own political party. In reality, it is easy to imagine that a politician can (gladly) overlook this assumption, enabling him to strive for the maintenance of his own position. It is of course incorrect to assume that all politicians are necessarily corrupt. But every politician who is trying to be re-elected will naturally (have to) try to increase his personal power and influence so that he can command respect and thus conquer an important office, which will in turn increase his standing, and so on. If, to make sure he succeeds in his attempt, he turns to political corruption, part of the reason is provided by the political system that allows and incites him to do so. Political corruption can easily develop in a welcoming environment, brought about by the defaults in the political-administrative system that are deliberately not remedied or even kept secret. What makes this possible is a failure or even lack of control on the exercise of political power.

If curbing corruption is deemed necessary, it needs to be done through a combination of measures in several areas. Firstly, the environment should be made less welcoming to corruption. Secondly, the work of the government has to be improved. Thirdly, the functioning of the government should be under constant, thorough supervision by well-equipped controlling bodies. Some changes in the law will help to enforce all this. In the end, all reforms can be bundled into the notion of democratic transparency, an increase of which is imperative if corruption is to be suppressed.

Bibliography

Bouman, H., *Ambtelijke Willekeur en Corruptie in Nederland*, Baarn: Het wereldvenster, (1978).

De Clercq, B J., "Politieke Beroepsethiek en Politieke Corruptie", *Res Publica*, (1980), pp 633-655

Deysine, A., "Political Corruption: a Review of the Literature", *European Journal of Political Research*, N.7, (1980), pp. 447-462.

Hoetjes, B J.S., "Het Voorkomen en Voorkómen van Corruptie - een Ecologisch Perspectief", *Civis Mundi*, N1, (1979), pp. 5-15

Mény, Y , *La Corruption de la République*, Paris: Fayard, (1992)

Simon, D. & Eitzen, S., *Elite Deviance*, Boston: Allyn and Bacon, (1990), third edition.

Weber, M., "Politics as a Vocation", in Gerth, H & Wright Mills, C., *From Max Weber Essays in Sociology*, New York: Oxford University Press, (1973), pp. 77-128

Reports of the
EGPA Permanent Study Groups

# Report of the Study Group on Agriculture

J. Chr. Van Dalen[*]

The theme of the study group was -and will be for the near future- "government and the agri-chain".

Agri-culture, or (as is said more fashionable nowadays) "agribusiness", is in a turbulent transition. Within EU-countries agribusiness policies and practices are changing at different pace, but in general faster than ever before. It is recognised that agribusiness is contributing to several negative phenomena like pollution, traffic congestion, and violations of public health. However, agribusiness is catering to people with necessary healthy food, is delivering degradable plastics, and nowadays is increasingly offering leisure environment-friendly activities in natural contexts.

The production of agri-based goods and services requires a long journey along several stages through complicated networks. The network is composed of private businesses, co-operatives, governmental and semi-governmental bodies and mixtures of them all. The special path through the network leading to the sale of a product is called a chain: a generalised notion of the classic production column.

Interestingly, the chain "from farmer to consumer", or "from seed to mouth", is nowadays developed as a splendid analytical vehicle to analyse what is happening in agri-business. It is applicable to the primary sector of farmers as well as to all stages of processing and selling food to the consumer and to the later stages of recycling (or coping otherwise with) partly used products. The extensive use of chain analysis makes it possible to check for quality, environmental care, food safety, effectiveness of public policies, and many other aspects.

The place and function of government is often underestimated in chain analysis. However, government certainly has strong influences on the functioning of different chains. Policies and the administration of policies on pricing, competition, taxation, pollution, public health, infrastructure, regional planning and other subjects certainly are quite influential. Besides, it has to be recognised that policies are formulated and executed by different governmental bodies (e.g. ministries) at different levels.

Sometimes the administration of policies has counter effects, because they are intervening at some stage in the chain, while at other stages these interventions are generating serious problems (e.g. the former butter surplus in Europe) or perhaps at other stages the interventions are obstructed, and generate reverse effects. The withdrawal of government as a direct intervening, controlling or evaluating body is one of the remarkable examples in the field. Other examples are produced by internationalisation, revolutionary shifts in citizens' consumption behaviour (which by the way is now creating many environmental problems),

---

[*] Prof. Jan Chr. Van Dalen, University of Wageningen, The Netherlands.

the fast introduction of information technology, and the increasing number of forms of organisational co-operation within industries, as well as between industries.

In the study group we discussed more extensively the consequences of a chain approach focused on rural development. Nowadays the farmer is no longer the supplier of raw material to industry only. The primary sector is developing as a multi-process-/multi-product sector, stimulated by introducing environmental care in the context of recreational and nature purposes. The role of government and public administration in this context is changing by introduction of new forms of contracting, public-private relationships, integration of policies from different origins of design training and education schemes, the direction of innovation processes. From the discussion it may be concluded that there is a need for co-ordination in many respects.

Moreover, it could be concluded that there is a need for more and deeper knowledge related to the function and the scope of government intervening somewhere in the agri-chain. A need to be covered by more research into the essence and the (side)effects of policies and administration.

The case of rural development is particularly interesting because it urges the explicit elaboration of the roles of "public" and "private". The discussion concerned some experimental cases, having many consequences for the business sector as well as government and the administration of policies.

It might be stipulated that in The Netherlands we are intensively experimenting with the chain approach. The so called Foundation for Agri Chain Competence is a splendid policy experiment generating some 60 projects on improving of the effectiveness of agree-chains (including conditions for nature preservation, pollution, diminishing traffic congestion, improving infrastructure and generating new applicable knowledge).

Report of the Study Group on Informatization in Public Administration

I. Snellen & W. Van de Donk[*]

During its closing session in Budapest (1996) the Permanent Study Group "Informatization in Public Administration" concluded that researchers on the subject - despite their empirical research efforts and their growing fund of study results - still have much work to do. They still have to convince many of their colleagues in the public administration discipline of the importance of Information and Communication Technology (ICT) for the structure and functioning of public authorities now and in the future.

Not only practitioners and academics, but also handbooks on public administration excel in neglecting ICT as core-technologies -that both enable and provoke more or less radical changes- of public administration.

A second conclusion was, that a concerted effort is needed to provide our colleagues in the discipline with systematic insight in the way in which ICT developments impact the practice of public administration as well as the basic tenets of its discipline. The endeavour initiated by the members of the study group is to re-think and re-phrase the basic concepts and doctrines of public administration discipline for the INFORMATION AGE.

To get the discussion of the study group started, a framework of basic concepts of public administration discipline was presented in the call-for-papers and an example of a doctrine, fundamentally affected by ICT developments (I.Th.M. Snellen: Street Level Bureaucracy), was annexed to the call for papers. The framework of concepts, accepted as the basis for submitting papers, looks like follows: *(please see document next page)*.

The number of papers presented at the meetings of the Permanent Study Group in Leuven does not allow for comment upon each of them. They will just be mentioned in the list below. It may be remarked that they were very well spread out over the framework of concepts. The significance of ICT-developments for the **Politics-Administration dichotomy** was highlighted in Frissen and Zuurmond. The shape of the **Trias Politica** in an information age in de Mulder. The changing positions and roles of the **Executive and legislative** in Wassing and Kordelaar. The shifting boundaries in the **Framework of Jurisdictions** of public administration in Bekkers. The ICT induces dynamics of relationships between different **Layers of Government** in Hoetink and Bekkers. The re-definition of the roles of political bodies and public authorities representing **Administration and Society** was discussed on the basis of the papers by Hoff & Löfgren, Smith, Depla, Edwards and Poupa. A re-definition of relationships between **Citizens and the State** on the basis of papers by Webster and Hoff and Rosenkrands.

---

[*] Prof. Dr. Ignace Snellen, Erasmus University Rotterdam, The Netherlands. Dr. Wim Van de Donk, Tilburg University, The Netherlands.

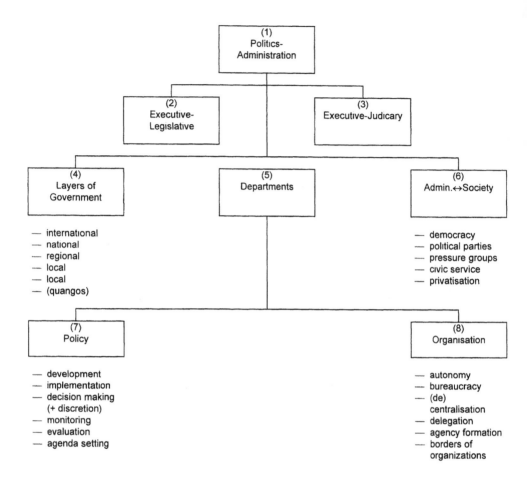

The influence of ICT-developments at the level of **Local Government** was focused upon by Pratchett, Vintar, Almeida and Endo.

The foreboding of changes taking place as far as **Policy making** in an information age are concerned were discussed by Margetts, Andersen and Van de Donk. The **(inter) organisational** aspects of public administration in an information age in Zouridis, Grimmers, Snellen, Bellamy, Lips, Damchak, Friis & La Porte.

Two of the papers Van den Hoven and Raab were focused on one of the general themes of the Leuven conference being **Responsibility, Accountability and Trust**. They were discussed during a common meeting with one of the working groups. One of the conclusions of that common meeting was that informatization is challenging the way we think about some of the core concepts in the field of public administration, e.g. the concept of responsibility. A comparable claim was found, finally, in the paper of Taylor. In this paper the general gist of the discussions during three fruitful days was summarised: informatization is like an X-ray, it is forcing us to re-consider existing concepts, norms and choices that are forming the body of knowledge of public administration. Taylor claims that: "for the student of informatization in is forcing us to re-consider existing concepts, norms and choices that are forming the body of knowledge of public administration. Taylor claims that: "for the student of informatization in public administration (...) information is the centrepiece of our understanding and, from that understanding we can research and understand public administration to a level which has previously been impossible to achieve."

On the basis of the body of papers and some additional contributions an attempt will be made to publish a handbook "Public Administration in an Information Age". The date of publication will be the beginning of May 1998. If we succeed, the book will be presented at an international conference that will be organised in Tilburg (May, 14, 1998). Members of EGPA will receive an invitation to participate.

Public Administration in an Information Age - List of Papers

Taylor	Informatization as X-ray: Understanding Contemporary Public Administration
Edwards	Towards an Informed Citizenry: ICT and electoral choice
Smith	Political Parties in the Information Age: From Mass Party to Leadership Organization?
Frissen	Public Administration in Cyberspace. A Postmodern Perspective
Snellen	Street Level Bureaucracy in An Information Age
Lips	Organization public service delivery in an information age
Bekkers	Beyond the Boundaries of Public Organization: wiring public organizations and shifting organizational boundaries
Bekkers	The Ambivalence of Transparency New Forms of Steering and ICT in the Dutch Sheltered Working Places
Webster	Changing Relationships between Citizens and the State: The Case of Closed Circuit Television Surveillance Cameras
Bellamy	ICT and the Criminal Justice System
Helen Margetts	Computerizing the Tools of Government?
Kim V. Andersen	Electronic Models in Decision Making
Paul Depla	Citizen Consultation in Dutch Local Government and Technology
Richard De Mulder	The Digital Revolution: from trias to tetras publica
Jens Hoff and Karl Loffgren	Political Parties and Computer Mediated Communication in Denmark: general use and strategy
Jens Hoff and Jacob Rosenkrands	The Citizen Card Debate in Denmark: great expectations-small results
Patrick Hoeting	Visions on ICT-induced Dynamics in Intergovernmental Relations
Jorgen Svensson	Informatization and Policy Implementation
Gerard Wassink and Patries Kordelaar	Changing Roles in Quality Management of Legislation
Klaus Grimmer	Structuring Administrations with Help of IaC Technology
Lawrence Pratchett	Technological Bias in an Information Age: An analysis of ICT policymaking in local government
Stavros Zouridis	ICT and the Organization Chart of Public Administration

Mirko Vintar	BPR and Workflow Management in Local Administration Context: some practical aspects
R.J. Beliz Pestana de Almeida	SAFIRA: Financial and administrative system of the autonomous region of the Azores
Tetsuya Endo	Key Persons and Organizational Strategy of Municipal Governments in Information Network Society
Christine Poupa	Changing Power Relationships within Public Administration: an example in Switzerland with Internet
Kees Schalken	Virtual Communities as a Public Sphere for Democracy

papers for the common session with working group I on Responsibility

Raab	Electronic Confidence: trust, information and public administration
Van den Hoven	Moral responsibility, Public Office and Information Technology
Cope & Sweeting	The paradox of responsibility in local governance. The local democratic deficit in Britain
D.W Parsons	Fuzzy in Theory and Getting Fuzzier in Practice. post-modern reflections on responsibility and public administration and management.

papers-proposals that are taken in for the book-project

Zuurmond	From Bureaucracy to Infocracy
Klaus Lenk	Electronic Federalism
Demchak, Friis, LaPorte	Public Agencies: effectiveness versus transparency
Van de Donk	Beyond Incrementalism: informatization and public policy-making
Kilian en Wind	Interorganizational Relationships: ICT as object and medium

Report of the Study Group on Personnel Policy

D. Farnham, S. Horton & A. Hondeghem[*]

Last year in Budapest the Personnel Policy Study Group began a new project on *The Flexibility of Staffing and Personnel Systems in the Public Service*. Five of these papers were incorporated into a symposium on *Employment Flexibilities in Western Europe* published in the *Review of Public Personnel Administration* (Summer 1997) at the University of South Carolina.

This year, in Leuven, additional papers on flexibilities were presented and we moved closer to achieving our objective of producing an international book on personnel flexibilities, to be published in 1999.

Twenty conference delegates attended the Study Group which met continuously over two days. Seven papers were presented covering the wide range of flexibilities identified as part of our study framework. These included numerical, temporal, contractual and pay flexibilities and career mobility.

Two papers looked specifically at pay flexibility. One, on Italy, examined the new system introduced in 1993, designed to bring the determination of Civil Service pay closer to the private sector model of collective bargaining and to decentralise decision making on a range of issues including performance related pay, pay differentials and funding pay increases. In practice, the system remains highly centralised because of the intervention of central government, the power of the public sector unions and resource constraints.

A comparative paper on pay flexibility in the UK and Germany also pointed to moves towards decentralisation. In both countries, the major driving forces were to reduce public expenditure and increase productivity. However, there were notable differences in the means and developments in each country. These were identified as a function of: (i) different political structures providing frameworks for public employment; (ii) relations between employer and employee representatives; (iii) the legal basis for pay determination; and (iv) the influence of different private sector pay models in the two countries.

Two papers focused on the need for flexible behaviour in responsive organisations. The first, a study of the Flemish Community Committee in Brussels, identified a personnel strategy designed to create both a flexible organisation and a culture conducive to achieving and maintaining personal commitment in a situation of unpredictability and rapid change. The second, based on research conducted in an English Health Trust, pointed to the need to enable

---

[*] Prof. dr. David Farnham, University of Portsmouth, Department of Business and Management, United Kingdom. Mrs. Sylvia Horton, University of Portsmouth, School of Social and Historical Studies, United Kingdom. Dr. Annie Hondeghem, Catholic University of Leuven, Public Management Centre, Belgium.

staff to deal flexibly with the public, if improved quality of service was to be achieved. The implications of this for selection, training and rewards were highlighted.

There were three national studies, one relating to Belgium and two to the UK. The first examined recent changes in personnel management in Flanders, following the new agreement for decentralisation in 1993. Only half of local authorities have established their own personnel statutes and, where they have, there is evidence of a high degree of standardisation and more rigidity than in the past. There appears to be very limited scope for exercising personnel flexibilities because of excessive steering by the Flemish government.

In the UK Civil service a similar gap between the rhetoric and the reality of personnel reforms was also identified in another paper. Although there is evidence of some real decentralisation there is also increased centralisation. The paper points to the dual movements to strategic centralisation and operational decentralisation simultaneously.

The final paper on the UK was a theoretical paper presenting two models of people management in the public sector - traditional people management (TPM) and new people management (NPM). Examining five key characteristics related to employment practices in public organisations, the paper pointed to evidence of a movement away from TPM to NPM and from standardised to flexible practices. The conclusions were guarded, however, and highlighted the gap between espoused policies and actual practice. It also pointed to variations between different parts of the public sector and the presence of strong elements of continuity as well as of change. Key barriers to change were identified such as public professions, trade unions and the public service ethic.

Group discussions focused particularly on the lessons to be learned from the papers. The conclusions reached were, first, that the spread of flexibilities was not uniform and that variations both nationally and internationally have to be explained. Second, the unexpected and unintended outcomes and consequences of espoused policies needed to be explored further. Third, there is a need to move beyond description and analysis to the evaluation of flexibilities for governments, employers, employees and the public, i.e. all public service stakeholders.

The group agreed to continue with the project as originally planned and to produce final papers for publication in 1999. The papers to be prepared for the Paris Conference are to consist of both national papers and thematic, comparative papers.

A clear framework for both the national studies and the thematic papers was agreed to and participants volunteered to take responsibility for the production of selected papers for Paris. Former members of the group are to be contacted and invited to offer contributions. All readers of this report are also invited to contact the convenors if they are interested in joining the project.

In conclusion - the quality of the papers presented at this year's conference was of a high standard and led to very stimulating debates. The outcome of our final deliberations augurs well for the future of the Study Group.

Finally, the convenors of the group would like to thank all the participants for making the Leuven Conference such a success and they look forward to meeting them again in Paris.

Report of the Study Group on Quality and Productivity in the Public Services

G. Bouckaert & H. Summa[*]

So far, the study group has concentrated mostly on organisational aspects of the efficiency, effectiveness, quality, and satisfaction in government. During the last two years, in Budapest (1996) and Leuven (1997) the emphasis was on the financial cycles which monitor and control the efficiency and effectiveness of policy and management. Therefore the link between performance on the one hand, and budgets, accounts, and audits on the other hand, was a major topic of the study group.

Financial cycles are recurrent and allow for a procedural and institutional approach (data gathering, processing, reporting, interpreting; division of labour; distribution of responsibilities, mechanisms of accountability), for an ex ante, ex nunc and ex post approach (before, during and after), for an internal and external approach (line departments with self evaluation, and inspections of finance or courts of audits with external evaluations). This financial cycle coincides with a policy cycle which also may include performance indicators on economy, efficiency, effectiveness and quality which may be used for policy preparation, contracts, monitoring and control, and evaluation.

A logical next step for the group is to focus on the further use of performance measurement systems in the policy cycle.

In the public sector new forms of control are emerging. Traditional forms of input controls are being replaced by different performance management agreements.

A first major element in such a performance management approach is structural. This results in the creation of agency-like organisations within the public sector as hived-off organisational entities separated from traditional governmental departments and dedicated to service delivery. Such an administrative decentralisation may involve the reallocation of activities from the centre to executive agencies, public enterprises or quasi-non-governmental organisations.

A second element relates to the steering, monitoring and feedback mechanisms. This implies the replacement of the traditional hierarchical relationship between the centre (Minister, Mayor) and the devolved organisation by a relationship based on an "internal" quasi-contract, in which the objectives and the resource framework for the organisation are set (e.g. United Kingdom: Framework Documents, Finland: Result Agreements, Canada: Business Plans, New Zealand: Performance and Purchase Agreements,....) Obviously, these trends are to be observed at the national, regional as well as at the local level.

---

[*] Prof. Dr. Geert Bouckaert, Catholic University of Leuven, Public Management Centre, Belgium. Ms. Hilkka Summa, European Commission.

The emphasis in the future will be on the second element. This includes topics like, e.g.:

- different types and levels of arrangements (e.g. individual-institutional, written - unwritten);
- the preparation of the arrangements, the negotiation process, the renegotiation and the role and power of the actors involved (e.g. line departments-financial departments);
- the format and content of the arrangements (e.g. objectives, targets, resources...);
- incentives and sanctions;
- the forms and the extent of operational autonomy for the devolved units;
- the implementation, the monitoring and evaluation of these performance arrangements;
- the impact assessment of performance arrangements on the efficiency, effectiveness, client orientedness and public accountability of the devolved organisations; this may imply the impact on the internal management (human resources, financial, organisational) in the devolved organisations, on the role and functioning of the central department and on the overall co-ordination of governmental policies;
- links and synergies with market-type mechanisms.

An overview of these elements using this information provides elements to assess the added value of performance measurement in the public sector.

*Ethics and Accountability in a Context
of Governance and New Public Management*
EGPA Annual Conference, Leuven 1997
IOS Press, 1998

Report of the Study group on Public Budgeting and Accounting

M. Hogye & F. Sabbe[*]

In preparing and discussing papers in the Leuven conference, the study group continued its activities in the field of the management and organisation of tax administration. This year a new dimension of investigation, ethics in taxation and tax administration, was introduced.

In the call-for-papers, participants from Western and Central and Eastern European Countries were requested to deal with the following questions:

- measuring, estimating and evaluating tax compliance, tax evasion and avoidance;

- analysis of the origins of tax evasion and avoidance with a focus on the ethics and responsibility of tax administration (legal, political, economic, cultural-historical and other origins, role of the black and grey economy);

- organisational and managerial capacity of tax administration to improve tax compliance, political intervention and the effects of tax compliance (e.g. hidden subsidies and employment policy).

According to the preliminary applications, we expected several papers to be presented in the conference. However, only four persons, two from Hungary, could participate in the discussion, and only one paper was presented (M. Pásztor, Tax Fraud: heritage, habit or gambling - the example of supplementary wages).

Despite this unfavourable situation, a very useful and interesting discussion took place. The meeting offered us a forum for international debate. We had the opportunity to present and analyse some ethical questions related to tax administration, in particular the phenomena of tax evasion and avoidance. All the participants contributed meaningful ideas on the basis of their own experiences.

In the group meeting the participants also discussed necessary changes in the Study Group's activities for the future. They decided to change the name of the Study Group to *Public Finance and Management*, to attract potential participants for future conferences, and to cover a wider range of topics for analyses.

---

[*] Prof. dr. Mihaly Hogye, Center for Public Affairs, Budapest University of Economic Sciences, Hungary.
Ms. Francisca Sabbe, Catholic University of Leuven, Public Management Centre, Belgium.

Report of the Study Group on Co-operation in Continuing Education, Training, Research and Consulting between Eastern and Western Europe

G. Jenei[*]

The Permanent Study Group had three sessions. Four papers were discussed. Two of them dealt with the context, the other two dealt with the content of the co-operation. The discussions were stimulating with the participation of regular members of the group and of special guests as well. Sometimes the participants came to an agreement, sometimes they were divided, and in many cases they were sceptical.

There were common points in the discussions and we were able to draw some conclusions concerning international co-operation and ethics[1]:

1. Ethics is an integral part in all stages of co-operation from the sporadic personal contacts to institutional partnerships. Different ethical issues emerge relative to the individual, the organisational, national and international levels, and a special relationship can be observed between levels and stages.

2. Different forms of co-operation on ethical issues have been evolving among West and East European countries in the 1990's. They fall into two dimensions.

2.1. The first is the relationship between different scholars. The question is whether they can understand each other in the exchange of experiences or in joint actions. And their different ethical codes, sets of moral principles or value systems may make co-operation easier or they may introduce obstacles which have to be overcome.

Co-operation is a cross cultural matter. It often happens that misunderstandings in co-operation are expressed in ethical terms. Human behaviour is deeply rooted in the culture. And the behaviour of a person oriented by a value system based on individualism can conflict with a person who is oriented by a value system based on collective values. On the other hand the person with a collective value orientation can easily miss the distinction between a philosophy of individualism and the expression of a person's own self-interest and personality.

Co-operation has intensified in the 1990s between Western and Eastern Europe. Different forms of co-operation have been evolving in public administration and education.

---

[*] Prof. dr. György Jenei, Centre for Public Affairs Studies, Budapest University of Economic Sciences, Hungary.

Eastern Europe has been fragmented. In this regard, we usually speak about a learning process, a knowledge transfer. There were illusions in the beginning. It was thought that Western public administration practices could be directly implemented in Eastern Europe. However, we now realise that a learning process is needed to adapt to Western performance standards.

Participants in training programmes returned to their working places after finishing the programme and tried to implement what they had learned. However, the consequences of that were many misunderstandings and failures. The acquired knowledge did not work in reality, given their organisational, political and cultural environment.

During the training programme the practitioners simulated games, but now they had to fulfil what they learned on the battle field. They could not imitate the game; they had to play the real game.

What were the reasons for these failures?

In light of these failures people became sceptical and they began to refuse the Western European pattern of administration.

In reaction, a group of West-European experts tried to force the East Europeans to adapt Western practices, but they did not understand why these efforts were unsuccessful. There were accusations that the Eastern Europeans did not want to apply the new practices.

We were convinced that this was a simplified explanation. Behind the failures and unsuccessful attempts you can observe differences between teaching public administration and working on the improvement of public administration. You can teach public administration theories, methods and techniques and students can understand them. But these bodies of knowledge function in special political, economic, social and institutional frameworks in Western Europe. They embody traditional mechanisms, generally accepted values and norms, and attitudes of Western Europe. The framework and the value system, however, cannot be exported. That is why the assimilated knowledge can not be quickly implemented. The political, legal, institutional frameworks and value systems in Central-Eastern Europe are quite different from Western Europe.

(In brackets from that point of view Eastern Europe is also not unique. There are deep differences among the different countries of the region.)

2.2. Second, ethical issues can involve differences in civil servants and civil services. The crucial point is whether, for ethical requirements of the day-to-day work in the public administration, more autonomy, business-like managerialism, and blurring the boundaries between public and private have the same consequences in the East and West.

For example: In the last decades efficiency and effectiveness have been of increasing importance in the public sector. This process resulted in changes and shifts in the ethical requirements of public administration. The traditional bureaucratic role is outdated. Under new circumstances, public administration has undertaken broader responsibility. But there is an emerging anxiety that broader responsibility may threaten or weaken the legal state (in the German term: the 'Rechtstaat'). There is also a concern that this growing autonomy of the bureaucrats and the expansion of business-like managerialism will damage the integrity of civil servants and the sound, ethical basis of the public sector. This may especially be a problem in the case of the Central-Eastern European countries, where the legal state and constitutionalism are not strong historical traditions and where political systems were oppressive.

In the history of public administration in Central Eastern Europe, there has been no Weberian period. This form of administration was not developed - because it was not forced either by the civil society or by special legislation. Indeed, the very essence of bureaucratic activities is to execute the orders given by the legitimate power on a legal basis and transparent for society.

Even if power was influenced, the decision making process has been carried out in the shadows, without any legitimised responsibility. Politicians were encouraged to break the law and they took action without a legal basis. The problem is whether the trend of new public management can be applied in Central Eastern Europe directly without having a strong Weberian tradition. It would be a great step forward for these countries to set up a traditional bureaucratic ethics based on the theory of Weber.

Theoretically the third option would be a parallel process, building a public administration based on legalism and adopting a business-like managerialism in the public sector at the same time. But we were sceptical whether this very complicated task can be managed in practice. Can legalism and managerialism be developed in parallel without resulting in a serious value vacuum in the public administration?

In the Central Eastern European region there is already a value vacuum. Sometimes there is a lack of values because the old values have disappeared or been weakened and the new values are not yet entrenched. In other cases you can see value conflicts when the old and the new values impact events at the same time.

3. A crucial conclusion of the discussions was that ethical standards and value systems of public administration are influenced by the value system of the society and the political system. Special examples were discussed from Central-Eastern Europe.

In the case of corruption for instance - especially in the East-European region - it is a requirement that the civil servant has to support his family using, and often misusing, the opportunities provided by his position. On the other side of the coin people show a tax evasion practice which can be characterised by the following slogan: „When you do not cheat the state, you steal from your family." This in itself is an ethical statement, but not one that conforms to a Weberian notion of administration.

In Eastern Europe the whole political system is influenced by clans. They are the main actors. It is obvious that the day-to-day life and actions of the public administration has to follow the expectations of the clans. The consequence is that corruption is built into the system. This type of civil service can not function without corruption. Every service has its fee. Under this system, it is seen as immoral when civil servants require more than the traditional price of the service or when they fail to provide the promised services.

The conclusion of the discussion was that only the transparency of the tax collection and - generally speaking - of services can be successful when there are institutionalised opportunities for individuals and groups to influence decisions.

4. The compatibility of ethical and cultural standards came up frequently. We conceived co-operation as a mutual learning process and not as a transfer of knowledge. In this approach the main questions were:

- Are we motivated enough to learn?
- Can we apply in practice what we have learned?

The mutual learning process depends on the compatibility of ethical standards and cultures in the different societies. It is not only an East-West related problem, but sometimes you have to adapt projects from one part of Eastern Europe to another part.

The Muslim republics of Central Asia are also involved in the co-operation and in the mutual learning process as well. This raised the problem of whether these autocratic systems - in which the whole power of the former communist party is concentrated in the hands of the President - should be supported by Western Europe? The answer was yes, because Islam fundamentalism may be the only realistic alternative.

On the other hand, culturally we can find common points with the strong social-value orientation and solidarity of Islam culture.

5. Last but not least, it was emphasised that ongoing public sector reforms also generate a need for new values and ethical standards. The strong push for a more direct democracy creates strong requirements for the integrity of civil servants. The complex nature of public issues and the lack of public understanding of these problems affects the perceived integrity of civil servants.

In this turbulent era when fundamental changes and continuities influence events, the reform efforts in public administration must at the same time include the ethical factors as well.

It is necessary because of different reasons. First, there is a continuing push for more 'direct' democracy in the region and social groups gain more opportunities for participation. In that case the integrity of the public servants has a growing importance.

There is an increasing complexity of public issues and people often do not understand the essence of the issues. It means that they have lost much of their ability to participate meaningfully in the public sector. And sometimes they blame the integrity of the public servants without understanding the ongoing processes.

Secondly, large bureaucracies are being transformed, flattened. The information age increasingly substitutes ad hoc and temporary for permanent forms. The increasing autonomy of public agencies gives a growing importance to the ethical components of the personality of civil servants. It is crucial how they are committed to public values. Do they have a strong orientation to serve the public or do they have hidden or expressed oppressive temptations?

Thirdly, the amount of information available is great. Effective communication in many cases were more important than effective actions. Much information is false; bad information drives out good. Journalist, radio and TV talk shows often focus on successes and failures and miss what is really going on. Under these circumstances the transparency of the civil service has a growing importance. They have to learn how to communicate, and this is also a technical issue. But in the long run the crucial issue is whether the performance of the public sector is convincing, or not, and it is decisive what people think of and how they evaluate public servants' integrity.

Government usually must operate under laws. If they want to get out from under a law, they should go to the legislative body to get the law changed. But there are many pressures on the everyday activities of the public administration and they have to provide quick solutions for the challenges they face. The consequence is that there are basically two different attitudes in the public sector. Public servants on the local level spend a lot of their time on day-to-day management. Planning and implementing are their main focus. Here you should not overemphasise the legal side of public administration. In many cases you need risk-takers because only these persons can cope with the difficulties. We have to add that many of them are risk-averse and they can find an excuse in the prescription of laws and regulations. The main difference between the public administration and the public management attitude is that the public management perspective takes the public and the private sector challenges as essentially the same, a generic activity of managing. The public administration perspective, on the other hand, sees fundamental differences between the public and private sectors: the primary purpose of the government is to implement laws passed by the Parliament.

There are tensions inside the public sector. Civil servants have a different set of values and demands of the institutions for which they work. The younger civil servant are not ready to follow the value interests of their predecessors. These tensions are often expressed in ethical terms as well.

Notes

[1] The conclusions are based on four papers. They are as follows:
- *Some Considerations on the Training Programme to Support the Independence of the Judiciary and Practising Lawyers in Uzbekistan*, Prof. Katlijn Malfliet, Institute for European Policy, Katholieke Universiteit, Leuven

- *Some Considerations on the Relation of Ethics and International Cooperation,* Prof. György Jenei, Center for Public Affairs Studies, Budapest University of Economic Sciences
- *A Case Study of East-West Co-operation of France, Holland and Russia,* Svetlana Khapova, Stavropol State Technical University
- *Ethics in International Cooperation A case study,* Dr. ir. Frits van den Berg, Consultant, The Netherlands

*Ethics and Accountability in a Context
of Governance and New Public Management
EGPA Annual Conference, Leuven 1997
IOS Press, 1998*

L'évolution de la contractualisation
dans le secteur public depuis 1980

Yvonne Fortin et Hugo Van Hassel[*]

Le thème retenu pour 1997 portait sur « la contractualisation, une forme de partenariat entre le secteur public et le secteur privé pour la gestion des services publics ».

Huit rapports ont été présentés, dont trois sur la police et l'activité policière, notamment au Royaume-Uni.

<u>A service based typology for contract management</u>. Karin Bryntse, Department of Business Administration, School of Economics and Management, Lund University, Sweden.

L'auteur avait, en 1996, présenté dans le cadre du même groupe d'étude, un rapport qui débouchait sur le thème de 1997. En 1997, à Leuven, Karin Bryntse résume ainsi l'objectif de son travail qui n'est pas encore achevé :

> « The aim of this paper is to analyse and discuss how different service characteristics influence the design of contracting arrangements for the delivery of local government services. The analysis is based on empirical material concerning contracts for technical services as highway maintenance, parks maintenance, refuse collection and water&sewerage, and social services. Interviews have been carried out with client officers in local authorities in Sweden, England and Germany. »

L'auteur construit, à partir de théories économiques, théories des organisations, et à partir de travaux sur les contrats de service et de fournitures, portant aussi bien sur le secteur public que le secteur privé, un cadre théorique très minutieux, riche, mais clair et solide et à l'occasion critique. Ainsi, par exemple, l'auteur observe que la notion d'incertitude, telle qu'elle résulte des travaux de Williamson notamment, ne se rapporte pas à la nature des activités, mais plutôt au comportement de la nature humaine et est liée à l'opportunisme et à la rationalité limitée (bounded rationality). L'auteur met en lumière trois grandes catégories d'incertitudes: incertitude de la demande (uncertaintly of demand); incertitude des conditions de production; incertitude du financement.

Ses conclusions, après analyse des situations concrètes ci-dessus mentionnées, sont les suivantes :

> « A general result from the analysis is that the complexity, risk potential and relative importance/stability of funding seems to be determinating factors for the design of contract management structures. Complexity is thereby defined as a cluster of uncertainty, asset specificity and the need for co-ordination with other activities and actors. This aligns to some extent with the arguments for the transaction cost theory (Williamson, 1991, 1996),

---

[*] Yvonne Fortin, GAAP-Groupe d'Analyse des Politiques Publiques, Ecole Normale Supérieure, France.
Prof.dr. Hugo Van Hassel, Catholic University of Leuven, Public Management Centre, Belgium.

which predicts long-term relational contracting in situations with high degrees of uncertainty and asset specificity (which includes competence). However it is argued that the factor of risk is not fully recognised within the transaction cost theory. The potential consequences of delivery failures should not be interpreted as simply a question of risk of individualistic opportunism. It is rather related to the characteristics of the specific services in combination with difficulties to specify tacit knowledge of services. The relative importance is another special aspect that needs consideration, which in a local government context has to be related to stability of funding. A general conclusion is that the service characteristics matter and that there is a need for a differentiation of contract management strategies. This need of differentiation can be seen as something that maybe not has been fully recognised in traditional hierarchical management of local government, where uniformity is (used to be?) a dominating value (Stewart, 1992). »

<u>Governance by Contact. Creating Public-Private Partnership in Denmark</u>. Carsten Greve, Assistant Professor, Institute of Political Science, University of Copenhagen, Denmark.

L'auteur résume lui-même ainsi son rapport:

« This paper discusses contracts in public-private partnerships in Denmark. First, a distinction is made between a 'hard' and a 'soft' version of contracts with the latter emphasising co-operation and mutual trust. Then the government's quest for a 'shared-power' society is explored. Four types of public-private contracting are presented and related to the hard/soft distinction; Contracting out, strategic contracting out, development contracts and investors agreements in joint-stock companies. The conclusion is that Denmark is moving towards the soft version of contracts, here termed governance by *contact*. »

Le rapport, très bien documenté, analyse le rôle joué par les différentes formes de contractualisation en général et de partenariat public/privé en particulier dans le processus global de modernisation et de renouveau du secteur public: il ne s'agit plus seulement d'économiser les deniers publics; il s'agit de plus en plus, pour le gouvernement central et les collectivités locales de définir une stratégie de coopération entre le secteur public et le secteur privé, stratégie visant à se substituer à la politique de privatisation pure et simple, jugée souvent inadaptée. En bref, « The government vision is that of a shared power world, as suggested by Kettl ».

Toutefois, l'auteur n'hésite pas à pousser son analyse au delà des objectifs clairement affichés par les promoteurs des différentes formes de contractualisation. Comme l'ont également fait plusieurs rapporteurs en 1996 et en 1997, il relève, qu'en pratique, contractualiser peut être une tactique visant à se débarrasser, en la transférant à d'autres par contrat, d'une responsabilité difficile à assumer directement sans subir des contrecoups dévastateurs (politiques notamment).

En conclusion de la partie consacrée aux quatre grandes catégories de contrats qui, au Danemark, reflètent la coopération entre le secteur public et le secteur privé, il insiste sur un point essentiel, celui du risque encore trop peu étudié. Il écrit à ce propos: « We know little about what level of risk and what level of success the government (both state and local) is willing to accept ».

A son avis, la question de la responsabilité et de sa mise en oeuvre posent des problèmes difficiles qu'il convient d'aborder dans un esprit ouvert et non sous un angle strictement juridique.

Il insiste sur le rôle joué au Danemark par les forum où s'instaure le dialogue entre les détenteurs d'enjeux, dialogue qui porte sur les résultats, les erreurs, la façon de les corriger et de les éviter à l'avenir. Il évoque à ce propos le concept de confiance, parlant de 'trust based contracts' ainsi que de 'sanctions négociées'.

Dans l'explosion contractuelle que connaît le Danemark, à l'instar de nombreux pays, l'auteur estime que les contrats correspondent tantôt à un modèle relationnel hiérarchique, tantôt à un modèle de relations en réseau, mais que l'option choisie n'est pas laissée au hasard.

> « The government places faith in both a model of hierarchy and a model of network. When it comes to placing responsibility, the government point to the purchaser/provider model which is a hierarchy re-established. When it comes to obstacles of co-ordination of many independent decisions, the government points to dialogue and co-operation which could be interpreted as a network model. »

Analysant un ensemble de rapports gouvernementaux récents et plus particulièrement le rapport de 1997, intitulé « Denmark as a Spearhead country », Carsten Greve entrevoit une amorce de contrat social implicite: « In short, there is an implicit element of a societal 'contract with Denmark' surrounding the project », « The initiative (Denmark as a Spearhead country) links the management of contracts with the wider aspect of societal and democratic governance ».

Le traditionnel pacte socio-politique, le célèbre « contrat social » cher à Rousseau, se teinterait d'économie, voire deviendrait un pacte socio-économique. C'est une analyse visionnaire qui nous est proposée.

Public Service Provision in UK Local Authority Quasi Markets 1989-1997: Issues of Contract, Governance and Accountability. Peter Vincent-Jones, Sheffield Hallam University, United Kingdom.

> Public services throughout the world are increasingly being provided through market and quasi-market arrangements involving privatisation, contracting out, internal markets, franchising, management contracts, and partnership companies. This paper considers what might be learned about the problem of choice of governing instrument for public services provision from the unique experience of compulsory competitive tendering (CCT) in the UK since 1988. An analytical framework drawing on agency and transaction cost theories is developed and illustrated with reference to criteria of accountability, trust, effectiveness, quality, consumer voice, citizen participation and redress for poor performance. The attempts by metropolitan local authorities in the north of England to solve internal contracting problems in the provision of buildings cleaning, refuse collection and housing management services under CCT are analysed with reference to these criteria. Some tentative conclusions are offered about the potential role of internal contracting, contracting out, and externalisation on the abolition of CCT and its replacement by a new duty of demonstrating 'best value' in public services provision. The paper argues that internal contracting between local authority clients and competitive in-house agencies may be a viable form of institutional arrangement for services provision in future in appropriate circumstances. The paper explores the idea that internal quasi-market contracting may

> operate as a publicly accountable mechanism whereby relationships between a number of client, contractor and consumer parties may be governed without formal recourse to legal norms in a co-operative network that extends beyond the boundaries of the local authority organisation. »

C'est ainsi que l'auteur résume sa recherche. La combinaison de différentes approches théoriques appliquées à chacune des catégories de détenteurs d'enjeux permet à Peter Vincent-Jones de porter une appréciation critique mais soigneusement justifiée du fondement de la stratégie gouvernementale. Elle le conduit à regretter un usage qu'il juge inapproprié du raisonnement économique par le gouvernement central dans le domaine étudié.

L'auteur insiste beaucoup sur l'importance des relations entre les différents détenteurs d'enjeux impliqués ou concernés par un contrat et réserve à la confiance une place centrale.

Dans une digression fort à propos, il relève que si l'adoption de 'mécanismes juridiques' ('legalistic mechanism') est en général considérée comme une réponse à un déficit de confiance, « in the present context, however, the new accounting and contracting systems have not developed in response to perceived trust deficits, but have been compulsorily imposed within pre-existing trusting environments with the purpose of securing efficiency reforms ».

Le rapport apporte la démonstration que le bon fonctionnement du système contractuel dépend en grande partie d'une coopération confiante et d'une intégration progressive des détenteurs d'enjeux (stakeholders) au processus contractuel.

<u>Contracting and public/private sector partnership in transport in the United Kingdom</u>. Dr. Enid Wistrich, Middlesex University, United Kingdom.

Ce rapport est publié ci-après. Son grand mérite est d'avoir pris en compte, à partir d'outils d'analyse économiques, juridiques, politiques et sociologiques, un domaine extrêmement complexe, de l'avoir examiné en prenant en compte son évolution dans le temps et d'avoir amorcé une comparaison entre les secteurs du transport routier et ferroviaire de voyageurs.

S'agissant du transport ferroviaire de voyageurs, l'auteur démonte chaque pièce du puzzle, l'examine sous tous les angles, se place du point de vue de chacun des détenteurs d'enjeux et conclue en ouvrant des pistes de réflexion générales.

Une session spéciale a été consacrée aux problèmes de gestion posés par la police qui ont fait l'objet de trois rapports.

Le premier, <u>The rise of Audit in British Policing</u>. Stephen P. Savage, Stephen Cope et Sarah Charman, s'inscrit dans le prolongement direct des travaux présentés en 1996 par ces mêmes auteurs, travaux qui analysaient le rôle joué par l' « Association of Chief Police Officers of England, Wales and Northern Ireland (ACPO) » dans l'élaboration d'une nouvelle politique en matière de police. En 1997, leur attention s'est portée sur l'Audit Commission et l'Inspection Générale (Her Majesty's Inspectorate of Constabulary - HMIC).

Les auteurs résument ainsi les conclusions de leurs recherches :

> « We argue that the Audit Commission has played a crucial role in the reform of the police, not just in terms of its specific influence over Kenneth Clarke's (the Minister) reform package, but more generally in facilitating the development of a managerial philosophy within the policy service which has affected the organisational culture of police management. In turn this cultural change has generated a degree of internally-led reform, in which police managers have sought to drive the reform agenda from within rather than simply allow reform to be imposed from without. This stance has not been the approach of some other public sector professions. »

Les auteurs montrent comment les trois principaux protagonistes que sont l'Audit Commission, l'ACPO et l'Inspection Générale, malgré des intérêts divergeants ou une situation parfois de concurrence, ont développé des relations de partenariat véritable sur la base desquelles s'est construite et continue de progresser la réforme.

Dans le second rapport, Policing Bureaucracy, l'auteur, Barry Loveday, appréhende la police en tant que profession, c'est à dire en tant que corps de métier ayant ses techniques, ses méthodes, sa culture propres. Il cherche à comprendre et à mesurer l'impact que cette profession a eu sur des points clé de la réforme comme la redéfinition de ce qui constitue le noyau dur de l'activité policière, la définition d'une politique (policy) policière, ou le pilotage, l'évaluation, le contrôle des résultats. Pour ce faire, il décortique les rapports que la police entretient avec les autorités 'de tutelle' tant centrales que locales qui ont elles aussi été remodelées.

Il montre que « Ironically, the overall impact of change may well have been to enhance and strengthened the position of professionals in the police service vis-à-vis central and local government ».

Cette situation, selon l'auteur, s'explique tantôt par l'action directe ou indirecte des membres de la police, tantôt par la conception ou le fonctionnement proprement dits des structures, nouvelles ou remodelées, instaurées par le gouvernement et qui, faute d'avoir joué le rôle initialement prévu, ont été en quelle que sorte captées par la profession, ou sont en voie de l'être.

Le troisième rapport, Regulating Private Security - International Perspectives on Improving Accountability and Performance, présenté par Mark Button, porte sur un domaine où la contractualisation se développe rapidement, mais en se faisant discrète.

Les entreprises privées de sécurité se multiplient, leurs activités augmentent et se diversifient. En outre, si elles opèrent pour l'essentiel, à l'heure actuelle, dans le secteur privé, elles ont aussi commencé à investir la sphère publique et, comme l'écrit l'auteur : « for a variety of reasons, the industry is also undertaking many functions that use to be associated with the public sector. Combined with this many private security personnel assume - through a variety of means - police-like powers and undertake police-like functions. Yet in many countries they are subject to no or very ineffective statutory controls ». Effectuant un large tour d'horizon international, l'auteur constate que seule une réglementation adaptée serait à même de garantir un niveau de responsabilité et de performance suffisant.

Il élabore ainsi des modèles de réglementation à partir des deux critères qu'il estime être les plus importants: le champ d'application et le fond de la réglementation (width and depth). Il conclut que le modèle le plus efficace aurait pour caractéristique d'être général, c'est à dire large, en ne négligeant aucun point essentiel.

Il termine son rapport par l'avertissement suivant:

> « As the private sector continues to challenge the monopoly of the state even in areas of criminal justice it is essential that the same - if not higher - standards of ethics and accountability are applied. The history of private sector involvement in the criminal justice system in the Eighteenth and Nineteenth Centuries - at least in England - is a sorry one of corruption and ineffectiveness. If we are to avoid a return to the past it is essential that more research is undertaken on how the role of the private sector can be improved and made properly accountable ».

Le grand mérite de cette étude est d'avoir analysé un champ où la contractualisation plus particulièrement sous sa forme partenariale - public/privé - est de nature à faire courir des risques majeurs à la liberté individuelle qui est au coeur de toute démocratie.

En 1996, Guy Peters avait présenté un rapport où il analysait les raisons pour lesquelles la gestion contractuelle par objectifs était très peu développée en interne, dans le secteur public, au niveau fédéral, en Amérique du Nord.

En 1997, dans son rapport intitulé « <u>The Contract State in the United States: multiple goals for a single instrument</u> », après avoir rappelé que « Contracting in the United States also has a history of being used as a multi-purpose instrument » et que la contractualisation investit tous les domaines de l'action publique, Guy Peters axe son analyse sur le caractère multi fonctions et multi usages de la contractualisation. On en use et, à l'occasion, on en abuse.

L'auteur insiste sur le fait que, plus encore que les caractéristiques techniques de l'outil contractuel, ce sont les motifs et les objectifs qui ont présidé au choix de cet outil qui importent.

> .... « Thus, the use of contracting for the United-States (or indeed for any other country) cannot be understood without taking into account the broader political objectives of government. Contracting is not a simple technical exercise; it is one more instrument among many others through which governments attempt to steer their economy and society ».

Si les tenants de la contractualisation insistent sur sa souplesse, face à des situations différentes, l'auteur montre que la spécificité des problèmes, comme celle des co-contractants du gouvernement peuvent entraîner des effets pervers (conflit d'intérêts; rupture d'égalité devant le service).

De même, toujours à partir d'exemples concrets, il tempère fortement l'affirmation courante selon laquelle la contractualisation générerait quasi automatiquement un renforcement de la responsabilité. Il identifie plusieurs freins ou obstacles: des freins économiques (coût respectif des procédures de suivi et de contrôle d'une part, de la fraude d'autre part); des freins sociologiques (pouvoir et influence d'un groupe, d'une profession donnés qui leur permet d'échapper à un contrôle authentique; 'dérive bureaucratique' quasi inhérente à toute négociation du fait de la nécessité d'arriver à un accord; ....); socio-politiques enfin.

Comme d'autres rapporteurs, l'auteur dénonce lui aussi l'utilisation de l'outil contractuel comme moyen d'éluder sa responsabilité et d'éviter d'avoir à rendre compte des résultats (mesures de performance) et/ou de se protéger contre d'éventuelles retombées politiques dans des domaines politiquement très sensibles (contrôle des naissances, avortement).

Enfin, l'auteur dénonce certaines contradictions entre la culture américaine soucieuse de s'assurer du bon usage des deniers publics par le recours éventuel au juge d'une part, et une contractualisation, qui pour remplir pleinement ses promesses, doit demeurer souple, adaptable.

« Contracting out is a useful tool for government, but it, like all tools, also have some possible costs that must be considered. Those costs become particularly manifest in societies which tend to resort to legal means for redressing problems, and in societies that are placing increasing demands on government for strict accountability for its actions. Unfortunately, the United States fits both of those categories so that although the well-developed commercial culture of the US might appear to make contracts an especially useful device, it may have more negative consequences in the US than in many other countries. »

Selection of Papers of the Permanent Study Groups Related to the Conference Theme

# Risks in Value for Money-related Performance Measurement

J. Vakkuri & P. Meklin[*]

1. Introduction

This is a study of risks in value for money-related performance measurement[#]. The focus is on a methodological approach. The main purpose of the paper is to shed light on risks theoretically and to link them to a few practical measurement problems. To accomplish this, risks are examined in an illustrative fashion in the context of performance measurement of Finnish universities. The aim is to connect examples from Finnish universities with wider theoretical problems of measuring 'value for money'.

The text is organised as follows. First, theoretical background for performance measurement and its relations to value for money-related performance measurement is considered. On the basis of accounting methodology value for money is seen as a 'principal', and the measurement of value for money is seen as a 'surrogate'. (Ijiri, 1967; 1975.) These elements are combined with the context where value for money is analysed. Second, empirical evidence of the measurement of value for money in the Finnish university context is presented. Third, risks are categorised on the basis of Smith's (1995) formulation. Finally, the categories are applied to highlight the risks of performance measurement in the Finnish university context.

2. The Basics of Performance Measurement

Performance measurement is a special language where "real world" phenomena are given symbolic meanings. In the accounting literature the "real world" is usually defined as a principal, whereas measures as symbolical meanings are called surrogates. (Ijiri, 1967: 4-6.) The basic aim of performance measurement is to systematise the relationships between these two elements.[1]

The conception of the "real world" is an ontological assumption, which is why two major approaches regarding performance measurement can be put forward (Swoyer, 1987; Porter, 1995). First, we may adopt an approach where performance measurement is seen as a systematisation of "real" objects. The only problem is to find the "right" surrogates for the real world phenomena. Using this approach performance measurement is an extension of measurement in natural science, which is why measurement theory includes the concept of indirect measurement (Ellis, 1966: 54). This world is the world of quantities.

---

[*] Jarmo Vakkuri & Pentti Meklin, University of Tampere, Department of Administrative Science, Finland.
[#] We are grateful to Professor Pertti Ahonen and senior lecturer Jukka Nummikoski for their valuable comments on an earlier draft of this text.

Secondly, we may adopt a more constructivistic view where performance measurement is seen as a transformation of meanings and a strategy of communication (Porter, 1995). Phenomena are not "out there" to be discovered. They are also socially constructed. Performance measurement is therefore not just a form of objective recording of social phenomena. It is also a form of social practice representing different schools of thought, cultures, paradigms and modes of behaviour. (Hopwood & Miller, 1994.)

2.1. Value for Money-related Performance Measurement and the University Context

The basic principles and the two approaches described are also relevant in value for money-related performance measurement. Here, the function of the language of measurement is the same, but the "real world" phenomenon (i.e. the principal) must be accorded a more detailed focus. What then, is the more detailed focus? Even though the concept of value for money is ambiguous, it has been seen as a general theoretical concept for an accountable public sector. (Glynn, 1993; cf. Mayston, 1993; Trow, 1996.) It can also be considered operational as a concept by means of which certain characteristics of public sector activities can be evaluated. These characteristics include the three Es' known as economy, efficiency and effectiveness, which derive their scientific origin from (neoclassical) economics (Dogramaci & Färe, 1988; Lovell, 1993), organisation theory (Cameron, 1986) and political science (Pollitt, 1993; Ahonen & Salminen, 1997).

Difficulties in using the concept of value for money in practice are widely known. As Henry Mintzberg has stated regarding the concept of efficiency

> "I believe the root of the problem lies not in the definition of the term but in how that definition is inevitably put into operation. In practice, efficiency does not mean the greatest benefit for the cost; it means the greatest measurable benefit for the measurable cost. In other words, efficiency means demonstrated efficiency, proven efficiency, above all calculated efficiency" (Mintzberg, 1989: 331.)

The same problem concerns the case of value for money. Demonstrating value for money is complicated unless some specific performance measures are introduced.

In addition to conceptual and methodological problems there is more to be taken into account. In the public sector value for money is brought about by activities that are carried out in organisations. Therefore despite the universal nature of the value for money-related phrases in neoclassical economics (cf. Mäki et al., 1993) it has a contextual nature defined according to the variety of functions among the public sector organisations. In the light of the previous discussion the basic theoretical setting is illustrated in Figure 1.

In Figure 1 there is a theoretical distinction between value for money (principal) and the measurement of value for money (surrogate). While principal refers to theoretical conceptions of the elements of value for money, surrogates are seen as operationaldevices, by means of which the elements of value for money are put into practice[2]. Both are needed. In fact, the complexity of a measurement process is a by-product of these interrelations. Moreover, there is a contextual emphasis. The assumption of the universal applicability of performance measurement in different organisation contexts is a mere assumption. In the university context measurement practices, instead of reflecting methodological imperatives, should reflect basic understanding of universities' activities.

The performance of universities is measured, not because it is an object of the inquiry itself (cf. Leontief, 1961), but because it serves some rational purposes.

Figure 1. Basic elements in value for money-related performance measurement

```
┌─────────────────────┐         ┌─────────────────────┐
│   Principal         │         │   Surrogate         │
│                     │◄───────►│                     │
│  Value for money    │         │  The measurement    │
│  -Economy           │         │  of value for money │
│  -Efficiency        │         │                     │
│  -Effectiveness     │         │                     │
└─────────────────────┘         └─────────────────────┘
              ▲                         ▲
               \                       /
                \                     /
                 ▼                   ▼
              ┌─────────────────────┐
              │   The university    │
              │   context           │
              └─────────────────────┘
```

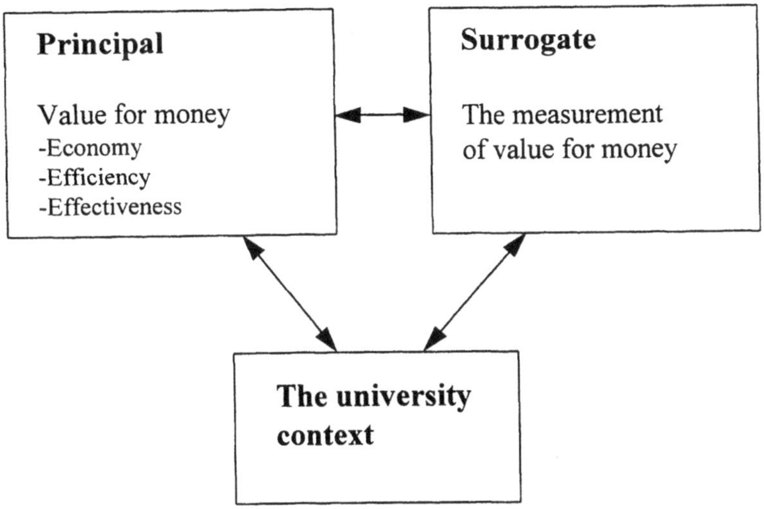

2.2. Value for Money-related Performance Measurement — Snapshots from the Finnish University Context

None of the value for money concepts is uncontroversial. The meaning attached to the concepts varies according to the theoretical sources from which they originate. There is a theoretical level, which is mainly related to the optimising principles in neoclassical economics, especially in production theory and welfare economics. (see e.g. Lowe, 1977; McKenzie, 1983). On the other hand, for public sector purposes there seems to be an "official" interpretation of the concepts introduced, for example, by the Ministry of Finance (VM, 1988; on local government see KRANK, 1989). Finally, there is a large variety of interpretations provided by experts and consultants in different handbooks (e.g. National Audit Office, 1996).

The measure of 'economy' usually refers to the capability of an organisation to produce outputs at the minimum cost. The traditional idea stemming from neoclassical economics is to see economy as a principle of 'economising', a "technique" without any inherent value attached to it (Lowe, 1977; Nell, 1996). The measures of 'economy' in the context of university organisations are surrogates for the phenomenon of "producing" cheaply. (Glynn, 1993.) The efficiency component in value for money involves a comparison of the universities' activities against a performance standard (Lovell, 1993; Glynn, 1993). Because the setting of a standard is complicated in the university context, there is a demand for techniques allowing universities themselves to set their performance standards. This has been a starting point for techniques like Data Envelopment Analysis (DEA) and benchmarking where it is possible to "let the data speak for themselves" (Charnes et al., 1994: 426).[3] The effectiveness dimension in value for money attempts to take into consideration effects of universities' activities in relation to their basic objectives (Glynn,

1993: 50). Is a university increasing value for money when it performs economically and efficiently? The answer of the value for money rhetoric is negative, because 'economy' and 'efficiency' do not reveal whether a university performs well enough in relation to its basic objectives.[4] (Also Carter et al., 1992; Cave et al., 1991.)

In the Finnish university context the measures of economy are usually interpreted as unit costs partly due to the "official" interpretation of the concepts. Therefore ratios such as

- Costs / Students
- Costs / Undergraduate degrees (master's degrees)
- Costs / Post-graduate degrees (licentiate degrees and doctoral degrees)

are the basic vocabulary in different lists (see KOTA, 1994; cf. Cave et. al., 1991). Moreover, comparisons between academic disciplines on the basis of their unit costs are seen as signals of 'economising' the taxpayer's money. It may appear economical to have education in law instead of art or human science education (Helsingin Sanomat December 17, 1995)! Interdisciplinary comparability is not the only problem in the measures of economy. Even intradisciplinary assessments lack perspective, as they tend not to give the measures of economy a sufficient contextual emphasis.

Due to improved cost accounting systems, measures of economy have become essential in Finnish universities. Efficiency measurement is not far behind. In Finland sophisticated measurement of input-output efficiency of universities is present (Mäkilä, 1995; cf. Vakkuri, 1997; Vakkuri & Mälkiä, 1996.) Examples of less sophisticated measures of efficiency can be found in KOTA[5].

- Number of post-graduate degrees / Number of professors and associate professors.

This is considered as a measure of "post-graduate efficiency". On the other hand, a measure of "undergraduate efficiency" is calculated as a following ratio

- Number of undergraduate degrees / Total number of teaching staff.

The case in point is that there have not been any attempts to construct performance standards for input-output relations, which would be the case in the efficiency measurement. Therefore, from a conceptual point of view, a large part of the "efficiency" measurement has in fact been "productivity" measurement, which is measurement without a comparison between observed and optimal values of inputs and outputs. (Lovell, 1993.)

Generally speaking, performance measurement of Finnish universities can be illuminated by the constructivistic approach. Value for money-related performance measurement in the Finnish university context is not theory-based. Rather it is data-based or criteria-based (cf. Cameron, 1986), meaning that there is no specific theoretical "model" in the background. The nature of the measurement process can be considered an ad hoc process, where, after examining the data base, the performance measures are calculated from the data available and afterwards given a theoretical meaning. Epistemologically, this is an example of limitations of empirical knowledge (Wilson, 1996: 177), because there can be no certainty as to how much the individual's conception of 'economy' and 'efficiency' has been influenced by the base data.[6] Accordingly, as to the risks involved this may lead to tunnel vision (more on this in Chapter 3).

Measurement of 'effectiveness' is even more intelligible from the constructivistic angle. At Finnish universities effectiveness is usually measured with models regarding the effects of teaching (see OPM, 1996: 27). The ratio is simple.

- Number of graduates employed / Number of graduates (%)

It is not surprising that during the high unemployment in the 1990's the number of graduates employed has become one of the most important measures of effectiveness. The lists of academic unemployment rates by discipline are seen as indications of the effectiveness or ineffectiveness of a university. However, it should be noted that in some cases it is easier for a specialised university (e.g. technical university or a business school) than for a multidisciplinary university to "prove" effectiveness in this respect. Multidisciplinarity means diversification, different types of disciplines. Therefore there may also be a greater variance in the measures of academic unemployment.

3. Risks in Value for Money-related Performance Measurement

3.1. Seven Theoretical Aspects of Risks in Value for Money-related Performance Measurement

Despite its rational objectives, value for money-related performance measurement may have unintended impacts and consequences. They may be even dysfunctional (cf. Bouckaert 1993b). Smith (1995: 200-212) makes a distinction between seven dimensions of the impacts of performance measurement. In this chapter those elements are regarded as risks of performance measurement, which under certain circumstances may result in secondary consequences that are both non-controllable (cf. Bernstein, 1996: 197-214) and unintended in nature (cf. Hayek, 1936). It is also important to point out that based on different decision-making and evaluative situations the risks may be interpreted differently. The actual meaning is dependent upon how performance measurement information is used (cf. Ijiri, 1975: 45-47). Therefore, to combine performance measurement with resource allocation[7], financial rewards or organisational development may have their distinct characteristics as to the risks involved.

A sophisticated performance measurement system cannot be established without a detailed and credible database. However, the idea of a database covering the entire domain of an organisation's activities is unrealistic for such reasons as the transaction costs of information gathering (Williamson, 1985: 18-22). In this regard the danger lies in a situation where the real world is narrowed to the "measurable" area of an organisation's activities, to tunnel vision.[8] The phrase "if you cannot measure it, it does not exist" (Yankelovich, 1972; quoted in Gray, 1993: 21) entails severe problems especially as far as public sector activities are concerned.

Secondly, due to the multi-dimensional nature of organisational goals public sector performance measurement is a complex exercise as opposed to the ideal situation in business where profit is the key criterion. The impossibility of constructing a single and an aggregate measure, such as profit, is not a catastrophe per se. It is a simple signal of the distinctive nature of the organisational characteristics of the public sector. Yet, as regards performance measurement, lack of congruency between different goals is a problem, and may cause a situation known as suboptimisation. In such a situation organisations as parts of larger organisations prefer to pursue their own goals, which are different from the higher order goals. Instead of "total optimisation", the system may pursue suboptimisation at the different organisational levels. In the public sector, where many activities are based on spill-over effects and externalities, this may lead to considerable controversy.

Thirdly, many functions of the public sector have long-term implications. To see the effects of a programme or the effects of the activities of an organisation requires patience. On the other hand, performance measurement usually tends to concentrate on the short term. The reason for this "impatience" of a performance measurement system is related to data, and especially to its comparability over time. Smith calls this the problem of myopia. Accordingly, the problem of comparability over time tends to limit the time horizon of not only the measurer, but also the decision-maker and the user of the measurement information. (See also e.g. March, 1994.)

Fourthly, public sector organisations are not homogeneous. This is why there are rarely any objective and universal performance standards against which activities could be compared (Smith & Mayston, 1987: 181). However, in order to produce valid and reliable information on value for money in some context, it is logical to make assumptions creating convergence among organisations. The assumption of convergence is not as considerable a risk as those concrete actions made with that assumption in mind. Standardising the activities of organisations makes them more easily measurable, as simultaneously inducing them to move towards the "average" (Cf. Golany & Roll, 1989: 239).[9]

To be an "average" university or university department may not be a virtue. On the contrary, it can also be seen as an indication of ossification. Fifthly, Smith (1995: 208) argues that with a detailed performance measurement system there is a profound risk that the organisation system becomes ossified. It fails to react to new challenges and opportunities. This is because there is no guarantee that the performance measurement system is capable of capturing new innovative ideas. Where this is the case, it may be more tempting for organisations to 'run with the pack' (Smith, 1995: 208) than to innovate. Furthermore, to be innovative may not be rational for organisations if they cannot make sure that their innovative actions are measured by the performance measurement system. Thus in addition to the issue that the area of innovativeness may be limited by the static performance measurement, organisations may be prevented from creating innovations at all. This problem is also related to the suboptimisation problem discussed above.

Sixthly, performance measurement may create an incentive structure where organisations see greater potential gains in altering their behaviour according to the measurement system than according to other actors. In the "optimal" performance measurement system this is not a problem, because the measurement system reflects the "real" nature of the activities[10]. In the "non-optimal" system this reflects the competitive situation of organisations under the rules of game specified by the measurement system. In this sense the problem is not competition, it is rather the problem of destructive competition (Axelrod, 1984).

Finally, performance measurement as a form of social practice is related to social activities, one of which might be called "creative accounting", the misrepresentation of performance measurement information. Since performance measures are surrogates for "real" performance, there is the question of the congruence between behaviour and reported behaviour. Organisations can do the job in both ways: improve their performance or "improve" reports of their performance. For example, in the efficiency measurement this is regarded as a special problem in the case of non-parametric techniques with no sophisticated devices for controlling statistical errors (cf. Bauer, 1990).

3.2. Risks in the Finnish University Context

Tunnel vision in measurement is perhaps one of the most serious risks in the university context. In fact, a large part of active debate on the performance measurement of universities in Finland is associated with this risk. Speculations have been put forward whether universities are transformed more into 'pulp factories' than into accountable knowledge-intensive public organisations (on institutional logic see Townley, 1997). The most considerable risk related to tunnel vision problems is to make an assumption of quantifying everything in the universities' activities.

The risk can be seen as two-fold. First, to accept the view that performance measurement is one type of social practice implies that it should itself produce value for money for decision-makers and decision-making processes. A value for money evaluation is itself supposed to be an activity with a high level of value for money. (Cf. Mayston, 1993.) It would be awkward to consciously use "irrational" means to achieve "rational" ends.[11] Accordingly, it is most probable that the transaction costs of establishing an optimal and detailed performance measurement system in the university context are high. This is why there is a tendency to concentrate on the "most easily measurable" areas of universities' activities (see e.g. OPM, 1996). The measures of 'economy' and 'efficiency' are therefore bound to be the basic elements of the performance measurement system. This is also why the risk of tunnel vision is possible.

Signals of suboptimisation can be found in the Finnish context. The idea of replacing quantity with quality is especially problematic (cf. Pollitt, 1990). Partly due to the national higher education policy Finnish universities have increased the turn-out of degrees, especially post-graduate degrees. The processes have become more efficient in the sense that with a decreasing amount of taxpayers' money more degrees are "produced" (On the cutbacks e.g. Malkki & Kinnunen, 1997).

These measures are at variance with the academic unemployment measures. It may not seem relevant for Finnish universities to be responsible for confirming the appropriate links between higher education and working life. For example, it is often economical and efficient to educate people in fields where workplaces are scarce, because the idea of 'economising' may concern only a producer, not necessarily a customer. (Cf. Nell, 1996; Pollitt, 1993.) In this sense suboptimisation between the three Es' is a problem. Additionally, suboptimisation between different universities or different university departments within the same university is part of reality. In this chapter this element is combined with the risk of gaming.

In the Finnish examples of performance measures, myopia is indicated in a failure to consider universities as providers of long-term effects. The time scale usually ranges from one year to three years. Because one year is conceived to limit the time horizon, a two or three year horizon is used to take the time dimension into account. This reflects the basic assumption that the variation in output measures can be unbiased by extending the time scale in a universal manner.

Methodologically, the problem is not that of broadening the time scale of the measures. If needed, as a result of the improved cost accounting systems and the increased accuracy of the output indicators, performance measurement can be extended to cover many more years than at present. The risk is the static nature of such measurement systems. For example, if reliable performance measurement is affected by the changing nature of universities over time, it can be debated whether this is an advantage or disadvantage. It is an advantage if the static nature and the low level of adaptation among universities is a virtue. On the other hand, it is a disadvantage if universities as knowledge-intensive organisations are expected to react to changing circumstances in a distinctive manner. (For a more detailed discussion, see March, 1994.) In this respect value for money is a concept which is sensitive towards different periods of time.

Analysis of value for money is a procedure in which universities are compared against criteria of value for money. The criteria are universal in the sense that they are applied equally to different types of universities. We are assuming similarities among universities, while looking for dissimilarities in their capability to produce value for money. Therefore, unit costs are assumed to have a similar meaning in the natural sciences and in the human sciences. In the same manner the employment ratios are treated as equal whether we are concerned with law or art education.

However, because of the differences between fields of science, disciplines, scientific cultures and different modes of creating knowledge, there are theoretical constraints in the notion of a unified and homogeneous university sector. This sets limitations for comparisons because of the distinctive nature of production functions among disciplines. Looking at the Finnish university context it cannot be disregarded that universities consist of different sets of disciplines. In Finland there are 9 multidisciplinary universities, 3 technical universities, 3 business schools and 4 colleges of art. The major risk is that these universities with different sets of disciplines with different production functions are not comparable with each other (cf. Vakkuri & Mälkiä, 1996). Value for money is influenced by the disciplinary context in which it is analysed.[12]

For measurement purposes it is possible to assume that there are no problems with comparability. In fact, the next practical step is to increase the "optimality" of a performance measurement system by increasing convergence among disciplines and universities. Here we encounter the risk of distorting the effects of scientific "dissimilarity", one of the basic principles in creating and mediating knowledge. Thus performance measurement may not be able to cover all dissimilar ways of increasing taxpayers' value.

In the Finnish context the risk of ossification is related with the previous risk. Three dimensions of value for money can be considered as constraints, as a mechanism of controlling the use of money invested by taxpayers. However, there is another approach, which does not neglect the possibility that there can exist innovative and different ways to produce value for money. (Cf. Dent & Ezzamel, 1995.) The last aspect is closely associated with the activities of universities, because the unpredictable and chaotic nature of research activities may not be compatible with the fairly static nature of performance measurement. In fact, this has been among the widely debated questions in the performance measurement of Finnish universities. (Laukkanen & Stenvall, 1996; Helenius et al., 1996; on European dimension see Trow, 1996.)

Finnish universities and indeed other public sector organisations are at a stage of metamorphosis (Ahonen & Salminen, 1997). The administrative system of universities has been changed: it is more decentralised and deregulated. This is one of the preconditions for a new gaming situation. As far as value for money-related performance measurement is concerned, there is a risk of destructive gaming. This means that the competitive situation between and within universities is organised around the performance measurement system. In such a situation it is most essential for the University of Tampere to confirm that all of its resources are used to produce its own outputs. It is not useful to pursue co-operation with other universities unless there are co-operation outputs used to measure such activities.

Therefore, unit costs and ratios such as number of post-graduate degrees / number of professors and associate professors are not improved by helping students graduate in another university. In fact, they can be improved by encouraging post-graduate students, especially those who are to qualify in the near future, to complete their studies at the University of Tampere. This is a problem, because the boundaries of scientific expertise are not always compatible with the administrative boundaries of universities. Therefore, the risk of double standards for universities' activities may arise. According to Kaukonen (1996) the first of these is used for satisfying evaluators and the other is used to develop the content of scientific work.

The risk of misrepresentation embraces both moral and methodological aspects. A person may find it tempting to "improve" the performance of a university by means of creative accounting, if it has a direct effect on the success of the university and him/herself. Interpreting Smith (1995: 211), universities are vulnerable in this respect, because the audit of the outputs of universities would be a massive task. Therefore, complete control over the correct representation of performance measurement information includes costs which may exceed the benefits accruing.

Methodologically, however, there is a large variety of options to influence the measurement rankings. In fact, output measures are the tricky part in the case of universities. Time variations in output measures (especially number of post-graduate degrees) have considerable effects on the performance measures of the universities. Therefore, the measures of economy and efficiency may be distorted by using "creative" rolling averages. Because the number of post-graduates in a Finnish university is fairly small, the relative change in the measure may have significant effects on its ranking.[13]

The measure of effectiveness calculated as the academic employment rate is more vulnerable than the previous measures. When is it possible to report that a student is employed? Should a working position be permanent or temporary? If temporary, how temporary? In this age of "temporary jobs" this is indeed a crucial question. Additionally, should one criterion be that the student is employed by an organisation, whose basic function relates to an area of expertise equal with his or her studies? Further, how is equality defined in this regard? However, it is complicated to separate the effect of higher education in a case where it is easy to argue that a person would have been employed anyway.

Finally, it is essential to point out one thing. In order to avoid misrepresentation and fraud there is one logical conclusion, which is to limit performance measurement to the "most easily measurable" areas. This is because in those areas there are not as many methodological difficulties as in the more problematic areas of universities' activities. However, it is interesting to see that there we encounter the risk from which we started this discussion, the risk of tunnel vision.

4. Summary and Discussion

Value for money-related performance measurement is a combination of different approaches and perspectives, both theory-laden and empirically based. Being methodological, the chain of argument in this paper has practised the science of "muddling through" by attempting to see the interrelations between the "real world" and the measurement of the "real world". Moreover, the idea of value for money has been given the type of contextual emphasis, which, we argue, is most relevant as far as universities are concerned.

To see the practice of public sector performance measurement as a risky business may not be fashionable in Finland at the moment. This is because, as indicated earlier, characteristics of risks may vary according to distinctive types of using performance measurement information. The tone of the discussion is different if we are concerned with resource allocation or organisational development.

This text has been more tentative than exclusive in the sense that an extensive empirical analysis of risks in the Finnish university context has not been provided. However, our discussion indicates that theory-based "risk management" of performance measurement is needed in one way or another. At least in the Finnish context this would serve as both a scientific device for structuring discussion and creating a more comprehensive basis for performance measurement. Although it is important to "prove" value for money or the absence of value for money, sometimes it is equally important to clarify the analytical perspectives involved in the development of performance measurement practices. The categorisation and analysis of risks is one essential part in this type of process.

In the Finnish university context metamorphosis towards a more sophisticated performance measurement system is still going on. An approach is needed where performance measurement is considered to include risks and costs that may not be covered by the benefits of the system. Even though these costs and risks are not seen as operational and quantifiable, they may redirect attention to areas where the most severe problems exist. Methodologically speaking, the major problem may not lie in our ability to find correct principal-surrogate relations in the university context. The basic problem may be that it is not "efficient" to attempt to achieve that goal. In doing so, instead of increasing value for money, we may end up decreasing it.

Notes

[1] In measurement theory different theoretical problems associated with systematising these relationships are presented. These include validity, representation and uniqueness problems. (For more on these see Ellis, 1966; Berka, 1983.)

[2] Note the two ontological approaches mentioned earlier.

[3] There are a great number of properties in DEA and other benchmarking-related techniques which limit dogmatic interpretations (Bardach, 1994; Bouckaert, 1993a; Vakkuri, 1997). Issues like the construction of the input-output model, sensitivity towards statistical errors and problems related to appropriate combination of universities or university departments analysed are examples of such limitations. And finally, if we "let the data speak for themselves", it is usually assumed that the data "speaking for themselves", are reliable and cover all the different activities of universities. This is not always the case, at least not in the Finnish context.

[4] The complex interrelations between the concepts 'efficiency' and 'effectiveness' have been noted. Both are related to an external standard. While in 'effectiveness' the standard may be seen to regard the achievement of desired results set politically, in 'efficiency' the focus is on the standards set for input-output ratios. The distinction is far from simple, because desired results may also refer to outputs or input-output ratios. (Carter et. al., 1992; Glynn, 1993.)

[5] KOTA is a statistical system including basic data on the costs, inputs and outputs of universities. The system is maintained by the Ministry of Education.

[6] From the standpoint of the paradigm of neoclassical economics this is not regarded as a problem, because "...quantification in this instance is more than a methodological device employed by the investigator: it is an object of the inquiry itself" (Leontief, 1961: 118).

[7] In Finland the establishment of a new budgeting system is planned for universities where a major part of the resources of universities will be allocated on the basis of performance indicators (OPM, 1996). These plans have contributed to discussions on performance measurement. However, in this paper the risks are seen from a more general perspective in order to analyse theoretical background for different types of measurement practices.

[8] The traditional meaning of the "measurable" area regarding many knowledge-intensive activities and organisations can also be questioned. This aspect has been emphasised by Grilliches (1994).

[9] Despite the innovative methodological possibilities performance measurement is usually seen only as a form of central control (Dent & Ezzamel, 1995). For example, DEA (Data Envelopment Analysis) method has traditionally been used as a method for centralised performance control instead of strategic self-evaluation of organisations. Both these approaches are present in the DEA toolbox. The question is how the toolbox is utilised. (Vakkuri & Mälkiä, 1996.)

[10] This is a theoretical situation where 'surrogates' are correctly specified according to measurement principles reflecting the "real" nature of the 'principal'.

[11] Knudsen (1993) refers to this as a self-reference problem.

[12] It is reasonable to add that there do not exist independent and universal criteria which do not reflect the basic assumptions of science policy. For example, methodological solutions in the performance measurement of research activities are usually associated with certain fields of science and their scientific cultures. (Cf. e.g. Kaukonen, 1996.)

[13] There are different nuances in misrepresentation. Namely, creative accounting can be "creative" also in the sense that it maximises the reported performance within the boundaries of measurement rules.

Bibliography

Ahonen, Pertti & Salminen, Ari, *Metamorphosis of the Administrative Welfare State. From Depoliticisation to Political Rationality,* Berlin/New York: Peter Lang, (1997).

Axelrod, Robert, *The Evolution of Cooperation,* New York: Basic Books, (1984).

Bardach, Eugene, "The Problem of Best Practice Research", *Journal of Policy Analysis and Management.* V. 13, (1994), pp.260-268.

Bauer, Paul. W., "Recent Developments in the Econometric Estimation of Frontiers", *Journal of Econometrics* 46, (1990), pp.39-56.

Berka, Karel, *Measurement. Its Concepts, Theories and Problems,* Dordrecht: D.Reidel, (1983).

Bernstein. Peter L, *Against the Gods. The Remarkable Story of Risk,* New York: John Wiley & Sons, (1996).

Bouckaert, Geert, "Efficiency Measurement from a Management Perspective. A Case of the Civil Registry Office in Flanders", *International Review of Administrative Sciences.* V. 59, (1993), pp. 11-27. (Bouckaert 1993a.)

Bouckaert, Geert, "Measurement and Meaningful Management", *Public Productivity & Management Review.* V. XVII, N. 1., Fall (1993), pp. 31-43. (Bouckaert 1993b.)

Cameron, Kim, "Effectiveness as Paradox: Consensus and Conflict in Conceptions of Organizational Effectiveness", *Management Science* V. 32, N. 5, (1986), pp. 539-553.

Carter, Neil & Klein, Rudolf & Day, Patricia, *How Organisations Measure Success. The Use of Performance Indicators in Government,* London: Routledge, (1992).

Cave, Martin & Hanney, Stephen & Kogan, Maurice, *The Use of Peformance Indicators in Higher Education A Critical Analysis of Developing Practice,* Second Edition, London: Jessica Kingsley, (1991).

Charnes, Abraham & Cooper, William & Lewin, Arie.Y. & Seiford, Lawrence.M., Eds., *Data Envelopment Analysis. Theory, Methodology and Applications.* Boston: Kluwer Academic, (1994).

Dent, J & Ezzamel, M., "Organisational Control and Management Accounting", in Holloway, Jacky & Lewis, Jenny & Mallory, Geoff, Eds., *Performance Measurement and Evaluation.* London: Sage, (1995).

Dogramaci, Ali & Färe, Rolf, Eds., *Applications of Modern Production Theory Efficiency and Productivity,* Boston: Kluwer Academic, (1988).

Ellis, Brian, *Basic Concepts of Measurement.* London: Cambridge University Press, (1966).

Glynn, John, *Public Sector Financial Control and Accounting,* Second edition, Oxford: Blackwell Business, (1993).

Golany, B & Roll, Y, "An Application Procedure for DEA", *OMEGA: International Journal of Management Science,* V. 17, N. 3, (1989). pp. 237- 250.

Gray, Rob: *Accounting for the Environment. The Greening af Accountancy,* Part II, London: Paul Chapman Ltd, (1993).

Grilliches, Zvi, "Productivity, R & D, and the Data Constraint", *American Economic Review,* V. 84, N. 1 (March 1994), pp. 1-23.

Hayek, Friedrich A., *Economics and Knowledge.* Presidential Address Delivered Before the London Economic Club. Reprinted in Economica IV (1937), pp. 33-54.

Helenius, Börje & Hämäläinen, Esa & Tuunainen, Juha, Eds., *Kohti McDonalds-yliopistoa. Nakokulmia suomalaiseen korkeakoulu-ja tiedepolitiikkaan,* Gummerus, (1996). [Towards a McDonalds-university. Aspects on the Finnish higher education and science policy].

Helsingin Sanomat (National newspaper) 17.12. 1995. Korkeakoulutuksen tehokkuus ratkeaa uudella mittarilla. Oikeustiede ja lääketiede kärjessä, humanistiset alat tehottomimmat. [The problem of efficiency in higher education is solved with a new measurement technique Law and medical science the most efficient, human sciences the most inefficient].

Hopwood, Anthony G. & Miller, Peter, Eds., *Accounting as Social and Institutional Practice*. Gambridge University Press, (1994).

Ijiri, Yuji, *The Foundations of Accounting Measurement. A Mathematical, Economic and Behavioral Inquiry*, New Jersey: Prentice Hall, (1967).

Ijiri, Yuji, *Theory of Accounting Measurement*, Sarasota (FL): American Accounting Association, (1975).

Kaukonen, Erkki, "Tiedepolitiikka ja tutkimuksen arvioinnin ongelmat" [Science policy and problems in evaluation of research activities], in Laukkanen, Reijo & Stenvall, Kirsti Eds., *Arviointi koulutus- ja tiedepolitiikassa*, Tampere: Tampereen yliopisto, (1996), pp. 35-56.

Knudsen, Christian, "Equilibrium, Perfect Rationality and The Problem of Self-Reference in Economics" in Mäki, Uskali & Gustafsson, Bo & Knudsen, Christian, Eds., *Rationality, Institutions & Economic Methodology*. London: Routledge, (1993).

Kunnallisen alan rationalisointineuvottelukunta (KRANK), *Suositus kunnallisen palvelutoiminnan tuloksellisuuden arvioinnissa käytettävistä käsitteistä ja niiden sisällöistä* [The committee of the rationalization of local government services, A recommendation for the content of concepts in the evaluation of local goverment services April 7, (1989)].

Laukkanen, Reijo & Stenvall, Kirsti, Eds., *Arviointi koulutus- ja tiedepolitiikassa*, Tampere: Tampereen yliopisto, (1996). Hallintotiede A 9. [Evaluation in education and science policy].

Leontief, Wassily, "The Problem of Quality and Quantity in Economics" in Lerner Daniel, Ed., *Quantity and Quality The Hayden Colloqium on Scientific Method and Concept*, New York: The Free Press of Clencoe, (1961).

Lovell, Knox. A., "Production Frontiers and Productive Efficiency" in Fried, Harold.O. & Lovell, Knox C.A. & Schmidt, Shelton S., Eds, *The Measurement of Produductive Efficiency. Techniques and Applications*, New York: Oxford University Press, (1993).

Lowe, Adolph, *On Economic Knowledge. Toward A Science of Political Economics*, Enlarged Edition, New York: M.E. Sharpe Publisher, (1977).

Malkki, Pertti & Kinnunen, Juha, *Voimavarojen muutokset ja saastopaätokset 1990-luvulla korkeakouluissa*, Kuopion yliopisto, (1996), Yhteiskuntatieteet 42. [Changes in financial resources and cutback decisions at Finnish universities in 1990's].

March, James G., *Three Lectures on Efficiency and Adaptiveness in Organizations*, Helsinki: Svenska Handelshögskolan, (1994), Swedish Scool of Economics and Business Administration, Research Reports 32.

Mayston, David, Principals, Agents and the Economics of Accountability in the New Public Sector, *Accounting, Auditing & Accountability Journal*, V. 6, N. 3, (1993), pp. 68-96.

McKenzie, Richard B., *The Limits of Economic Science Essays on Methodology*, Boston: Kluwer-Nijhoff, (1983).

Mintzberg, Henry, *Mintzberg on Management. Inside Our Strange World of Organizations*, Free Press, (1989).

Mäki, Uskali & Gustafsson, Bo & Knudsen, Christian, Eds., *Rationality, Institutions and Economic Methodology*. London: Routledge, (1993).

Mäkilä, Atro, *Korkeakoulujen tehokkuuden arviointi Data Envelopment Analysis-menetelmalla.* Opetusministeriö, (1995), Korkeakouluneuvoston julkaisuja 2/1995. [Efficiency evaluation of universities by means of DEA method].

Nell, Edward J., *Making Sense of a Changing Economy Technology, Markets and Morals,* London: Routledge, (1996).

Opetusministeriö (OPM). *Yliopistojen tulosohjauksen kehittaminen, Yliopistolaitoksen tulosohjauksen kehittamistyoryhman loppuraportti,* Opetusministeriö, (1996). Opetusministeriön työryhmien muistioita 36: 1996 [Ministry of Education The development of result-oriented management of universities].

Pollitt, Christopher, "Measuring University Performance: Never Mind the Quality, Never Mind the Width?", *Higher Education Quarterly.* V., N. 1. Winter (1990), pp. 60-81.

Pollitt, Christopher, *Managerialism and the Public Services Cuts or Cultural Changes in the 1990s?,* 2. Edition. Oxford: Blackwell Publishers, (1993).

Porter, Theodore M., *Trust in Numbers. The Pursuit of Objectivity in Science and Public Life,* Princeton: Princeton University Press, (1995).

Smith, Peter & Mayston, David, "Measuring Efficiency in the Public Sector", *OMEGA. International Journal of Management Science,* V. 15, N. 3, (1987), pp. 181-189.

Smith, Peter, "Outcome-related Performance Indicators and Organisational Control in the Public Sector", in Holloway, Jacky & Lewis, Jenny & Mallory, Geoff, Eds., *Performance Measurement and Evaluation,* London. Sage, (1995).

Swoyer, Chris, "The Metaphysics of Measurement", in Forge, John Ed., *Measurement, Realism and Objectivity Essays on Measurement in Social and Physical Sciences,* Dordrecht: D. Reidel, (1987).

Taulukoita KOTA-tietokannasta 1994. Helsinki: Opetusministeriö, (1995). Koulutus- ja tiedepolitiikan linjan julkaisusarja. [Ministry of Education: Measures from the KOTA data base].

Townley, Barbara, "The Institutional Logic of Performance Appraisal", *Organisation Studies* (1997), Issue 2, pp. 261-285.

Trow, Martin, "Trust, Markets and Accountability in Higher Education. A Comparative Perspective", *Higher Education Policy,* V. 9, N. 4, (1996), pp. 309-324.

Vakkuri, Jarmo, *DEA-menetelman teoreettisista ominaispiirteista ja tietosisalloista. Tarkastelukohteena erityisesti korkeakoulujen laitostason arviointi,* Julkaisematon lisensiaattitutkimus. Tampereen yliopisto, (1997). [On the Theoretical Properties and Assumptions in DEA method, Performance Analysis of University Departmens, Unpublished licentiate thesis].

Vakkuri, Jarmo & Mälkiä, Matti, *The Applicability of DEA Method in Performance Analysis. The Case of Finnish Universities and University Departments,* Tampereen yliopisto, (1996), Hallintotiede C 12.

Valtiovarainministeriö (VM), *Ohjeet toiminta- ja taloussuunnitelman laatimiseksi vuosille 1990-94,* N. TM 8812. [Ministry of Finance: Instructions for Preparing the Finance and Policy Plan for the Years 1990-1994. Helsinki, May 4, (1988)].

Value for money handbook. National Audit Office, (1996).

Williamson, Oliver, *The Economic Institutions of Capitalism Firms, Markets, Relational Contracting,* New York/London: The Free Press, (1985).

Wilson, Catherine: Instruments and Ideologies: The Social Construction of Knowledge and Its Critics. *American Philosophical Quarterly,* Vol. 33, No. 2. (April 1996), p. 167-181.

Yankelovich, D. *Corporate Priorities A Continuing Study of the New Demands on Business.* Daniel Yankelovich Inc 1972.

Contracting in the Public Services :
the case of transport in the UK

E. Wistrich[*]

1. Introduction

For the purposes of this paper, contracting is defined in a broad sense as a device for clarifying respective rights and duties in an agreement between persons or organisations in a process of exchange (Hardern, 1992). The contract may be a 'discrete 'or classical one written for business purposes involving the purchase and supply of goods or services, outlined in a legal document and enforceable by the courts of law. Or it may be a 'relational' contract which places less importance on legal documents and more on developing trust and norms of behaviour over a longer relationship but which also relies on hierarchy and command in the organisation. (Macneil, 1980).

Contracting has become an important tool in present day public sector management. It is seen as a method of instituting a principal/agent relationship and overcoming the problems of self interested behaviour in public bureaucracies. In agency theory, the objectives of the service are set by the principals, either politicians or senior managers, and the agents carry out the operations. The contract relationship allows the terms of the work to be set out and the performance subsequently monitored. It is a tool well suited to a government which wishes to restrict its role in operations to purchasing and allow competition for service delivery among service providers (Boston et al., 1996; Self, 1993). It has therefore been used extensively in the break up of former state monopoly services and the introduction of market provision. The problems which may arise from contracting stem from two sources. The first comes from transaction costs. Every contract has its costs of preparation, execution and audit and these increase with the number of contracts and their complexity. 'Relational 'contracts which rely on trust have lower transaction costs, but they are subject to a different hazard. In a complex contract which relies on high professional expertise, the agents or providers are likely to have an advantage in information over the purchaser, which will enable them to negotiate a more favourable contract and reduce efficiency. This advantage is marked where investment in fixed assets is high and not transferable and where there is therefore little competition. The choice therefore may be between a large number of limited legally enforced contracts high in transaction costs, or fewer longer term trust based relational contracts, lower in transaction costs but open to exploitation by the agents . Relational contracts are also said to be used in those public services where professionals play an important role (Bennett & Fairlie, 1996).The second source of difficulty arises from the differentiation and fragmentation of a service which was previously unified as a state monopoly. Coordination of service and overall policy planning is harder to achieve. These issues will be further examined in the account which follows.

---

[*] Dr. Enid Wistrich, Middlesex University, United Kingdom.

2. Is 'Transport' a public service?

'Transport' is a very broad term defined as carrying people and goods from one place to another. It involves the means of carriage (cars, buses, trains and planes), and the track which carries them. Transport in Britain has moved between 'public service' and market operation over different periods of time, with varying modes of organisation and ownership. State finance is used for capital expenditure for roads and railways. More recently loss making railway services have been subsidised to keep them running for social reasons, and schemes for concessionary fares for the elderly and disabled on public transport have been subsidised raising the question of the extent to which public transport is a social service worthy of state funding. The idea that personal mobility is a welfare objective is a recent one (Wistrich, 1990), but was accepted as applied to public transport by the recent Conservative government which retained concessionary fare subsidies.

As a group of operations and services, transport therefore has a mixed role. For the carriage of freight, it is a commercial service, operated by the private sector on 'common carrier' networks requiring some public financing and regulation. For the carriage of passengers, it varies from a commercial service operated by coaches, taxis, lorries and planes, and a self service of privately owned cars, to a service with strong welfare elements in the case of public passenger transport. Overall, it has important consequences for both economic and environmental public issues. Transport may be placed largely in the category of a public utility supplying basic, essential services, requiring a high level of capital finance and of public regulation, but with some elements of a tax financed public welfare service and a significant public interest.

We may expect contracting to be used in transport for various aspects of the sector. First, the 'classic' or discrete limited term contract can be used to supply equipment, to carry out routine operations (e.g. maintenance), for skilled specific operations (e.g. computer traffic light systems) and for some direct service delivery (e.g. coach services). Second, a recent development to draw on private sources for capital finance requires more complex contracts to build networks or provide services. Third, the need to regulate access to a finite track of networks, requires contracts which give monopoly privileges for a limited period of time; these are described as franchises. Fourth, the public interest factors of safety, standards of performance, coordinated service and prevention of monopoly abuse have to be enforced and the means include a combination of licensing, franchising and government regulation. The total picture is therefore likely to be complex, with an extensive framework of institutions and powers, varying from one aspect of infrastructure and service provision to another. Such a requirement is not easy to construct and to operate as a unified whole. It has to cope with risk and different patterns of accountability, and, to be effective, requires the development of trust as well as the legal powers and sanctions typical of contracts. (Walsh, 1995; Hardern, 1992). The analysis which follows attempts to assess the various frameworks and types of contract.

3. Contracting and overland transport

3.1. Road Transport

3.1.1. Road building and maintenance

The building and maintenance of local roads has in Britain always been a local authority function. Since the 1930s, main roads of national importance and motorways have become increasingly important as car and lorry transport are now the predominant overland freight and passenger modes. Construction has been financed through capital funding as part of public sector borrowing. The work is commissioned by the public authorities and carried out through construction and service contracts. From 1980-97, competitive tendering for construction projects was compulsory for local authorities, and the design of new roads and the supervision of building contracts has increasingly been transferred by contract to the private sector, all as part of the Conservative government's move to privatise civil service and local government work. In 1997, the new Labour government withdrew the compulsory requirement on local authorities to put these contracts out to tender. A second and more recent move has been to try to attract private capital resources into the funding of public sector projects. Its underlying aim has been to control the total level of public expenditure and thus restrain inflation. It was thought that the long term need to modernise the road infrastructure could be better achieved if private finance was drawn in for investment, and the charge on Treasury funding minimised. The Private Finance Initiative announced in 1992 was put forward as the answer to the problem and is discussed below.

3.1.2. Road passenger transport

Road passenger transport is the area where market deregulation and liberalisation of transport has been most applied (Wistrich, 1996). Private cars and lorries have always had free access to the road network. In the 1980s licensing was abolished for long distance coach services and the majority of local bus services. Under the 1985 Transport Act, local buses and their drivers require only safety licenses and can enter or leave the service market at will, on any routes, provided they give 42 days notice to the local transport authority. Contracting procedures are however used by local authorities to provide for additional services to meet social needs. For example, if bus companies find it unprofitable to run evening or weekend services on particular routes, the local authority may contract to provide any additional services it wants and subsidise them from public funds within the limits of expenditure allowed. To do so, it must first specify the services required and secure competitive tenders before awarding the contracts. Franchising bus services on specified routes remains the practice in London and in Northern Ireland. In London, London Regional Transport is the franchiser and franchises are awarded to bus fleets which were previously part of an integrated public operation but are now separate business units, today mostly sold and operated as private firms. In spite of talk of total deregulation in London by the Conservative government, it was never carried out. Franchising is likely to remain in the future and may be extended to other parts of the country by the new Labour Government.

Contracting thus at present plays a relatively small role in road passenger transport because of the measures of privatisation and deregulation introduced in the 1980s and 1990s. British practice (except in London) contrasts with that in Sweden (Nordell, 1993) and New Zealand

(White, 1995) where county and regional authorities plan the network provision and contract for private operators.

3.2. The railways

The organisation of a rail system is both large scale and complex. The vertically integrated nationalised corporation which owned the service from 1948-94 had a substantial central organisation and hierarchy, uniform practices and a full personnel service covering many grades, combined with regional decentralisation of service operations,. The corporation built its own locomotives and rolling stock and had its own police. It still owned and operated hotels built in the nineteenth century near its main railway stations. In this context, the role of contracting was limited. The 1968 Transport Act allowed local Passenger Transport Authorities formed from local authorities outside London to contract with the railways for the provision of local and suburban services to supplement and coordinate with their bus services. Contracts no doubt supplied goods and equipment necessary to operations, or leased land and other services. Capital finance came from state sources, as did subsidy for the operating deficit. However, as competition from road and air transport reduced railway use, the reluctance of governments to invest and subsidise the railways became more marked.

Privatisation was not at first considered by the Conservative governments of 1979-97 because of poor supply and demand factors, high fixed costs and mixed use by both freight and passengers, all of which were thought to favour a single organisation (Beesley & Littlechild, 1983; Nash & Preston, 1993). However, the privatisation urge backed by a powerful desire of government to reduce its expenditure on subsidies and public borrowing for the railways brought reconsideration. The Railways Act of 1993 privatised the system, basically by subdividing it in a different way and then by creating a competitive environment. The organisation in the 1970s had regional operating units accepting both freight and passenger service and responsible for all aspects of operations on its lines. Then in the 1980s, sector management replaced it, each sector intended as a business unit. Freight had its own sector, as did the passenger services Intercity, Network SE which served the London area. The 1993 Act however divided British Rail differently into two parts; Railtrack for track and infrastructure, and operations run by operating units franchised for limited periods, plus a series of other operating units for stations, depots, coach and engine maintenance, catering etc. All these were hived off from British Rail, transformed into companies and sold into the private sector.

The structure is therefore fragmented from the previously integrated one and is intended to operate in the open market. However, it requires extensive linkages in order to operate successfully, and a careful system of public supervision to ensure safety and coordination, to provide necessary subsidies and to prevent monopoly abuse. These are largely secured by means of licenses, contracts or franchises. Contracting therefore plays a key role in the new, privatised system and is a good ground for testing the value of the method.

4. Contracting, licensing and regulation in railway operations

The 'players' in the new railway system are numerous. There are first two new public authorities concerned directly with licensing, regulating and franchising, - the Office of Rail Regulator and the Office of Passenger Rail Franchising. Then there is the large monopoly company Railtrack which owns the lines, signaling equipment, stations and depots. Next come the 25 passenger train operating companies (TOCS) which are franchised to run services, and in the future the Act intends there to be a number of non-franchised companies who will also operate services on contract. There are also the freight companies who contract with Railtrack to operate freight services. Lastly come the numerous companies who lease or contract to provide services to the operators. There are for example three rolling stock leasing companies (ROSCOs), OBS Services which provides catering, OHS Services for occupational health services, Business Systems which owns computer centres and RSP which owns software for ticketing and settlement schemes; all these and many others formerly belonged to British Rail and have been separated and sold off (OPRAF, 1996a).

From the viewpoint of the railway operating companies, the system is complicated and formidable to negotiate. A company first has to obtain a license to operate from the Office of the Rail Regulator. It then has to negotiate an access agreement with Railtrack which has to be approved by the Regulator to ensure that the agreement and the charges made do not inhibit competition, promotes efficiency and the use of the railway network, and protects the interests of users. Next it has to apply for a franchise to operate for a fixed period (usually 7-15 years) over a rail network. The franchise is obtained from the Office of Passenger Rail Franchising which sets out service performance obligations, restrictions on fare levels, and pays subsidies from government. Alternatively, it may, in the future, after securing its access agreement with Railtrack, choose to operate a service on one or more railway routes on an 'open access' basis, without a franchise and thus without a rail subsidy or franchise obligations. The Rail Regulator has to approve such agreements and has decided that he will only approve open access after 1999 where the competition will not in his view damage improvements to services. For the franchised companies, once the franchise is obtained the operating company has to negotiate contracts with a rolling stock company to lease stock, with station and depot facility owners for the use of their facilities, and with the Transport Police and various other firms for services necessary for their operation.

The franchise agreement obtained from the Office of Passenger Rail Franchising sets out a series of obligations which the franchisee must meet. The first is a minimum level of services set out in the Passenger Service Requirement (PSR), which are run according to a timetable. There must be adequate coach capacity to operate services. There are obligations to provide information about the services at stations and to participate in ticketing arrangements with other rail operators. The franchisee must accept restrictions on fare levels set by OPRAF, and make a minimum commitment of capital finance. It must publish an approved Passengers' Charter and conduct customer satisfaction surveys. The franchise agreement includes the amount of government subsidy to be paid to the company. Lastly, it sets out the penalty regime for instances when the trains are canceled or are not punctual. (OPRAF, 1996b)

Both the Rail Regulator and the Rail Franchising Director have responsibilities for reviewing the performance of contracts they have approved or issued, and may impose penalties as part of enforcement. One recent example concerns South West Trains which was the first rail franchise awarded in December 1995 and receives an annual subsidy of £m54. In January 1997, the company dismissed one tenth of its drivers as part of a cost cutting exercise. It then found it had to cancel many services because it had too few drivers to operate its trains; nearly 200 services were canceled in one week (Guardian 4/3/97). The Franchise Director may fine companies if they do not meet service targets, and take action for breach of contract if cancellations exceed the limits set for any three four-week periods over three years. He warned SWT of possible action, but decided not to impose a discretionary £m1 fine because service recovered to required levels in April (Local Transport To-day, 1997). SWT is however in line for breach action if it is 'called in' again by the Franchise Director before March 2000.

Railtrack has similarly run into trouble with the Rail Regulator. It had inherited a large shortfall on investment for renewing track and stations and had agreed a substantial investment programme with the Rail Regulator. But it failed to invest more than £m43 of the £m720 investment required in the first year of privatisation, despite making profits of some £m300 (Guardian, 1997). The incoming Labour Government called for tougher regulations and sanctions for the Regulator. The Regulator then proposed a modification to Railtrack's license requiring the company to give details on its expenditure of its subsidy, and to be publicly accountable for delivery of its network management plans. Railtrack initially resisted stronger scrutiny but eventually agreed to the amended license requirements (Local Transport To-day, 1997) The amended license gives the Regulator powers to investigate, and if necessary enforce, the carrying out of Railtrack's obligations. Railtrack now has to publish its criteria for carrying out its duties, together with an annual statement on how it will be done, and another on its annual performance (ORR, 1997). The Rail Regulator intends to hold regular meetings with Railtrack to monitor and review license compliance and progress in achieving agreed objectives.

5. Contracting and public/private sector partnership

Privatisation in the transport industry was clearly intended to increase efficiency and standards of service to customers through business methods and a competitive environment. Another important motive was to involve the use of private capital and thus reduce the burden on public funds. But the very large sums involved in major projects made investment unattractive to the private sector without some support from public funds. So the movement to involve private sector moneys has two aspects - to attract private funding into projects where the state has primary responsibility such as road building, and to create new joint projects where the public sector leads or has a substantial stake.

The Private Finance Initiative was announced in 1992 to create a framework for such funding. The PFI aims to encourage both free standing projects by the private sector and joint ventures of both the private and public sectors. The rules set out specify in advance the contribution the state will make and the risks it is prepared to take and seeks to transfer the greater part of the risk to the private sector. A project is identified and prepared and then private partners are selected by a competitive tender process. The partners then conclude a contract to carry out the project. The PFI is intended for all aspects of public sector activity, but its greatest use (80% of all projects) has been in transport. A Department of Transport estimate of 1994 showed transport projects being developed of a value of nearly £m10,000 (Terry, 1996), most of these for the railways. For example, the two largest are for the Channel Tunnel Rail Link (£m2.7) and London Crossrail (£m2.8) which is still being developed. Others now being constructed are the Heathrow Express Rail Line and the Midland (Birmingham) Metro. Of these, the Channel Tunnel Rail Link is financially free standing, but the others are joint capital ventures. A smaller number of projects are for road and bridge construction, for example the Birmingham North Relief Road and the Second Seven Crossing.

The PFI includes the first attempts to build and operate roads under the Design/Build/Finance/Operate (DBFO) schemes, to the value of £m380 in 1994. DBFO operates through competitive tender. It allows a private firm to carry through a total process from design to operation of new roads. It operates straightforwardly where the operator can recoup his costs by charging customers directly, as in toll payments. But in Britain toll payments are rare, applying only to new bridges and tunnels and there is substantial public resistance to them. "Shadow tolls" have been proposed as a method of overcoming this problem; these are payments to the provider by government based on the volume of monitored road use (Glaister and Travers, 1994). Local authorities were given powers in 1991 to contract with private sector firms to build new roads and charge tolls on them and some are now considering whether to do so. For example, the City of Edinburgh is currently considering combining with neighbouring local Councils to invite private sector firms to build a city by-pass road and to collect toll payments from it. In this case, the contract would include direct remuneration of costs from charges. Such a move is a further step in the direction of road pricing, which is unpopular with the public, but is necessary if there is to be more widespread road building by the private sector.

6. Transaction costs and competition in transport contracting

Transaction costs are high where there are many contracts involved in a service, its finance and operation. For any individual contract, the costs will be high where it is felt necessary to specify outputs in some detail because questions of quality have to be carefully defined and measured prior to monitoring. They are low when the goods or services required are simple, uniform or easily measured and assessed. We might therefore expect the transaction costs of a contract to build and maintain a road to be relatively low, provided the engineering was straightforward and the purchaser was experienced in preparing and monitoring similar contracts. A contract or series of contracts for a complex set of structures, as for example a transport interchange, will have higher transaction costs, as would one involving private and public finance or new design features. The large number of contracts which a railway operating company has to arrange also suggests high transaction costs.

The franchising process for railway operations is a complex one which grants a near monopoly contract for a fixed period. Although specialised machinery assets are involved (the rolling stock), the arrangements for leasing ensure that no company bidding for the contract is penalised for not owning rolling stock. After the franchise is granted, there are substantial costs in monitoring its progress. When the franchise period expires and a new franchise has to be negotiated, the existing franchise holder will have both experience and specialised knowledge which will give it a competitive advantage. It is likely that the franchiser and the franchisee will have developed a relationship with a significant amount of mutual trust and moved away from reliance solely on the wording of contracts for specification and monitoring purposes. The economist Oliver Williamson thinks that complex, idiosyncratic transactions involving specialised assets and knowledge incur high transaction costs. He suggests that these circumstances weigh against the use of competitive contracting (Williamson, 1985; Walsh, 1995; Coulson, 1997). It will therefore be interesting to see how tendering and franchising operate in railway transport operation in the future.

Turning to competition, there are consistent signs that the market is moving towards monopolies in transport operations. There have been numerous takeovers among bus fleets, absorbing the many small companies which were set up at privatisation, often based on management and employee buyouts or former municipally owned bus fleets. To-day there are seven major bus companies which in 1995 had over 60% of market share (Cheek, 1995). Stagecoach is one of these large companies which has also moved into rail and now runs two train operating companies. One company, National Express, dominates the long distance coach market. It has moved into both the bus and rail markets and owns five rail franchises (OPRAF, 1996b). In the case of railway freight, one company,EWS, now has a 80-90% share of all rail freight operations. Large firms in the bus and freight business appear increasingly to be taking over the rail operating companies.

7. Contracting and accountability

7.1. to Passengers - the use of contracts for monitoring

The intention of privatisation is that the market will offer greater choice of service and improve both efficiency and performance standards. The Conservative government's policy for privatising and deregulating buses had the expectation that deregulation would make services "far more responsive to the needs of the traveling public" and that "the spur of competition is the way to deliver more responsive services" (Citizen's Charter, 1991). Similarly, privatisation of the railways would be "the most effective way of making sure that passengers get a better deal". To improve service on the railways, it was decided to institute a Passenger's Charter for British Rail. Similar Charters are now incorporated into the franchise agreements of the TOCs and must meet a standard as least as high as British Rail's on, for example, standards of punctuality and reliability for train services. Compensation for breach of those standards may be claimed by passengers and information is given on how to make complaints. The Charters are therefore intended as an enforceable contract between the companies and their customers and individual customers and firms have a direct means of monitoring service and requesting redress for any specified shortfall.

Road passenger transport does not have the same machinery for passenger accountability. The former Traffic Commissioners who were responsible for licensing all bus services were abolished in 1995. Since the bus system was wholly deregulated outside London, it was anticipated that competition between companies would ensure that customers received good service. There is no formal specific avenue for making complaints about bus services. National Express, for example, is one of the largest operators but has no Passengers' Charter. Local authorities have a voice only in respect of their contracts for subsidised services. London Regional Transport and Passenger Transport Authorities have powers in relation to the franchises which they grant.

7.2. to State Authorities - the use of contracts for monitoring

The Rail Regulator has a statutory duty "to protect the interests of users of railways"(Art.1a Railways Act, 1993). He has stated that he sees his objective "to promote the public interest" and "to facilitate a 'fit for purpose' matrix of contracts and licenses which balances different interests, is capable of efficient operation, requires regulatory approval reasonably administered and puts the customers of the new railway first" (Swift, 1995). More recently, he has set out objectives for the improvement of services for passengers(ORR, 1997). The Regulator has powers to amend licenses and has now used these powers in relation to Railtrack to secure increased surveillance of its performance. He may be consulted but has no direct powers over fare levels and minimum service levels. These are within the jurisdiction of the Franchise Director as part of the franchise agreements (ORR, 1995). The agreements are contracts which may be enforced by the Franchise Director, who can fine operating companies or terminate their franchises (OPRAF, 1996b).Both the Rail Regulator and the Franchise Director are appointed by the Secretary of State who defines their powers and may issue 'guidance' to them, but they are otherwise independent. They are accountable to the Courts and to Parliament, but not to government (ORR, 1994).

It is helpful to match the 'consumerisation' of transport services to the broad categories suggested for public services by Hood, Peters and Wollmann. Their analysis outlines four archetypical forms of public service 'consumerism' : coproduction, representation, product choice and regulation (Hood et al., 1996). Coproduction and representation are described as 'active' controls and product choice and regulation as 'passive', but while product choice is direct consumer control, regulation is indirect. It is suggested that product choice benefits individual consumers most within the powers set out by regulators. Regulation and representation work best for active and articulate groups and others able to press their case. The new transport systems clearly emphasise product choice and regulation. While regulation is traditional in British public service, the use of contracting and Charters has shifted the emphasis towards court procedures and individual legal redress and away from representation. However the standards set out in rail passengers' charters are selected by the train operating companies who thus define their own performance expectations. Although the Charters have to be approved by the Franchise Director and the companies are obliged to carry out customer satisfaction surveys, they are essentially tools of management. Thus the regulatory system increases management's commitment to customer service. The Rail Regulator's recent statement of objectives for operators emphasises a number of service improvements such as access for the disabled, stable and robust timetables and improved passenger information (ORR, 1997). He has now used his enforcement powers under the 1993 Act to issue an order to 25 operating companies requiring them to ensure that 90% of telephone calls to the National Rail Inquiry scheme are answered in accordance with agreed performance standards, with a progressive financial penalty to be paid on the shortfall. This suggests that charters are not seen as a sufficiently powerful method of ensuring good customer service.

The Labour Government in power since May 1997 has decided to leave the industry in private ownership but will increase ministerial "guidance", which indicates that there will be more political control. The Secretary of State has said that the Franchise Director must consult Ministers before retendering a new or failed tender (Guardian 2/10/97). A new Strategic Rail Authority may be set up in line with a promise by the Labour Party at the election.

8. Reflections and Conclusions

Contracting is a key measure in the 'new institutional economics', a part of the new public management. It stems directly from the emphasis on competition and market structures which should provide incentives to managers and increase consumer choice (Rhodes, 1996). In the case of both road passenger and rail transport, markets were established and a large monopoly (British Rail) broken up and privatised. Full competition was introduced into the bus and coach industry by deregulation to allow open access except for London. In the case of the railways, the monopoly Railtrack had to be preserved, but competition was introduced for the service operators. Contracting takes the form of franchise agreements, providing a near monopoly for a limited period of time. Licensing for access to Railtrack is another contractual arrangement since conditions are attached to the license which is awarded. While 'classical' contracts can be used for much road construction and for relatively simple operations, complex and large scale projects require a complicated series of contracts. Such contracts will be based on professional judgments and skills, involve expensive assets, and are likely to require much negotiation. Transport projects of major importance involving both private and public finance will fall into this category and the transaction costs will be high. High transaction costs will also be a feature of the complex railway contracting system where operating companies have to conclude numerous contracts with the regulating authorities, Railtrack, the stations, and providers of rolling stock, repairs etc. There has as yet been no authoritative attempt to quantify these costs, but they have to be understood as part of the price of introducing competition through contracting. The British reforms are likely to provide useful experience for future developments. For example, the European Commission has recently produced a White Paper outlining a system of contracts and franchises similar to the British one for rail operations in the Community (CEC, 1996).

Contracting in transport has clarified two important aspects of the service. The first is subsidy from public funds where the amount of subsidy is now related to the service requirement, is transparent and appears in the contract agreements. In the case of local buses, the subsidy is attached to a specific contract for additional services which are not commercially viable and which is then put out to competitive tender. For railway operations, the subsidy is identified in the franchise agreement, and for Railtrack in its license. The second aspect is monitoring where the service offered by rail operators is set out in the franchise and can be checked and if necessary regulated. In addition, the rail Passengers Charters provide a basis for passenger monitoring and redress.

The weakness of contracting in transport lies in three areas - coordination of service, strategic policy formation and political accountability. First, in relation to coordination, because the operations are differentiated for contracting purposes, the service becomes fragmented. For both railways and buses, coordination of service is of great importance to passengers. It is much harder to achieve where there are numerous different companies operating. The same is true for coordination between road and rail. Second, contracting makes the formation of strategic policies in transport more difficult. The power to take decisions is distributed not only to the operating companies and Railtrack but also, in the case of railways, to two independent regulatory authorities. While the Rail Regulator states as his chief purpose the promotion of "the public interest"(Swift, 1995), his powers are limited to those set out by statute, and he is also subject to notes of "guidance" from the Secretary of State. The latter is best placed to consider strategic policy issues, for example the balance of development between road and rail. However there is now the further point of political accountability. The regulators are responsible to the Courts and to Parliament but not to the government, and the Minister's powers are less direct than in the case of a full public service. This may be appropriate to a public utility where commercial considerations are important, but it makes long term coordinated planning more difficult and it affects political accountability. The question of distancing operations from political control is a perennial problem, as much evident when there were nationalised transport industries. It will be interesting to see if contracting and regulation as methods have greater success in promoting good planning without interference with operations.

Finally, there is the more general issue of how useful contracts are when they deal with complex issues involving professional judgment, raised by Walsh (1995) and others. If it is the case that they increasingly rely on the building of long term relationships based on trust, they may lose their ability to check and monitor the providers, and Williamson's proviso that such services are less suitable for contracting will apply. This question will only be answered when more experience of how the new systems work, particularly the railways, is available.

Bibliography

Beesley M. & Littlechild S, "Privatisation: Principles, Problems and Priorities", *Lloyds Bank Review* ,N.149 (1983) pp 1-20

Bennett C. & Fairlie E ., "Contracting in Theory and Practice: some Evidence from the NHS" ,*Public Administration* , V.74 N 1 (1996) pp 49-66.

Boston J., Martin J., Pallot J., and Walsh P. *'Public Management - the New Zealand model'*, Auckland : OxfordUniversity Press, (1996)

Cheek C ,"Britain's Bus Industry" , *Local Transport To-day* V. N (1995) pp 13-17

Citizen's Charter,'*The Citizen's Charter - Raising the Standard*" Cm1599, London : HMSO

Commission of the European Communities, "*A strategy for revitalising the Community's railways*" , COM(96)421, Brussels : CEC (1996)

Coulson A "Transaction Cost Economics and its implications for local governance", *Local Government Studies*, V.23 N. 1 (1997) pp 107-113.

Glaister S. and Travers T. "*Tolls and Shadow Tolls*", London : Greater London Group,London School of Economics.

Guardian (4/3/97) 'Company that ran off the rails" 4/3/97 London

Guardian (27/6/97) 'Railtrack backtracks on subsidy" 27/6/97

Guardian (2/10/97) 'Prescott tears up rail sales rules'

Harden, I. '*The Contracting State*' , Buckingham : Open University Press (1992)

Hood C. Peters G, and Wollmann H., "Sixteen ways to consumerize public services", *Public Money and Management* , V.16 N.4 (1996) pp43-50

Local Transport To-day, "*Railtrack accepts call for greater accountability*" N.215 (3/7/ 1997)

Macneil I.R. (1980), 'The social contract' London : Yale University Press(1980)

Nash C.& Preston J. , 'The U.K.' in OECD "*Privatisation of the Railways*", London : OECD (1993).

Nordell O., ' Rail Privatisation Deregulation Swedish Style', Report of Transport Coordinators, Conference in *Local Government Review* Summer (1993)

Office of Passenger Rail Franchising, *'Passenger Rail Industry Overview*", London: OPRF , (1996)

Office of Passenger Rail Franchising, *Annual Report 1995-6,* London: OPRF (1996)

Office of the Rail Regulator, *Annual Report 1993/4,* London : ORR (1994)

Office of the Rail Regulator, *Annual Report 1994/5*, London : ORR (1995)

Office of the Rail Regulator, *Press Notice 97/18,* London: ORR (1997)

Parris H. , *'Government and Railways in nineteenth century Britain'* , London: Routledge & Kegan Paul , (1965).

Rhodes R., "The New Governance- Governing without Government", *Political Studies* V.44 N.4 (1996) pp652-657.

Self P., *'Government by the Market? The Politics of Public Choice'*, London: Macmillan (1993)

Swift J.,"Regulation and the Railways: the role of the independent regulator" Lecture to the Institute of Mechanical Engineers, Dec. 4, London (unpublished) (1995)

Terry F., 'The Private Finance Initiative - Overdue Reform or Policy Breakthrough?', *Public Money & Management* V. 16 N. 1(1996) pp9 -16

Transport,Department of, *Press Notice 21/5/97* London

Walsh K.,"*Public Services & Market Mechanisms· Competition, Contracting & the New Public Management*' ", London : Macmillan (1995)

White P., 'Bus & Coach Deregulation', *Global Transport,* V.1 N.1 (1995), pp31-4

Williamson O.,'*The Economic Institutions of Capitalism*" , New York :Free Press (1985)

Wistrich E. ,'Transport' in N. Deakin & A.Wright , Eds. *'Consuming Public Services'* , London:Routledge (1990) pp 35-55.

Wistrich E. , 'Privatisation & regulation - the case of transport in the UK' in L. Montanheiro , E.Rebelo, and G.Owen ,Eds. *'Public & Private Sector Partnerships: working for change*' , Sheffield : Pavic Publications, Sheffield Hallam University (1996) pp 651-660.

About EGPA

The European Group of Public Administration

The European Group of Public Administration (EGPA) was set up in 1974 as a working group of the International Institute of Administrative Sciences (IIAS) to strengthen contacts and exchanges among European scholars and practitioners. EGPA is now a regional group of IIAS.

- **Its objectives**

    * to organise and encourage the exchange of information on developments in the theory and practice of public administration;
    * to foster comparative studies and the development of public administrative theory within a European perspective;
    * to facilitate the application of innovative ideas, methods, and techniques in public administration; and
    * to include young teachers, researchers, as also civil servants in its activities.

- **Its activities**

    To achieve its objectives, EGPA, whose primary function is to serve as catalyst and intermediary, uses the following means:

    * *organises and sponsors conferences and small scale study meetings*

        The annual conference is the core activity of EGPA. It is held in a different European country every year. It is normally hosted by a member organisation. Each year, the theme selected for the conference is a topic of major concern for public administration in Europe.

    * *sets up study groups*

        Each Study Group is managed by a Director and a Chairperson, and is necessarily comprised of academics and practitioners. Papers contributed by members are country studies or comparative studies, which are discussed in the meetings of the groups during the annual conference. The work of each group is geared towards a publication or series of publications.

        EGPA has seven Study Groups, which develop the following topics:

        - Agriculture
        - Informatization in Public Administration;
        - Personnel Policies;
        - Quality and Productivity in the Public Sector;

- Public Finance and Management;
- Co-operation in Permanent Education, Training, Research and Consultancy between Eastern and Western Europe;
- The Development of Contracting in the Public Service since 1980

* *sponsors publications*

- The EGPA Yearbook published annually;
- Scientific studies resulting from the study groups' research;
- The International Review of Administrative Sciences (IRAS) to which EGPA contributes;
- The IIAS Newsletter to which EGPA contributes.

- **Its address**

European Group of Public Administration, c/o IIAS, rue Defacqz 1, box 11, B-1000 Brussels, Belgium (Tel.: 32-2-538.91.65, Fax.: 32-2-537.97.02, e-mail: geapegpa@agornet.be).

Publications of EGPA

Books

* *Les responsabilités du fonctionnaire.* Paris, Cujas, 1973, 223 pp.

* *The Public's Servant.* Finnpublishers, 1981, 160 pp.

* *Développement industriel régional; centralisation ou décentralisation - Regional Industrial Development; Centralization or Decentralization.* Brussels, International Institute of Administrative Sciences, 1981, 426 pp.

* *Consultative Mechanisms of Central Government - Les organismes consultatifs de l'Administration centrale.* Hugo Van Hassel & Jozsef Varga. Brussels, International Institute of Administrative Sciences, 1985, 130 pp.

* *Changing Agriculture in Europe : Policy making and Implementation - L'agriculture européenne en mutation : l'élaboration et la mise en oeuvre des politiques.* Bernard Hoetjes & Carlo Desideri. Brussels, International Institute of Administrative Sciences, 1987, iv & 318 pp.

* *New Trends in Public Administration and Public Law.* Hugo Van Hassel, Mihaly Hogye & György Jenei (Eds.). EGPA Yearbook. Annual Conference, Budapest 1996. Budapest, European Group of Public Administration & Center for Public Affairs Studies Budapest, 1997, 449 pp.

Occasional Papers

Series in which 23 papers were published from 1983 to 1988. These papers were specially prepared for the series or discussed during EGPA meetings. They were selected for the series by an editorial board headed by Jan Kooiman, Netherlands.

1/83 **KASTELEIN**, J., *Management and Organisation in Central government.* 22 pp. + ann.

2/83 **McMAHON**, Laurie & al., *Power Bargaining and Policy Analysis. What Prescriptions for Practitioners.* 33 pp.

3/83 **KIVINIEMI**, Markku, *Research on Structural Changes in Public Sector Organisation: Findings and Perspectives.* 25 pp.

4/83 **SMITH**, Brian C., *Access and the Reorganisation of Local Government in Britain.* 47 pp.

1/84 **DERLIEN**, H.-U., *Programme Evaluation in the Federal Republic of Germany.* 21 pp.

2/84 **KLINKERS**, Leo & **GUNN**, Lewis, *Survey among European Experts of Training and Education in Public Administration.* Final Report. 20 pp. + ann.

3/84 **MAARSE**, Hans, *Some Problems in Implementation Analysis.* Final Report of the workshop on « Methodological Aspects of Policy Implementation Analysis ». EGPA Conference on Policy Implementation with Special Reference to Agriculture. Dublin: 3-5 September 1984. 17 pp.

4/84 **AQUINA**, Herman J., *Implementation and the Strategic Use of Evaluation.* 19 pp.

1/85 **HANNEQUART**, A., *Production publique et Science de l'Administration publique.* 43 pp.

2/85 **KIVINIEMI**, Markku, *Local Government Reforms as Related to Structural Changes in the System of Public Administration.* 40 pp.

3/85 **WILLIS**, David, *Distributional Coalitions and Functional Interest Representation in the EEC: Problems, Diagnoses and Cures.* 72 pp.

1/86 **PEETERS**, C., **VERBEKE**, A. & **WINKELMANS**, W., *Effective Public Policy Formulation: The Belgian Inland Navigation Case.* 27 pp.

2/86 **WASS**, Douglas, Loyalty, *Neutrality and Commitment in Career Civil Service.* 23 pp.

3/86 **SPANOU**, Calliope, *Fonctionnaires et groupes de pression: le cas du ministère de l'environnement en France.* 31 pp.

4/86 **BODIGUEL**, Jean-Luc, *Les relations entre Administration et Partis politiques dans la France contemporaine.* 21 pp.

1/87 **HELANDER**, Voitto & **STAHLBERG**, Krister, *Corporatism and Bureaucracy.* 26 pp.

2/87 **BRESSERS**, Hans & **HONIG**, Mac, *A Comparative Approach to the Explanation of Policy Effects.* 28 pp.

3/87 **HANNEQUART**, A., *Evaluation and Public Policy. A Conceptualisation of the Case of Industrial Policy in Belgium.* 16 pp.

4/87 **AF URSIN**, Klaus, *Ethically Questionable Phenomena in Central Administration.* 29 pp.

1/88 **HOULIHAN**, Barrie, *Managing with Less: the Changing Roles of Professional Officers in the Local Policy Process.*

2/88 **HERWEYER**, Michiel, *Hard Cuts and Soft Spoils.* 16 pp.

3/88 **POLLITT**, Christopher et al., *Improved Organisational Performance. Dream and Reality in Health Service.* 36 pp.

4/88 **VAN DE DONK**, W. and **SNELLEN** I., *Knowledge-based Systems in Public Administration.* 28 pp.

International Review of Administrative Sciences

The members of the Group collaborate to the International Review of Administrative Sciences (IRAS), the journal of the International Institute of Administrative Sciences (IIAS), published quarterly, in French, English and Arabic. The French version is published by E. Bruylant and the English version by Sage publications.

Books published by the EGPA Permanent Study Groups

* I. Th. Snellen, W.B.H.J. van de Donk & J.-P. Baquiast (Eds.), 1989, *Expert Systems in Public Administration. Evolving Practices and Norms*. Amsterdam/New York/Oxford/Tokyo: Elsevier Science Publisher (ISBN 044488038, viii & 323 pp.)

* P.H.A. Frissen & I.Th.M. Snellen (Eds.), 1990, *Informatization Strategies for Public Administration*, Amsterdam/New York/Oxford/Tokyo: Elsevier Science Publishers (ISBN 0444888004, viii & 193 pp.).

* P.H.A. Frissen, V.J.J.M. Bekkers, B.K. Brussaard, I.Th.M. Snellen & M. Wolters (Eds.), 1992, *European Public Administration and Informatization*, Amsterdam/ Oxford/Washington/Tokyo: IOS Press (ISBN 9051991118, 636 pp.).

* W.B.H.J. van de Donk, I. Th. Snellen & P.W. Tops (Eds.), 1995, *Orwell in Athens. A Perspective on Informatization and Democracy*. Amsterdam/Oxford/Tokyo/ Washington D.C.: IOS Press (ISBN 905199219X, xii & 289 pp.).

* J.A. Taylor, I. Th.M. Snellen & A. Zuurmond (Eds). *Beyond BPR: Institutional Transformations in Public Administration. Ideas, Cases and Opportunities*, Amsterdam/ Oxford/Washington/Tokyo: IOS Press (ISBN 9051993099, xi & 258 pp.).

* D. Farnham, S. Horton, J. Barlow and A. Hondeghem (Eds.), *New Public Managers in Europe: Public Servants in Transition*. Macmillan, 1996. 308 pp.

* I.Th.M. Snellen and W.B.H.J. van de Donk (Eds.), *Public Administration in an Information Age. A Handbook*. IOS Press, 1998.

Author Index

Bouckaert, G.	243	Meklin, P.	263
Bovens, M.	41	Montanheiro, L.	189
Daurmont, O.	73	Ould Daddah, T.	v
De Clercq, B.	167	Parsons, W.	87
Depré, R.	vii	Raes, K.	197
Dorbeck-Jung, B.	45	Reichard, C.	123
Fabre, R.	59	Richards, D.	151
Farnham, D.	239	Robben, K.	219
Fortin, Y.	253	Sabbe, F.	245
Gulyàs, G.	167	Smith, M.J.	151
Hogye, M.	245	Snellen, I.	235
Hondeghem, A.	1,239	Staes, P.	139
Hood, C.	9	Summa, H.	243
Horton, S.	239	Vakkuri, J.	263
Hubeau, B.	107	Van Dalen, J.Chr.	233
Jann, W.	107	Van de Donk, W.	235
Jean-Pierre, D.	207	Van Hassel, H.	253
Jenei, G.	247	Van Rillaer, J.	35
Maes, R.	111	Vermeulen, P.	171
Maguire, M.	23	Wistrich, E.	279
Massey, A.	41		

CPSIA information can be obtained
at www.ICGtesting.com
Printed in the USA
BVHW04*0040040918
526190BV00006BA/93/P